# Games and Human Behavior

## Essays in Honor of Amnon Rapoport

T0330748

# Games and Human Behavior

## Essays in Honor of Amnon Rapoport

### Edited by

**David V. Budescu**
*University of Illinois at Urbana-Champaign*

**Ido Erev**
*Technion – Israel Institute of Technology*

**Rami Zwick**
*Hong Kong University of Science and Technology*

Psychology Press
Taylor & Francis Group

New York   London

The final camera copy for this work was prepared by the author, and therefore the publisher takes no responsibility for consistency or correctness of typographical style.

Reprinted 2009 by Psychology Press

Cover design by Kathryn Houghtaling Lacey

**Library of Congress Cataloging-in-Publication Data**

    Games and human behavior : essays in honor of Amnon Rapoport / edited by David. V. Budescu, Ido Erev, Rami Zwick.
       p.  cm.
    "Based on a workshop that took place in August 1996 in Chapel Hill, NC, in honor or Professor Amnon Rapoport's 60th birthday"—Pref.
    Includes bibliographical references and indexes.
    ISBN 0-8058-2658-0 (cloth : alk. paper) —
    ISBN 0-8058-2659-9 (pbk. : alk. paper).
    1. Small groups—Mathematical models. 2. Coalition (Social sciences)—Mathematical models. 3. Game theory. 4. Group decision making. 5. Rapoport, Amnon. I. Rapoport, Amnon. II. Budescu, David V. III. Erev, Ido. IV. Zwick, Rami.
    HM133.G35   1998
    302—dc21                      98-15206
                                     CIP

10  9  8  7  6  5  4  3  2  1

*To Amnon – friend, colleague, and teacher*

# Contents

# Preface

This volume is based on a workshop that took place in August 1996 in Chapel Hill, North Carolina, in honor of Professor Amnon Rapoport's 60th birthday. Amnon is one of the pioneers and leaders in the experimental study and quantitative modeling of human decisions in social and interactive contexts. During the first 30 years of his distinguished career, Amnon published 4 books and close to 200 research papers and chapters in leading psychological, management, decision theory, economics and political science journals, and is recognized as a leading authority in many of these areas.

In the domain of individual decision making, Amnon's work has been primarily on decisions under risk and multistage (dynamic) decision models. His work on large groups has dealt with voting systems, power measures, and coalitions. However, in our opinion his most important and influential work, and the one he enjoys and values most, is in the domain of decisions in small interactive groups. This includes theoretical and empirical research on:

- cooperation and competition among individuals and groups,
- bargaining processes and coalition formation,
- voluntary contribution to public goods,
- consumption behavior of common (and limited) resources,
- tacit cooperation and coordination in groups, and
- bargaining with incomplete information.

As a rule, Amnon's work is theory-driven and, in most cases, the theory is represented formally by mathematical (primarily, but not exclusively, game theoretical) models. At the same time he is a meticulous and rigorous, yet imaginative and creative experimentalist. In fact, he was one of the pioneers of computerized experimentation in the domain of individual and group decision making.

The impetus for the workshop, in addition to honoring Amnon on his 60th birthday, was the growing interest in the development of a descriptive (experimentally based) variant of game theory that combines psychological and economical elements, and appeals to both disciplines. In recent years more and more social scientists have combined in their work the theoretical framework of traditional game theory to model the environment in which decisions are made, and the experimental methodology to study actual human behavior under these structures. Game theory has always been a favorite model in economics and it has recently become more popular in social psychology as well. Conversely, the experimental method that has been the cornerstone of scientific psychology for the last century has become more popular and acceptable in economics (in the last 15 years a new field of "experimental economics" has emerged). The hope is that this convergence of models and methods in the two disciplines would lead to new insights on human behavior under a variety of (natural or artificially induced) incentive structures.

A distinctive characteristic of Amnon's research work is its interdisciplinary scope and appeal. In this spirit, a major goal of the workshop, and this volume, is to encourage and facilitate constructive communication across the boundaries separating these disciplines, and between psychologists and economists. Indeed, about half the participants in the workshop were psychologists and the other half were economists.

Because of his expertise in game theory, his interest in interactive and strategic decisions, and his strong experimental background, Amnon is one of the very few researchers whose work is relevant in both psychology and economics and whose contributions are recognized and appreciated in both disciplines. Thus, it is fitting that the workshop (held in his honor) and this volume brought together some of the leading researchers from both fields, as well as many of his former students and collaborators.

Amnon was a member of the celebrated first class in psychology at the Hebrew University in Jerusalem and obtained his PhD in quantitative psychology at the University of North Carolina (UNC) at Chapel Hill. His career was divided almost equally between Israel (The Hebrew University in Jerusalem and Haifa University) and the United States (UNC at Chapel Hill and University of Arizona). He also held visiting positions at the University of Michigan, the University of Illinois at Urbana-Champaign, Netherlands Institute of Advanced Studies, and the Hong Kong University of Science and Technology. However, there is a special place in his heart for Chapel Hill. Thus, the fact that the workshop took place on the UNC campus in Chapel Hill made the occasion more special for Amnon and for many of his former colleagues and students.

This book consists of 16 chapters coauthored by 25 contributors (14 trained in psychology and 11 trained in mathematics, economics, or business administration). We have organized the 16 chapters in five sections: 2 chapters on psychology and economics, 3 chapters on learning in experimental games, 3 chapters on market and coordination games, 3 chapters on bargaining, fairness and equity, and 5 chapters on social dilemmas and coordination.

Except for the first section that is theoretical in nature, all other chapters describe original experimental work or summarize empirical research in a certain domain.

## ACKNOWLEDGMENTS

We owe thanks to many for the successful completion of this volume. First, we acknowledge all the contributors who have also served as referees on some of the other chapters. Special thanks to other colleagues who attended the workshop and graciously agreed to review some chapters: Maya Bar-Hillel, Randy Bender, Jerry Busemeyer, Rachel Croson, Xiao-Ping Chen, Joachim Meyer, Robert Slonim, John van Huyk, Thomas Wallsten, and Eyal Winter. The Society of Mathematical Psychology agreed to sponsor the workshop in conjunction with its annual meeting and the local organizing committee, headed by Jonathan Marshall and Thomas Wallsten, went out of its way to help us organize the workshop. Special thanks to Norman Li and Adrian Rantilla for the splendid and dedicated work in preparing and formatting all the chapters, figures and tables for publication, and to Lawrence Earlbaum Associates for supporting this project.

Finally, many thanks to Amnon who brought us all together through his contagious enthusiasm for this exciting research area.

*David Budescu*
*Ido Erev*
*Rami Zwick*

# Part I

## On Psychology and Economics

# 1     The Psychological and Economical Perspectives on Human Decisions in Social and Interactive Contexts

**Rami Zwick**
*Hong Kong University of Science and Technology*

**Ido Erev**
*Technion – Israel Institute of Technology*

**David Budescu**
*University of Illinois at Urbana-Champaign*

In recent years many social scientists have come to realize the value of a theoretical framework that uses traditional game-theoretic concepts to model the environment in which decisions are made, and of meticulous and careful experimental work on interactive decisions. Our common hope is that a combination of these two components would lead to breakthroughs and new insights on human behavior under various (natural or artificially induced) incentive structures. This goal has been a major driving force of Rapoport's work for a long time (Kahan & Rapoport 1984; Rapoport 1990) and it is fitting that the workshop in his honor focuses on the most recent developments toward this goal. Most chapters in this volume summarize experimental studies designed to explore to what degree nonstandard motives (e.g., fairness, pride, retaliation, trust, etc.) guide human behavior in strategic settings (modeled by games), and how people learn to adapt to the objective incentive structure. This chapter sets the stage for the rest of the book by discussing some of the traditional differences between psychologists and economists in the study of human choice behavior.

## ON PSYCHOLOGY AND ECONOMICS

A fair amount has been written over the years on the interplay between economics and psychology. Most of the surveys were written by, and for, economists (for recent surveys see Earl, 1990; Lewin, 1996; Rabin, in press; Sugden, 1991; and for a review for psychologists see Lopes, 1994). Because psychology is, in general, less formal (mathematical) than economics, some speculate that economists can master the psychological content of a specific content area easier and quicker than psychologists can understand and appreciate the methodological rigor of economical models. This may begin to explain why mainstream economists believe that economics without psychological and sociological research is inadequate (Simon, 1986) and that "there are gains to be had from seeking help from psychology in at least some areas of their research" (Earl, 1990, p. 718).

Psychologists seem to be more skeptical in their views regarding the potential contribution of economics to psychology, as well as the effect of psychological research on studies in economics. The sharpest criticism is expressed by Lunt (1996) who argued that "economists are not ready, prepared or even vaguely interested in changing their core assumptions as a response to psychological work" (p. 283). A somewhat more positive view is expressed by Lopes (1994), who believed that

> Psychologists and economists have different perspectives on the world. With effort, any of us could learn to see from the other perspective. But we cannot do both at once, and it is not easy to maintain the alien perspective for long. Still, the effort is worthwhile. (p. 198)

In the introduction to the proceedings of the Conference on the Behavioral Foundations of Economic Theory, held in October 1985 at the University of Chicago, Hogarth and Reder (1986) wrote that

> it is possible that the two disciplines (economics and psychology) will continue to ignore each other for many years to come. Indeed, given the different substantive interests that motivate inquiry in the two disciplines, we believe that the bulk of most work in both areas will continue to develop in their present separate ways. (p. S200)

The chapters in this volume illustrate how economists and psychologists (and in some cases, jointly) study closely related issues using similar methodologies. In our view, the volume attests to the fact that psychologists and economists *do* learn from each other and *can* work together to improve our common understanding of human behavior. Thus, this collection supports Lopes' position and, in our opinion, refutes Hogarth and Reder's bleak scenario.

The goal of the introductory chapter is to highlight some of the differences between the assumptions commonly invoked (explicitly or implicitly) by economists and psychologists in the study of human choice. We believe that better understanding of these differences can facilitate accumulation and communication of knowledge across disciplinary boundaries. There are eight basic assumptions. In each case we highlight the contrast between the traditional views of psychologists and economists and examine the degree to which recent research managed to reduce the gap between the two disciplines in this context.

Before reviewing the differences between economics and psychology it is instructive to speculate on their origin. In our opinion, the two disciplines have distinct views on human choice behavior simply because they examine the same behavior from different perspectives that are dictated by their respective scopes and interests. *Psychology* is usually defined as the study of the thought processes and behaviors of humans and other animals in their interactions with their environments. Among other things, psychologists study sensory perception, emotion, motivation, problem solving, use of language and other mental tasks, group interaction, adjustment to social and physical environments, and the normal and abnormal development of these processes. *Economics* is traditionally considered to be the study of how human beings allocate resources to produce various commodities and how those goods are distributed for consumption among all members of a society. A basic tenet of economic theory is that resources are scarce, or at least limited, and that not all human needs and desires can be met. A major concern of economists is how to distribute these resources in the most efficient and equitable way.

This volume focuses on the domain where the two disciplines intersect – the study of human choice behavior. As the previous definitions indicate, this domain is but a small subset of their respective topics of inquiry. The tendency in every scientific field is to adopt assumptions and methodologies that apply to the largest possible number of content subareas (in fact, the boundaries of a discipline are delineated by the commonalties underlying all its subdomains). One implication of this tendency to establish broad and general common grounds across contexts is that some of the unique features associated with specific contexts are downplayed and even obscured. It is reasonable to attribute the differences between the traditional assumptions of psychology and economics on choice to the different contexts in which the two disciplines embedded this behavior.

One corollary of this analysis is that the existing differences are not inevitable. It is possible to imagine that the two disciplines could have developed in slightly different directions that would have favored alternative sets of underlying assumptions. And, more important for our goals, it is equally easy to envision how they could both shift focus and converge toward a new common core of axioms and a unified methodology. We hope that this volume makes a contribution in this direction.

# TRADITIONAL DIFFERENCES AND CURRENT VIEWS

To appreciate the significance of the differences between the economic and psychological perspectives, it is instructive to compare chapters on consumer behavior in economics and marketing textbooks (the latter are heavily influenced by the psychological view and research literature). The uninitiated reader may not even realize that both chapters presume to explain the same phenomena. The psychological (marketing) treatment of consumer behavior emphasizes the interaction between individual differences and environmental and situational influences. In particular, effort is devoted to study the cultural context of consumption, social class and status, reference groups, family and household influences, individual differences in economic and cognitive resources, needs, involvement, motivation, knowledge, expertise, attitude, personality and lifestyle. Psychological processes such as attention, comprehension, memory, and cognitive and behavioral theories of learning, persuasion, and behavior modification constitute an integral part of any treatment of consumer behavior in marketing. We refer to all these factors jointly as "the social context of consumer behavior." In sharp contrast, the economic treatment of consumer behavior emphasizes utility maximization and the theory of consumer demand, ignoring for the most part the social context and framing within which consumers operate.

The main differences between the assumptions traditionally invoked by economics and psychologists can be summarized along the eight dimensions that are reviewed next. Note that for the most part we do not discuss the commonly considered differences in methodology.[1] We believe that methodological differences are derivatives of the more fundamental differences discussed in this chapter.

## What Is Scarce?

Economists assume that environmental resources are scarce but, ironically, consider the mental resources available to the actors whose behavior is modeled to be unlimited. Psychologists, on the other hand, have always been interested in studying the mechanisms that allow humans and other animals to cope with, and adapt to, an environment that is characterized by subjective information overload (see research by Miller, 1956; Navon & Gopher, 1979). Most traditional economic models presume that scarcity is a characteristic of the external domain whereas abundance is typical in the internal mental realm. Most psychological models, on the other hand, presume that the locus of scarcity is internal. Just as fat has replaced starvation as the number one dietary concern in the developed world, information overload has replaced scarcity as an important emotional, cognitive, and social problem in many psychological models.

Recently, however, there are some indications that these traditional positions could be replaced with a compromise that recognizes the importance of considering both types of scarcity. With the wider acceptance of Simon's (1957) notion of bounded rationality, some economists are willing to concede that in principle scarcity of resources may apply to homoeconomicus, as well as to the physical environment in which a person operates. At the same time social psychologists have become more involved in the study of social dilemmas, consumption of finite common resources and voluntary contributions to public goods (e.g., Dawes, 1980; Komorita & Parks, 1995) – situations that involve scarce environmental resources. Indeed, almost all the chapters in this volume implicitly assume scarcity of both environmental and cognitive resources.

## Normative Versus Descriptive

It is tempting to relate the differences between psychology and economics to the traditional distinction between *normative* (how one ought to behave) and *descriptive* (how one actually behaves) theories. We consider this classification to be too sharp and artificial, and believe that it does not represent fairly and accurately either discipline.

In their groundbreaking book *Games and Decisions*, Luce and Raiffa (1957) stated that

> it is crucial that the social scientist recognize that game theory is not descriptive, but rather (conditionally) normative. It states neither how people do behave nor how they should behave in an absolute sense, but how they should behave if they wish to achieve certain ends (p. 63).

Propositions of normative theory are generally tautological; they are derived logically from definitions and axioms and, as such, are analogous to mathematical theorems. For a proposition to be of interest to behavioral scientists (and, in particular, to economists and psychologists) and to qualify as scientifically meaningful, it must say something about the real world and be falsifiable by some conceivable observation of behavior.

Traditionally, game theorists have been insensitive to the data produced in experimental and nonexperimental settings and have even dismissed these data as irrelevant. As Kadane and Larkey (1983) noted,

> When anomalies occur between theory and data as they have frequently in the past 30-plus years, there may be a flurry of activity to conduct new experiments with new procedures that produce data consistent with the theory. Such a procedure asserts that the anomaly resulted from faults in the experimental procedures and not faults in the theory (p.1377).

For the most part, this is no longer the dominant approach in game theory. For example, Rubinstein (1991), in his comments on the interpretation of game theory, wrote:

> I approach this paper with the view that game theory is not simply a
> matter of abstract mathematics but concerns the real world. We are
> attracted to game theory because it deals with the mind. Incorporating
> psychological elements which distinguish our minds from machines
> will make game theory even more exciting and certainly more
> meaningful. (p. 909)

Similarly, Roth (1991) warned that

> if we do not take steps in the direction of adding a solid empirical
> base to game theory, but instead continue to rely on game theory
> primarily for conceptual insights (deep and satisfying as they may
> be), then it is likely that long before a hundred years, game theory
> will have experienced sharply diminishing returns. (p.108)

In fact, there is a growing attempt by economists to refine game theoretical
models that traditionally rely on idealized representations of human abilities and
motivations to accommodate cognitive limitations and social context (e.g.,
Rabin 1993). In such an endeavor, new data lead to revisions or extensions of
the original models and the models are then used to produce new predictions for
testing. This view is no different than the one that quantitative psychologists
have adopted and applied consistently for the last fifty years, in a variety of
areas (e.g., Coombs, Dawes, & Tversky, 1970) including judgment and decision
(e.g., Rapoport & Wallsten, 1972).

## The Relative Value of Generality and Accuracy

All scientists would agree that a good model should be general *and* accurate, but
there are differences of opinion concerning the relative importance of these two
desirable properties. Psychological research uses a paradigm that relies heavily
on controlled laboratory experimentation and hypothesis testing. This paradigm
tends to emphasize and overweight accuracy over generality. As a result,
psychological models tend to be localized in nature, often recognizing individual
differences and context effects. Quite frequently they rely on ad hoc
assumptions and qualifiers that may vary from one model to the next and cannot
always be formulated mathematically. It is fair to say that mainstream
contemporary psychology has abandoned the search for general principles and
has accepted the fact that human behavior is better described by a variety of
more modest and narrow laws and rules that are invoked based on context
and/or situation-specific cues. In the behavioral decision-making domain, this
view is exemplified in the work of Payne, Bettman, and Johnson (1993) on the
adaptive nature on human decision processes.

On the other hand, the traditional approach in economics relies on the idea that behavior can, and should, be explained by a few general principles that may be applied to almost every conceivable situation. From the perspective of the marginal utilitarian, for example, the theory of utility transformed economics into science by making it possible to derive economic laws from a single fundamental law of human nature – the strive to maximize expected return (utility) – which can be deduced from a small set of compelling axioms of rationality.

It appears that, unlike the scarcity disagreement, the accuracy versus generality disagreement cannot be resolved easily. Although psychologists can argue reasonably that experimental data suggest that generality is too costly (in the sense that it requires very complex models), economists have good reasons to continue their search for general models. Localized models cannot be applied easily outside the lab because one rarely knows which of the numerous available models that often make contradictory predictions matches best the current circumstances.

Interestingly, two Nobel laureates in economics (Selten and Simon) appear to support the "psychological" view that generality is not necessarily the dominant dimension. In the Nancy L. Schwartz Memorial Lecture, Selten (1989) said:

> I do not accept the criticism against the use of ad hoc assumptions. Look at human anatomy and physiology: bones muscles, nerves, and so on. Human anatomy and physiology cannot be derived from a few general principles. Let me say something else in defense of ad hoc assumptions. Experiments show that human behavior is ad hoc. Different principles are applied to different decision tasks. Case distinctions determine which principles are used where. It is better to make many empirically supported ad hoc assumptions than to rely on a few unrealistic principles of great generality and elegance. (pp. 22-23)

And,

> It can be hoped that eventually many theories of limited range will grow together and evolve into a comprehensive picture of the structure of human economic behavior. Only painstaking experimental research can bring us nearer to this goal. (p. 27)

Similarly, Simon (1993) wrote:

> Instead of political science or history as derivative of economic analysis, there is a need for economics based upon the facts of history and political and social life. Such an economics will have little to say *a priori* but will reason from numerous painfully gathered facts. (p. 160)

## Rationality

> The human mind is something of an embarrassment to certain
> disciplines, notably economics, decision theory, and others that have
> found the model of the rational consumer to be a powerfully
> productive one. (Schelling, 1985, p. 191)

In economics, the rationality assumption constitutes a dominant paradigm that
has no counterpart in contemporary psychology. Psychologists and economists
consider a person to be rational if the person makes consistent and coherent
decisions in pursuit of his or her own objectives and goals. However, in
economics this is often an "if and only if" definition whereas in psychology a
much weaker "if" definition is considered appropriate. Traditionally, economists
believe that goal-directed behavior portrays the most interesting economic
activities and they emphasize the role of conscious choices. Psychologists, on
the other hand, believe that conscious choices (and behavior) reveal just the tip
of an iceberg, and that components such as instincts, habits, conditioned and
innate drives, and so on that cannot necessarily be portrayed as goal-oriented,
remain hidden below the surface. Psychologists believe that in many
circumstances, including important economic ones, these hidden drives are at
least as important and influential as deliberate thinking in determining behavior.
A more extreme position is that in some cases (for example, in contingent
valuation applications) people do not have built-in opinions and preferences
waiting to be revealed; rather, one's preferences and goals are constructed,
refined, and occasionally revised during the decision process. Clearly, the
economic goal-directed definition of rationality is not suitable for evaluating
behavior in such cases.

When asked and frequently, without being asked, people give reasons and
justifications for their actions, but both economists and psychologists tend to
discount these reasons as ex-post rationalization of, rather than rationale for,
action. However, although economists ignore these data altogether and rely
solely on observed and measurable behavior (the revealed preference doctrine),
some psychologists find this verbalization a rich source for inquiry into the
cognitive and subconscious processes underlying behavior (the traditional raw
data of the clinical psychologists). Nonbehavioral information, some
psychologists argue, may be more enlightening than actual behavior for the
understanding of individual motivation, especially when moral considerations
dominate choice.

Another often-made distinction is that in economics rationality is viewed in
terms of the choices it produces (substantive rationality), whereas in psychology
and other social sciences, it is assessed in terms of the processes it employs
(procedural rationality; Simon, 1986). Consequently, for a model to be credible
in economics, it has to work at the output end (i.e., to be valid in a predictive
sense), whereas the psychological plausibility of the process (i.e., its descriptive
validity) is not quite relevant. This view is best expressed in Friedman's (1953)

essay on the methodology of positive economics in which he argues that when economists make behavioral assumptions about individuals, these assumptions need not be accurate, and they may even be wildly implausible, as long as aggregate data such as prices and quantities behave *as if* the assumptions are accurate. Psychological models, on the other hand, strive to achieve a different balance between these two aspects. In fact, purely empirical prediction, without a reasonable understanding of its underlying process, has a bad reputation in some areas of psychology.

Finally, quantities and entities that are considered stable inputs in economic models, such as preferences and probabilities, are often considered by psychologists to be temporary outputs of rule-driven processes and context-specific problem-solving constructions.

The traditional justification for retaining the strong rationality assumption in economics, even in the face of contradictory results is the strive for generality. As discussed earlier, there are good reasons to believe that in some cases loss in generality can be very costly. And, the rationality assumption appears to facilitate construction of models that are general and provide a good approximation of behavior even when they are not exactly accurate (see Savage, 1954, for a discussion of this point). The belief that the rationality assumption is necessary to achieve generality follows from the argument that there is only one way to be rational, but many ways to behave irrationally. Erev and Roth (in press) pointed out that this argument is not strictly correct: The literature on equilibrium refinement shows that there is more than one way to be rational, and the robust results obtained in learning studies suggest that generality can be obtained without invoking a strong assumption of rationality. This state of affairs leads many economists to consider alternative, more general definitions of rationality, thus moving them closer to the psychologists' view. Indeed, none of the contributors to this volume (economists or psychologists) invokes the rationality assumption as a sole explanation of the behavior observed in their studies.

## How Should the Incentives Be Modeled and Studied

The economic definition of rationality emphasizes conscious, goal-directed behavior and assumes that each player's objective is to maximize his or her expected utility. However the theory postulates practically nothing about the sources, nature, components, and determinants of this utility. Nevertheless, in actual applications of the theory, utility is habitually equated with income, wealth, or profit. Money is taken to be the primary source of utility presumably because money can buy products and services that, ultimately, lead to satisfaction, happiness, and fulfillment of other goals. For example, cooperation in mixed-motive situations (e.g., voluntary contribution to public goods or self-restrained consumption of limited resources) is viewed as an anomaly and poses a major theoretical challenge to standard economic theory (e.g., Dawes &

Thaler, 1988).

The implication that people desire only (or primarily) economic gains is a far stronger assumption than utility maximization, and it is unquestionably false, in the empirical sense. Psychologists recognize that money (income) cannot be equated with, and in some cases does not necessarily contribute to, well being, happiness, and life satisfaction and that many decisions are driven, at least in part, by cognitive processes and emotional considerations that are far removed from profit maximization. People's behavior, including their economic behavior, is deeply affected by habits, tradition, emotions, and social and moral values such as friendship, love, loyalty, pride, shame, remorse, envy, spite, self-esteem, sense of commitment, respect for duty, and so on. Furthermore, psychologists acknowledge that the factors motivating human choice are often context-dependent, may vary across individuals, and may change over time.

Economists and psychologists agree that human behavior can be affected by a wide set of incentives. But they do not necessarily agree on the methodological and operational aspects involved in the study and modeling of these incentives. Following von Neumann and Morgenstern (1947), there is almost universal agreement in economics that the incentives can be modeled by quantitative utilities. Because utilities are clearly related to money, experimental examination of the effect of incentives relies on manipulations of the monetary outcomes. Many psychologists believe that real-life incentives are complex and cannot be captured and quantified as simple utilities. Consequently, their effects cannot be studied experimentally by focusing exclusively on monetary incentives. These psychologists try to induce these "social motivations" through experimental instructions ("imagine that you are a business man who...") that highlight motives other than money. For example, such instructions may emphasize the context of decisions, their emotional components, or their personal relevance. In other cases they attempt to induce comparative processes ("in such situations, a typical participant achieves a certain level of success"), or emphasize group memberships and loyalties.

Amnon Rapoport was one of the first psychologists to accept, and consistently follow, the economic convention of paying subjects in experiments as a function of their decisions (and ultimate performance). This methodology is now quite standard in the study of social (group) decision making, but not necessarily in other branches of psychology.

Monetary incentives are appealing because they are easy to quantify, explain (to the experimental subjects), and justify (to fellow researchers). In addition, their effects appear to be relatively uniform across subjects (all subjects have monotonically increasing utility functions for money, but not everyone reacts similarly to other cues induced by special instructions). It is quite clear, however, that the endorsement of this methodology is, to a large degree, a matter of convenience and convention. It certainly should not be interpreted as an admission that other nonmonetary motives are unimportant, or irrelevant. In fact, one of the major challenges for a psychoeconomical descriptive theory of interactive decision making is to find an appropriate way to model the joint effects of the monetary *and* social factors. Practically all the chapters in this volume include such attempts.

## Framing Effects

A fundamental tenet of traditional game theory and economics is that the effects of the environment on behavior are mediated by the incentive structure. Thus, in developing descriptive models of choice behavior, the effects of the environment can be captured, and abstracted, by the incentive structure. Empirical evidence from psychological experiments cast serious doubts on this assumption. Kahneman and Tversky (1979, 1984) showed that it is possible to manipulate environmental factors such that they affect behavior in a systematic fashion, without altering the incentive structure. They labeled this phenomenon – minor modifications in the presentation of simple choice problems leading to major changes in revealed preferences – "the framing effect."

Although framing effects are robust and persistent, there seem to be no serious attempts to incorporate them in economical (and for that matter, psychological) models, and to give up the abstraction of the environment by the incentive structure. The concern is that because there are so many possible "frames," general models that allow for such effects would be impossible to construct unless a general theory of framing is developed. And, unfortunately, it is unlikely that such a theory would be developed in the foreseeable future.

Most chapters in this volume bypass the framing problem by focusing on relatively abstract context-free frames. For example experimental studies of social dilemmas do not use terms such as "contribution," "donation," or "consumption" when communicating with the subjects because of strong connotations and normative associations. The justification for this convention is that these abstract context-free cases provide good approximations of the average or typical behavior across the multiple possible frames. Roth and Erev (1995), for example, approached this problem by distinguishing between initial tendencies and learning. They assume that framing affects initial tendencies, but learning is sensitive primarily to the incentive structure.

Both approaches appear sensible! However, we need to acknowledge that there is little evidence to justify either assumption beyond common sense and wishful thinking.

## Learning and Equilibrium

Much of the research in economics involves equilibrium analysis. Its underlying assumption is that collective choices and markets are at equilibrium. At Nash equilibrium, no individual has positive incentives to change his or her behavior unilaterally. Two major interpretations of Nash equilibrium in the context of rational players were suggested. The first assumes that the game is played only once (and a repeated game is "repeated" once), and the players have sufficient knowledge and ability to analyze it in a rational manner. Players reach the equilibrium by "thinking their way there," so their observed choices reveal stable features of underlying preferences. This is a cognitive interpretation of equilibrium. The second interpretation does not require that participants in the game know its structure or any other facts at the outset. The assumption is that if people face a similar situation numerous times they learn to adopt better strategies by a trial-and-error process. A Nash equilibrium is considered a stationary point in this process. Players get to the equilibrium by adjusting their behavior in response to the demands of the environment and the behavior of their partners. These internal processes increase or decrease the individuals' tendency to respond to certain external stimuli. This is a learning interpretation of equilibrium.

*Learning* is defined by psychologists as an enduring change in the neural mechanisms of behavior that results from experience with environmental events. The study of the general principles of learning has always been a central topic in scientific psychology, and has engendered some of its major achievements (e.g., Pavlov's work on classical conditioning and Skinner's work on operant learning). These principles are assumed to apply in practically every aspect and facet of human behavior. Economists however have studied learning only to the extent that this process can be used to justify equilibrium concepts.

The relationship between learning and equilibrium has received a lot of attention recently in experimental game theory, which is reflected in this volume. This research indicates that: (a) whereas convergence toward equilibrium is very quick in some settings (e.g., the market entry game studied by Rapoport, Seale, Erev, & Sundali, 1998; chap. 8, this volume), extremely slow learning is observed in other settings (e.g., ultimatum games studied in Roth & Erev, 1995), (b) in some settings initial learning (first 400 trials) does not move behavior toward equilibrium (some of the matrix games studied by Erev & Roth, in press; chap. 4, this volume), and (c) fairly general models (Erev & Roth, in press) can describe the learning process in various games quite well. These results stress the importance of studying and understanding the learning process per se, and not just as a justification of equilibrium. All the learning chapters in this volume indicate that a clear shift toward the more general (psychological) interpretation of learning is taking place in experimental economics.

Before we conclude this section we wish to discuss learning and adaptation in a more general framework, of socialization and formal education and their treatment, or lack of, in psychology and economics. These comments are not intended to highlight differences between the two disciplines but rather to emphasize some important aspects that are currently neglected by both.

Most cultures and societies endorse some norms and values that contradict the basic tenets of rationality. The well-known proverb "if there is a will, there is a way" encourages us to ignore base rates; idealization of extreme forms of heroism for a common cause (e.g., sacrificing one's life for one's country) promotes disregard to the most basic elements of self-interest and survival over the benefit to society; the high value some institutions attach to perseverance (e.g., "never quit" and "finish the job" even if that job is no longer as important to us as it was when originally started) reinforces sunk-cost effects. Barney (the purple menace to economists) who preaches that "sharing is fun" and "sharing is caring" socializes children growing up today. Clearly the need to promote such pro-social behaviors indicates that, in most people's minds, these are not inherited tendencies. What might be inherited is our preparedness to *learn* such attitudes but not the attitudes and behaviors. This conclusion is consistent with much of the modern cross-cultural work in psychology (e.g. Triandis, 1995) that distinguishes between individualistic and collective cultures, and traces the impact of this distinction on behavior of individual members of these societies.[2]

Another interesting issue is the dual action of learning and teaching. It is well understood in developmental psychology that while parents are shaping their children's behavior, they are also conditioned by their children's behavior to react in certain ways. This is also captured in the classic cartoon reproduced in several psychological textbooks in which one laboratory mouse brags to its colleague "Boy do I have this guy conditioned. Every time I press the bar he drops in a pellet of food." Players in games (even if they are played only once) are simultaneously "students" and "teachers." As teachers they have their own theory of effective teaching, based on introspection, experience, and beliefs about how others learn. Some are convinced that "sparing the rod spoils the child," emphasizing the role of punishment in education, whereas others believe in the effectiveness of "the carrot." In any case, subjects in games are not only dynamic learners but also active teachers, shaping (consciously or not) the behavior of their opponents and partners. Surprisingly, this dual effect is completely ignored in economic modeling and, for the most part, in behavioral psychology.

Finally, most models of reinforcement learning in games emphasize only one type of instrumental contingency, namely, positive reinforcement. For the most part they ignore other types of reinforcement such as positive punishment (if the subject performs the instrumental response, it receives the aversive stimulus; otherwise not), negative reinforcement (the response turns off or prevents the presentation of the reinforcer), and negative punishment (the instrumental response prevents the delivery of an aversive stimulus – for example, explaining fair behavior as punishment avoidance, see Bolton & Zwick, 1995). Such omissions (in a different context) led Lunt (1996) to suggest that "economists work with simplified and anachronistic applications of psychological theory" (p. 283).

## Social Context and "Hot and Cold" Cognition

The psychological assumptions underlying models in economics have become more prominent recently. Leading economists and game theorists attempt to formulate theories that allow for imperfect rationality or weaken established assumptions and hypotheses (e.g., Machina,1982; Selten, 1975). In most instances bounded rationality is equated with limits on memory (capacity and selectivity) and mental computation, and these confines are used to address experimental anomalies or to offer a dynamic for selection among multiple equilibria. Consequently, experimenters (economists and many psychologists) make every attempt to strip the subjects of sources of argumentation and emotion. In effect, the experiments are designed to reduce the effect of "hot cognition" and see how people act when all distractions from "cold rationality" are removed. However, it is possible that some of the more interesting behavioral anomalies, especially those that are evident in games, are due to emotional impulses induced by social constraints and norms rather than to cognitive limitations, and seem to be much more fundamental and difficult to address (Lewin,1996). The social context of human economic behavior is at the core of game theory and, therefore, it is quite surprising that sociological and social psychological approaches to economic behavior have had relatively little impact even in the field of experimental economics.

For example, Bolton and Zwick (1995) argued that the major source for the violation of economic rationality in the ultimatum game is not limited cognitive capacity but rather powerful emotional reactions to what players view as unfair treatment by the first movers. Although this explanation is offered in the economics literature, it is essentially a modified utility interpretation. The same analysis offered in the psychological literature examines the state of mind that leads from judgment of unfairness to likely anger to acting spitefully. Pillutla and Murnighan (1996) argued, for example, that anger is a better explanation for the rejections than the mere perception that offers are unfair.

In game-theoretic formulations the desirability of an action is equated with the value of its consequences. In other words, players maximize their utilities by picking a "best" strategy from a set of well-defined distinct alternatives. Given the feasibility of a strategy, the only issue that affects one's choice is the strategy's direct and indirect effectiveness in promoting the player's objective function. Interestingly, in Adam Smith's writing, there is a distinct assessment of actions that is not identified with the evaluation of the useful consequences of that action when seen on its own. This view is not generally shared in contemporary economics but is echoed in the psychological literature on the relationship among beliefs, attitudes, intentions, and behavior.

There is an ongoing controversy in the psychology literature (that is not echoed in economics) regarding the origins of attitudes. Many psychologists do not accept the view that all attitudes are belief-based (cold cognitive), and point to the direct influences from affect (emotions/hot cognition) to attitudes. The existence of such a direct link may suggest that some behaviors are not determined only by the beliefs about their consequences, but also by the emotional residues of those actions. Further, the attitude-behavior relationship may be weaker when behavior is susceptible to social influence. For example, in the popular theory of reasoned action (Ajzen & Fishbein 1980), consumption behavior is subject to both attitudinal and social influence variables. Attitudinal or personal components and normative or social components determine intentions, which are the immediate antecedents of behavior. That is, one forms attitudes not only toward the consequences, but also toward the action itself. In such a model, attitudes toward consequences may be fixed, whereas attitudes toward the action are contingent on its social context.

There is, of course, nothing in the economic idea of assessment of consequences to prevent it from being influenced by the nature of the process that leads to the final outcomes. However, such dependency is seldom acknowledged in practice. In fact, many experimental economists employ anonymity and double-blind procedures to eliminate the effects of social context. In contrast, many social psychologists are interested primarily in the specific effects of varying social contexts and emotional climate on interactive actions.

## SUMMARY

In this chapter we have highlighted the major differences between the traditional economic and psychological approaches to the study of choice behavior, and summarized some recent trends in both disciplines. Our analysis suggests that the gap between economists and psychologists on some of these dimensions appears to be shrinking. Researchers in both disciplines tend to agree that: (a) in most cases both environmental and mental resources are scarce, (b) the strong assumption of rationality should be weakened, (c) some of the important effects of incentives can be studied conveniently by manipulating monetary outcomes, (d) framing effects cannot be ignored but their presence does not necessarily invalidate the game theoretical abstraction of the incentive structure, (e) learning is more than a justification for equilibrium, and (f) quantitative models are useful for the development of a good descriptive theory.

Practically all the contributors to this volume endorse (implicitly, and in some cases explicitly) these emerging common assumptions. This is amply reflected in their experimental work and their theoretical models. We started our chapter by asking a deceptively simple question "Can psychologists and economists cooperate in the study of human decisions in social and interactive contexts?" Although we can not conclude it with an equally simple answer, we are encouraged by the recent developments in experimental economics and behavioral decision theory, and we hope that in the not-too-far future, the answer will be an unqualified "yes." We hope that the collection of chapters in this book contribute toward this end.

# ENDNOTES

1. Camerer (1995, 1996), for example, emphasized that the difference between psychological and economic experiments should not be overstated. There is a substantial overlap across disciplines in methods and substantial variation within disciplines. However, the typical differences in methods are worth analyzing because they usually follow from different background presumptions about human nature and different target domains investigators hope to generalize. Among the important differences are: psychologists use natural stimuli, economists prefer abstract stimuli; psychologists do not pay because incentives usually complicate instructions; psychologists presume that subjects are cooperative and intrinsically motivated to perform well; psychologists do not repeat the tasks – they are interested in initial behavior, economists are interested in equilibrium.
2. This argument is a bit tricky and possibly circular. To establish this claim fully we would need to show that in societies that do not teach such behaviors (if such societies exist) these behaviors are nonexistent. The fact that something is taught does not necessarily imply that it would not have emerged otherwise in the absence of teaching (think of toilet training). Societies may achieve other secondary goals by teaching and preaching their values.

# REFERENCES

Ajzen, I., & Fishbein, M. (1980). *Understanding attitude and predicting social behavior.* Englewood Cliffs, NJ: Prentice-Hall.

Bolton, G. E., & Zwick, R. (1995). Anonymity versus punishment in ultimatum bargaining. *Games and Economic Behavior, 10,* 95-121.

Camerer, C. (1995). Individual decision making. In J. Kagel & A. E. Roth (Eds.), *Handbook of experimental economics* (pp. 587-703). Princeton, NJ: Princeton University Press.

Camerer, C. (1996). Rules for experimenting in psychology and economics, and why they differ. In W. Albers, W. Güth, P. Hammerstein, B. Moldovanu, & E. van Damme (Eds.), *Understanding strategic interaction: Essays in honor of Reinhard Selten* (pp. 313-327). Berlin: Springer.

Coombs, C., Dawes, R. M., & Tversky, A. (1970) *Mathematical Psychology.* Englewood Cliffs, NJ: Prentice-Hall.

Dawes, R. M. (1980). Social dilemmas. *Annual Review of Psychology, 31,* 169-193.

Dawes, R. M., & Thaler, R. H. (1988). Anomalies: Cooperation. *Journal of Economic Perspectives, 2*(3), 187-197.

Earl, P. E. (1990). Economics and psychology: A survey. *The Economic Journal, 100,* 718-755.

Erev, I., & Roth, A. (in press). Predicting how people play games: Reinforcement learning in experimental games with unique, mixed strategy equilibria. *American Economic Review.*

Friedman, M. (1953). The methodology of positive economics. *Essays in positive economics.* Chicago: University of Chicago Press.

Hogarth, R. M., & Reder, M. W. (1986). Editors' comments: Perspectives from economics and psychology. *The Journal of Business, 59* (4 part 2), 185-207.

Kadane, J. B., Larkey, P. D. (1983). The confusion of is and ought in game theoretic contexts. *Management Science, 29*(12), 1365-1379.

Kahan, J.P. & Rapoport, A. (1984), *Theories of coalition formation*. Hillsdale, NJ: Lawrence Erlbaum Associates.

Kahneman, D., & Tversky, A. (1979). Prospect theory: An analysis of decisions under risk. *Econometrica, 47,* 263-291.

Kahneman, D., & Tversky, A. (1984). Choice, values, and frames. *American Psychologist, 39,* 341-350.

Komorita, S. S., & Parks, C. D. (1995). Interpersonal relations: Mixed motive interaction. *Annual Review of Psychology, 46,* 183-207.

Lewin, S. B. (1996). Economics and psychology: Lessons for our own day from the early twentieth century. *Journal of Economic Literature, 34*(3), 1293-1323.

Lopes, L. L. (1994). Psychology and economics: Perspectives on risk, cooperation, and the marketplace. *Annual Review of Psychology, 45,* 197-227.

Luce, D. R., & Raiffa, H. (1957). *Games and decisions*. New York: Wiley.

Lunt, P. (1996). Rethinking the relationship between economics and psychology. *Journal of Economic Psychology, 17,* 275-287.

Machina, M. J. (1982). Expected utility analysis without the independence axiom. *Econometrica, 50,* 227-324.

Miller, G. A. (1956). The magical number seven plus or minus two: Some limits on our capacity to process information. *Psychological Review, 63,* 81-97.

Navon, D., & Gopher, D. (1979). On the economy of the human processing system. *Psychological Review, 63,* 81-97.

Payne, J. W., Bettman, J. R., & Johnson, E. J. (1993). *The adaptive decision maker.* Cambridge University Press.

Pillutla, M. M., & Murnighan, J. K. (1996). Unfairness, anger, and spite: Emotional rejections of ultimatum offers. *Organizational Behavior & Human Decision Processes, 68,* 208-224.

Rabin, M. (1993). Incorporating fairness into game theory and economics. *American Economic Review, 83,* 1281-1302.

Rabin, M. (in press). Psychology and economics. *Journal of Economic Literature.*

Rapoport, A., Seale, D. A., Erev, I., & Sundali, J. A. (1998). Equilibrium play in large group market entry games. *Management Science, 44*(1), 119-141.

Rapoport, A., & Wallsten, T. S. (1972). Individual decision making. *Annual Review of Psychology, 23,* 131-176

Rapoport, A. (1990). *Experimental studies of interactive decisions.* Dordrecht, Holland: Kluwer.

Roth, A. (1991). Game theory as a part of empirical economics. *The Economic Journal, 101,* 107-114.

Roth, A. E., & Erev, I. (1995). Learning in extensive-form games: Experimental data and simple dynamic models in the intermediate term. [Special Issue] *Games and Economic Behavior, 8,* 164-212.

Rubinstein, A. (1991). Comments on the interpretation of game theory. *Econometrica, 59*(4), 909-924.

Savage, L. J. (1954). *The foundations of statistics.* New York: Dover.

Schelling, T. C. (1985). The mind as a consuming organ. In J. Elster (Ed.), *The multiple self* (pp. 177-195). New York: Cambridge University Press.

Selten, R. (1975). Re-examination of the perfectness concept for equilibrium points in extensive games. *International Journal of Game Theory, 4,* 25-55.

Selten, R. (1989, May). *Evolution, learning, and economic behavior*. Paper presented at the Nancy L. Schwartz Memorial Lecture, Kellogg Graduate School of Management, Northwestern University, Chicago.

Simon, H. A. (1957). *Models of man*. New York: Wiley.

Simon, H. A. (1986). Rationality in psychology and economics. *Journal of Business, 59*(2), 209-224.

Simon, H. A. (1993). Altruism and economics. *American Economic Review, 83*(2), 156-161.

Sugden, R. (1991). Rational choice: A survey of contributions from economics and philosophy. *The Economic Journal, 101*, 751-785.

Triandis, H. C. (1995) *Individualism and collectivism*. Bolder: Westview Press.

von Neumann, J., & Morgenstern, O. (1947). *Theory of games and economic behavior*. Princeton, NJ: Princeton University Press.

# 2    Experimental Demand, Clear Incentives, Both, or Neither?

## Robyn M. Dawes
*Carnegie Mellon University*

Psychologists are concerned that experimental demand may invalidate the results of their experiments; the concern is that subjects may respond to cues in the experimental situation that signal the experimenter's intent, and hence behave in the way experimenters wish for reasons independent of the hypotheses the experimenters are attempting to evaluate. In contrast, experimental economists are concerned that a lack of clear incentives may invalidate the results of their experiments; confusion on the part of the subjects about the incentive structure that the economics experimenter has built into the situation is considered to be a potential impediment to evaluating economic hypotheses. The problem is that clear incentives provide subjects with an understanding of the experimenters' intent, and such intent is best conveyed through clear incentives. In many situations, the negatively valued experimental demand of the psychological experimenter is equivalent to the positively valued incentive clarity of the economics experimenter. When the purpose of the experiment is to determine whether subjects are able to respond appropriately to demands/incentives, this identity is benign. When, however, the intent of the experiment is to test hypotheses about subjects' systematic deviations from the incentive/demands of the situation (as in experiments investigating altruistic choice), this equivalence is not so fine. In these situations, it presents both the psychological and the economics experimenter with a quandary that is not easily resolved.

## EXPERIMENTAL DEMAND, CLEAR INCENTIVES, BOTH, OR NEITHER?

Subjects of experiments make constrained choices. Such choices may be economic ones (e.g., how much to invest in an experimentally created public good), expressive ones (e.g., where to place a check mark on a rating scale communicating attitudes toward sterile needle exchange programs), creative ones (e.g., deciding what an ink blot "looks like"), physiological ones (e.g., change in skin conductance on listening to a favorable statement about members of a minority group against which one is supposedly not prejudiced), and so on. The purpose of experiments is to garner information from such responses. If there is no constraint on them, then no information can be gathered because it is impossible to interpret them. Conversely, if there is total constraint, no information can be gathered either because subjects "could not have done otherwise."

Clearly (and trivially) some moderated degree of constraint is necessary in order to obtain the desired information, and this moderate degree may be different depending on the nature of the information. The point of this note is that the concerns of psychologists about constraints and those of experimental economists often tend to be quite different. In general, experimental psychologists are concerned about providing too much constraint, which can result in subjects' simply responding to the experimental demand of the situation, when this demand leads the subjects to behave in ways that they feel that they "have to" behave. (Yes, it would be nice to have unanimity within experimental conditions, but, again, not because subjects believe they "could not have done otherwise.") In contrast, experimental economists are often more concerned that responses are too unconstrained because the incentives that guide behavior are not clear. (In what follows, to avoid the trivial definition of "incentives" in terms of "revealed preference," the term refers to those parts of the experimental situation that experimenters, subjects, or both acknowledge to be important influences on behavior.)

This chapter considers monetary incentives, which are chronically used by experimental economists, and are often used by psychologists. Its major point is compatible with that of Lopes (1994) who wrote:

> Psychologists and economists also worry differently about experiments. Economists worry that subjects will not "tell the truth" unless incentives make truth-telling compatible with maximizing utility. Psychologists expect subjects to tell the truth, but worry about experimental demand and select subjects who are naive with respect to the theory under test. (p. 218)

As Lopes goes on to point out, one response psychologists have developed to their own concerns is to use deception, so that the purpose of the experiment will not be "clear" – and then worry that the subjects' expectations of deception will lead them to behave in ways incompatible with having believed the deception! In contrast, one way experimental economists deal with lack of clarity is to repeat the choice situation with such clear monetary incentives and feedback that only a nincompoop could fail to understand how she or he is expected to [should] "behave"! At the end of this process, subjects are hardly "naïve" – as desired by psychologists.

The concern about experimental demand that psychologists have is often couched in terms of the possibility of reactive arrangements. To quote Campbell and Stanley (1963):

> *Reactive arrangements.* In the usual psychological experiment, if not in educational research, a most prominent source of unrepresentativeness is the patent artificiality of the experiment setting and the student's knowledge that he [*sic*] is participating in an experiment. For human experimental subjects, a higher-order problem-solving task is generated, in which the procedure and experimental treatment are reacted to not only for their simple stimulus values, but also for their roles as cues in divining the experimenters' intent. (p. 20)

In contrast, consider the statement of an experimental economist (Ledyard, 1995) about monetary public goods games:

> It is possible to provide an environment in which at least 90% of subjects will become selfish Nash players. Heterogeneous payoffs and resources, complete and detailed information, particularly about the heterogeneity, anonymity from others and the experimenter, repetition and experience, and low marginal payoffs will all cause a reduction in rates of contribution, especially with small numbers. Add unanimity to the mechanism and rates will go to zero. It is possible to extinguish any trace of "altruism" in the lab. It is [also] possible to provide an environment in which almost all of the subjects contribute toward the group interest. Homogeneous interest, little or rough information, face-to-face discussions in small groups, no experience, small numbers and high marginal payoffs from contributing will all cause an increase in contributions. (p. 172)

Let us consider the latter quote from the perspective of the former. One way of structuring the environment involves basically no "altruistic" contributions whereas another way yields such departures from the game theory predictions. The psychologist critic concerned with experimental demand would point out that the former finding involves some "beating of subjects over the head" through constant repetition, feedback, complete and detailed information, and anonymity. So naturally the subjects act in accordance with standard "economic" (i.e., Nash) theory when the experimental situation is arranged in this manner. The response of the experimental economist is that the whole purpose is to find out exactly those characteristics of the environment that will yield near universal choice in accord with economic principles. Hence, making the monetary incentives clear through repetition and feedback is desirable, not undesirable (Tullock, 1993). The experimental psychologists might counter by asking the experimental economists why they do not just give the subject an IQ test instead – to understand that subjects are capable of interpreting their "messages" correctly. The possible response is that economic rationality is in fact intelligent behavior, so what is wrong with relating it to intelligence? Why not test economic rationality even more directly in an economic situation?

In the area of assessing altruistic contribution to public goods, the contrast in the positions is quite stark. Why, the psychologist could ask, do you think you could learn anything about such contributions by repetitively stressing that the only adaptive – and hence expected – behavior is "rational" failure to contribute? Clear incentives convey the nature of this rationality, and subjects are punished for ignoring these incentives. Why, the experimental economist may counter, do you think you could learn anything about altruistic contributions to public goods in a one-shot experiment, where people are presented with a rather unique situation that is confusing and ambiguous and you never give them a chance to learn the consequences of their own behavior? Thus, the experimental psychologist may be impressed by high, irrational, contributions to public goods in one-shot decisions, or in the first round of repeated play, whereas the experimental economist may be impressed by the very low rate of such contributions by later rounds. In fact, the same experiment may simultaneously demonstrate to the experimental psychologist that subjects are quite altruistic (or "group regarding," see Dawes, van de Kragt, & Orbell, 1988), counter to the rational, selfish individual assumed by the economist – and convince the experimental economist that these assumptions are correct.

There is one type of experiment in which these conflicting analyses converge. This is the type of experiment designed to determine whether subjects are capable of responding to rational incentives; the double auction experiments first begun and extensively studied by Smith (1986) constitute such experiments. The question is basically "can the market work as it is meant to, that is, do we obtain the equilibrium prices that economic theory predicts?" Here, there is no conflict between the demand interpretation and the incentive interpretation. The experimental psychologist running such an experiment wants the subjects to respond to the cues about the behavior that the psychologist deems appropriate, as does the experimental economist. Of course, there may be a subtle difference in the interpretation of the positive results; the experimental economist may conclude that market mechanisms *do* work (alternatively, that subjects are rational economic agents), whereas the experimental psychologist may conclude that market mechanisms *can* work (alternatively, that subjects can learn to be rational economic agents when the situation demands such learning). But that distinction does not lead to much of a brouhaha.

Critical disagreement arises when the variable of interest, such as altruistic contribution, is defined in terms of defying (overcoming, ignoring, negating, etc.) the economic incentives in the experimental situation. The best way to study such behavior, according to the experimental psychologist, would be to present the situation in as neutral a manner as possible, to make the incentives clear, but to assiduously avoid providing a message that subjects are "supposed" to respond to them. According to the experimental economist, the best way to study such a variable is to make the incentives crystal clear.

Van de Kragt, Orbell, and Dawes (1983) discovered a mechanism that might best be described as group designation of a minimal contributing set as a solution for step-level public goods problems. For example, groups were presented with a public goods problem where at least five of nine people had to sacrifice a $5.00 endowment, anonymously, in order for all group members to obtain a $10.00 bonus. When they were allowed to discuss this problem, group members typically urged everyone to contribute their $5.00, but then many pointed out that an agreement specifying universal contribution would provide an incentive not to contribute, because if at least five others did in fact contribute, the noncontributing member would receive both the $10.00 bonus and keep the $5.00 endowment. Spontaneously, a large majority of groups (10 of 12 in the original experiment) within 10 minutes of discussion created a mechanism for solving this dilemma. They designated which 5 people should contribute; sometimes a few people volunteered, although usually the contributing members were chosen by lot. Those not in the designated contributing set of contributors were not to contribute. Thus, each person within that set understood that his or her contribution was essential to his or her receipt of the $10.00 bonus – as well as to everyone else's receipt of that bonus. The subjects had themselves spontaneously transformed the public goods game into an assurance game. And it worked. It always worked, even when experimenters explained the mechanism to subjects and chose those in the designated contributing set by lot, rather than allow the subjects themselves to create the mechanism: "Outcomes in the minimal contributing set cases were the result of overwhelming conformity, on the part of designated contributors and designated noncontributors alike, to the roles that had been specified to them by the group" (van de Kragt, Orbell, & Dawes, 1983, p. 114).

The problem was that not only was each individual's contribution critical for his or her own receipt of the $10.00 bonus, but for everyone else's as well. The experimental manipulation that unconfounded these two considerations was to form the designated contributing set as before, but then introduce a payoff function that provided the $10.00 bonus for each person within the set if *all 4 others* within it contributed, and the $10.00 bonus for those outside the set if *all 5* members of it contributed. Here, the payoff to the designated individual was independent of his or her own choice about contribution, but that contribution was absolutely necessary if anyone else in the room was to receive the $10.00 payoff. When subjects were not allowed to discuss the situation, contribution rates for those in the set were minimal – 28%. When, however, subjects were allowed to discuss the situation, almost everybody in the designated set contributed, as before. In fact, 24 out of 25 subjects did, whereas in the earlier experiments all had. See the details of this experiment in Dawes, van de Kragt, & Orbell (1988) and van de Kragt et al., (1986).

Did the subjects understand the incentives clearly? They were quizzed before making their choices, and these choices were not requested until every subject in all experiments answered the quizzes correctly. But did they really understand the consequences of their choices (the true incentives)? None of them experienced these consequences until after the choice was made, and the choice was never repeated. Suppose that the experiment had been iterated. What would have happened? We do not know. Would it have been important if the behavior was different? The psychologists wary of experimental demand could easily say "no," whereas the economists concerned with creating a clear economic experiment could easily say "yes."

One possible criterion for deciding whether an experiment is too constrained is to ask whether the finding that subjects did not behave as they actually did would be a priori absurd, or at least difficult to conjecture (Dawes, 1991). The problem with this criterion is that of who decides what is absurd or unusual. This criterion can be used quite simply to decide that our government should not spend millions of dollars to determine that HIV-infected infants who are dying will perform more poorly on cognitive tasks than do those that are not dying, or that *National Geographic* articles portray Western (White) societies in more favorable terms than African (Black) societies. Ideally, we could use the criterion that people who are unfamiliar with the theories predict the behaviors they expect in the experiments, and the other behaviors would defy plausibility. But suppose such peoples' "intuitions" are so good that they predict what the theory to be evaluated predicts? Then have we learned anything? The problem is that we must decide what is implausible to whom and plausible to whom else – and in situations that are far more ambiguous than those that can be dismissed as unworthy of investigation because results in the direction opposite that hypothesized are so improbable.

Consider, for example, the quotation from Ledyard at the beginning of this chapter. The next sentence concerning contribution is: "why and how this all [contributing, as opposed to behaving in accord with a Nash equilibrium] works remains a mystery" (p. 172). A mystery to whom? Contributing in a monetary social dilemma situation may be somewhat mysterious behavior to a game theorist, whereas failing to do so may present a mystery to a social psychologist. In summary, the trick of inserting the word "not" in the results and deciding whether they would still be believable can work on occasion, when the judgment is clear, but turns out to be ambiguous in exactly those situations where we most need guidance for deciding whether the experiment provides information.

Conversely, we can use the judgment that "anything might happen" in an experiment to conclude that there is too little constraint on subjects' choice. Here we would ask whether to expect behavior to be consistent with various theories, or to be chaotic. Again, we have the problem of whom to ask. For example, a believer in the validity of the Rorschach ink blot tests may conclude that the subject must choose between good versus poor form responses that follow certain principles (determinates), whereas a critic familiar with the literature that projective interpretation of the responses does not yield knowledge may conclude that this deficiency occurs because there is too little constraint.

These conflicting views about demand versus clear incentives arise outside experimental situations as well. The Spanish composer Enrique Granados (of Goyescas fame) died in a manner wholly consistent with the extreme romanticism of his music. On March 24, 1916: "The *Sussex* was torpedoed by a German submarine in mid-channel; Granados was picked up by a lifeboat, but he saw his wife struggling in the sea and dived in to save her. Both were drowned" (Ruiz-Pipo, 1980, pp. 628-629). Clearly, Granados understood the consequences of his behavior only after he made the choice – and he had no opportunity to repeat it. Suppose, now, that an omnipotent experimenter (OE) decided to make the incentives clear. OE halts time when a drowning Granados – summoning forth his last, heroic effort of denial – sees a bright light and old friends a millisecond before they deceptively urge him into oblivion. He is then placed back on the lifeboat, and Trial 2 commences. OE repeats the process. Suppose that by Trial 9 Granados no longer jumps out of the lifeboat. What would we conclude about human behavior, about altruism, about response to clear incentives, about the rational person model of human behavior? About the nature of human impulsivity? Or even about the nature of love? Has Granados simply gotten the message about what OE expects of him and decided that it is time to succumb to it rather than to death? Or were the first eight acts those of a confused individual in a unique situation never before experienced (and never to be experienced again) – and hence not representative of ordinary human choice in the ordinary world? Representative or not, diagnostic or not, important or not?

My own response to these questions is that the quandary is a quandary, and there is no easy way out. Experimentation is an inherently ambiguous and flawed way of understanding human behavior. We must, however, take Winston Churchill's advice for evaluating representative democracy and consider the alternatives. They are worse.

## ACKNOWLEDGMENT

This chapter was supported in part by the National Science Foundation, grant SES-9008157. Any opinions, conclusions, or recommendations are those of the author and do not necessarily reflect the views of the National Science Foundation.

# REFERENCES

Campbell, D. T., & Stanley, J. C. (1963). *Experimental and quasi-experimental designs for research*. Chicago: Rand McNally.

Dawes, R. M. (1991). The importance of alternative hypotheses – and hypothetical counterfactuals in general – in social science. Division One William James Book Award Address on August 16, 1991. *The General Psychologist, 28*(1), 2-7.

Dawes, R. M., van de Kragt, A. J. C., Orbell, J. M. (1988). Not me or thee but we: The importance of group identity in eliciting cooperation in dilemma situations: Experimental manipulations. *Acta Psychologica, 68,* 83-97.

Ledyard, J. O. (1995). Public goods: A survey of experimental research. In J. H. Kagel and A. E. Roth (Eds.), *The handbook of experimental economics* (pp. 111-194). Princeton, NJ: Princeton University Press.

Lopes, L. L. (1994). Psychology and economics: Perspectives on risk, cooperation, and the marketplace. *Annual Review of Psychology, 45,* 197-227.

Ruiz-Pipo, A. (1980). Enrique Granados. In S. Sadie (Ed.), *The new grove dictionary of music and musicians, Vol. 7.* (pp. 628-629). London: Macmillan.

Smith, V. L. (1986). Experimental methods in the political economy of exchange. *Science, 234,* 167-173.

Tullock, G. (1993, August). *Psychology and economics: Mediating the difference*. Paper presented at the 1993 meeting of the Economics Science Association, Tucson, AZ.

van de Kragt, A. J. C., Orbell, J. M., & Dawes, R. M. (1983). The minimal contributing set as a solution to public goods problems. *American Political Science Review, 77,* 112-122.

van de Kragt, A. J. C., Orbell, J. M., Dawes, R. M., Braver, S. J., & Wilson, L. A. (1986). Doing well and doing good as ways of solving social dilemmas. In H. Wilke, D. Messick, & C. Rutte (Eds.), *Social dilemmas* (pp. 177-203). Frankfurt am Main: Verlag Peter Lang.

# Part II

## Learning in Experimental Games

# 3   Experience-Weighted Attraction Learning in Games: Estimates From Weak-Link Games

**Colin Camerer**
*California Institute of Technology*

**Teck-Hua Ho**
*University of Pennsylvania*

How does an equilibrium arise in a game? For decades, the implicit answer to this question was that players reasoned their way to an equilibrium, or adapted and evolved toward it in some unspecified way. Theorists have become interested in the specific details of how adaptation and evolution work. Much of this interest revolves around models in which players change their strategies or learn, and what equilibria might result under various learning rules. Our research is motivated by a different question: Which learning models describe human behavior best? This chapter proposes a general experience-weighed attraction (EWA) model and estimates the model parametrically using a small set of experimental data.

Our main contribution is that the general model contains two very different, well-known approaches as special cases. One approach, *belief-based models*, starts with the premise that players keep track of the history of previous play by other players and form some belief about what others will do in the future based on that observation. Then they choose a best-response strategy that maximizes their expected payoffs, given the beliefs they formed. This class of models includes Cournot (1960) best-response dynamics and fictitious play (Brown, 1951).

The other approach, *choice reinforcement models*, assumes that strategies are reinforced by their previous payoffs, and the probability of choosing a strategy depends in some way on its cumulative stock of reinforcement (e.g. Bush & Mosteller, 1955; Cross, 1983; Erev & Roth, 1997; and Roth & Erev, 1995). Reinforcement models are belief-free: Players care only about the payoff strategies yielded in the past, not about the history of play by others that created those payoffs. As a result, reinforcement may lead players to choose dominated strategies, which are not the best responses to any beliefs about what others will do.

Some studies have evaluated each of the different approaches empirically, but few have compared them directly (e.g. Chen & Tang, 1996; Erev & Roth, 1997; and Ho & Weigelt, 1996). Indeed, it seems almost impossible to have a unifying framework that includes these two different approaches as special cases. One way to see the apparent incompatibility is to highlight the information players are assumed to use in the two approaches. Except during the formation of initial attractions, which may depend on the payoff matrix, the choice reinforcement approach implicitly assumes players do not use full knowledge of the payoff matrix. Choice-reinforcing learners who know the list of strategies but not their payoffs will play exactly the way as if they had the matrix or tree in front of them, holding initial reinforcements constant. Belief-based learners use the payoff matrix to calculate expected payoffs of strategies, given their beliefs, but pay no attention to their own payoff history. Both approaches assume players do not pay attention to other players' payoffs. How can a single approach include them both? The keys to a unifying approach are two modeling features.

The first key feature is to separate cumulative reinforcement or attraction of strategies into two components. One component represents the amount of experience (possibly discounted to reflect forgetting, or the players' awareness that nonstationarity implies old experience is not as useful as new). The second component represents the average payoff attraction that experience suggests. These two features are necessary to capture belief models in which prior beliefs have strength, and they also suggest an interesting way to expand choice reinforcement.

The second key feature is expanding how strategies are reinforced. In the choice reinforcement approach, when Player 1 picks strategy $s^i_1$ and Player 2 picks $s^j_2$, strategy $s^i_1$ is reinforced according to the payoff $\pi_1(s^i_1, s^j_2)$ and unchosen strategies $s^k_1$ ($k \neq i$) are not reinforced at all. In our approach, the unchosen strategies *are* reinforced based on a multiple $\delta$ of the payoffs $\pi_1(s^k_1, s^j_2)$ they would have earned. (The default approach implicitly assumes $\delta = 0$.)

When $\delta = 1$, and previous attractions depreciate at the same rate as the strength or weight of previous experience, reinforcing each strategy according to what it would have earned is behaviorally equivalent to a belief-based model. The equivalence occurs because reinforcing all strategies based on past payoffs is the same as computing expected payoffs based on beliefs that arise from past history. The expansion of reinforcement with $\delta = 1$ also nudges choice reinforcement away from its behaviorist roots toward something more cognitive, intelligent, and probably more realistic.

We also replace the best-response feature of belief models with better response or quantal response (e.g. Fudenberg & Levine, 1996; Ho & Weigelt,

1996; and McKelvey & Palfrey, 1995, 1996). In quantal response models, strategies with higher payoffs are chosen more often, but the strategy with the highest payoff is not chosen all the time (except in the limiting case of extremely payoff-sensitive response functions). Introducing this feature puts best-response models and reinforcement models on a similar statistical footing and uses more information than other measures, like hit rate measures of the proportion of correct predictions.

Next we describe the general EWA model. We describe choice reinforcement and belief-based models (with geometrically declining weights), show how they are special cases, and give psychological interpretations to the EWA parameters. We also give a simple example to further sharpen intuition. We conclude by reporting parameter estimates from one small set of experimental data.

# THE EXPERIENCE-WEIGHTED ATTRACTION (EWA) MODEL

There are $n$ players indexed by $i$ ($i = 1, ..., n$). $S_i$ is the strategy space of Player $i$ and for this chapter, $S_i$ consists of $m_i$ discrete choices, that is, $S_i = \{s^1_i, s^2_i, ..., s^{m_i}_i\}$. $S = S_1 \times ... \times S_n$ is the Cartesian product of the individual strategy spaces and is the strategy space of the game. $s_i \in S_i$ denotes a strategy of Player $i$, and is therefore an element of $S_i$. $s = (s_1, ..., s_n) \in S$ is a strategy combination, and it consists of $n$ strategies, one for each player. $s_{-i} = (s_1, ..., s_{i-1}, s_{i+1}, ..., s_n)$ is a strategy combination of all players except $i$. $\pi_i(s_i, s_{-i})$ is the payoff function of Player $i$ and is scalar valued.

Let $s_i(t)$ be the strategy actually chosen by Player $i$ in the $t$th play of the game. Similarly, $s_{-i}(t) = (s_1(t), ..., s_{i-1}(t), s_{i+1}(t), s_n(t))$ are the strategy combinations for all players except $i$ at time $t$ respectively.

The core of the model is two state variables that are updated after each round. The first variable is $N(t)$, which we interpret as the number of observation-equivalents of past experience. (This number will not generally equal the number of previous observations, due to forgetting and the number $N(0)$ of observation-equivalents of prior experience.) The second variable is $A^j_i(t)$, the attraction of a strategy after period $t$ has taken place. In reinforcement approaches, $A^j_i(t)$ is a stock of reinforcement or past rewards (including some initial reinforcement or propensity). In belief-based models, $A^j_i(t)$ corresponds to expected payoff of strategy $s^j_i$ in $t + 1$, given beliefs based on history through $t$. We use the new, neutral term attraction, which is used in marketing literature on brand choice, because attractions can be either propensities or expected payoffs.

The class of learning models predicts how frequently players choose strategies at each round. $A^j_i(t)$ determines the period $t + 1$ choice probabilities. Specifically, the probability with which Player $i$ chooses a strategy $j$ for period $t$

+ 1 is:

$$P_i^j(t+1) = \frac{e^{f(A_i^j(t))}}{\sum_{k=1}^{m_i} e^{f(A_i^k(t))}}, t \geq 0 \qquad (1)$$

where $f(.)$ is some monotonically increasing function that connects attraction to choice probability. The special cases of power functions $f(x) = ln(x^\lambda)$ and logit choice functions, $f(x) = \lambda \cdot x$, have been used in previous work.

The variables $N(t)$ and $A_i^j(t)$ begin with some prior values, $N(0)$ and $A_i^j(0)$. These prior values can be thought of as reflecting pregame experience, due to either learning transferred from different games or introspection. $N(0)$ can be interpreted as the number of periods of actual experience that is equivalent to pregame thinking. In belief-based models, $A_i^j(0)$ will be equal to expected payoffs given initial prior beliefs.

Updating of these variables is governed by two rules. First,

$$N(t) = \rho \cdot N(t-1) + 1, t \geq 1. \qquad (2)$$

The parameter $\rho$ can be thought of as a depreciation rate or retrospective discount factor that measures the fractional impact of previous experience, compared to one new period.

The second rule updates the level of attraction. A key component of the updating is the payoff that a strategy yielded or would have yielded in a period. The model weights hypothetical payoffs that unchosen strategies would have earned by a parameter $\delta$, and weights payoff actually received from chosen strategy $s_i(t)$, by an additional $1 - \delta$ (so they receive a total weight of 1). Using an indicator function $I(x, y)$ that equals 1 if $x = y$ and 0 if $x \neq y$, the weighted payoff can be written $[\delta + (1 - \delta) \cdot I (s_i^j, s_i(t)] \cdot \pi_i(s_i^j, s_{-i}(t))$.

Remember that the initial condition is $A_i^j(0)$. The rule for updating attraction sets $A_i^j(t)$ to be a weighted average of the weighted payoff from period $t$ and the previous attraction $A_i^j(t-1)$, according to:

$$A_i^j(t) = \frac{\phi \cdot N(t-1) \cdot A_i^j(t-1) + [\delta + (1-\delta) \cdot I(s_i^j, s_i(t)] \cdot \pi_i(s_i^j, s_{-i}(t))}{N(t)}.$$

$$(3)$$

The factor $\phi$ is a discount factor that depreciates previous attraction.

The next section briefly discusses psychological interpretations of some of the parameters. In Camerer and Ho (1996), we show that $\delta = 0$, $N(0) = 1$, and $\rho = 0$ imply choice reinforcement in which only chosen strategies are reinforced.

More remarkably, when $\delta = 1$ and $\rho = \phi$ and initial attractions are equal to expected payoffs given initial beliefs, the attraction of each strategy corresponds exactly to its expected payoff when beliefs are formed as a geometrically weighted average of observed history. Then the choice reinforcement and belief-based approaches can be directly compared by measuring $\delta$, $\rho$, and $N(0)$.

## Psychological Interpretation of Parameters

A psychological interpretation can be given to each of the parameters in the model. Sensible interpretations are important in judging how good a model is. Parameters with natural interpretations are better because they can be measured in other ways and theorized about more fruitfully.[1]

### 1. Attraction depreciation $\phi$
To economists, the parameter $\phi$ is naturally interpreted as depreciation of past attractions. Roth and Erev (1995) called $\phi$ forgetting. However, a low $\phi$ may also reflect the players' intuitive understanding that they should abandon old predispositions gradually because other players may be changing their strategies (even if they remember their earlier payoffs perfectly well).

### 2. Experience depreciation $\rho$
The parameter $\rho$ depreciates the experience measure $N(t)$. It captures something like decay in the strength of prior beliefs, which could be different than decay of initial attractions (captured by $\phi$). In a game-theoretic context, $\rho$ can be interpreted as the degree to which players realize other players are adapting, so that old observations on what others did become less and less useful. In this view $\rho$ is an index of perceived nonstationarity.

### 3. Imagination $\delta$
The parameter $\delta$ can be interpreted as a combination of information about foregone outcomes and the ability to imagine them.[2] Roth and Erev (1995) suggested that a desirable feature for a learning model is that it not depend on information unobservable to the players. A corollary principle is that the model should use all information that is available (unless there is some good reason to think players do not). The general EWA model with $\delta > 0$ uses available information about payoffs that <u>could</u> have resulted. This information is ignored in choice reinforcement (when $\delta = 0$ players care only about their actual payoff).

The implicit cognitive assumption is that players do not realize what other strategies would have earned, or they do not attend to or imagine them. When $\delta = 1$, the incremental weight to the actual payoff, $1 - \delta$, is zero; hypothetical or imaginary payoffs have equal cognitive weight.

When players do not know foregone payoffs it is natural to take $\delta = 0$ as a sign of their ignorance. Thus, our model is at least as widely applicable as choice reinforcement to domains in which foregone payoffs are unknown (like animal learning and many kinds of naturally occurring games humans play). Similarly, in games with very large strategy spaces, it is plausible that $\delta$ is lower than in simpler games because scarce attention must be divided across a wider number of foregone payoffs.

### 4. Initial attraction and weight $A^j_i(0)$, $N(0)$

The term $A^j_i(0)$ represents the initial attraction, which might be derived from some analysis of the game, from surface similarity between strategies and strategies that were successful in similar games, and other factors.

The term $N(0)$ represents the strength of the initial attractions relative to later reinforcement, and can be interpreted as the unit-for-unit relative weight of prior experience (or introspection) compared to actual payoff experience. Thus, $N(0)$ captures something like stubbornness of players (or in belief models, the strength of prior beliefs relative to likelihood evidence from experience).

Notice that $N(0)$ should not be interpreted as the amount of pregame thinking, per se – instead, it is the relative amount of pregame thinking compared to thinking during the game. As a result, it is hard to guess a priori how task variables would affect $N(0)$. For example, when stakes are higher subjects may take longer to respond but they may also think carefully about how to respond to actual experience, so the effect on $N(0)$ is not clear. Similarly, if the game is repeated for many periods, subjects may think more carefully before playing (because their thinking has a longer payback period), which suggests a higher $N(0)$. Or they might think less carefully before playing because they realize they will get a lot of experience to learn from, which suggests a lower $N(0)$.

These interpretations suggest other ways to measure the parameters that might interest psychologists. For example, if we think $\phi$ and $\rho$ reflect memories of previous outcomes, then standard measures of memory – like accuracy and speed of recall – should correlate with $\phi$ and $\rho$. And if $\delta$ is interpreted as attention to foregone payoffs from unchosen alternatives, then values of $\delta$ should correlate with other measures of attention (such as eye movements or looking times in an information retrieval system, as in Camerer, Johnson, Sen, and Rymon (1993)).

## CHOICE REINFORCEMENT MODELS

Excluding the generalization feature that spreads reinforcement of the chosen strategy to neighboring strategies, the choice reinforcement model begins with initial propensities $A^j_i(0)$ and updates them according to

$$A_i^j(t) = (1 - \phi)A_i^j(t - 1) + I(s_i^j, s_i(t)) \cdot \pi_i(s_i^j, s_{-i}(t)). \qquad (4)$$

Early models often updated probabilities directly (i.e. $A_i^j(t) = P(s_i^j(t+1)))$. In the form studied by Erev and Roth (1996), $f(x) = ln(x)$ so the predicted choice probability is

$$P_i^j(t+1) = \frac{e^{ln(A_i^j(t))}}{\sum_{k=1}^{m_i} e^{ln(A_i^k(t))}} = \frac{A_i^j(t)}{\sum_{k=1}^{m_i} A_i^k(t)}. \qquad (5)$$

**Proposition 1:** *Assume* $\delta = 0$, $N(0) = 1$, *and* $\rho = 0$. *That restricted model is the same as a simple version of choice reinforcement.*[3]
*Proof: See Camerer and Ho (1996).*

The basic idea is simple: Fixing $N(0) = 1$ and $\rho = 0$ means that $N(t) = 1$ for $t \geq 0$, so the $N(t)$ term in Equation 3 disappears. Fixing $\delta = 0$ means that only chosen strategies are reinforced.

In the EWA model, $N(t)$ allows initial attractions and later experience to be weighted differently, essentially controlling the strength of initial attractions in a way that is not present in most choice reinforcement models. These effects can be seen most directly by computing the attraction after two periods, $A_i^j(2)$, which is

$$A_i^j(2) = \frac{\phi^2 \cdot A_i^j(0) \cdot N(0) + \phi \cdot \pi_i(s_i^j, s_{-i}(1)) + \pi_i \cdot (s_i^j, s_{-i}(2))}{\rho^2 \cdot N(0) + \rho + 1}. \qquad (6)$$

Notice that the parameter $\phi$ controls the relative weight of different chunks of experience – the first period payoff is weighted by $\phi$ whereas the second period payoff is weighted by one. The parameter $N(0)$ (along with $\phi$) controls the tradeoff between initial attractions and actual payoff experience. Thus, by choosing $N(0)$ small (large), the effect of prior experience in the form of $A(0)$ is short-lived (long-lasting). For example, if $N(0) = \varepsilon$, then initial attractions wear off immediately after play begins. Alternatively, a very large $N(0)$ means that experience barely changes attractions. In choice reinforcement, the relative impact of the initial attractions and the relative impact of different pieces of experience are controlled by one parameter ($\phi$), so prior experience ($A(0)$) and old payoff experience must be discounted at the same rate. Whether these two effects need to be separate is, of course, an empirical question. That question is answered by the parameter estimates of $N(0)$ and $\rho$.

## BELIEF BASED MODELS

Adaptive players are those who base their responses on beliefs formed by
observing the history of others. Although there are many ways of forming
beliefs, we consider a fairly large class of models that includes familiar ones like
fictitious play and Cournot best-response as special cases. We consider models
in which initial beliefs of opponents' strategies are expressed as a ratio of
hypothetical counts of observations of strategy $s^k_{-i}$, denoted by $C^k_{-i}(0)$. (For
simplicity, assume there are only two players.) These observations can then be
naturally integrated with actual observations as experience accumulates.
Furthermore, we assume that past experience is depreciated or discounted by a
factor $\rho$ (presumably between zero and one). (For these models to be a special
case of the EWA approach, this factor $\rho$ is the same as $\phi$ as used earlier – in a
sense, the belief approach imposes the restriction that prior experience and
actual experience are depreciated at the same rate, which is not true for EWA.)

Formally, the prior beliefs for Player $i$ about choices of others are specified
by a vector of frequencies of choices of strategies $s^k_{-i}$, denoted by $C^k_{-i}(t)$
normalized by the sum of those frequencies. We define the sum of those
frequencies by

$$N(t) = \sum_{k=1}^{m_{-i}} C^k_{-i}(t).  \tag{7}$$

Note that $N(t)$ is not subscripted because the count of frequencies is assumed to
be the same for all players. Thus, the initial prior $b_0(s^k_{-i})$ is:

$$b_0(s^k_{-i}) = \frac{C^k_{-i}(0)}{N(0)}  \tag{8}$$

with $C^k_{-i}(0) \geq 0$ and $N(0) > 0$. Beliefs are updated by depreciating the previous
count by $\rho$, and adding one for the strategy actually chosen by the other player.
That is,

$$b_t(s^k_{-i}) = \frac{\rho \cdot C^k_{-i}(t-1) + I(s^k_{-i}, s_{-i}(t))}{\sum_{h=1}^{m_{-i}} [\rho \cdot C^h_{-i}(t-1) + I(s^h_{-i}, s_{-i}(t))]}.  \tag{9}$$

Expressing beliefs in terms of previous-period beliefs,

$$b_t(s^k_{-i}) = \frac{\rho \cdot b_{t-1}(s^k_{-i}) + \dfrac{I(s^k_{-i}, s_{-i}(t))}{N(t-1)}}{\rho + \dfrac{1}{N(t-1)}}.$$  (10)

Expected payoffs are just taken over beliefs in each period, according to

$$A^j_i(t) = E_\pi(s^j_i \mid b_t(s^k_{-i})) = \sum_{k=1}^{m_{-i}} \pi_i(s^j_i, s^k_{-i}) \cdot b_t(s^k_{-i}),$$  (11)

when written as a function of $A^j_i(t-1) = E_\pi(s^j_i \mid b_{t-1}(s^k_{-i}))$, this is

$$A^j_i(t) = E_\pi(s^j_i \mid b_t(s^k_{-i})) = \frac{\rho \cdot N(t-1) \cdot A^j_i(t-1) + \sum_{k=1}^{m_{-i}} \pi(s^j_i, s^k_{-i}) \cdot I(s^k_{-i}, s_{-i}(t))}{\rho \cdot N(t-1) + 1},$$  (12)

which can also be written as

$$A^j_i(t) = E_\pi(s^j_i \mid b_t(s^k_{-i})) = \frac{\rho \cdot N(t-1) \cdot A^j_i(t-1) + \pi(s^j_i, s_{-i}(t))}{\rho \cdot N(t-1) + 1}.$$  (13)

Written in this form, the relation between belief-based models (in which attractions are expected payoffs) and the EWA model in Equation 3 should be apparent. Next we state our second proposition.

*Proposition 2: Assume $\delta = 1$ and $\rho = \phi$ in the EWA model, and the $A^j_i(0)$ are expected payoffs given initial beliefs (based on relative frequencies $C^k_{-i}(0)$). That restricted model is the same as geometric weight belief-based models.*
*Proof: See Camerer and Ho (1996).*

Furthermore, in the quantal response or logit form, $f(x) = \lambda \cdot x$, so

$$P^j_i(t+1) = \frac{e^{\lambda \cdot A^j_i(t)}}{\sum_{k=1}^{m_i} e^{\lambda \cdot A^k_i(t)}}.$$  (14)

The parameter $\lambda$ measures sensitivity of players to expected payoffs. Sensitivity could vary due to psychophysical concerns of whether subjects are

**Table 3.1**
**Stag Hunt**

|   | $\underline{L}$ | $\underline{R}$ |
|---|---|---|
| T | 8 | 9 |
| B | 4 | 10 |

highly motivated or not.

The main virtue of this parameter-rich approach is that three kinds of familiar belief models are special cases. Cournot best-response dynamics correspond to $\phi$ = 0; previous attractions are immediately discarded and only the last observation counts in determining beliefs. Fictitious play corresponds to $\phi = 1$; all previous observations count equally in determining beliefs. Furthermore, more complicated rules can be constructed by letting $\phi$ vary with time, with player's payoffs, and so on. In the strict best-response versions of all these approaches $\lambda$ = $\infty$ because players are assumed to always choose the best-response. But these versions are sure to be rejected because a single prediction error makes the likelihood zero, so noisy adaptive models with finite $\lambda$ are a natural extension (see Fudenberg & Levine, 1996), and are estimated later.

## AN EXAMPLE

An example will help illustrate how EWA is a bridge that spans choice reinforcement and belief models. We use a two-player version of stag hunt as an example. Table 3.1 shows the row player's payoffs.

To illustrate, we take only row Player 1's perspective (and drop the Player 1 subscript for brevity). Suppose the history of play is T, L in period 1. The row player's actual payoff was 8.

First consider a belief model in which the initial experience-equivalents are $C^L(0)$ and $C^R(0)$, so $N(0) = C^L(0) + C^R(0)$. Then the preplay initial expected payoffs are

$$A^T(0) = \frac{C^L(0) \cdot 8 + C^R(0) \cdot 9}{N(0)} \qquad (15)$$

$$A^B(0) = \frac{C^L(0) \cdot 4 + C^R(0) \cdot 10}{N(0)}. \qquad (16)$$

Player 1's history of observations of the column player's moves is L in period 1. Suppose the player updates beliefs by weighting each period's previous stock of cumulated observations by $\rho$, then adding one for each observed choice by the other player. Then after period 1 the beliefs are (cf. Equation 10):

$$b_1(L) = \frac{\rho \cdot C^L(0) + 1}{\rho \cdot N(0) + 1} \tag{17}$$

$$b_1(R) = \frac{\rho \cdot C^R(0) + 0}{\rho \cdot N(0) + 1}. \tag{18}$$

To cement intuition, keep in mind the extreme cases $\rho = 0$ (Cournot best-response dynamics) and $\rho = 1$ (fictitious play). After period 1, the expected payoffs are

$$\begin{aligned} A^T(1) &= 8 \cdot b_1(L) + 9 \cdot b_1(R) \\ &= \frac{(\rho \cdot C^L(0) + 1) \cdot 8 + (\rho \cdot C^R(0) + 0) \cdot 9}{\rho \cdot N(0) + 1} \end{aligned} \tag{19}$$

$$\begin{aligned} A^B(1) &= 4 \cdot b_1(L) + 10 \cdot b_1(R) \\ &= \frac{(\rho \cdot C^L(0) + 1) \cdot 4 + (\rho \cdot C^R(0) + 0) \cdot 10}{\rho \cdot N(0) + 1} \end{aligned} \tag{20}$$

With a little algebra on the previous equations, updated expected payoffs can be expressed as a function of the previous expected payoffs, like so (cf. Equation 12)

$$A^T(1) = \frac{\rho \cdot A^T(0) \cdot N(0) + 8}{\rho \cdot N(0) + 1} \tag{21}$$

$$A^B(1) = \frac{\rho \cdot A^B(0) \cdot N(0) + 4}{\rho \cdot N(0) + 1}. \tag{22}$$

Now switch to choice reinforcement. After the first period choice reinforcement will have updated attractions (cf. Equation 4)

$$A^T(1) = A^T(0) \cdot \phi + 8 \qquad (23)$$

$$A^B(1) = A^B(0) \cdot \phi \qquad (24)$$

The trick is to think of a sensible general form for which Equations 21, 22, 23, and 24 are special cases. Starting with the choice reinforcement attractions, three features must be added: (a) The foregone payoff 4 must be added to $A^B(1)$ with a weight $\delta$. Then if $\delta = 0$ the choice reinforcement attractions apply, and if $\delta = 1$ the actual payoff 8 and the foregone payoff 4 are both weighted equally, as in the belief-based expected payoffs (Equations 21 and 22), and (b) the choice reinforcement attractions must be divided by the factor $(\rho \cdot N(0) + 1)$. Think of this term as a way of scaling attractions so that they are like expected payoffs (Equations 21 and 22) or, if $\rho = 0$, the scaling factor is 1 and the choice reinforcement attractions can grow beyond the scale of payoffs, and (c) the initial attraction $A^j(0)$ must be weighted by the experience-equivalent factor $N(0)$.

Adding these three features gives updated attractions

$$A^T(1) = \frac{\phi \cdot A^T(0) \cdot N(0) + 8}{\rho \cdot N(0) + 1} \qquad (25)$$

$$A^B(1) = \frac{\phi \cdot A^B(0) \cdot N(0) + \delta \cdot 4}{\rho \cdot N(0) + 1}. \qquad (26)$$

The connection between this form and the two special cases should be almost transparent. When $\rho = 0$, $N(0) = 1$, and $\delta = 0$ (Equations 25 and 26), the choice reinforcement equations (Equations 23 and 24) result. When $\phi = \rho$ and $\delta = 1$ (Equations 25 and 26) and the initial attractions $A^T(0)$ and $A^B(0)$ are expected payoffs determined by the initial beliefs, then the belief-based model attractions (Equations 21 and 22) result.

The general forms (Equations 25 and 26) are the EWA model (see Equation 3).

The class of adaptive belief models that emerge as special cases of our general model is admittedly rather special because it only permits geometrically declining weight on past observations (see also Chen & Tang, 1996; Fudenberg & Levine, 1996).

However, this class could be expanded without too much loss of parsimony by allowing $\phi$ to depend on time, on the spread of reinforcements, expected payoffs, and so forth.

# PARAMETER ESTIMATION FROM EXPERIMENTAL DATA

We estimated the values of model parameters from one sample of experimental data on weak-link coordination games. We picked weak-link games because the data were easy to obtain and the results help highlight the differences among choice reinforcement ($\delta = 0$), the belief models ($\delta = 1$), and the more general EWA approach. In fact, because the sample is small and the learning process does not appear to have converged after only five periods, the data provides a conservative test of differences between models. Any differences are likely to loom larger in larger data sets with more periods over which learning can take place.

## The Likelihood Function

The weak-link data have seven strategies, numbered 1-7, and we use data from 60 subjects and five periods. Thus, the log of the likelihood function for the EWA model is

$$LL(A^1(0),...,A^7(0),\delta,\phi,\lambda,N(0),\rho) = \sum_{i=1}^{60} \sum_{t=1}^{5} log(P_i^{s_i(t)}(t)).$$

(27)

The probabilities $P_i^{s_i(t)}(t)$ are given by Equation 1. Initial attractions are estimated and subsequent attractions are updated according to Equation 3. The initial experience weight $N(0)$ is estimated, and subsequent values $N(t)$ for $t > 1$ are updated according to Equation 2. An implicit assumption in the exponential (logit) choice model is that disturbances are added to attractions that have a double exponential distribution (Yellott, 1977).[4]

## Weak-Link Games

Weak-link games are $n$-person versions of stag hunt. In the weak-link games, players choose a strategy from some ordered set, and their payoff depends positively on the lowest strategy picked by any player and on the difference between their strategy and the lowest one. This game was first studied experimentally by Van Huyck, Battalio, and Beil (1990), and later studied by Knez and Camerer (1996) and Camerer, Knez, and Weber (1996). The data we use are from Knez and Camerer (1994).

The weak-link game captures social situations in which a group's output is extremely sensitive to its weakest link – friends must wait for their slowest

**Table 3.2**
**Weak-Link Game**

|       |   |       |       | Min {$X_i$} |       |       |       |       |
|-------|---|-------|-------|-------------|-------|-------|-------|-------|
|       |   | 7     | 6     | 5           | 4     | 3     | 2     | 1     |
|       | 7 | 1.30  | 1.10  | 0.90        | 0.70  | 0.50  | 0.30  | 0.10  |
|       | 6 | -     | 1.20  | 1.00        | 0.80  | 0.60  | 0.40  | 0.20  |
| $X_i$ | 5 | -     | -     | 1.10        | 0.90  | 0.70  | 0.50  | 0.30  |
|       | 4 | -     | -     | -           | 1.00  | 0.80  | 0.60  | 0.40  |
|       | 3 | -     | -     | -           | -     | 0.90  | 0.70  | 0.50  |
|       | 2 | -     | -     | -           | -     | -     | 0.80  | 0.60  |
|       | 1 | -     | -     | -           | -     | -     | -     | 0.70  |

arrival before they get seated in a restaurant, a chemical recipe or meal is ruined by one bad ingredient, a dyke bursts if it has a single leak, and so forth.

Table 3.2 shows payoffs in the weak-link games. Players pick a number from 1 to 7. Player $I$'s payoffs from choosing $x_i$ (in dollars) is $.60 + .10 \cdot min(x_1, x_2, . . ., x_n) - .10 \cdot (x_i - min(x_1, x_2, . . ., x_n))$.

Subjects were University of Chicago undergraduates playing in groups of three. In these experiments, subjects were told only the minimum choice in the entire group (including their own). Strictly speaking, the EWA model with $\delta \neq 0$ should not necessarily apply to these data because subjects who chose the minimum in a period could not be sure whether others did or not. Thus, our estimates essentially test a joint hypothesis that learning follows EWA (or its special case rules) and that subjects who chose the minimum know what the minimum of the other two choices was. If the latter hypothesis is false, that should give choice reinforcement (which does not require the hypothesis, because beliefs are not formed) an advantage over the other theories. We also assume that players care only about the minimum of others (because only the minimum is relevant for their payoffs), and essentially treat the other two players as a composite whose minimum is the composite's strategy choice.

Table 3.3 shows the actual frequencies of number choices across five periods. There is wide dispersion in first period choices, with a large percentage of choices of 7 (the payoff-dominant equilibrium choice). Notice that 1, 3, and 4 are also chosen frequently, but 2, 5, and 6 are not. As we see, explaining the precise nature of these first period choices is a challenge that belief-based models fail to meet. The problem arises because it seems likely that players use different decision rules that are not always consistent with any single set of beliefs. The choice of 1 is minimax; any player who thinks about choosing 2 probably chooses 1 instead. The choice of 7 is payoff-dominant; any player considering 6 probably just chooses 7. But any set of beliefs that explain the

**Table 3.3**
**Observed Frequencies of Choices Over Rounds**

| | Period | | | | |
|---|---|---|---|---|---|
| Choices CHI (n=300) | 1 | 2 | 3 | 4 | 5 |
| 1 | 0.133 | 0.100 | 0.167 | 0.217 | 0.283 |
| 2 | 0.050 | 0.100 | 0.117 | 0.050 | 0.083 |
| 3 | 0.133 | 0.117 | 0.183 | 0.183 | 0.217 |
| 4 | 0.183 | 0.183 | 0.183 | 0.167 | 0.150 |
| 5 | 0.067 | 0.067 | 0.067 | 0.067 | 0.033 |
| 6 | 0.017 | 0.067 | 0.033 | 0.050 | 0.017 |
| 7 | 0.417 | 0.367 | 0.250 | 0.267 | 0.217 |

frequent choices of 1, 3, and 4, and the most frequent choices of 7, do so by assigning expected payoffs that are monotonically increasing from 1 to 7. Those beliefs cannot explain why 5 and 6 are so rare.[5] Second, there is a trend toward smaller numbers (particularly 1 and 3), so there is evidence of learning, which models should be able to capture. Third, because all payoffs are positive, all strategies will be positively reinforced. As a result, the choice reinforcement model may struggle to explain why players so frequently switch their strategies to strategies they never picked before, and often, to new strategies which are best responses to the minima previously observed. For example, consider a player who chooses 7 and observes a minimum of 5. In choice reinforcement, the strategy 7 is reinforced with payoff .90 and no other strategy is reinforced. In general reinforcement, the strategy 5 is reinforced by $\delta \cdot 1.10$. We frequently see players' best responding to the previous minima, switching from 7 to 5 in our example. These switches are hard to explain unless $\delta$ is substantially different from zero. We report estimates using the logit or quantal response form of the probability response function (corresponding to $f(x) = \lambda \cdot x$).[6]

Table 3.4 reports the results. In the EWA first, the values of $A^j_i(0)$ are relatively similar, although $A^2(0)$ and $A^6(0)$ are slightly lower, fitting the lower frequencies of strategy 2 and 6 evident in Table 3.3. However, the high value of $\lambda$, 6.16, inflates these small differences in $A^i(0)$ into substantial differences in choice probabilities, thus accounting for the wide dispersion and a substantial number of choices of 1 and 7 in the first period. The estimate of $N(0)$, 2.19, indicates that prior attractions carry about twice as much weight as each period of experience. This reflects the fact that relatively slow learning occurs across the five periods (which, in the EWA model, means that a period of actual experience counts only half as much as the experience embedded in initial attractions). The estimate of $\phi$ is .582, much lower than the depreciation rate of .999 used in earlier simulations by Roth and Erev (1995) and Erev and Roth

**Table 3.4**
**Weak-Link Data, Exponential $P^j_i(t)(n = 300)$**

| Parameters | EWA | Choice Reinforcement ($\delta$=0) | | Belief-Based Models ($\delta$=1) | | |
|---|---|---|---|---|---|---|
| | | $\rho$ free | $\rho = 0$ | $\rho = \varphi$ free | $\rho=\varphi=0$ | $\rho=\varphi=1$ |
| $A^1(0)$ | 0.763 | 1.131 | 1.153 | 0.700 | 0.700 | 0.700 |
| $A^2(0)$ | 0.656 | 0.834 | 0.806 | 0.715 | 0.726 | 0.701 |
| $A^3(0)$ | 0.765 | 1.104 | 1.119 | 0.730 | 0.752 | 0.701 |
| $A^4(0)$ | 0.834 | 1.214 | 1.253 | 0.745 | 0.778 | 0.702 |
| $A^5(0)$ | 0.716 | 0.797 | 0.746 | 0.760 | 0.804 | 0.703 |
| $A^6(0)$ | 0.658 | 0.449 | 0.358 | 0.755 | 0.830 | 0.703 |
| $A^7(0)$ | 1.000(f) | 1.472 | 1.565 | 0.791 | 0.855 | 0.704 |
| $\lambda$ | 6.157 | 2.884 | 2.319 | 21.98 | 7.106 | 552.078 |
| $\varphi$ | 0.582 | 0.552 | 0.527 | 0.525 | 0.000(f) | 1.000(f) |
| $\delta$ | 0.652 | 0.000(f) | 0.000(f) | 1.000(f) | 1.000(f) | 1.000(f) |
| $N(0)$ | 2.187 | 1.000(f) | 1.000(f) | 11.08 | 5.933 | 120.617 |
| $\rho$ | 0.198 | 0.216 | 0.000(f) | 0.525 | 0.000(f) | 1.000(f) |
| LL | -358.058 | -386.787 | -387.163 | -438.546 | -471.300 | -441.795 |
| $\chi^2$ | | 57.46 | 58.22 | 160.98 | 226.50 | 166.18 |

(1997). Most importantly, the estimate of $\delta$ is .652. This indicates that a general model in which foregone payoffs are partially reinforced (contrary to choice reinforcement) but not reinforced as fully as actual payoffs (contrary to belief models) fits better.

In choice reinforcement the estimates are similar to the EWA model, except the levels of $A^j_i(0)$ are about 50% higher. Because, $N(0)$ is restricted to equal one in this case, higher levels of initial attraction are needed to reflect the primacy of initial experience over actual experience. The $\chi^2$ statistic testing the choice reinforcement restrictions ($\delta = 0$, $N(0) = 1$, and $\rho = 0$), reject those restrictions with a $\chi^2(3) = 58.22$ ($p < .001$).

The belief models are even more strongly rejected. The values of $A^j_i(0)$ are expected payoffs given some beliefs (the belief that the minimum of others' choices is $j$ is $[C^j_{-i}/N(0)]$). As discussed earlier, explaining both the frequent initial 1, 3, 4, and 7 choices requires expected payoffs that are monotonically increasing. For example, for the general belief model with $\phi$ between zero and one, the estimated initial counts that determine prior beliefs $C^1_{-i}, \ldots, C^7_{-i}$ are 4.71, 0, 0, 0, 0, 0, and 6.38. But these beliefs cannot explain the low frequencies of 2 and 6 choices, and hence the log likelihoods of all three belief models are much more negative (worse-fitting) than for EWA. $\chi^2$ statistics reject all three forms at very low $p$-values.

**Table 3.5**
**Model Prediction Errors**

| | EWA Model (actual - predicted) | | | | |
|---|---|---|---|---|---|
| | 1 | 2 | 3 | 4 | 5 |
| 1 | .017 | -.028 | -.005 | .009 | .047 |
| 2 | -.011 | .039 | .020 | -.082 | -.033 |
| 3 | .037 | -.026 | -.005 | -.016 | .010 |
| 4 | .046 | -.010 | -.039 | -.021 | -.010 |
| 5 | -.006 | -.006 | .002 | .022 | -.012 |
| 6 | -.047 | .041 | .007 | .026 | -.006 |
| 7 | -.037 | -.008 | .021 | .066 | .008 |

| | Choice Reinforcement (actual − predicted) | | | | |
|---|---|---|---|---|---|
| | 1 | 2 | 3 | 4 | 5 |
| 1 | -.004 | -.041 | .041 | .078 | .119 |
| 2 | -.007 | .020 | .021 | -.064 | -.015 |
| 3 | -.010 | -.040 | .041 | .031 | .057 |
| 4 | -.014 | -.003 | .006 | .006 | -.003 |
| 5 | .007 | -.016 | -.014 | -.005 | -.040 |
| 6 | .007 | .035 | .036 | -.035 | -.050 |
| 7 | .023 | .045 | .058 | -.010 | -.067 |

| | Belief Models (actual − predicted) | | | | |
|---|---|---|---|---|---|
| | 1 | 2 | 3 | 4 | 5 |
| 1 | .096 | .042 | .050 | .006 | .037 |
| 2 | -.005 | .0163 | -.034 | -.171 | -.109 |
| 3 | .052 | -.016 | -.027 | -.042 | .015 |
| 4 | .066 | .011 | -.043 | .007 | .011 |
| 5 | -.100 | -.130 | -.109 | -.018 | -.026 |
| 6 | -.219 | -.128 | -.070 | -.008 | -.042 |
| 7 | .108 | .209 | .233 | .229 | .113 |

Within the class of belief models, fictitious play ($\phi = 1$) fits much better than Cournot ($\phi = 0$). Indeed, the fictitious play restriction is only rejected (relative to the general belief model) at $p = .025$.

Table 3.5 shows the model prediction errors – actual frequencies from Table 3.3 minus frequencies predicted by the models (using the likelihood-maximizing parameter values) – for each choice and period. Several facts are notable. EWA predicts fairly accurately throughout, missing choice frequencies by more than .05 only twice. Choice reinforcement predicts quite accurately in the first period, but predicts increasingly less accurately across periods. In that sense, reinforcement does not capture evolution of choices over time – learning – particularly well. The belief model makes substantial errors in all periods.

Averaging squared deviations (MSD) across all the strategy period categories in Table 3.5, EWA has an MSD of .00091, choice reinforcement has .00159, and the belief-based model has .01014. Using another criterion, EWA has absolute deviations greater than .05 in 2 of 35 strategy-period cells whereas reinforcement has 7 and belief-based models have 16.

The deepest apparent flaw in the belief models is the inability to explain the nonmonotonic pattern of first period choices (it severely overpredicts initial choices of 5 and 6) and persistent underprediction of choices of 7. The latter feature occurs because the belief model mistakenly predicts that players choosing 7 will best respond to lower minima by moving to lower numbers, which they do infrequently. At the same time, the choice reinforcement approaches cannot account for the increasing frequency of choices of 1. The EWA model avoids both of these prediction errors: It fits first period choices by allowing unrestricted values of $A^j_i(0)$ in period 1 (they need not be expected payoffs given prior beliefs). But by allowing some degree of best-response, it can explain why players switch away from 7 toward 1 (but not as often as complete best-response predicts).

## CONCLUSION

We propose a new model of learning in games in which initial attractions are weighted by the amount of experience equivalence they have. Attractions are updated by the payoffs actually received, or some fraction of the payoffs that would have been received (given the other players' moves).

One advantage of this model is that it includes two seemingly different approaches, choice reinforcement and belief-based models as special cases. Thus, the model shows that there is a surprising family resemblance between reinforcement learning and belief-based learning. It also provides a natural way to do model comparison by testing the special cases as restrictions of the EWA model.

It is important to note that EWA is not the same as simply taking a weighted average of probabilities (or attractions) from the choice reinforcement and general belief models, because EWA is not linear in the parameters $\delta$, $N(0)$, and $\rho$, which distinguish those two special cases. Indeed, direct econometric comparisons show that in two classes of coordination games, the weighted average model fits much worse than EWA (Camerer & Ho, 1997). The weak-link analysis shows why this is so. EWA is able to combine the best parts of both specialized models, but uses them to explain different parts of the learning process: EWA uses flexibility in initial attractions of choice reinforcement to fit the first period, and uses the tendency toward best response in belief models to capture changes over time (but without using the full force of best-response and overlearning). Thus, EWA combines the strengths of two different approaches, and avoids their weaknesses.

Initial parameter estimates suggest the general model provides a substantial improvement over either choice reinforcement or belief models. Further parameter estimates and discussion of what the parameters of the model represent (or independent estimates of them) are necessary to fully understand the model and its uses. Estimates reported elsewhere show that EWA improves substantially on choice reinforcement and belief models in dominance-solvable games and other coordination games, and improves modestly in constant-sum games with unique mixed-strategy equilibria (Camerer & Ho, 1996). In further work we found that allowing parameters to vary over time improves fit, and suggests that $\delta$ and $\lambda$ are increasing over time (consistent with increasing imagination and response sensitivity; cf. McKelvey & Palfrey, 1995).

In addition, we see the EWA model as a platform onto which other features can be added. For example, Erev and Roth (chap. 4, this volume) point out that in many games, the sensible domain of decision rules that are reinforced during learning are not just stage-game strategies, but include repeated-game strategies and other heuristic rules. EWA learning allows any set of strategies or rules $S^j_i$. In addition, the model does not include sophistication because Player $i$ does not use information about Player $j$'s payoffs (both historical and the full payoff matrix). This is not a deliberate omission; in future research we hope to be able to include sophistication parsimoniously.

Because the model we presented does not currently incorporate strategic sophistication, it could be used to fit individual choice data in which players learn about state probabilities or choice utilities over time (e.g. animal learning or consumer choices of brands).

## ACKNOWLEDGMENTS

This research was supported by NSF grants SBR-9511001 and SBR-9511137. We have had helpful conversations with Bruno Broseia, Lief Gkioulekas, Yuval Rottenstreich, Roberto Weber, two referees, and Ido Erev; excellent research assistance from Hongjai Rhee; and comments from participants in the Society for Mathematical Psychology conference (July, 1996), the Russell Sage Foundation Summer Institute in Behavioral Economics (July, 1996), and the Economic Science Association meetings (October, 1996).

## ENDNOTES

1. For example, as just noted, the choice reinforcement and belief approaches predict that players use different sets of historical and payoff information. These theories

about what information subjects will ask for or attend to can therefore be interpreted as predictions.

2. Busemeyer and Myung (1992) have a somewhat related similarity parameter in their adaptive approach.

3. This model is a restricted version of Roth and Erev (1995) and Erev and Roth (1997), which include a cutoff parameter to extinguish strategies with low reinforcement, a reference point that is updated over time, and a generalization parameter that spills over reinforcement from one strategy to unchosen neighboring strategies.

4. In the exponential choice model, one of the initial attractions must be normalized for identification (e.g., $A^7(0)$) because $P^j_i(t)$ is invariant to adding an arbitrary term to all initial attractions.

5. The inability of belief-based models to explain the frequencies may be a consequence of the implicit assumption that all players have the same beliefs. There are not enough data to estimate different beliefs for each player, but models that allow more than one segment of parameters may fit better.

6. This form fits these data better than the power form, which has log likelihoods for EWA, choice reinforcement (with $\lambda = 1$), and belief models of -363.74, -412.22, and −437.92. The power form uses two fewer parameters because $\rho$ only appears in the dominator of the attraction-updating equations (and hence divides out when attraction ratios are taken), and the initial experience count $N(0)$ also disappears because the probabilities associated with any set of initial attractions $A^j_i(0)$ are the same as those with $A^j_i(0) \cdot N(0)$ for positive $N(0)$. The parameter estimates and restriction test results do not change much between the exponential and power forms.

# REFERENCES

Brown, G. (1951). Iterative solution of games by fictitious play. In *Activity analysis of production and allocation*. New York: Wiley.

Busemeyer, J. R., & Myung, I. J. (1992). An adaptive approach to human decision making: Learning theory, decision theory, and human performance. *Journal of Experimental Psychology: General, 121*, 177-194.

Bush, R., & Mosteller, F. (1955). *Stochastic models for learning*. New York: Wiley.

Camerer, C. F., & Ho, T. (1996). Experience-weighted attraction learning in games. *Econometrica*.

Camerer, C. F., & Ho, T. (1997). EWA learning in games: Heterogeneity and time-variation. *Journal of Mathematical Psychology*.

Camerer, C. F., Johnson, E., Sen, S., & Rymon, T. (1993). Cognition and framing in sequential bargaining for gains and losses. In K. Binmore, A. Kirman, & P. Tani (Eds.), *Frontiers of game theory* (pp. 27-48). Cambridge, MA: MIT Press.

Camerer, C. F., Knez, M., & Weber, R. (1996). *Timing and virtual observability in ultimatum bargaining and weak-link coordination games*. Caltech Working Paper No. 970, May, Pasadena, CA.

Chen, Y., & Tang, F. F. (1996). Learning and incentive compatible mechanisms for public goods provision. *Journal of Political Economy*.

Cournot, A. (1960). *Recherches sur les principes mathematiques de la theories des richesses* [Researches in the mathematical principles of theory] (N. Bacon, Trans.). London: Haffner.

Cross, F. G. (1983). *A theory of adaptive economic behavior*. New York: Cambridge University Press.

Erev, I., & Roth, A. (1997). Modeling how people play games: Reinforcement learning in experimental games with unique, mixed strategy equilibria. *American Economic Review*.

Fudenberg, D., & Levine, D. (1996). *Theory of learning in games*. Manuscript submitted for publication.

Ho, T. H., & Weigelt, K. (1996). Task complexity, equilibrium selection, and learning: An experimental study. *Management Science, 42*, 659-679.

Knez, M., & Camerer, C. (1994). Creating expectational assets in the laboratory: Coordination in weakest-link games. *Strategic Management Journal, 15*, 101-119.

Knez, M., & Camerer, C. (1996). *Increasing cooperation in social dilemmas through the precedent of efficiency in coordination games*. University of Chicago Working Paper, August, Chicago, IL.

McKelvey, R. D., & Palfrey, T. R. (1995). Quantal response equilibria for normal form games. *Games and Economic Behavior, 10*, 6-38.

McKelvey, R. D., & Palfrey, T. R. (1996). *Quantal response equilibria for extensive form games*. Caltech Working Paper 947, January, Pasadena, CA.

Roth, A., & Erev, I. (1995). Learning in extensive-form games: Experimental data and simple dynamic models in the intermediate term. *Games and Economic Behavior, 8*, 164-212.

Van Huyck, J., Battalio, R., & Beil, R. (1990). Tacit cooperation games, strategic uncertainty, and coordination failure. *The American Economic Review, 80*, 234-248.

Yellott, J. (1977). The relationship between Luce's choice axioms, Thurstone's theory of comparative judgment, and the double exponential distribution. *Journal of Mathematical Psychology, 5*, 109-144.

# 4 On the Role of Reinforcement Learning in Experimental Games: The Cognitive Game-Theoretic Approach

**Ido Erev**
*Technion – Israel Institute of Technology*

**Alvin E. Roth**
*University of Pittsburgh*

Experimental investigation of choice behavior in repeated games reveals that in many settings the effect of experience can be predicted by simple reinforcement learning models. These models, which feature a slow adjustment process in response to accumulated reinforcements, appear to capture behavior when it is both consistent and inconsistent with equilibrium predictions (see e.g., Bornstein, Erev & Goren, 1994; Camerer & Ho, chap. 3, this volume; Erev and Rapoport, 1998; Erev & Roth, 1998; Mookherjee & Sopher, 1997; Rapoport, Erev, Abraham, & Olson, 1997; Rapoport, Seale, Erev, & Sundali, 1998; Roth & Erev 1995; Slonim & Roth, 1998; Tang, 1996).

Yet examination of the experimental psychology and gaming literatures also reveals robust learning phenomena that cannot be explained by simple reinforcement learning models. These phenomena include sequential dependencies (Rapoport & Budescu, 1992; Tolman, 1925), reciprocation (Rapoport & Chammah, 1965), transfer (e.g., Rapoport et al., 1998), expectation-based learning (Camerer & Ho, chap. 3, this volume), imitation (Bandura, 1969), and direction learning (Selten & Buchta, chap. 5, this volume).

Three classes of explanations can be provided to account for the apparent contradiction between the good descriptive power (in some settings) and the clear violations (in other settings) of simple reinforcement learning models. First, in line with the general approaches proposed by Camerer (1990), Camerer and Ho (chap. 3, this volume), Cooper and Feltovich (1996), Mookherjee and Sopher (1997), and Selten and Buchta (chap. 5, this volume), it can be argued that choice behavior and learning are game-specific. Thus, it is possible that in some games learning is best approximated by a reinforcement learning process, whereas other processes underlie learning in other games.

According to a second class of explanations reinforcement learning models do not capture a robust property of human behavior. Rather, human learning is better approximated by a different general learning (or other) rule whose predictions are similar to the predictions of reinforcement learning models in some games. An argument of this type is made in Fudenberg and Levine's (1997) book on learning theory and by Cheung and Friedman (1996).

Note that the first of the two classes of explanations presented, and to some extent the second, are rather pessimistic. The first implies that a general model of learning could be developed, if at all, only after we understand learning in a very large set of specific games (this model would predict which learning rule would be used in a new game). And the second suggests that the knowledge accumulated thus far in experimental research is of little value; we are yet to find a general principle of learning (unless one of the new proposals should prove surprisingly robust). The third class of explanations, proposed in our recent work (Erev & Roth, 1998; Roth & Erev, 1995) and referred to as cognitive game theory, is more optimistic. This approach conjectures that learning can always be approximated by reinforcement learning models in which people learn among cognitive strategies. Thus, whenever high level cognitive strategies play an important role, reinforcement models that ignore these strategies fail. This approach predicts that when the relevant cognitive strategies are understood (and much of the research in cognitive psychology focuses on that goal), the effect of experience can be predicted by a general model.

The main goal of this chapter is to review the evidence that suggests the role of reinforcement learning is best understood within the cognitive game theory framework. This chapter: (a) describes Roth and Erev's (1995) reinforcement learning model; (b) reviews results that demonstrate that this simple model provides a good approximation of behavior in repeated games in which players cannot reciprocate; (c) summarizes six violations of this model (and of the simple reinforcement learning approach); (d) presents the cognitive game-theoretic explanation of these violations, and discusses the value and limitations of this approach; and (e) presents conclusions and directions for future research.

## ROTH AND EREV'S REINFORCEMENT LEARNING MODEL

In Roth and Erev (1995), we proposed a reinforcement learning model built on a linear quantification of Thorndike's (1898) law of effect (similar quantifications were suggested by Bush & Mosteller, 1955; Harley, 1981; Herrnstein, 1970; and Luce, 1959). To the basic quantification we added three additional important characteristics of human and animal learning: generalization (and experimentation), recency, and effect of reference points (Erev & Roth, 1996b).

## Basic Assumptions and a One-Parameter Model

The family of models we considered can be summarized by four main assumptions. For expository purposes these assumptions are presented with the specific quantification assumed by a basic one-parameter model.

**A1. Initial propensities.** At time $t = 1$ (before any experience has been acquired) each Player $n$ has an initial propensity to play $k$th pure strategy, given by some nonnegative number $q_{nk}(1)$. In the basic model, each player will be assumed to have equal initial propensities for each pure strategy, that is, for each Player $n$,

$$q_{nk}(1) = q_{nj}(1) \text{ for all pure strategies } k, j. \tag{1}$$

**A2. Reinforcement function.** The reinforcement of receiving a payoff $x$ is given by an increasing function $R(x)$. In the basic model the reinforcement function is set to

$$R(x) = x\text{-}x_{min}, \tag{2}$$

where $x_{min}$ is the smallest possible payoff.

**A3. Updating of propensities.** If Player $n$ plays $k$th pure strategy at time $t$ and receives a reinforcement of $R(x)$, then the propensity to play strategy $j$ is updated as a function of $R(x)$. The basic model assumes a linear function,

$$q_{nj}(t+1) = \begin{cases} q_{nj}(t) + R(x) & \text{if } j = k \\ q_{nj}(t) & \text{otherwise} \end{cases} \tag{3}$$

**A4. Probabilistic choice rule.** Following Luce (1959) the probability $p_{nk}(t)$ that Player $n$ plays his $k$th pure strategy at time $t$ is

$$P_{nk}(t) = \frac{q_{nk}(t)}{\sum q_{nj}(t)} \tag{4}$$

where the sum is over all of Player $n$'s pure strategies $j$.

Note that the model satisfies the law of effect (Thorndike, 1898) and the power law of practice (Blackburn, 1936). Pure strategies that have been played and have met with success tend to be played with greater frequency than those that have met with less success, and the learning curve will be steeper in early periods and flatter later (because nonnegative reinforcements imply $\Sigma q_{nj}(t)$ is an increasing function of $t$, so a reinforcement of $R(x)$ from playing pure strategy $k$ at time $t$ has a bigger effect on $p_{nk}(t)$ when $t$ is small than when $t$ is large).

*The Single Parameter of the Basic Model.* It follows from the probabilistic choice rule (Eq. 4) and our assumption that each player's initial propensities are all equal that at the initial period of the game each player chooses each strategy with equal probability. However we have not made any assumption that fixes the sum of the initial propensities, which appears in the denominator of Eq. 4, and therefore influences the rate of change of choice probabilities, that is, the speed of learning (which is also influenced by the size of the rewards). The basic model's sole parameter, $s(1)$, which we call the *strength* of the initial propensities, is introduced to determine the ratio of these two determinants of the learning speed. Let $X_n$ be the average absolute payoff for Player $n$ in the game. The initial strength parameter for Player $n$ is defined as $s_n(1) = \Sigma q_{nj}(1)/X_n$, and we assume that this is a constant for all players, that is, $s_n(1) = s(1) > 0$ for all Players $n$.

Note that this definition and the probabilistic choice rule yield the initial propensities $q_{nj}(1) = p_{nj}(1)\, s(1)\, X_n$, where $p_{nj}(1)$, the initial choice probability is given by $p_{nj}(1) = 1/M_n$, where $M_n$ is the number of Player $n$'s pure strategies. Thus the initial propensities are determined by the observable features of the game and by the strength parameter $s(1)$.

## A Three-Parameter Model

It is easy to see that the basic model can come to adjust too slowly. That is, if $s(1)$ is low it predicts fast initial learning, but extremely slow learning in the longer term (when the propensities are large relative to the obtained reinforcements). To address this problem we (Roth & Erev, 1995) introduced responsiveness to the model by adding two weaker psychological assumptions: experimentation and a recency effect. The first of these can be viewed as an extension of the law of effect:

> **Experimentation (or Generalization):** Not only are choices that were successful in the past more likely to be employed in the future, but similar choices will be employed more often as well, and players will not (quickly) become locked in to one choice in exclusion of all others.

The second additional feature of individual learning modeled in Roth and

Erev (1995), can be viewed as an interaction between the law of effect and the power law of practice.

**Recency.** Recent experience may play a larger role than past experience in determining behavior.

In Roth and Erev (1995) we called this "forgetting."
These two assumptions were quantified in Roth and Erev by the following modification of Eq. 3 (assumption A3), the updating function:

$$q_{nj}(t+1) = (1-\phi)q_{nj}(t) + E_{nk}(j, R(x)) \tag{5}$$

In Eq. 5, $\phi$ is a forgetting (or recency) parameter that slowly reduces the importance of past experience, and $E$ is a function that determines how the experience of playing strategy $k$ and receiving the reward $R(x)$ is generalized to update each strategy $j$.

Experimental investigation of generalization suggests that strategies that subjects find similar to the selected strategy will be affected by the reinforcement. Brown, Clark, & Stein (1958) observed a normal generalization distribution. In games in which similarity of strategies can be linearly ordered (such as those studied in Roth & Erev, 1995) we chose a three step function to approximate the generalization function, as follows:

$$E_{nk}(j, R(x)) = \begin{cases} R(x)(1-\varepsilon) & \text{if } j = k \\ R(x)\varepsilon/2 & \text{if } j = k-1, \text{or } j = k+1 \\ 0 & \text{otherwise} \end{cases} \tag{6}$$

where $\varepsilon$ is an experimentation/generalization parameter. For games when only two strategies are considered, or when the $M_n \geq 2$ strategies do not have an apparent linear order, the generalization function is reduced to a two step function:

$$E_{nk}(j, R(x)) = \begin{cases} R(x)(1-\varepsilon) & \text{if } j = k \\ \dfrac{R(x)\varepsilon}{(M_n - 1)} & \text{otherwise} \end{cases} \tag{7}$$

Another way to think of these two functions is that when the strategy sets allow similarity judgments to be made, players will generalize their most recent experience in a way that leads to experimentation among the most similar strategies. When no similarity judgments can be made, players simply retain some propensity to experiment among all strategies.

*Parameters.* The model has three parameters: the strength parameter $s(1)$ (as in the basic model) and the experimentation and forgetting parameters $\varepsilon$ and $\phi$.

## SUPPORTIVE EVIDENCE

### Analysis of Published Data Sets

To evaluate the models just described, Erev and Roth (1998) assembled and analyzed a data set consisting of all experiments we could locate involving play of 100 periods or more of games with a unique equilibrium in nontrivial mixed strategies. The reason for looking for so many periods of play is to observe intermediate-term as well as short-term behavior. The data sets assembled report repeated play of 11 games, under a variety of experimental conditions, from the experiments of Malcolm and Lieberman (1965), Ochs (1995), O'Neill (1987), Rapoport and Boebel (1992), and Suppes and Atkinson (1960). In addition, a replication study of one of the conditions reported in Suppes and Atkinson (1960) was added. Thus a total of 12 data sets were analyzed.

*Derivation of Predictions.* To derive the models' predictions for these experiments computer simulations were conducted, designed to replicate the characteristics of each of the experimental settings. In each case the simulated players participated in the same number of rounds as the experimental subjects. Two hundred simulations were run in each game under different sets of parameters. At each round of each simulation the following steps were taken:

1. Simulated players were matched (using the matching procedure of the experiment being simulated).
2. The simulated players' strategies were randomly determined via Eq. 4.
3. Payoffs were determined using the payoff rule employed in the experiment in question.
4. Propensities were updated according to Eq. 5.

*Parameter Estimation.* A grid search with a mean squared deviation (MSD) criterion was conducted to estimate the value of the free parameters. That is, the simulations were run for a wide set of parameters, and the parameters that minimized the distance between the model and the data (minimized the model's MSD score) were selected, for each of the tests presented.

### Main Results

Figure 4.1 presents the experimental and the simulation results in a sample of 3 of the 12 games. The payoff matrices are presented at the left-hand side of the

**Data Equilibrium Reinforcement Learning**

**Game:          Choice probability    1-parameter        3-parameter**

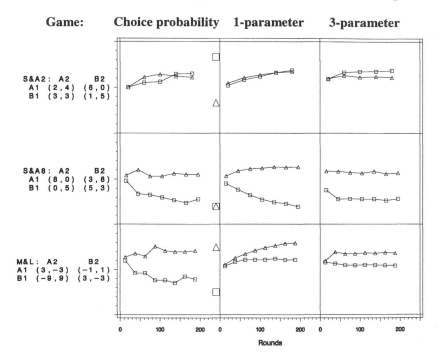

Fig. 4.1. Observed and predicted choice probabilities as a function of time over player type (P(A1) is represented by $\Delta$ and P(A2) by $\square$) in three of the games studied in Erev and Roth (1998). In the first two games (adapted from Suppes & Atkinson, 1960) each payoff unit increases winning probabilities (by 1/6 in Game S&A2, and by 1/8 in S&A8). In Game M&L (adapted from Malcolm & Leiberman, 1965) payoffs were directly converted to money.

figures. Each cell within the figure's frame is a graph that has the probability of a certain choice (ranging from 0 to 1) on the Y axis, and the rounds of the experiment (organized into blocks as in the data of that experiment) on the X axis. The first column of each figure summarizes the relevant experimental results. In each cell of this column, the mean probability with which Players 1 (row players) and Players 2 choose their first strategy (A) is plotted over time. (Player 1 choices are indicated by triangles, Player 2 choices by squares.) The equilibrium predictions for Players 1 and 2, respectively, are given by the triangle and square at the far right of each cell in column 1.

The remaining two columns present the behavior of virtual subjects that behave according to the one-parameter and three-parameter models. The parameters utilized to derive these curves are the ones that best fit the data over the 12 games. The estimated parameters were $s(1) = 54$ for the one-parameter model, and $s(1) = 9$, $\varepsilon = .2$, and $\phi = .1$ for the three-parameter model.

The top panel of Fig. 4.1 presents the results obtained in the mixed strategy experimental condition summarized in chap. 3 of Suppes and Atkinson (1960). The game played in this condition, referred to here as Game S&A2, has a unique mixed strategy equilibrium in which Player 1 chooses A1 with probability 1/3 and Player 2 chooses A2 with probability 5/6. It was played by 20 pairs of subjects for 200 rounds. The subjects were not informed that they were playing a two-person game. They were told that their task, in each of the 200 trials, was to predict which of two lights will be turned on. Subjects were run in pairs and the probability of a correct response was determined by the game payoff matrix (each point increases the probability of being correct by 1/6). Following each choice the subjects received accuracy feedback. Thus, although the subjects did not know that they were playing a game, the game is a description of the reinforcement structure (although subjects were not paid based on their performance, following Suppes and Atkinson's (1960) assumption that a "win" is a reinforcing event).

Suppes and Atkinson (1960) presented the choice proportions in blocks of 40 trials. The results (see top panel in Fig. 4.1) show that Player 2 appears to move toward the equilibrium prediction (the proportion of A2 choices increases with time). Player 1 initially moves away from the equilibrium. Only in the last two blocks is the proportion of A1 choices reduced.

The one-parameter model captures the initial learning trends (the simulated Player 2 moves immediately toward the equilibrium, whereas the simulated Player 1 starts moving in the opposite direction). Yet, this model fails to capture the late direction change in Player 2's behavior. The three-parameter model captures both the initial and the late trends.

The second panel in Fig. 4.1 summarizes the results obtained in a condition reported in chap. 4 of Suppes and Atkinson (1960), in which players knew that they were playing a game, but did not know the payoff matrix. At the equilibrium of this game (S&A8) both players choose A with probability .2. This game was played by 20 pairs of subjects for 210 rounds. Subjects were told that they were playing a two-person game in which they had to predict which of two lights will be turned on. They were told that the correct answer depends on their response, on the other subject's response, and on a random event. As in Game S&A2, the probability of correct responses were determined by the payoff matrix, which was not presented to the subjects.

The results (summarized by the proportions of A choices in blocks of 30 trials) are similar to the results obtained in Game S&A2. Whereas one of the players (Player 2) quickly learns to approach the equilibrium prediction, the other (Player 1) initially moves away from the equilibrium. For this data also, the one-parameter model captures the initial trends whereas the three-parameter model captures the whole learning curve.

The third panel in Fig. 4.1 summarizes the results for the study conducted by Malcolm and Lieberman (1965), which was designed to test the descriptive power of the minimax (maximin) equilibrium prediction. The payoff matrix was explained to the subjects, and the payoffs units were chips that were converted to money at the conclusion of the experiment. Nine pairs of subjects participated in 200 replications of the game. At the equilibrium of this game Player 1 chooses A1 with probability 3/4 and Player 2 chooses A2 with probability 1/4.

Malcolm and Lieberman present the choice proportions in blocks of 25 trials. Experience led both players toward the equilibrium prediction, but Player 1 appears to learn faster, reaching equilibrium by the forth block, whereas Player 2 approaches equilibrium slowly. Similar trends are exhibited by the simulated subjects.

## Summary Statistics and Ex Ante Prediction of Behavior

Ideally we would like to be able to predict behavior at every level of aggregation or disaggregation, for every game, for any length of play. Because the models we consider are computational, we can use them to simulate each experiment and predict the probability of each action over time. Erev and Roth (1998) compared the predictions of different learning models and of equilibrium by computing the MSD of the predicted and observed behavior over time, for each game, both for all subjects and for individual pairs.

For each model and each of the 12 experimental data sets we performed two tests of descriptive power and one test of predictive power, as follows. First, we found the best parameters for minimizing the MSD over all games, and computed the MSD for each game using these parameters. Then we found the best parameters for minimizing the MSD for each of the 12 games separately (i.e., by looking at a model that replaces each parameter of the original model with 12 distinct parameters, one for each game). Finally, we tested the predictive power of each model on each of the 12 games by estimating the model's parameters on the data from the other 11 games, using the model to predict behavior in the game of interest, and comparing the predicted path of behavior with the observed path. The predictions reported here are for the entire path of play of the game over all periods.

Table 4.1 gives the results of the aggregate data (i.e., pooling over all subject pairs for each game). For brevity we omit the other analyses here.

Each of the first 12 rows of the table represents one of the games (initials reflect the authors who first experimented on each game). The numbers are the MSD scores (lower is better), with predictions being compared to data in real time (i.e., round $n$ of the data is compared to round $n$ of the simulations). The

**Table 4.1**
**MSD Scores (100 x Mean Squared Deviation) Between the Distinct Predictions and the Experimental Results by Game and Over Games.**

| Game | Random | Equilibrium | One-Parameter | | | Three-Parameter | | |
|---|---|---|---|---|---|---|---|---|
| | | | *Best Fit* | *By Game (12 par.)* | *Predi ction* | *Best Fit* | *By Game (36 par.)* | *Predi ction* |
| S&A8 | 1.08 | 6.92 | 0.16 | 0.07 | 0.16 | 0.38 | 0.05 | 0.67 |
| S&A2 | 2.04 | 7.18 | 0.30 | 0.24 | 0.30 | 0.18 | 0.10 | 0.26 |
| S&A3u | 2.53 | 7.27 | 0.31 | 0.14 | 0.31 | 0.12 | 0.04 | 0.19 |
| S&A3k | 1.46 | 7.56 | 0.11 | 0.10 | 0.11 | 0.07 | 0.05 | 0.09 |
| S&A3n | 2.11 | 6.14 | 0.57 | 0.41 | 0.57 | 0.31 | 0.25 | 0.39 |
| M&L | 2.46 | 2.11 | 2.27 | 1.89 | 2.27 | 1.24 | 0.21 | 1.24 |
| On | 2.19 | 0.14 | 1.81 | 0.33 | 1.81 | 0.72 | 0.32 | 0.87 |
| R&B15 | 1.07 | 0.45 | 0.98 | 0.50 | 0.98 | 0.65 | 0.35 | 0.83 |
| R&B10 | 1.38 | 1.03 | 0.73 | 0.16 | 0.86 | 0.33 | 0.11 | 0.48 |
| Oc9 | 3.88 | 2.22 | 2.71 | 2.34 | 2.71 | 1.54 | 1.34 | 1.54 |
| Oc4 | 1.78 | 1.37 | 1.54 | 1.54 | 1.64 | 1.09 | 0.99 | 1.17 |
| Oc1 | 0.45 | 0.45 | 0.48 | 0.41 | 0.48 | 0.48 | 0.37 | 0.51 |
| Mean | 1.87 | 3.57 | 1.00 | 0.68 | 1.02 | 0.59 | 0.35 | 0.69 |

table reports the results for random choice, for the equilibrium predictions, and for the two models presented earlier. For each model, the table reports the three comparisons in order; first the MSDs for the parameters that minimize the MSD averaged over all games, then for the parameters (x 12) that separately minimize the MSDs for each of the 12 games, and then the MSD of the prediction for each game, using the parameters that best fit the other 11 games. The final row, which gives the mean over all games, gives a quick summary statistic by which the models can roughly be compared.

The table shows that the one-parameter reinforcement learning model outperforms the equilibrium prediction (and this remains true for *all* values of its one parameter; as $s(1)$ goes to infinity, the model approaches the random choice model). The model's descriptive and predictive power is further significantly improved by incorporating experimentation and forgetting into the three-parameter reinforcement model; this makes the model more responsive to a changing environment (i.e., an adaptive opponent).

Overall, the results support the notion that it may be possible to find learning models that can be usefully applied to a variety of games, rather than having to construct or estimate models separately for each game. For example, Table 4.1 shows that the three-parameter reinforcement model fit simultaneously to all games has a lower mean deviation (0.59) than does the one-parameter (x 12) model fitted to each game separately.

## Initial Propensities, Adjustable Reference Point, and Generalizability

Whereas the three-parameter model provides a good prediction of behavior in the games considered in Erev and Roth (1998), it is clear that this model is oversimplified. In Roth and Erev (1995; also Slonim & Roth, 1998) we noted that the simplification assumption of uniform initial propensities has to be replaced with estimated initials in order to account for behavior in sequential bargaining games in which players in different countries have different initial propensities to use specific strategies.

In addition, it is easy to think about situations in which the assumed reinforcement function in the one- and three-parameter models ($R(x) = x - x_{min}$) cannot provide a good approximation of behavior. For example, the addition of a dominated strategy that leads to a loss of $100 with certainty to each of the games considered earlier is not likely to affect human behavior, but has a strong effect on the predictions of the two models (when $x_{min}$ is very small relative to all other payoffs these models predicts very slow learning). To address this limitation we proposed (in Erev & Roth, 1996a) a generalization of the three-parameter model in which payoffs are evaluated relative to an adjustable reference point. The generalized model has five parameters.

This generalization has little effect in the experiments considered by Erev and Roth (1998), but improves the model's predictions in other settings. The value of the reinforcement learning model with adjustable reference was demonstrated in the context of simplified poker games (Rapoport et al., 1997), market entry games and step-level public good games (Erev & Rapoport, 1998), and probability learning tasks (Bereby-Meyer & Erev, 1998).

To evaluate the generalizability and predictive power of the model with the parameters that best describe previous experiments, Roth, Slonim, Erev, and Bereby-Meyer (1997) studied 40 randomly selected 2 x 2 probabilistic constant-sum games under distinct information conditions. The payoff matrix in these games is defined by four probabilities (the probability that Player 1 wins in each cell). The random games were created by a uniform and independent random drawing of each of the four probabilities. Three pairs of subjects were run for 500 trials in each randomly selected game.

The main result of this extensive study is a demonstration that the *ex ante* prediction of simple reinforcement learning models of the behavior of the average pair is more accurate (has a smaller MSD score) than a prediction that is based on the average of the other two pairs that played the same game. Thus, it has "human power" of more than 2. In comparison, the human power of the equilibrium prediction is less than 1.

**Table 4.2**
**A Matching Pennies Game**

|              | Column Choice |        |
| Row Choice   | A             | B      |
|--------------|---------------|--------|
| A            | 1,-1          | -1, 1  |
| B            | -1,1          | 1,-1   |

# VIOLATIONS OF SIMPLE REINFORCEMENT LEARNING MODELS

Despite the success that we have had in using reinforcement learning models to predict behavior in very simple strategic environments, it is clear that the model will need to be enriched if we are to extend it to more complex environments. Indeed, there is relatively large agreement among cognitive psychologists that reinforcement learning models are useful in predicting simple behavior, but fail to capture complex behavior. Six robust violations of reinforcement learning models are often used to justify this conclusion. These violations that have been observed both in psychological research and in experimental games are summarized here.

## Overalternation and the "Gambler's Fallacy"

While studying the behavior of rats in a simple T-maze task, Tolman (1925) discovered a robust violation of the law of effect. In each trial of his study, rats had to choose an arm in the T maze. Whereas the law of effect predicts an increase in choice probability following a reward, Tolman found a decrease. His subjects tended to alternate even after winning a reward in one of the two sides.

Interestingly, Rapoport and Budescu (1992) have found a similar phenomena in human behavior. In one of their experimental conditions, human subjects played a symmetrical zero-sum matching pennies game (cf. Table 4.2). Whereas their aggregate results (about equal choice of each alternative) are consistent with equilibrium and reinforcement learning, analysis of sequential dependencies reveal a clear violation of these two models.

Like Tolman's rats, Rapoport and Budescu's subjects exhibit a strong overalternation effect. In violation of the reinforcement learning prediction of a weak win-stay, lose-change dependency, their subjects tended to alternate even after winning.

Another robust sequential dependency that violates the law of effect was

**Table 4.3**
**A PD Game**

| Row choice | Column Choice | |
|---|---|---|
| | *C* | *D* |
| C | 1,1 | -10, 10 |
| D | 10,-10 | -1,-1 |

*Note.* Adapted from Rapoport and Chamman (1965).

documented in probability learning studies. In a typical study (see the review in Lee, 1971) decision makers are asked to predict which of two events (L or H) will occur. In each trial only one event occurs, and the occurrence probabilities are fixed throughout the experiment. These studies reveal slow learning that can be approximated by Roth and Erev's model, and a violation of this model known as the "gambler's fallacy": At least in the beginning of some of the studies decision makers tend to predict a change in the state of the world.

## Reciprocation

Rapoport and Chammah (1965) studied behavior in seven repeated prisoner dilemma games (PDG). Table 4.3 presents one of the games they studied. In keeping with the definition of the PDG, each player has a dominant strategy (to choose D), but the "rational" outcome (the DD cell) is inefficient (both players could benefit from a move to the CC cell).

Rapoport and Chammah's (1965) subjects were randomly matched at the beginning of the experiment and ran for 300 trials. Simple reinforcement learning models (like the Roth & Erev model) with only the stage game strategies "C" and "D" modeled predict convergence to the dominant strategy (see Bornstein et al., 1994). In violation of this prediction, an increase in C choices (cooperation) with time, and strong sequential dependencies, were observed in four of the seven games.[2]

## Transfer

People's ability to transfer knowledge from one set of situations to another set is probably the toughest challenge for students of learning. Simple reinforcement learning models ignore transfer altogether. Roth and Erev's model, for example, was designed to address situations in which the learners play one game repeatedly. When decision makers participate in a few similar games during the same experimental block the model fails to predict the observed between-games facilitation.

For example, in Rapoport at el. (1998) subjects participated in 10 market entry games in each of 10 experimental blocks. The results reveal that much of the learning occurred before the second block. A single experience with each of the games was enough. This observation is inconsistent with the much slower prediction of a simple reinforcement learning model to this task.

A clearer example was documented in a binary categorization task research. In Kubovy and Healy (1977) and Kubovy, Rapoport and Tversky (1971) subjects were asked to categorize stimuli to one of two categories. Whereas each stimuli was presented only once, subjects learned and improved with practice.

## Expectation-Driven Behavior

Whereas most comparisons suggest that reinforcement learning models provide a better approximation of behavior than expectation based models (see e.g., Camerer & Ho, chap. 3, this volume; Erev & Roth, 1998; Mookherjee & Sopher, 1997; Tang, 1996), it is clear that expectations affect behavior. For example, examination of large group multiple strategies games (Camerer & Ho, chap. 3, this volume; Cooper & Feltovich, 1996; Roth, Prasnikar, Okuno-Fujiwara, & Zamir, 1991; Van Huyck, Battalio, & Beil, 1991) reveals relatively fast learning that cannot be accounted for by reinforcement learning models (at least not given our quantification). Camerer and Ho (chap. 3, this volume) demonstrate that in the game they analyzed behavior is sensitive to outcomes of strategies that the decision maker has not selected. This sensitivity can be described as an attempt to maximize expected reward.

## Imitation

Another reasonable explanation for the quick learning just discussed is that subjects imitate successful others. Bandura (1969) argued that vicarious learning (imitation) is inconsistent with reinforcement learning, and should be thought of as an independent learning process. Bandura supported this assertion with the observation that children tend to imitate others even when this behavior is not reinforced.

## Direction Learning

Examination of the choice sequences of individual players often reveals consistent patterns that violate probabilistic models (like all reinforcement learning models). For instance, in games with a linearly ordered strategy space, some subjects consistently adjust their strategy in line to a direction-learning rule. Selten (1996) cited 10 studies in which some of the subjects can be categorized as "directional learners." To demonstrate the appeal of direction learning Selten presents an "archer" thought experiment. Obviously, a good archer has to adjust his or her behavior in line with a directional learning rule:

After missing the target to the left, the archer adjust the aim to the right. As noted by Selten, this trivial observation is not predicted by reinforcement learning models.

In line with Selten's suggestion, a strong knowledge of results (KR) effect was observed in motor learning research (Trowbridge & Cason, 1932). Subjects appear to learn faster when the feedback they receive includes directional and quantitative information in addition to the reinforcement.

## THE COGNITIVE GAME THEORETIC EXPLANATION

According to the cognitive game-theoretic approach (Erev & Roth, 1998), it is convenient to decompose models of dynamic choice behavior into three submodels: (a) an abstraction of the cognitive strategies; (b) the incentive structure (the game); and (c) the learning/adaptation rule. Under this decomposition the apparent inconsistency between the descriptive power and the violations of reinforcement learning models can be explained by the distinction between the assumed cognitive strategies and the assumed learning rule. Cognitive strategies can be task-specific (like stage game strategies), or general adaptive rules (repeated game strategies like the tit-for-tat (TFT) strategy). The results summarized earlier are consistent with the hypothesis that the general learning rule can be approximated by a reinforcement learning model. The six violations previously summarized are then explained by the conjecture that they reflect a utilization of repeated game-cognitive strategies. That is, if reinforcement learning goes on among a rich set of strategies (and not merely among stage game strategies), then the phenomena we have been discussing no longer appear to violate the hypothesis that the learning process can be approximated as reinforcement learning.

It is important to emphasize that the cognitive game-theoretic approach is not suggested here as a testable model. Rather, like traditional game theory it is a theoretical framework that can be utilized to construct testable models. Our main assertion is that if cognitive strategies and games are assumed to be situation-specific (a common assumption in cognitive psychology and game theory), there is no need to assume a situation-specific learning model. And to the extent that cognitive strategies and the game can be assessed, the assumption of a general learning rule can be utilized to facilitate construction of useful models of choice behavior.

For the current discussion, the main difference between this explanation and alternative explanations that assume situation-specific learning processes is the assumed predictability of violations of simple reinforcement learning (i.e., reinforcement learning over actions rather than strategies). The cognitive game-theoretic explanation implies that the frequency of violations is predictable: Subjects are expected to learn to use strategies that lead to violations when they are positively reinforced and to stop using them when they impair reinforcement. The situation-specific explanations can describe dynamic trends of this type (by fitting parameters), but currently do not have clear parameter-free predictions.

To evaluate the potential of the cognitive game-theoretic explanation this section discusses each of the observed violations. The discussion starts with a description of a cognitive strategy that could lead to the observed results. We then review studies that examine whether the magnitude of the violation (utilization of the assumed strategies) is affected by reinforcements. It is shown that in most cases clear learning effects that can be described as reinforcement learning among cognitive strategies are observed. In fact, the cognitive strategies explanation often coincides with the explanation provided (under different names) and supported in the psychological literature.

## Sequential Strategies and Dependencies

Sequential dependencies can be a result of repeated game strategies. For example, rats (and humans) can follow an alternation strategy. Thirty years of alternation research is summarized by Dember and Fowler (1958). This research concludes that animals have a natural tendency to alternate. This tendency is assumed to be effective in most natural settings. (A rat that has eaten all the food in one location may profit from searching elsewhere rather than returning immediately.) Yet, when animals are put in a situation in which this strategy is inefficient, they can learn to avoid it. Moreover, when animals are put in a situation in which alternation is adaptive (as in Green, Price, & Hamburger's 1995 study in which pigeons played a chicken game against an alternating computer), they can learn to increase the probability of alternation.

Similar conclusions were reached in the human probability learning literature. It was found that the gambler's fallacy phenomena that impair earnings disappears as subjects gain experience (Estes, 1964).

Thus, it appears that rats, pigeons, and humans have an initial tendency to follow sequential strategies and learn to adjust the probability of using these strategies based on their effectiveness.

Note that this conclusion implies that at least initially players use repeated game strategies even in zero-sum games. Thus, it apparently contradicts the results summarized earlier that show that behavior in these games can be predicted by a reinforcement-learning model among the stage game strategies. To understand this contradiction Rapoport et al. (1997) derived the predictions of the Roth and Erev model for zero-sum games under two models of the strategy space: only stage game strategies or stage game plus alternation and a gambler's fallacy strategies. Their results indicate that the addition of the sequential strategies has very little effect on the aggregate predictions for such games. Thus, the paradox is resolved by the conclusion that in zero-sum games the approximation of the strategy space by the stage game strategies is inaccurate but robust.

## Reciprocation Strategies

Reciprocation in repeated games is also observed widely enough for it to be sensible to think of reciprocation as a common repeated game strategy. For example, Axelrod (1984) argued that people follow the TFT strategy in PDG. Interestingly, Anatol Rapoport, who proposed the TFT strategy in Axelrod's tournament, did not use it to explain his experimental data. In fact, Rapoport and Chammah's (1965) data are not entirely consistent with the argument that players follow the TFT strategy. If players were simple TFT followers, reciprocation should have been observed immediately in all PDG. Rapoport and Chammah (1965) found a slow increase in reciprocation in some games and no increase in other games.

This observation is consistent with the view that TFT is a cognitive strategy. Erev and Roth (1996a) derived the prediction of a cognitive game-theoretic model for Rapoport and Chammah's (1965) games under the assumption of reinforcement learning among three cognitive strategies (TFT and the stage game strategies). This model reproduces the experimental results: it predicts an increase in reciprocation only when the experimental players learned to reciprocate.

## Transfer: The Example of Cutoff Strategies

Transfer is predicted by the cognitive game-theoretic approach (and by all other cognitive models) because cognitive strategies can apply to many situations. For example, learning to follow a reciprocation strategy in one setting is expected to increase the probability of using this strategy in a different but similar setting. Whereas many questions regarding transfer are still open (like the measurement of similarity), it is clear that transfer is consistent with models that assume cognitive strategies. Moreover, in specific settings in which similarity can be approximate, cognitive game-theoretic models appear to provide a good prediction of learning.

For example, Rapoport et al. (1998) found that transfer between similar market entry games is predicted by a model that assumes reinforcement learning among cutoff strategies. A similar cutoff reinforcement learning model was found to reproduce all the robust regularities observed in binary categorization under uncertainty studies (Erev, 1998). In a typical binary categorization task a decision maker (DM) is presented with an observation (e.g., a height of an individual) that can come from one of two overlapping populations (e.g., heights of males and females). The DM's task is to classify the observation (e.g., decide if it is a male or a female) given a well-defined reward structure.

Previous research demonstrate that behavior in categorization tasks can be approximated by signal detection theory (SDT, Green & Swets, 1966). The relatively good approximation made SDT one of the most important tools for applied psychologists (see e.g., Swennsen, Hessel, & Herman, 1977; Wallsten & Gonzalez-Vallejo, 1994). This theory assumes that DMs consider cutoff strategies (e.g., respond male if the likelihood ratio of male exceeds a certain cutoff), and select the cutoff that maximize expected utility. Yet, careful examination of the difference between the predictions of SDT and the observed behavior reveals robust violations of this theory. Although the violations appear to decrease as DMs gain experience, they do not disappear even after thousands of decision trials with immediate feedback.

Different learning models were proposed to address the different violations of SDT (see Busemeyer & Myung, 1992 and an early review in Kubovy & Healy, 1977). Erev (1998) reviewed the known violations and compared previous explanations to a model that assumes reinforcement learning among cognitive cutoff strategies. This model is identical to the model presented earlier with the exception that at each period the DM selects a cutoff (that implies a decision) rather than one of the stage game strategies. Even without fitting parameters to specific experiments, the cutoff reinforcement learning model was found to capture 16 behavioral regularities and to outperform all previous explanations (typically post hoc alternative models).

## Best Reply to Observed Statistics

The findings that people are affected by observed nonreinforcement events can be explained by the assumption that this information is utilized by certain cognitive strategies. For example, subjects who use a fictitious play strategy (Robinson, 1951) might explicitly calculate expected values (under the typically false assumption of a stationary world) and select the alternative that maximizes expected reward.

To test the hypothesis that best reply rules are strategies (rather than general learning models), it is useful to consider the evidence for best-reply behavior in games in which best reply to observed statistics is reinforcing. For example, in the Van Huyck et al. (1991) average opinion games, the optimal response is to match the population average. In these and similar games behavior can be described by a fictitious learning rule (Crawford, 1994), and as noted by Camerer and Ho players weigh nonreinforcement events. On the other hand, in market entry games in which matching other players is typically not reinforcing (and the best reply rule can lead to large losses), behavior is inconsistent with best-reply rules (Erev & Rapoport, 1998). An interesting and related analysis of the best-reply strategies is provided by Stahl (1996).

## Imitation Strategies

Miller and Dollard (1941) provided an influential account of imitation within the reinforcement learning (operant conditioning) paradigm. In controlled experiments they established that the probability of imitation is a function of the probability of reinforcement of previous imitative behavior. Bandura (1969) criticized this account and argued that a cognitive element has to be added to explain why children initially tend to imitate successful (and significant) others. He proposed a theory of imitation to account for this observation. Clearly, however, the required cognitive element can also be added by the assumption that people tend to follow cognitive imitation strategies that specify who should be imitated. This cognitive game-theoretic assumption is consistent with both Miller and Dollard's (1941) and Bandura's (1969) results. It is also consistent with the current view of learning by observation (Mazur, 1994).

## Directional and Correctional Strategies

The observation that directional feedback and other information about outcomes facilitates learning can be accounted for by the assumption that people can follow directional strategies. For example, an archer can adjust ·to the observation that the wind carries arrows to the left by following a directional strategy that implies a correction to the right.

There are two types of evidence that suggest that directional learning is better abstracted as a cognitive strategy than as a learning rule. First, it turns out that the provision of feedback about outcomes after each trial during the learning period can have a negative effect (see e.g., Winstein & Schmidt, 1990). It appears that when this information is always provided subjects may learn to rely on it and, as a result, do not develop alternative and more robust strategies.

A second line of evidence includes observed behavior in games in which direction learning loses its effectiveness. Duffy and Nagel (1997; and see Nagel, chap. 6, this volume) found that the evidence for direction-learning behavior decreases with experience in a beauty contest (guessing) game when these strategies are not reinforced.

# ON THE VALUE AND LIMITATIONS OF THE COGNITIVE GAME-THEORETIC APPROACH

As noted earlier, the fact that violations of simple reinforcement learning models can be accounted for within the cognitive game-theoretic framework does not imply that this framework is accurate. Moreover, the general framework is not testable; thus, the accuracy question is not relevant. The important question is "is it useful?"

The results summarized earlier provide reasons to conjuncture that this approach is likely to be useful. The most encouraging observation is the apparent robustness of the predicted choice probabilities to certain inaccuracies in the exact modeling of the cognitive strategies. It seems that even a rough approximation of these unobserved strategies can lead to nontrivial predictions. As noted in Erev and Roth (1998) the fact that learning curves in matrix games in which players cannot reciprocate can be predicted from the assumption of stage game strategies does not imply that this assumption is an accurate approximation of the cognitive strategies. In fact, as the sequential strategies observed in these games suggest, this assumption is violated. The model appears to succeed because the predicted curves in this wide set of games are robust to the assumed cognitive strategies. To further explore this assertion we ran simulations of the constant-sum games studied in Roth et al. (1997) with simulated players who consider all the cognitive strategies mentioned that can be used in these games (alternation, gambler's fallacy, imitation and best reply to expectations). In line with Rapoport et al.'s (1997) results, addition of these strategies had a clear effect on the sequential dependencies, but only a mild effect on the aggregate choice probabilities. This does not imply that the exact cognitive strategies can be ignored. As noted earlier, in games that allow players to reciprocate an abstraction of a reciprocation strategy is needed to predict aggregate choice probabilities.

Another indication of the potential robustness of cognitive game-theoretic model comes from the study of models that assume learning among cutoff strategies. For example, Erev (1998) assumes that in binary categorization decisions DMs learn among 101 cutoff strategies. Whereas this assumption cannot be correct, Erev's model was found to account for 16 robust behavioral regularities that have been explained by six distinct models. Moreover, the cognitive game-theoretic model outperforms each of these six situation-specific models.

Finally, note that each of the cognitive strategies considered earlier was introduced in previous research. Thus, whereas some of these strategies are suggested here in a post hoc manner, it seems that it is possible to base a cognitive game-theoretic model on robust models developed in traditional cognitive research.

These results imply that even if there are infinitely many cognitive strategies that players might consider, a rough approximation of these strategies may be sufficient to predict choice probabilities. And this rough approximation can be obtained in an ex ante way for wide sets of well-defined situations.

## CONCLUSIONS

The results just reviewed show that whereas simple reinforcement learning models (that assume learning among stage game strategies) provide a good approximation of behavior in some games, the predictions are violated in other games. The violations summarized earlier suggest that people (and other animals) "try to be smarter" than simple reinforcement learners. Each of the six violations of pure reinforcement learning can be summarized as an attempt to increase payoffs. Sequential dependencies, best reply, and directional learning can represent an attempt to efficiently reply to regularities in the world;

reciprocation maximizes earning by tacit cooperation; and transfer and imitation can facilitate efficient utilization of accumulated knowledge.

As noted in the beginning of the chapter, the contradiction between the predictive power and the clear violations of simple reinforcement learning models can be addressed by three distinct theoretical approaches: An "as if" approach implies that players do not follow reinforcement learning rules but sometime behave as if they do. A game-specific learning approach implies that the extent to which players use reinforcement learning rules changes from game to game. And the cognitive game-theoretic approach implies that reinforcement learning determines choices among cognitive strategies. The results reviewed earlier summarize evidence that favors the cognitive game-theoretic account. This evidence suggests that the frequency of apparent violations of the law of effect may be predictable.

It should be emphasized that the support to the cognitive game-theoretic approach does not imply that the alternative approaches are wrong. Clearly, the reviewed evidence does not contradict the view that different models (or parameters) are needed to approximate learning in different games (Camerer & Ho, chap. 3, this volume; Selten, 1996). Rather, it suggests that reinforcement learning models can be used to predict which learning rule will best approximate behavior in a specific setting. For example, Camerer and Ho (chap. 3, this volume) suggest that it may be possible to describe the different models by a single functional form with game-specific parameters. In their research they show that in a simplified case the parameters can be estimated. The current results suggest that it may be possible to predict the value of the "best" parameters.

Strictly speaking, the current results do not even rule out the possibility that people never follow reinforcement learning rules. Roth and Erev's model is suggested here as an approximation of a slow adjustment process among cognitive strategies that appears to characterize behavior in games. Other approximations are, of course, possible. Yet, given the good fit provided by the current model to data described earlier, we conjecture that alternative models may use other theoretical terms (like beliefs) but are unlikely to be described by very distinct functional forms. (In Erev and Roth, 1998, we show that the main difference between our quantification of the law of effect and probabilistic fictitious play models can be summarized by three noncentral parameters.)

Finally, it is instructive to note that the cognitive game-theoretic approach represents a relatively minor modification of traditional game theory. The distinction between strategies and actions that we make here in connection with the reinforcement learning rule is a familiar one in traditional game theory. What we are proposing is that it may be possible to replace a general model of perfectly rational behavior (utility maximization, supplemented by assumptions of equilibrium behavior) with a general model of boundedly rational learning, supplemented by an empirically informed model of what strategies players consider.

The open question is how the cognitive strategies should be modeled. Advances in cognitive psychology and judgment and decision-making research suggest that good approximations can be obtained. This research suggests that in a wide set of situations, people tend to utilize relatively small sets of adaptive cognitive strategies. These strategies, often referred to as heuristics (Tversky & Kahneman, 1974), decision rules (Busemeyer & Myung, 1992; Payne, Bettman, & Johnson, 1993), production rules (Anderson, 1982), or algorithms (Gigerenzer, 1996), are assumed to be used because they typically achieve good outcomes with relatively little cognitive effort. Yet, as demonstrated by Tversky and Kahneman (1974), in certain settings they can lead to counterproductive behavior (biases); in these settings people initially tend to follow inefficient strategies. Cognitive game theory may allow us to predict in which strategic environment initial behavior is likely to persist.

In summary, like traditional game theory, cognitive game theory assumes a general decision rule among situation-specific strategies. The major difference is the attempt to replace the rationality assumption with a simple general learning rule, supplemented by an empirically based model of the strategy sets perceived by players. Our reading of the psychological literature suggests that the law of effect is the only property of learning sufficiently general so as to be able to drive learning in games with a wide variety of information conditions,[3] and that initial strategies can be approximated. The fact that initial cognitive strategies are not always adaptive suggests that learning among these cognitive strategies can lead to nontrivial testable predictions.

## ENDNOTES

1. In addition to these models we also considered a four-parameter variant of Camerer and Ho's model (see chap. 3, this volume). This model, which generalizes reinforcement learning and belief learning, did not outperform the three-parameter model on these data.
2. Similar results were obtained by Rapoport and Moskowitz (1966). And see Komorita and Parks (chap. 13, this volume) for a review of related studies.
3. Including situations in which individuals are not aware of the fact that they are learning to make more adaptive decisions. And repeated games are often played with very little awareness. For example, driving involves many repeated perceptual games: in a common scenario one of two drivers has to slow down to prevent an accident. Although we play this and similar games every day we are rarely aware of the fact that we make decisions and update our strategies. Yet, experimental studies of games of this type (Erev, Gopher, Itkin, & Greenshpan, 1995; Gilat, Meyer, Erev, & Gopher, 1997) show adaptive learning among cognitive strategies that can be described by Roth and Erev's quantification of the law of effect.

# REFERENCES

Anderson, J. R. (1982). Acquisition of cognitive skill. *Psychological Review, 91*, 112-149.

Axelrod, R. (1984). *The evolution of cooperation.* New York, NY: Basic Books.

Bandura, A. (1969). *Principles of behavior modification.* New York, NY: Holt, Rinehart & Winston.

Bereby-Meyer, Y., & Erev, I. (1998). On learning to become a successful loser: Comparison of alternative abstractions of learning in the loss domain. *Journal of Mathematical Psychology.*

Blackburn, J. M. (1936). *Acquisition of skill: An analysis of learning curves.* (IHRB Rep. No. 73).

Bornstein, G., Erev, I., & Goren, H. (1994). Learning processes and reciprocity in intergroup conflicts. *Journal of Conflict Resolution, 38*, 690-707.

Brown, J. S., Clark, F. R. & Stein, L. (1958). A new technique for studying special generalization with voluntary responses. *Journal of Experimental Psychology, 55*, 359-362.

Busemeyer, J. R., & Myung, I. J. (1992). An adaptive approach to human decision making: Learning theory, decision theory, and human performance. *Journal of Experimental Psychology: General, 21*, 177-194.

Bush, R., & Mosteller, F. (1955). *Stochastic models for learning.* New York, NY: Wiley.

Camerer, C. (1990). Behavioral game theory. In R. Hogarth (Ed.) *Insights in decision making: A tribute to Hillel J. Einhorn.* Chicago: University of Chicago Press.

Cheung, Y. & Friedman, D. (1996). *A comparison of learning and replicator dynamics using experimental data.* Mimeo, University of California, Santa Cruz.

Cooper, D., & Feltovich, N. (1996). *Reinforcement-based learning vs. Bayesian learning: comparison.* (Working paper 305), University of Pittsburgh.

Crawford, V. P. (1994). Adaptive dynamics in coordination games. *Econometrica, 63*, 103-143.

Dember, W. N., & Fowler, H. (1958). Spontaneous alternation behavior. *Psychological Bulletin, 55*, 412-428.

Duffy, J., & Nagel, R. (1997). On the robustness of behavior in experimental "P-beauty contest" games. *Economic Journal, 107*, 1684-1700.

Erev, I. (1998). Signal detection by human observers: A cutoff reinforcement learning model of categorization decisions under uncertainty. *Psychological Review, 105*(2), 280-298.

Erev, I., Gopher, D., Itkin, R., & Greenshpan, Y. (1995). Toward a generalization of signal detection theory to N-person games: The example of two-person safety problem. *Journal of Mathematical Psychology, 39*, 360-375.

Erev, I., & Rapoport, A. (1998). Coordination, "magic," and reinforcement learning in a market entry game. *Games and Economic Behavior, 23*, 146-175.

Erev, I., & Roth, A. (1996a). *A cognitive game theoretic analysis of reciprocation.* Paper presented at the workshop on Games and Human Behavior in the honor of Amnon's Rapoport 60th birthday, Chapel Hill, NC.

Erev, I., & Roth, A. (1996b). *On the need for low rationality, cognitive game theory: Reinforcement learning in experimental games with unique, mixed strategy equilibria.* Mimeo, The University of Pittsburgh.

Erev, I., & Roth, A. (1998). Predicting how people play games: Reinforcement learning in experimental games with unique, mixed strategy equilibria. *American Economic*

*Review.*

Estes, W. K. (1964). Probability learning. In A. W. Melton (Ed.), *Categories of Human Learning* (pp. 89-128). New York, NY: Academic Press.

Fudenberg, D., & Levine, D. K. (1996). *Theory of learning in games* [draft]. Available at: http://levine.sscnet.ucla.edu/papers/contents.htm.

Gigerenzer, G. (1996). *Introducing satisfying models of inference and how they affect our notions of sound reasoning and rationality.* Paper presented at the meeting of the society of Judgment and Decision Making, Chicago, IL.

Gilat, S., Meyer, J., Erev, I., & Gopher, D. (1997). Beyond Bayes' theorem: The effect of base rate information in consensus games. *Journal of Experimental Psychology: Applied, 2,* 83-104.

Green, D. M., & Swets, J. A. (1966). *Signal detection theory and psychophysics.* New York, NY: Wiley. (Reprinted in 1988; Los Altos, CA: Peninsula Publishers)

Green, L., Price, P. C., & Hamburger, M. (1995). Prisoner dilemma and the pigeon: Control by immediate consequences. *Journal of Experimental Analysis of Behavior, 64,* 1-17.

Harley, C. B. (1981). Learning the evolutionary stable strategy. *Journal of Theoretical Biology, 89,* 611-633.

Herrnstein, R. J. (1970). On the law of effect. *Journal of the Experimental Analysis of Behavior, 13,* 243-266.

Kubovy, M., & Healy, A. F. (1977). The decision rule in probabilistic categorization: What it is and how is it learned. *Journal of Experimental Psychology: General, 106,* 427-446.

Kubovy, M., Rapoport, A., & Tversky, A. (1971). Deterministic vs. probabilistic strategies in detection. *Perception & Psychophysics, 9,* 427-429.

Lee, W. (1971). *Decision theory and human behavior.* New York, NY: Wiley.

Luce, D. R. (1959). *Individual choice behavior.* New York, NY: Wiley.

Malcolm, D., & Lieberman, B. (1965). The behavior of responsive individuals playing a two-person, zero-sum game requiring the use of mixed strategies. *Psychonomic Science,* 373-374.

Mazur, J. E. (1994). *Learning and behavior.* Englewood Cliffs, NJ: Prentice-Hall, Inc.

Miller, N. E. & Dollard, J. (1941). *Social learning and imitation.* New Haven, CT: Yale University Press.

Mookherjee, D., & Sopher, B. (1997). Learning and decision costs in experimental constant sum games. *Games and Economic Behavior, 19,* 97-132.

Ochs, J. (1995). Simple games with unique mixed strategy equilibrium: An experimental study. *Games and Economic Behavior, 10,* 202-217.

O'Neill, B. (1987). Nonmetric test of the minimax theory of two-person zerosum games. *Proceedings of the National Academy of Sciences, USA, 84,* 2106-2109.

Payne, J. W., Bettman, J. R., & Johnson, E. J. (1993). *The adaptive decision maker.* Cambridge, England: Cambridge University Press.

Rapoport, Am., & Boebel, R. B. (1992). Mixed strategies in strictly competitive games: A further test of the minmax hypothesis. *Games and Economic Behavior, 4,* 261-283.

Rapoport, Am., & Budescu, D. V. (1992). Generation of random series in two-person strictly competitive games. *Journal of Experimental Psychology: General, 121,* 352-363.

Rapoport, Am., & Moskowitz, A. (1966). Experimental studies of stochastic models for the prisoner dilemma. *Behavioral Science, 11,* 444-458.

Rapoport, Am., Erev, I., Abraham, E. V., & Olson, D. E. (1997). Randomization and adaptive learning in a simplified poker game. *Organizational Behavior and Human Decision Processes, 69,* 31-49.

Rapoport, Am., Seale, D. A., Erev, I., & Sundali, J. A. (1998). Coordination success in market entry games: Tests of equilibrium and adaptive learning models. *Management Science, 44,* 119-141.

Rapoport, An., & Chammah, A. M. (1965). *Prisoner dilemma.* University of Michigan Press.

Robinson, J. (1951). An iterative method of solving a game. *Annals of Mathematics, 54,* 296-301.

Roth, A. E., & Erev, I. (1995). Learning in extensive-form games: Experimental data and simple dynamic models in the intermediate term. *Games and Economic Behavior* [Special Issue: Nobel Symposium], *8,* 164-212.

Roth, A. E., Prasnikar, V., Okuno-Fujiwara, M., & Zamir, S. (1991). Bargaining and market behavior in Jerusalem, Ljubljana, Pittsburgh, and Tokyo: An experimental study. *American Economic Review, 81,* 1068-1095.

Roth, A. E., Slonim, B., Erev, I., & Bereby-Meyer, Y. (1997). *On the predictive power of reinforcement learning models: Predicting behavior in randomly selected games.* Mimeo, University of Pittsburgh.

Selten (1996). *Learning direction theory.* Paper presented at the workshop on Games and Human Behavior in honor of Amnon's Rapoport 60th birthday, Chapel Hill, NC.

Slonim, R., & Roth, A. E. (1996). *Financial incentives and learning in ultimatum and market games: An experiment in the Slovak republic.* Econometrica.

Stahl, D. O. (1996). *Evidence based rule learning in symmetric normal-form games.* Working Paper, University of Texas.

Suppes, P., & Atkinson, R. C. (1960). *Markov learning models for multiperson interactions.* Palo Alto, CA: Stanford University Press.

Swennsen, R. G., Hessel, S. J., & Herman, P. G. (1977). Omission in radiology: Faulty search or stringent reporting criteria? *Radiology, 123,* 563-567.

Tang, F. (1996). *Anticipatory learning in two-person games: An experimental study. Part II. Learning.* Discussion Paper B-363, University of Bonn, Germany.

Thorndike, E. L. (1898). *Animal intelligence: An experimental study of the associative processes in animals.* Psychological Monographs, 2.

Tolman, E. C. (1925). Purpose and cognition: The determiners of animal learning. *Psychological Review, 32,* 285-297.

Trowbridge, M. H., & Cason, H. (1932). An experimental test of Thorndike's theory of learning. *Journal of General Psychology, 7,* 245-260.

Tversky A., & Kahneman, D. (1974). Judgment under uncertainty: Heuristics and biases. *Science, 185,* 1124-1131.

Van Huyck, J., Battalio, R. & Beil, R. (1991). Strategic uncertainty, equilibrium selection, and coordination failure in average opinion. *Quarterly Journal of Economics, 106,* 885-909.

Wallsten, T. S., & Gonzalez-Vallejo, C. (1994). Statement verification: A stochastic model of judgment and response. *Psychological Review, 101,* 490-504.

Winstein, C. J. & Schmidt, R. (1990). Reduced frequency of knowledge of results enhances motor skill learning. *Journal of Experimental Psychology: Learning, Memory, and Cognition, 16,* 677-691.

# 5     Experimental Sealed Bid First Price Auctions with Directly Observed Bid Functions

**Reinhard Selten**
**Joachim Buchta**
*University of Bonn*

In the literature one finds quite a number of experimental papers on first price sealed bid auctions with independent private values (Cox, Roberson, & Smith, 1982; Cox, Smith, & Walker, 1983, 1985a, 1985b, 1988; Kagel, Harstad, & Levin, 1987; Kagel & Levin, 1985; Walker, Smith, & Cox, 1987). In these studies bid functions have been estimated from the data. In some cases it was assumed that all subjects had the same bid functions and in others separate bid functions were estimated for each subject, but in all cases it had been assumed that bid functions do not change in the course of the experiment.

The new feature of the experiment presented here consists in the fact that bid functions were not estimated but directly observed. This makes it possible to check whether bid functions have the properties predicted by game-theoretic analysis. It can also be explored how bid functions are changed by experience.

In our experiment three bidders compete for 50 periods; private values are uniformly and independently distributed over the interval [0,100]. It is well known that under these conditions risk-neutral equilibrium requires that for three competitors the bid is two thirds of the private value. In experiments the bids tend to be higher. In the literature this fact has been explained by the assumption that subjects are risk-averse (Cox, Robertson, & Smith, 1982). This interpretation of the data does not agree well with our findings as we show later.

We look at the data in the light of an approach that we call "learning direction theory." This approach is not yet a full-fledged learning theory because it only explains directions of change without any attempt to predict amounts of change. The same kind of theory has been applied successfully in several other studies (Kuon, 1994; Mitzkewitz & Nagel, 1993; Nagel, 1993; Selten & Stoecker, 1986).

Learning direction theory predicts that subjects tend to lower or not increase their bids at last period's value if they have obtained the object because in this case they might have been able to buy it at a lower price. Similarly it is predicted that subjects tend to increase or not lower their bids at last period's value if it was sold to another competitor below this value. In this case they lost the opportunity to make a profit by a bid slightly higher than the price. Learning direction theory is based on the idea that after an experience subjects think about what might have been a better decision in the last period. They then adjust their behavior accordingly. Of course, this does not conform to the full rationality of economic theory, but it does conform to the bounded rationality of experimental subjects.

## THE EXPERIMENTAL DESIGN

The data were gathered in three sessions involving 9, 6, and 12 subjects, respectively, subdivided into independent subject groups of three subjects each that stayed together during all 50 periods. There was no interaction across subject groups.

In each of the nine independent subject groups the three subjects interacted in sealed bid first price auctions for 50 periods. The subjects interacted anonymously via computer terminals. The private value of the object was uniformly distributed over the interval [0,100]. Only one object was sold in every auction.

At the beginning of every period each subject had to specify a piecewise linear bid function shown on the computer screen. The corners of the bid function could be fixed by a graphical input mode or could be entered numerically. The program then automatically computed the linear connections between adjacent corners and showed them on the screen. The input precision was two decimal points but otherwise the number of corners was not limited. The subjects had the option not to change their bid functions from one period to the next. Only in the case of a change, new corners had to be specified. It was also possible to make a direct linear connection between two corners whereby intermediate corners were eliminated. Bids higher than the private value were not permitted. Several changes could be made consecutively and the result of each change was immediately visible on the screen. Finally, the subjects had to confirm that they did not want further changes.

After the subjects had determined their bid functions an object value was drawn randomly and bids were determined accordingly. The object was sold to the highest bidder at the price of the bid. After the auction the price was made public to all three participants. Hidden information about values and bids of the competitors was not revealed. As far as this is possible, common knowledge about the rules was established by the introductory talk.

The subjects had the possibility to look at a table on the screen that showed

**Table 5.1**
**The Last Nonmonotonous Bid Function**

| Period of Last Nonmonotonous Bid Function | Number of Subjects |
|:---:|:---:|
| 50 | 6 |
| 40 – 49 | 3 |
| 30 – 39 | 3 |
| 4 – 5 | 2 |
| Always monotonous | 13 |

the corners of the current bid function. Another table, which was also available, exhibited the subject's history of past play.

After each auction period the profits of the highest bidders were added to his or her account. At the end of the session money payoffs were determined by an exchange rate of DM 0.30 per point.

All sessions were performed in 1992 at the Bonn Laboratory of Experimental Economics. Subjects were separated from each other and interacted anonymously by formal bids only. Each session lasted for 3 – 4 hours including an introductory talk of about 30 minutes and exercises guided by a computerized learning program by which subjects were made familiar with the technique of fixing piecewise linear bid functions.

# ARE BID FUNCTIONS MONOTONOUS?

All theoretical models proposed in the literature (Cox, Roberson, & Smith, 1982) including those involving risk aversion and/or incomplete information yield monotonously increasing bid functions. Surprisingly, in our experiment we observed many bid functions that were decreasing over parts of the range.

We speak of a new bid function if a bid function has been changed from the previous period to the current one. In all sessions, 475 new bid functions were observed. Two hundred and nineteen (46%) of these new bid functions are decreasing over parts of the range. It is quite possible that in the beginning some subjects did not have a sufficient understanding of the strategic situation and others indulged in a certain playfulness, which led them to misuse the graphical program to draw interesting landscapes. However, the phenomenon of nonmonotonicity is not an initial effect. Among the 383 new bid functions in periods 6 to 50 there are 174 (45%) that are nonmonotonous. Here, we use the word *nonmonotonous* in the sense that a bid function is decreasing over parts of

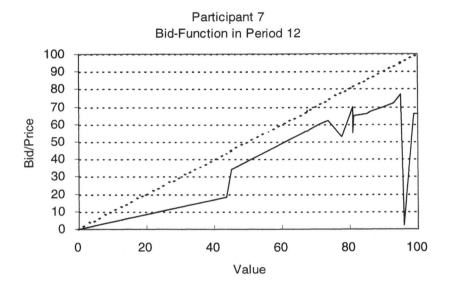

Fig. 5.1. The bid function of Subject 7 in period 12.

the range. Similarly, *monotonous* is used in the sense of not decreasing.

Of the 27 subjects, only 15 specified monotonous bid functions in periods 6 to 50. Table 5.1 gives an impression of when subjects had a nonmonotonous bid function for the last time in the course of play.

It can be seen that those 12 subjects who specified nonmonotonous bid functions in periods 6 to 50 did not switch to monotonicity until late in the session. The phenomenon of nonmonotonicity is quite persistent even if there seems to be a weak tendency to more monotonicity with increasing experience. Figure 5.1 shows an example of a nonmonotonous bid function observed in the experiment.

At the moment we can only speculate about the reasons why some subjects specify nonmonotonous bid functions. One often finds sudden drops of the bid function in the high parts of the range that may be due to the desire to have a small chance to make an extraordinarily high profit. This goal can be achieved by specifying very low bids for a small interval of high values.

Especially in the last two periods some subjects substantially decrease their bids in the high part of the range, presumably, in order to provide a last chance for a high profit. In order to exclude such end effects as well as initial effects from the evaluation of the data, we often restrict our attention to periods 5 to 48.

**Table 5.2**
**Linearity in Bid Functions**

|                   | Period 5 | Period 48 |
| ----------------- | -------- | --------- |
| Exactly linear    | 5        | 2         |
| Not exactly linear | 22      | 25        |

Note. Entries show numbers of subjects.

**Table 5.3**
**Measures of Determination of the Ray-Approximations of Observed Bid Functions**

|                                      | Period 5 | Period 48 |
| ------------------------------------ | -------- | --------- |
| Minimum                              | .889     | .780      |
| Median                               | .996     | .997      |
| Maximum                              | 1.000    | 1.000     |
| Number of subjects with $R^2 > .99$  | 18       | 22        |

# ARE BID FUNCTIONS LINEAR?

Relatively few of the bid functions are exactly linear. Table 5.2 shows that this does not change with experience.

Even if exact linearity is the exception rather than the rule, approximate linearity is very common. For each observed bid function we determined a ray approximation by computing a linear regression through the origin which, for the sake of simplicity, was based on integer values only in the range [0,100]. The extent to which a bid function is approximately linear can be judged by the measure of determination $R^2$ connected to this ray approximation. Table 5.3 gives an impression of the distribution of the measures of determination in periods 5 and 48.

Within the range of the measures of determination shown in Table 5.3 considerable deviations from the visual impression of linearity are possible.

Table 5.4
Slopes of the Ray-Approximations of Observed Bid Functions

|                                    | Period 5 | Period 48 |
|------------------------------------|----------|-----------|
| Minimum                            | .520     | .463      |
| Median                             | .785     | .791      |
| Maximum                            | .949     | .980      |
| Average distance from the median   | .089     | .073      |

Thus, the ray approximation of the bid function of Fig. 5.1 has a measure of determination of $R^2 = .936$. Only bid functions whose ray approximations have very high measures of determination can really be considered as approximately linear. In Table 5.3 we have drawn an arbitrary border line at $R^2 = .99$. Already in period 5 the measure of determination is higher for most subjects. In this sense, we can say that approximately linear bid functions are very common.

## SLOPES OF THE RAY APPROXIMATIONS

Table 5.4 gives an impression of the distributions of the slopes of the ray-approximations in periods 5 and 48.

Table 5.4 conveys the impression that the distribution of the ray approximation slopes does not change much from period 5 to period 48. The medians show that most of the slopes are higher than 2/3 , the slope of the risk-neutral equilibrium bid function. An interpretation of this fact in terms of risk aversion would require that some subjects, the more risk-averse ones, have high slopes both in periods 5 and 48, whereas others, the less risk-averse ones, have low slopes in both periods. However, this is not the case. The Spearman rank correlation between the subjects' slopes in periods 5 and 48 is only + .197. Of course, this very low rank correlation is not significant.

It is interesting to see that the slopes of the ray approximations of a subject's bid functions exhibit considerable variation over time. The average of the absolute difference between the slopes of period 5 and period 48 taken over all 27 subjects is .128. This number is much higher than the average distances from the median shown in Table 5.4. The fact that from period 5 to period 48 the slopes travel farther than the distance to the median clearly indicates that an interpretation in terms of degrees of risk aversiveness is not adequate.

The slopes of the ray approximations do not show a clear tendency to decrease or increase over time. For 12 subjects the slope at period 48 is smaller

Participant 24
Bid-Function in Period 12

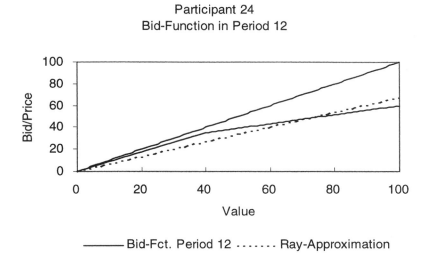

——— Bid-Fct. Period 12 ······· Ray-Approximation

Fig. 5.2. Example of a flat top (Subject 24 period 12).

than at period 5, for 13 subjects the slope at period 48 is greater than at period 5, and for 2 subjects the slope is the same in both periods.

## FLAT AND STEEP TOPS

Game equilibrium models of the first price sealed bid private value auction involving risk aversion predict bid functions with a *flat top* in the sense that for high values the slope is smaller than for low values (Cox, Roberson, & Smith, 1982). In the opposite case of higher slopes for high values we speak of a *steep top*. In order to examine whether flat or steep tops prevail in our data we have defined a measure called *top deviation*. The top deviation is the bid at 100 minus 100 times the slope of the ray approximation. As Figs. 5.2 and 5.3 illustrate, a negative top deviation corresponds to a flat top and a positive one to a steep top.

In period 48 we observe 15 subjects with positive top deviations, 10 with negative top deviations, and 2 have zero top deviations. (These are the two subjects with exactly linear bid functions in period 48.) The data do not show a clear tendency toward flat or steep tops in the bid functions of experienced individuals. This negative result also speaks against an interpretation of the distribution of slopes in terms of risk aversion.

Participant 7
Bid-Function in Period 37

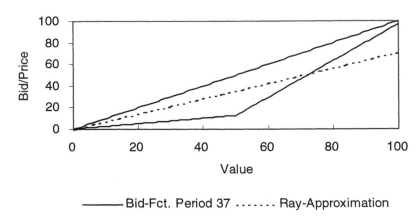

———— Bid-Fct. Period 37 ······· Ray-Approximation

Fig. 5.3. Example of a steep top (Subject 7, period 37).

# LEARNING DIRECTION THEORY

This section looks at the data in the light of an approach called learning direction theory. The name indicates that only the direction of learning is explained. The theory is qualitative rather than quantitative. It predicts the direction of change in response to experience but does not specify the amount of change.

As an illustration of the basic idea underlying the approach consider the example of a marksman who tries to shoot an arrow at the trunk of a tree. If he misses the trunk to the right, he will shift the position of the bow to the left and if he misses the trunk to the left, he will shift the position of the bow to the right. The marksman looks at his experience from the last trial and adjusts his behavior according to a simple qualitative picture of the causal relationship between the position of the bow and the path of the arrow.

Learning direction theory generalizes the kind of behavioral adjustment illustrated by the marksman example to repetitive decision tasks of the following kind: A parameter $p_t$ has to be fixed in a sequence of periods $t = 1, 2, \ldots, T$. After each period the decision maker obtains feedback information that permits qualitative conclusions on whether a parameter choice $p < p_{t-1}$ or $p > p_{t-1}$ might have been better in the last period. Of course, such conclusions require some qualitative causal picture of the relationship between the parameter and the degree of success achieved. Learning direction theory predicts $p_t \leq p_{t-1}$, if the feedback information indicates, that $p_{t-1}$ might have been too high and $p_t \geq p_{t-1}$, if there is reason to suppose, that $p_{t-1}$ might have been too low.

The theory does not exclude the case that the decision maker does not respond to his or her experience. However, if one responds, one is expected to respond in the right direction. The behavior predicted by learning direction theory is boundedly rational because it makes rational use of the qualitative conclusions drawn from the feedback information. Of course, this is very different from the full rationality usually assumed in economic theory. Whereas full rationality is ex ante in the sense that it looks to the future, the bounded rationality of learning direction theory is ex post in the sense that it looks at the past. The reasoning based on the feedback information does not really concern the question "What will be the best decision in this period?" but rather "What would have been a better decision in the past period?" Moreover, the reasoning is qualitative rather than quantitative. Qualitative conclusions are drawn on the basis of qualitative features of the feedback information. Accordingly we may say that learning direction theory involves qualitative ex post rationality.

Admittedly, learning direction theory does not provide a general, fully specified model of behavior. In every specific case one has to fill in suitable assumptions about the qualitative causal relationships guiding the interpretation of feedback information. Moreover, in applications to experimental data it will rarely be the case that the influences on behavior embodied in learning direction theory are the only ones that are present in the situation. Therefore, one cannot expect more than conformance to the weak prediction that disregarding cases of unchanged parameters more parameter changes will be in the right direction than in the wrong one.

In research on the end effect in 10 period prisoners dilemma (PD) supergames (Selten & Stoecker, 1986), the learning direction theory approach was applied to the period in which subjects intended to switch from cooperation to noncooperation toward the end of the supergame. It was postulated that this intended deviation period would shift in the direction toward the beginning after an experience in which the opponent deviated to noncooperation earlier or at the same time as the subject, and in the direction toward the end if the subject deviated first. In the first case, the subjects would have earned more by an earlier deviation and in the second case more might have been earned by a later deviation. In the relevant part of the experiment, after both cooperation and end effect had been learned, only 7 of 34 subjects ever changed their intended deviation periods in the wrong direction, each of them only once. Learning direction theory was strongly supported by the data.

In a study of Mitzkewitz and Nagel (1993), the learning direction approach was successfully applied to demands and offers in ultimatum games with incomplete information. Another application can be found in a guessing game study by Nagel (1993), in which each of 15 subjects had to name a number repeatedly with the aim of coming as near as possible to 2/3 (or 1/2) of the average of all numbers named. Further evidence in favor of learning direction theory has been found in the evaluation of alternate move bargaining experiments with incomplete information by Kuon (1994) where the approach was applied to characteristics of bargaining behavior like first demand and concession rate.

## APPLICATION OF LEARNING DIRECTION THEORY TO BID FUNCTION CHOICE

It was the intention of our study to generalize learning direction theory beyond decision tasks involving a single parameter to situations in which a whole function has to be fixed by the subjects. Admittedly we succeeded to do this only to a limited extent. It is difficult to say something about the way in which the bid function as a whole will be changed in response to last period's experience but learning direction theory suggests a hypothesis about changes at last period's value.

Let $v$, $b$, $p$ be last period's value, bid, and price respectively. We distinguish the following three "experience conditions".

| | |
|---|---|
| Successful bid: | $p = b$ |
| Lost opportunity: | $b < p < v$ |
| Outpriced value: | $v \leq p$ |

If we say that a change tends to be a decrease (increase) in an experience condition we mean that in this condition a decrease (increase) is more frequent than an increase (decrease). We now state the hypothesis suggested by learning direction theory.

**Bid Change Hypothesis.** A change of the bid for last period's value tends to be a *decrease* in the *successful bid* condition and an *increase* in the *lost opportunity* condition. No systematic tendency is expected in the outpriced value condition.

**Interpretation.** In the successful bid condition the subject could have obtained the object at a lower price. Of course, it is not clear how high the second bid was but a higher profit could have been made by some lower bid. Therefore, in the successful bid condition the feedback information suggests that a lower bid might have been better. Accordingly, the bid change hypothesis predicts a tendency toward a decrease of the bid.

In the lost opportunity condition the subject could have obtained the object by a bid slightly higher than last period's price. This means that the feedback information suggests that a higher price might have been better. Accordingly, the bid change hypothesis predicts a tendency toward an increase of the bid in the

**Table 5.5**
**Number of Bid Change Directions in the Three Experience Conditions in Periods 6 to 50**

|                    | Decrease | Increase | Unchanged | Row sums |
|--------------------|----------|----------|-----------|----------|
| Successful bid     | 49       | 8        | 348       | 405      |
|                    | .12      | .02      | .86       | .33      |
| Lost opportunity   | 9        | 47       | 94        | 150      |
|                    | .06      | .31      | .63       | .12      |
| Outpriced value    | 53       | 62       | 545       | 660      |
|                    | .08      | .09      | .83       | .55      |
| Column sums        | 111      | 117      | 987       | 1215     |
|                    | .09      | .10      | .81       | 1.00     |

*Note.* In each field absolute frequencies are shown above and relative frequencies are shown below. In the first three columns relative frequencies relate to the row sums in the last column relative frequencies relate to the column sum.

lost opportunity condition.

In the outpriced value condition the subject did not have any opportunity to make a positive profit by another bid in the last period. Therefore, the feedback information does not permit any conclusions on what might have been better. Accordingly, we do not expect any tendency towards a decrease or an increase of the bid in the outpriced value condition.

**Experimental Results.** Table 5.5 gives an overview over the bid changes in the three experience conditions.

Obviously, the numbers are in agreement with the bid change hypothesis. In the successful bid condition we observe 12% decreases and 2% increases. In the lost opportunity condition we find 31% increases and 6% decreases. In the outpriced value condition the table shows 8% decreases and 9% increases. Whereas in the successful bid condition and in the lost opportunity condition the numbers of changes in the right direction are five to six times as great as those in the wrong direction there is not much difference in the outpriced value condition.

A change of last period's bid occurs in 14% of all cases in the successful bid conditions and in 37% of all cases in the lost opportunity condition. We may say that the subjects are more inclined to react to the lost opportunity condition than to the successful bid condition. This is understandable because the feedback information is much clearer in the lost opportunity condition, where a subject can easily see the profit that could have been gained and where it is also obvious which bid should have been made. Of course, clarity arises only by hindsight, but this lies in the nature of ex post rationality.

The observations counted in Table 5.5 are not independent of each other. A meaningful test of the bid change hypothesis must look at aggregated data from each of the nine three-person subject groups that constitute our independent observations. In the successful bid condition there are more changes in the right direction than in the wrong direction in every group. (Cases of no change and periods 1 to 5 are not considered in this comparison and the following one.) In the lost opportunity condition there are more changes in the right direction than in the wrong one in eight of nine groups. In one group both numbers are equal. In both cases the null hypothesis that the probability for a higher number of changes is the same in both directions can be rejected by a binomial test in favor of the alternative predicted by the bid change hypothesis on a significance level of 2% (one-tailed). It is also interesting to notice, that in the lost opportunity condition no subject made more changes in the wrong direction than in the right direction. In the successful bid condition only 1 of 27 subjects had more changes in the wrong direction than in the right direction. (This subject had only one change in this condition.)

The data confirm the bid change hypothesis but this does not mean that learning direction theory captures all influences on observed behavior. The bid for last period's value was changed only in 228 (60%) of the 383 new bid functions in periods 6 to 50. Obviously learning direction theory cannot explain the changes in the remaining 40% of the cases.

# TYPICITY AND CONFORMITY

This section examines the question whether conformity to learning direction theory is a feature of typical subject behavior. The data confirm the predictions of learning direction theory but it is at least a theoretical possibility that this is mainly due to the behavior of a minority of subjects that is not really typical.

A measure of typicity has been introduced in research on the evaluation of strategy programs for a finitely repeated asymmetric Cournot duopoly (Selten, Mitzkewitz, & Uhlich, 1989). The strategies were described by a number of characteristics that were either present or absent in each case. The information about the characteristics of strategies can be summarized by an incidence matrix with rows for characteristics and columns for subjects and entries of one in the case that the strategy of the subject has the characteristic and zero otherwise. For the sake of brevity we speak of characteristics of a subject instead of

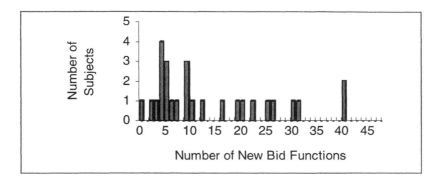

Fig. 5.4. Distribution of the numbers of new bid functions from period 6 on for the 27 subjects.

characteristics of a subject's strategy. On the basis of the incidence matrix numbers between zero and one called *typicities* were assigned both to characteristics and to subjects according to the following principles:

1. The typicity of a subject is the sum of the typicities of its characteristics.
2. The typicity of a characteristic is proportional to the sum of the typicities of the subjects with this characteristic.
3. The sum of the typicities of the characteristics is 1.
4. The typicities of subjects and characteristics form eigenvectors of AA' and A'A respectively, where A is the incidence matrix and A' its transpose. The eigenvectors are connected to the greatest eigenvalue that is the same one in both cases.

It follows by 1, 2, and 3 that the typicities of subjects and characteristics form right eigenvectors of AA' and A'A respectively. In addition to this it is required that these are eigenvectors connected to the common greatest eigenvalue. This eigenvalue is a positive real number if each of the characteristics is shared by some majority of the subjects (Kuon, 1993).

The method of computing typicities just described cannot be directly applied if important features of the subjects are naturally expressed by variables measured on an interval scale or a ratio scale. For this case Kuon (1993) developed a method that transforms the measurements to characteristics. The method can best be explained with the help of an illustrative example. One of the variables used for the exploration of what is typical in our case is the number of a subject's new bid functions from period 6 onward. Figure 5.4 shows the distribution of this variable.

One first determines a *typical interval* defined as the majority interval with the greatest occupation surplus. A *majority interval* is an interval that contains more than half of all subjects' values. The *occupation surplus* is the difference of the relative occupation (number of subjects with values in the interval divided by the total number of subjects) minus the relative length of the interval (length of the interval divided by length of the range). In our case [2,10] is the typical interval. Its occupation surplus is computed as follows:

| | |
|---|---|
| occupation: | 15 |
| relative occupation: | $15/27 = .556$ |
| relative length: | $9/44 = .204$ |
| occupation surplus: | .352 |

In our example the variable can assume only integer values. In such cases the length of an interval is the number of integer points in the interval. In the case of a continuous variable length is defined in the usual Euclidean way. It may happen that the maximal occupation surplus does not uniquely determine one of the majority intervals as the typical one. For this case Kuon defines the typical interval as the union of all majority intervals with maximal occupation surplus. This problem does not arise in the evaluation of our data.

The typicity analysis for the 27 subjects of our experiments is based on nine characteristics derived from the following variables:

1. Number of new bid functions from period 6 onward.
2. Fraction of nonmonotonic new bid functions from period 6 onward.
3. Period of last new bid function.
4. Mean slope of ray approximation (all periods).
5. Mean measures of determination (all periods).
6. Variance of slopes (all periods).
7. Variance of measures of determination (all periods).
8. Mean top deviation (all periods).
9. Number of non-negative top deviations (all periods).

Of course, the selection of the variables used for the typicity analysis is to some degree arbitrary. We have tried to cover the most important features of observed bid functions and their change over time.

It is our intention to examine whether subjects tend to conform the more closely to the bid change hypothesis the more typical they are. For this purpose

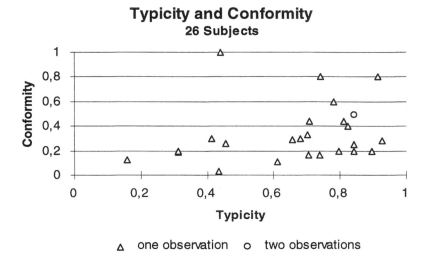

Fig. 5.5. Typicity and conformity.

we define a *conformity index* as the fraction of bid changes at last period's value in the right direction in the successful bid and lost opportunity conditions among all bid function changes from period 6 onward. Here, *right direction* means an increase in the lost opportunity condition and a decrease in the successful bid condition. The number of all bid function changes contains also those cases where the bid function was changed but not at last period's value. The conformity index shows which fraction of all bid function changes from period 6 onward is explainable by the bid change hypothesis. The higher the index is the more the subject conforms to the bid change hypothesis.

For one of the subjects a conformity index is not defined because this subject never changed the bid function. The Spearman rank correlation coefficient between typicity and conformity index for the remaining 26 subjects is .355. This is significant at the 5% level (one-tailed). The result indicates that the more typical a subject is the more it tends to conform to the bid change hypothesis.

Figure 5.5 provides a visual impression of the connection between typicity and conformity.

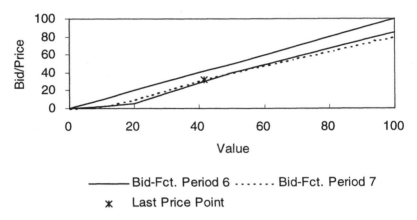

Fig. 5.6. Bid functions of Participant 3 for periods 6 and 7.

## BID FUNCTIONS OF THE MOST TYPICAL SUBJECT IN PERIODS 6 TO 11

This section illustrates behavior by the example of the most typical subject's bid functions in periods 6 to 11. This subject, participant 3, changed the bid function in each of the periods 7 to 11. Figures 5.6 to 5.10 show the old and the new bid function for each of the five cases. The figures also show the last price point, which indicates the subject's value and the price observed in the last period.

In Fig. 5.6, the last price point is above last period's bid function and below the line at which price equals value. This means that Participant 3 experienced the lost opportunity condition in period 7. The change of the bid function is in agreement with the bid change hypothesis. At last period's value the new bid function is above the old one. It is interesting to see that the increase of the bid function in the lower part was accompanied by a decrease in the upper part. Maybe, the subject wanted to behave as indicated by the bid change hypothesis without modifying the overall aggressiveness of the bid function.

As Fig. 5.7 shows, Participant 3 was in the outpriced value condition in period 8. Nevertheless, the participant changed the bid function. The change seems to be motivated by the desire to achieve a gestalt improvement. The new bid function is smoother than the old one. The kink at the value 10 is eliminated;

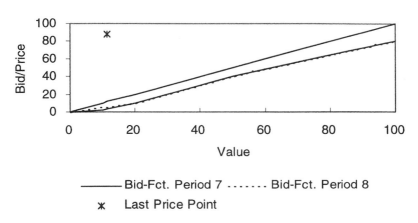

Fig. 5.7. Bid functions of Participant 3 for periods 7 and 8.

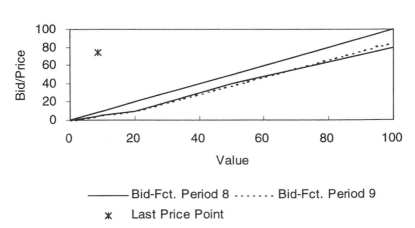

Fig. 5.8. Bid functions of Participant 3 for periods 8 and 9.

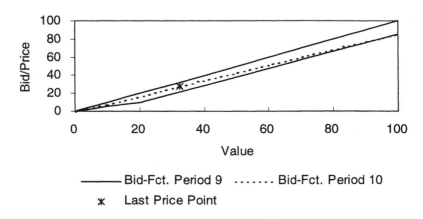

Fig. 5.9. Bid functions of Participant 3 for periods 9 and 10.

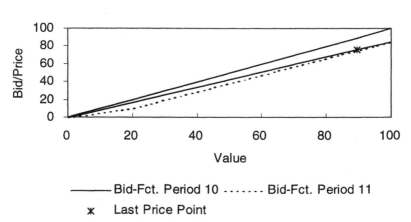

Fig. 5.10. Bid functions of Participant 3 for periods 10 and 11.

the new kink at value 20 is less sharp. We did not yet analyze bid function changes in the outpriced value conditions systematically but we have the impression that gestalt improvement is an important motive.

Figure 5.8 shows that in period 8, too, Participant 3 experienced the outpriced value condition. Again, the bid function change is a gestalt improvement. The kink at value 50 is eliminated by specifying a straight line for the interval [20,100].

In period 9, Participant 3 experienced the lost opportunity condition (see Fig. 5.9). As predicted by the bid change hypothesis, the new bid function is above the old one at last period's value. The new bid function is a straight line. We may say that a gestalt improvement is combined with the response to last period's experience.

In period 10, Participant 3 received the object (see Fig. 5.10), and lowered the bid at last period's value as predicted by the bid change hypothesis. Interestingly, the new bid function for period 11 is the bid function of period 9.

Admittedly, the behavior of the most typical subject is not representative of the whole sample because typicity is positively correlated to conformity to the bid change hypothesis. The behavior of less typical subjects is often much less easy to understand, particularly in cases of nonmonotonic bid functions.

# ARE PAYOFF INCENTIVES SUFFICIENTLY STRONG?

Harrison (1989) criticized first price sealed bid auction experiments with independent private values. He maintains that the incentives for optimization are typically very weak such that even sizeable deviations entail only very small losses of fractions of a penny. He argues that a subject will not find it profitable to go to the trouble to determine an optimal bid function under these circumstances. Harrison does not explain how the subject can find out that losses caused by the failure to optimize are very small without first having determined what is optimal. Presumably, a subject would have to compute the equilibrium bid function and the consequences of various deviations from it under the condition that it is used by the other players in order to find out whether it is worthwhile to spend the effort involved in this computation. However, a subject who has already computed what is optimal can behave accordingly even if the cost of deviation is small.

Quite apart from this inherent inconsistency of Harrison's critique we argue that at least in our case the incentive for optimization is not small. Suppose, a subject computes the risk-neutral equilibrium bid function at the beginning of the game before the first decision is made. The subject will then be able to use this function for all 50 periods of the game. The right measure of the incentives is not the gain in a single period but the gain over all 50 periods.

**Table 5.6**
**Losses by Deviations from the Equilibrium Ray Bid Function to the Average Ray Approximation of Observed Bid Functions**

|  | **Ray Bid Function Slopes of Opponents** | | |
|---|---|---|---|
|  | **_a,a_** | **_a,r_** | **_r,r_** |
| Own slope *a* | 125.00 | 107.14 | 96.84 |
| Own slope *r* | 105.44 | 92.45 | 83.33 |
| Loss in DM | 19.56 | 14.69 | 13.51 |
| Loss in $ (1 DM = $.6) | 11.73 | 8.81 | 8.11 |

*Note.* Entries in the first two columns are payoffs in DM obtained in fifty periods.

The risk-neutral equilibrium bid function is a straight line through the origin with the slope

$$a = \frac{2}{3} = .667. \tag{1}$$

Consider a risk-neutral player who wants to behave optimally. This cannot be done without forming expectations about the behavior of the others. If he or she expects that all players are risk-neutral and fully rational, the player will come to the conclusion to use the risk-neutral equilibrium strategy. Of course, the player also may form different expectations. We consider only the case that linear bid functions through the origin are used. This is not unreasonable because bid functions very often are nearly linear. We refer to linear bid functions through the origin as *ray bid functions*. The average slope of the ray approximations observed in the experiments are roughly equal to

$$r = \frac{7}{9} = .778. \tag{2}$$

In order to examine the consequences of deviations from optimal behavior it is reasonable to look at the advantage of using the ray bid function with the equilibrium slope *a* compared with using the ray bid function with the average slope *r* under the assumption that the opponents, too, use ray bid functions with slopes *a* or *r*. Table 5.6 shows payoffs in DM for the six possibilities that arise in this way. The loss is highest in the case of equilibrium strategies used by the opponents. From the point of view of rational theory this is the most relevant case. The loss is smaller but still considerable if one or two opponents use the ray bid function with average slope.

Interestingly, the ray bid function with slope $a$ is not only the equilibrium strategy but also the optimal bid function for a wide range of behaviors on the other side provided that the opponents use ray bid functions. The ray bid function with slope $a = 2/3$ is optimal if the slopes $s$ and $t$ of the opponents' ray bid functions are not smaller than 2/3. This can be seen as follows:

Let $v$, $u$, and $w$ be the values of the object for Players 1, 2, and 3, respectively, and assume that players 2 and 3 use the following bid functions:

$$b_2 = su \qquad (3)$$
$$b_3 = tw. \qquad (4)$$

We are interested in the expected value $E(b,v)$ of Player 1's payoff if the value is $v$ and the bid is $b$. Player 1 does not obtain any payoff unless $b_2$ and $b_3$ are smaller than $b$. (Cases of equality can be neglected.) We have $b > b_2$ if and only if

$$u < \frac{b}{s} v \qquad (5)$$

holds. Because $u$ cannot be greater than 1 this has the consequence that the probability for $b_2 < b$ is as follows:

$$\text{Prob}(b_2 < b) = \min\left[\frac{b}{s}, 1\right]. \qquad (6)$$

Analogously we have

$$\text{Prob}(b_3 < b) = \min\left[\frac{b}{t}, 1\right] P. \qquad (7)$$

This yields

$$E(b, v) = (b - v)\min\left[\frac{b}{s}, 1\right]\min\left[\frac{b}{t}, 1\right]. \qquad (8)$$

It follows that

$$B = (b-v)\frac{b^2}{st} \qquad (9)$$

is an upper bound of $E(b,v)$:

$$E(b,v) \le B. \qquad (10)$$

It can be seen easily that the maximum of B with respect to $b$ is obtained at

$$b = \frac{2}{3}v. \qquad (11)$$

The maximum of $E(b,v)$ cannot be greater than the maximum of its upper bound B. Therefore, if $E(b,v)$ and B coincide at $b = 2v/3$, then $E(b,v)$ assumes its maximum at this value, too. If $s$ and $t$ are both not smaller than 2/3 then $b/s$ and $b/t$ with $b = 2v/3$ are not greater than 1. This has the consequence that for $t \ge$ 2/3 and $s \ge$ 2/3 the bid function $b = 2v/3$ is optimal for Player 1. We can conclude that the ray bid function with the slope $a = 2/3$ is optimal for a risk-neutral player, as long as the opponents use ray bid functions with slopes at least as high.

## SUMMARY AND CONCLUSION

Our experiment differs from other experiments on sealed bid first price auctions with independent private values by the direct observation of bid functions. This makes it possible to examine the shape of bid functions without any assumption of constancy over time. Surprisingly, many bid functions are nonmonotonous. Nevertheless, most bid functions have high measures of determination and can be considered to be almost linear in this sense. Therefore, it is reasonable to concentrate attention on the slopes of the ray approximations. The distribution of these slopes does not change much from period 5 to period 48 but the slopes of the individual subjects show much movement over time. This throws doubt on conclusions from earlier experiments based on the assumption that subjects have constant bid functions. In particular, the explanation of bids higher than at risk neutral equilibrium by game theoretical models involving risk aversion is not in agreement with the data. There seems to be no systematic tendency towards flat or steep tops.

The movement of bid functions in time permits a partial explanation by learning direction theory. In earlier studies this theory has been applied to situations in which a one-dimensional decision parameter has to be fixed repeatedly over a number of periods. The theory focuses on the direction of change of the decision parameter. This direction is seen as determined by qualitative ex post reasoning on the basis of the feedback information. In our case the decision task requires the determination of a whole function and not just a single one-dimensional parameter. Nevertheless, learning direction theory can be applied to the question how the bid at last period's value can be expected to change in response to last period's experience. We have distinguished three experience conditions, the successful bid condition, the lost opportunity condition, and the outpriced value condition. The bid change hypothesis derived from learning direction theory predicts that in the case of a change of the bid at last period's value this bid tends to decrease in the successful bid condition and to increase in the lost opportunity condition. No systematic tendency is expected in the outpriced value condition. As we have seen, the bid change hypothesis is confirmed by the data. It has also been shown with the help of a typicity analysis that the more typical a subject is the more it conforms to the bid change hypothesis. The behavior of the most typical subject illustrates the fact that the bid change hypothesis does not fully describe the motivation of subjects. Bid functions may be changed for other reasons, for example, in order to achieve gestalt improvements. Finally we have argued that in our case the incentives for optimization are not small.

Our results show that a behavioral approach based on learning direction theory yields a better explanation of the data than normative game-theoretic models. Admittedly, the bid change hypothesis makes only weak predictions about relative frequencies of directions of change. But these predictions are derived without any parameter estimates. Game equilibrium models involving degrees of risk aversion or distributions over such degrees in games of incomplete information and possibly other parameters, like utilities of winning, fully specify behavior as a function of these parameters, but because these parameters have to be estimated, it is doubtful whether the predictions derived from such models are really stronger than those obtained from the bid change hypothesis. Moreover, a basic hypothesis underlying these models, namely constancy of bid functions over time, is clearly rejected by the data.

Some aspects of our data still need to be explored in more detail, in particular the surprisingly high frequency of nonmonotonous bid functions. At the moment we can only speculate about the reasons for nonmonotonicity. It seems possible that some subjects have a mixed attitude toward risk that induces them to behave risk-aversive in most of the range of possible values and risk-seeking in some subintervals of high values. Of course, this does not agree with classical ideas about the way in which decision makers relate to risk but, nevertheless, such behavior may be quite frequent in practice.

# ACKNOWLEDGMENT

Support by the Deutsche Forschungsgemeinschaft through SFB 303 is gratefully acknowledged.

# REFERENCES

Cox, J. C., Roberson, B., & Smith, V. L. (1982). Theory and behavior of single object auctions. In V. L. Smith (Ed.), *Research in Experimental Economics, Vol. 2* (pp. 1 – 43). Greenwich, CT: JAI Press.
Cox, J. C., Smith, V. L., & Walker, J. M. (1983). Test of a heterogeneous bidders theory of first price auctions. *Economic Letters, 12*, 207-212.
Cox, J. C., Smith, V. L., & Walker, J. M. (1985a). Expected revenue in discriminative and uniform price sealed-bid auctions. In V. L. Smith (Ed.), *Research in Experimental Economics* (Vol. 3, pp. 183-232). Greenwich, CT: JAI Press.
Cox, J. C., Smith, V. L., & Walker, J. M. (1985b). Experimental development of sealed-bid auction theory; calibrating controls for risk aversion. *American Economic Review, 75*, 160-165.
Cox, J. C., Smith, V. L., & Walker, J. M. (1988). Theory and individual behavior of first-price auctions. *Journal of Risk and Uncertainty, 1*, 61-99.
Harrison, G. W. (1989). Theory and misbehavior of first-price auctions. *American Economic Review, 79*, 749-762.
Kagel, J. H., Harstad, R. M., & Levin, D. (1987). Information impact and allocation rules in auctions with affiliated private values: A laboratory study. *Econometrica, 55*, 1275-1304.
Kagel, J. H., & Levin, D. (1985). Individual bidder behavior in first-price private value auctions. *Economic Letters, 19*, 125-128.
Kuon, B. (1993). Measuring the typicalness of behavior. *Mathematical Social Sciences, 26*, 35-49.
Kuon, B. (1994). Two-person bargaining experiments with incomplete information. *Springer lecture notes in economics and mathematical systems* (No. 412). Berlin, Heidelberg, New York.
Mitzkewitz, M., & Nagel, R. (1993). Experimental results on ultimatum games with incomplete information. *International Journal of Game Theory, 22*, 171-198
Nagel, R. (1993). Experimental results on interactive competitive guessing. *Discussion Paper No. B-236,* University of Bonn, Germany.
Selten, R., & Stoecker, R. (1986). End behavior in sequences of finite prisoner's dilemma supergames: A learning theory approach. *Journal of Economic Behavior, 47-70.*
Selten, R., Mitzkewitz, M. & Uhlich, G. R. (1997). Duopoly strategies programmed by experienced players. *Econometrica, 65*, 517-555.
Walker, J. M., Smith, V. L., & Cox, J. C. (1987). Bidding behavior in first price sealed bid auctions. *Economic Letters, 23*, 239-244.

# Part III

# Market and Coordination Games

# 6     A Survey on Experimental Beauty Contest Games: Bounded Rationality and Learning

**Rosemarie Nagel**
*Universitat Pompeu Fabra, Barcelona*

*Or, to change the metaphor slightly, professional investment may be likened to those newspaper competitions in which the competitors have to pick out the six prettiest faces from a hundred photographs, the prize being awarded to the competitor whose choice most nearly corresponds to the average preferences of the competitors as a whole; so that each competitor has to pick not those faces which he himself finds prettiest, but those which he thinks likeliest to catch the fancy of the other competitors, all of whom are looking at the problem from the same point of view. It is not a case of choosing those which, to the best of one's judgment, are really the prettiest, nor even those which average opinion genuinely thinks the prettiest. We have reached the third degree where we devote our intelligences to anticipating what average opinion expects the average opinion to be. And there are some, I believe, who practise the fourth, fifth and higher degrees.*

Keynes (1936, p. 156)

Many models of economic behavior are based on the assumption that agents select strategies that maximize utility believing that all others do the same (are equally rational), and that all agents believe that all others believe that all agents are rational, and so on. This chapter reviews experimental research on a simple guessing game called the beauty contest game (BCG), that facilitates an evaluation of this kind of depth of reasoning of agents. Models of bounded rationality are presented that explain deviations from theoretic predictions in that game. Furthermore, learning models that attempt to describe the behavior in repeated guessing games are discussed.

The basic beauty contest game is as follows. A certain number of players choose simultaneously a number from an interval, say, 0 to 100. The winner is the person whose number is closest to $p$ times the mean of all chosen numbers, where $p$ is a predetermined and known number less than one. The winner gains a fixed prize. If there is a tie, the prize is split among those who tie. The game is repeated several times within the same group.

The game was first introduced by Moulin (1986) and experimental data on numerous variations have been analyzed by Bosch and Nagel (1997a, 1997b), Camerer (1997), Camerer and Ho (1998, chap. 3, this volume), Duffy and Nagel (1997), Ho, Camerer and Weigelt (in press), Nagel (1994, 1995), Selten and Nagel (1998), Stahl (1996, in press), and Thaler (1997). Besides reviewing this research, I add one further variation of the game in which the payoff structure to the winner is altered and include the resulting data set in the analysis.

The game is *dominance solvable*, that is, the process of iterated elimination of weakly dominated strategies leads to one solution. This solution corresponds to the game's unique equilibrium in which everybody chooses 0. Thus, a rational player does not simply choose a random number or a favorite number, nor does a rational player choose a number above $100p$ because it is dominated by $100p$. Moreover, if a player believes that the others are rational as well, the player will not pick a number above $100p^2$, and if he or she believes that the others are rational and that they also believe that all are rational, then he or she will not pick a number above $100p^3$ and so on, until all numbers but zero are excluded. The concept of iterated dominance is an important concept in game theory; the beauty contest game is an ideal tool to study how many iterated levels subjects actually apply.

Because the race of iterated reasoning is similar to the one mentioned by Keynes (1936) in the context of the beauty contest thought experiment, the class of $p$-mean games and its variations have been called "$p$-beauty contest games" (Ho et al., in press) or "beauty contest game" (Duffy & Nagel, 1997).[1] By using the metaphor Keynes (1936) wanted to express that a clever investor has to "anticipate the basis of conventional valuation a few months hence, rather than...over a long term of years" (p.155) and thus decides to sell or buy stocks just a short time before the average does. The main task is to guess how far the average is reasoning. Of course, if everybody reasons this way, then the optimal time of selling or buying unravels. This means that people will sell or buy earlier and earlier if they believe that other market participants will also do so. The experience of unraveling in timing of transactions in many real-world markets, such as entry-level medical labor markets, clinical psychology internships, or postseason college football bowls, has been documented by Roth and Xing (1994). In these markets it is important to act earlier in time than the competition, but not too much earlier. A choice in our beauty contest game could represent the time choice of the decision maker (DM) in any of these markets.

There is theoretical research that studies other games in order to explore the idea of finite depth of reasoning (see, e.g., Amershi & Sunder, 1987; Aumann,

1992; Binmore, 1987; Kreps & Wilson, 1982; Selten, 1991; Stahl, 1993). Many experimental studies have tried to do this by concentrating on the degree of iterated dominance. For example, McKelvey and Palfrey (1992) and Nagel and Tang (1997) studied behavior in the centipede games, Beard and Beil (1994) and Schotter, Weigelt, and Wilson (1994) studied extensive form games, van Huyck, Wildenthal, and Battalio (1996) studied a five strategy prisoners' dilemma game (PDG), Camerer, Blecherman, and Goldstein (1995) studied an electronic (e-mail) game, Stahl and Wilson (1994) studied 3 x 3 games, and Rapoport and Amaldoss (1996) studied normal form games with mixed equilibria. The general finding of these experiments is that few subjects choose dominated strategies or play equilibrium strategies and a great majority of them reveal no more than three levels of iterated dominance.

Most of these games are mixed-motive games. Thus, concerns other than pure self-interest might be reasons for not using high levels of rationality; these other components could be, for example, altruistic behavior, reciprocity, or equity (for the importance of these concepts, see Bolton, chap. 9, this volume). Furthermore, some of these games do not allow us to discriminate between levels of reasoning higher than two or three because equilibrium is reached after two or three iterations of elimination of dominated strategies.

Unlike the mixed-motive games just mentioned, the beauty contest games are generally constant-sum, so one expects that nonstrategic aspects like fairness will not matter for explaining violations of iterated dominance. Thus, one can concentrate on matters of strategic reasoning. An additional advantage of this game is that it is easy to change the number of iterated eliminations of dominated strategies needed to reach equilibrium without complicating the structure of the game or changing its payoff structure. In some variations of the game the number of iteration steps to reach equilibrium is infinite as in the basic game, whereas in others the number is as low as three. The experimental results show that there are very few observations of reasoning levels higher than two, independent of the number of the required iterations steps.

Another feature of the beauty contest game is that behavior is often far from equilibrium in the first period and the choices gradually converge to equilibrium over time. This has been observed in many other studies, as for example in public good experiments (see Ledyard, 1995). Learning may not be as easy as repeating a successful choice of the previous periods, but rather asks for a more complicated way of updating. Several learning models have been tested to explain actual behavior over time in the beauty contest game: Iterated best-response models, learning direction theory, a simple reinforcement model, a rule-based reinforcement model, an experienced-weighted attraction model, and various others. The basic finding of most of the studies reviewed here is that over time players rarely learn to employ higher depth of reasoning. An exception is in the cases when players have previous experience with a similar game or when a single player has almost no influence on aggregate performance.

In the new treatment I introduce, I change only the payoff structure such that the winner's payoff is not a fixed prize but instead the winner receives $x$ where $x$ is his or her chosen number. Therefore, the game becomes a mixed-motive game rather than a constant-sum, while maintaining all other properties of the beauty contest game. Here I show a phenomenon resembling a beginning of a bubble observed in asset market experiments (see Sunder, 1995).

The chapter is organized as follows: First, I describe the basic beauty contest game and its theoretic solution, then I introduce the variations on the basic game in the literature and provide motivations of the studies. Next, I describe the experimental designs and summarize the data generated from the various studies. Because the results are often at odds with the theoretical predictions, I also review the descriptive models that have been introduced to explain many features of the data, and end by offering some concluding thoughts.

## GAME-THEORETIC ANALYSIS

Moulin (1986) introduced the beauty contest game as an example for explaining iterated elimination of weakly dominated strategies and sophisticated equilibrium. The typical beauty contest game has a number of parameters, almost all of which have been varied in the different studies in this area. The number of players is $n > 1$. All players simultaneously choose real numbers from an interval, say [0, 100]; the winner is the person whose number is closest to $p$ times the mean of all chosen numbers, where $p < 1$ (e.g., p = 2/3). The winner receives a fixed prize, and in the case of multiple winners the fixed prize is either split or allocated randomly to one of the winners. The other players receive nothing. The rules are made publicly known. In equilibrium all players have to choose 0. If all choose 0 no player has an incentive to deviate to another number. There are no other equilibria. If only integers are allowed then all choosing 1 is also an equilibrium.

The game-theoretic thought process, the iterated elimination of weakly dominated strategies leading to the equilibrium is as follows: For any $n>2$,[2] and for example $p = 2/3$, a rational player can eliminate all numbers above 100 x 2/3 = 66.667, which are weakly dominated by 66.667. The reason is that 2/3 times the mean (with the highest possible mean 100) can never be greater than 66.667. Therefore 66.667 is as good as any number above that and sometimes better. We obtain a new game with the interval [0, 66.667]. Now if the player believes that the others also eliminate numbers above 66.667, the number 66.667 x 2/3 = 100 x $(2/3)^2$ = 44.444 weakly dominates the numbers above 44.444, which leaves [0, 44.444]. If the player believes that all players are rational and that all believe that all players are rational the remaining interval is [0, 29.433]. Thus, we have reached iteration step three. The process, called iterated elimination of weakly dominated strategies, continues with analogous arguments of beliefs of one

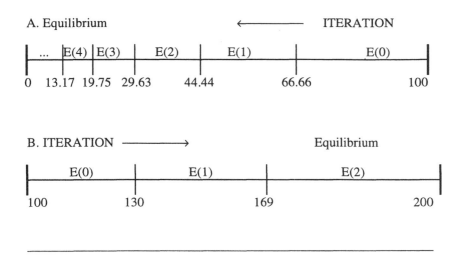

Fig. 6.1. (A) Infinite process of iterated elimination of dominated strategies for $p = 2/3$-mean game   (infinite threshold game). (B) Finite process of iterated elimination of dominated strategies for $p = 1.3$-mean game (finite threshold game). Adapted with permission from Ho et al. (in press).

another until all numbers except 0 are eliminated. The number of eliminations in this example is infinite. Figure 6.1 illustrates this process. Players who choose above 66.667 must be nonrational players, call the range $E(0)$. A player who chooses in the range $E(1)$ is rational and believes that the others are nonrational. A player who chooses in the range $E(2)$ is rational and believes that others are rational and so on.

It is quite clear that most players will not engage in a very high or even infinite levels of reasoning, at least in the first period. However, this game provides "an ideal tool" to study "where the hierarchy of iterated dominance reasoning breaks down" (Camerer, 1997). Later, I discuss models of reasoning processes that may describe actual behavior.

The calculation of the boundaries $100p^k$ neglects the influence of the considered player on the average. For a given number of players, $n$, the weakly dominating strategy is

$$\frac{p(n-1)}{n-p} \times 100 \qquad (1)$$

accounting for the influence of a single player on the mean. Iterated elimination step $k$ has the right-hand boundary

$$\left[\frac{p\,(n\,-\,1)}{n\,-\,p}\times 100\right]^{k+1} \qquad (2)$$

This analysis shows that the smaller the $n$, the smaller the calculated boundaries. For a large number of players, $100p^k$ is a good approximation. Ho et al. (in press) studied behavior in rather small groups (n = 3 or 7) and made use of the precise calculation, incorporating the influence of a single player.

Note that if $p = 1$ there are infinitely many equilibria in which all choose the same number. The original beauty contest game mentioned by Keynes (1936) can be formulated as a special case of $p = 1$. In Keynes' example the reasoning of higher steps all collapse into degree 1. If the investor has guessed the average face picked, then he or she also has to pick this face, whereas with $p < 1$, he or she wants to reason one level higher than the average. This $p = 1$ game is similar to pure coordination games (although it is still a constant-sum game) which have been studied extensively (see, e.g., van Huyck, Battalio, & Beil, 1990; Metha, Starmer, & Sudgen, 1994; and Ochs, 1995, for a survey). The game with $p = 1$ is not considered in this survey.

## VARIATIONS ON THE BASIC GAME

This section presents the variations on the basic game that have been studied experimentally. Table 6.1 summarizes the treatments analyzed and states the parameter values used. Note that in the last column the number in parenthesis gives the equilibrium prediction of each game and the number of iterative elimination steps to reach the equilibrium.

The first experimental study of the beauty contest game was conducted by Nagel (1994, 1995). The idea for this experiment was born in a game theory class by Roger Guesnerie who ran a demonstration experiment of the 2/3-mean game. I noticed (as a participant) that some numbers were quite prominent for actual behavior in the first period. My own choice was based on the simple rule 50 x 2/3 x 2/3. In the second period choices dropped, however, they were still far from equilibrium. I was interested in particular whether a simple iterated best-reply model, $50p^k$, $k = 1,2, \ldots$ and so on, could account for first-period behavior. To test this I varied the $p$-values, $p > 1$ or $p < 1$, and chose a rather large number of players within a session. For $p > 1$ and a [0, 100] interval to choose from, there are two equilibria: All choose zero or all choose 100. The latter is the perfect equilibrium (Selten, 1975). For $p > 1$, there are no dominated strategies and consequently there is no process of iterated elimination of dominated strategies leading to equilibrium. One may ask whether reasoning with $p > 1$ is therefore very different from the case when $p < 1$. Of further interest was whether players use higher reasoning steps over time and whether learning direction theory (see Selten & Buchta, chap. 5, this volume) can structure the data.

Stahl (1996, in press) reanalyzed Nagel's (1995) data set. Stahl (1996) studied which learning model out of a class of learning models could best explain behavior in the game. A variation of a reinforcement-based model tied with iterated best-reply behavior explained behavior best. Stahl (in press) tested whether more complicated types of players – Bayesian players – rather than iterated best-response types of players could help to explain the data even better. This is similar to Stahl and Wilson (1995) where these types of players were added to simple iterated best-reply players. The result is that adding more complicated types of players does not improve the description of behavior of the beauty contest data set.

Ho et al. (in press) varied the number of players to study the effect of different weights on the mean behavior by a single player. An iterated best-response model predicts that the smaller the number of players, the faster the convergence toward equilibrium. However, the data showed the opposite result. They also tested how behavior changes when the $p$-value is varied. For $p > 1$, and numbers in the interval [100, 200], the only equilibrium is that all choose 200, the upper bound of the interval. The iterated elimination process starts from the lower bound $100p$, $100p^2$ and so on (see Fig. 6.1). The number of eliminations is finite and differs for different $p > 1$. These games are called *finite threshold games* (FT) versus *infinite threshold games* (IT) for $p < 1$ and zero as the lower bound of the interval. A further question is whether players who have played one version of the game behave differently when they play another version within the same player group (for example, they play first an FT game and then an IT game). They tested an iterative best-response model against various other learning models, among them learning direction theory.

Camerer and Ho (in press) reanalyzed the Ho et al. (in press) data set. They proposed a general learning model called an experienced-weighted attraction (EWA) model, which contains a basic reinforcement model and a belief-based model as special cases (also see Camerer & Ho, chap. 3, this volume).

Duffy and Nagel (1997) studied the influence by a single player on aggregated performance. Although the number of players is kept rather large, the order statistic *mean* of the basic game is either changed to *maximum* or *median*, with $p = 1/2$. These two additional treatments assign very different weights to extreme choices. The median is hardly affected by these choices. On the other hand, if the maximum behavior determines the winning choice, a single player can completely influence the evolution over time. The question is whether the smaller a player's influence on the order statistic, the faster the convergence. In more economic terms one can ask whether in the median game players are more concerned with market fundamentals, such as the parameter $p$ or the previous

**Table 6.1a**
**Experimental Designs and Structure of the Games by Different Authors**

| Authors | Subject Pool | # of Sessions | # of Players | Winning Formular | Parameter p, c |
|---|---|---|---|---|---|
| Nagel (1995) | Univ. of Bonn undergrads | 3-4 | 15-18 (total 166) | $p$ x mean | $p = 1/2$, 2/3, 4/3 |
| Ho et al., (in press) | Southeast Asia business undergrads | 6-7 | 3 or 7 (total 277) | $p$ x mean | $p = 0.7$, 0.9; $p = 1.1$, 1.3 |
| Duffy & Nagel (1997) | Pittsburgh Univ. undergrads | 1 of 10 periods, 3 of 4 periods | 13-16 (total 175) | $p$ x median $p$ x mean $p$ x max. | $p = 1/2$ |
| Camerer & Ho (1998) | UCLA and Penn. undergrads | 4, 6-7 | 7 (total 147) | $p$ x (median + $c$) | $p = 0.7$, 0.8; $c = 18$ |
| Nagel (new) | Caltech undergrads | 4 (adtnl. w/ fixed prize) | 12-17 (total 59) | $p$ x mean | $p = 2/3$ |
| Bosch & Nagel (1997a) | Readers of *Expansion* | 1 | 3, 696 | $p$ x mean | $p = 2/3$ |
| Thaler (1997) | Readers of *Financial Times* | 1 | 1, 460 | $p$ x mean, comment | $p = 2/3$ |
| Selten & Nagel (1998) | Readers of *Spektrum* | 1 | 2, 728 | $p$ x mean | $p = 2/3$ |

**Table 6.1b**
**Experimental Designs and Structure of the Games by Different Authors**

| Authors | Range of Choices | Payoffs | # of Periods | Info. After Each Period | # of Iteration Steps |
|---------|------------------|---------|--------------|-------------------------|----------------------|
| Nagel (1995) | [0, 100] ; real numbers | Win : 20DM Lose : 0 Show : 5 | 4 | all choices (anon.); mean, $p$ x mean, winning #s | infinite for $p < 1$; n.a. for $p > 1$ |
| Ho et al., (in press) | [0, 100] if p<1; [100, 200] if p>1 | Win : $3.50 if $n = 7$, 1.50 if $n = 3$; Lose : 0 | 10 | mean, personal payoff | infinite for p < 1; 8 : p=1.1; 3 : p=1.3 |
| Duffy & Nagel (1997) | [0, 100]; real numbers | Win: $20/ period; Show : 5 | 4, 10 | all choices (anon.); $r$, $p$ x $r$, winning #s | infinite |
| Camerer & Ho (1998) | [0, 100]; real numbers | Win1:$7,28, Lose1:0; Win 2:5, Lose 2:-2 | 10 | median, personal payoff | infinite above or below equilib. |
| Nagel (new) | [0, 100]; real numbers | Win: $x$, $x$ is chosen #, (fixed 20); Show : 5 | 4 | all choices (anon.); mean, $p$ x mean, winning #s | infinite |
| Bosch & Nagel (1997a) | [1, 100]; decimals | Win: 100, 000 Pesetas | 1 | rel. freq. of choices; $p$ x mean, winning #s | 12 |
| Thaler (1997) | [0. . . 100]; integers | Win: 2 tickets to NY | 1 | abs. freq. of choices; $p$ x mean, winning #s | infinite |
| Selten & Nagel (1998) | [0, 100]; decimals | Win: 1000DM | 1 | rel. freq. of choices; $p$ x mean, winning #s | infinite |

market median, and less with speculation about actions of other players. In the maximum game, on the other hand, the main concern may be speculating about the actions of the *outliers*, those who choose high numbers. Game theoretically, there should be no difference, because the iterated elimination process is the same for all these treatments and in equilibrium all choose zero. Note that the equilibrium is weak for $p = 1/2$, because if everybody chooses zero, a unilateral deviation does not change the payoff for any player.

Camerer and Ho (1998) presented a game that has the equilibrium prediction in the interior of the interval of possible choices. The winner is the person who is closest to $p$ x (median + $c$), where $p < 1$ and $c$ is a positive constant. The equilibrium is that everybody chooses $cp / (1 - p)$. The parameter $p$ is varied. The process of iterative elimination of dominated strategies is infinite from below and above the equilibrium. This means starting at 100, $p(100 + c)$, $p^2(100 + c) + pc$, $p^3(100 + c) + p^2c + pc$, and so on leads with infinite steps to the equilibrium from above, while starting at 0, $pc$, $p^2c + pc$, $p^3c + p^2c + pc$, and so on leads with infinite elimination steps to the equilibrium from below. Furthermore, the authors vary the payoffs (high versus low payoff to the winner; zero payoff versus negative payoff to the losers) to see whether this makes a difference in behavior. Having the equilibrium in the inside of the interval of choices is interesting in that it allows study of the effects of overshooting or undershooting the equilibrium or to allow for errors on both sides on the equilibrium. Besides collecting the choices of the subjects, the authors recorded the time for responding and noticed that those who responded quickly and those who took much longer performed better than those with intermediate response times.

There is one new treatment called the ($p$-mean) variable payoff treatment. The game is a 2/3-mean game with the equilibrium at zero as in the basic game. In all treatments mentioned earlier the payoff to the winner is fixed. In the variable payoff treatment, the winner receives the $-value of his or her choice. Thus, if he or she wins and has chosen 5, the player receives $5. The equilibrium is in weakly dominated strategies. With this slight change, the equilibrium is not Pareto-optimal. That is outside the equilibrium the expected payoff is higher for all players. Here one can argue that choosing a high number (say, 100) can be interpreted as altruistic behavior. Although this player gives up any chance of winning, the player increases the actual prize of the winner if the other players anticipate an altruist and thus do not play zero. Other games similar to this game are the centipede game (see, e.g., McKelvey & Palfrey, 1992; Nagel & Tang, in press) and the finitely repeated PDG (e.g. Selten & Stoecker, 1986), with a Pareto-inferior equilibrium. The current game also resembles a Bertrand game.

Most of the experimental subjects were students. However, Thaler (1997) and Bosch and Nagel (1997a, 1997b) independently ran the 2/3-mean game with newspaper readers of *Financial Times* and *Expansion*, a business newspaper and Spanish daily, respectively. Selten and Nagel (1998) repeated the same experiment in *Spektnum der Wissenschalt*, a natural science magazine and

German monthly. Readers responded in one to three weeks either by letter, fax, or email. The results of Nagel (1995) were confirmed with the exception that up to 18% of the newspaper readers played equilibrium choices whereas none did in the lab study. Furthermore, some readers indicated in their comments that they used best-reply against an assumed probability distribution of choices whereas Nagel (1995) did not find those comments. Given that readers could communicate with others, some made inquiries or performed little experiments with their colleagues (one reader made his own experiment announcing the game in various international newsgroups on the internet) to find out about behavior of others. Some even wrote computer programs that produced the mean of a random number generated. "None of the computers . . . seemed to have a faulty chips: They all obtained 50 as the result of their simulation" (Thaler, 1997, p.4).

Camerer (1997) ran 2/3-mean games with business executives and found that they did not behave differently from students. Many colleagues have participated in a beauty contest experiment, which has been used as a demonstration experiment or as motivation of features for a subsequent talk; for example, by Camerer, Plott, Thaler, or myself, on topics like experimental market games, behavioral finance, relationship between experiments and game theory, or discussions about the beauty contest experiments. People trained in game theory typically choose numbers much lower than the general public. I do not discuss the data that have been generated by nonstudents in this survey any further. For a discussion, see Bosch, Nagel, and Satorra (1998).

The variations of the game are named according to the order statistic used; median game, mean game, maximum game. The treatment that pays the winner the dollar amount equal to the number chosen is called the variable payoff treatment.

## EXPERIMENTAL DESIGN

In all laboratory studies, the subjects were undergraduate students in various countries (see Table 6.1). They could participate only in one session. Typically, they had no experience with the game. When entering the room, subjects were seated far apart so that they could not see each other's work. Communication was strictly forbidden during the experiment. The experiments were conducted with pencil and paper. Each subject received written instructions (see the Appendix for a sample) and one response card for each round. In Nagel (1995), Duffy and Nagel (1997) and in the new design, subjects were asked for written comments.[3] The instructions were read aloud by either the experimenter or an administrator. The instructions contained the basic rules of the games with the number of players, the range of the possible choices, an explanation of how the winner is determined, the expected payoff for the winner in each period, the

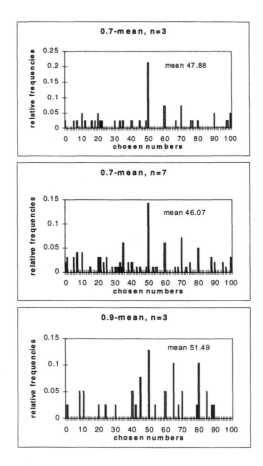

Fig. 6.2. Relative frequencies of first period choices in small groups of players. Reprinted with permission from Ho et al. (in press).

number of periods, and the information gathered after each round. Apart from Nagel (1995) and the new design, subjects were told how the order statistic is calculated. Each player knew that he or she would play within the same group of players during the entire session. Public information was written on the blackboard or announced. In Ho et al. (in press) subjects participated in two different treatments (first a treatment with $p > 1$ then with $p < 1$ or vice versa; the order was determined randomly) within the same group in order to test learning across different parameter settings. The experimental procedure of the two treatments was the same. All sessions lasted about 30 to 45 minutes. At the end

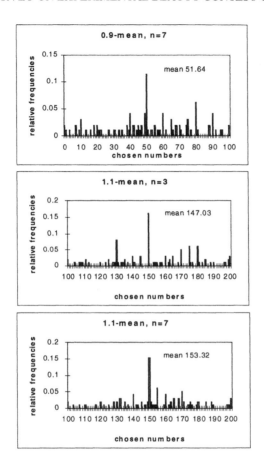

Fig. 6.3. Relative frequencies of first period choices in small groups of players. Reprinted with permission from Ho et al. (in press).

of a session subjects were paid in cash. Average earnings were around $10 in most sessions.

## DESCRIPTIVE SUMMARY OF THE DATA

This section presents a summary of the data from these studies. First period

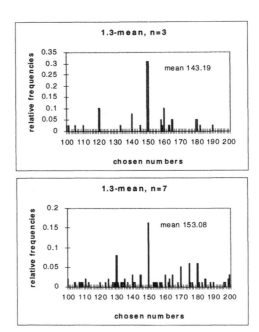

Fig. 6.4. Relative frequencies of first period choices in small groups of players. Reprinted with permission from Ho et al. (in press).

behavior is separated from the behavior in the other periods and models that have been introduced to explain many of the characteristic features of behavior discovered by the descriptive analysis are presented in the following section.

## First Period Choices

The first period choices are summarized in Figures 6.2 through 6.7. Each graph presents the relative frequency distribution of choices for each treatment separately. The equilibrium is chosen less than 2.5% of the time in all treatments, except for the 0.7(median+18) treatment, with 10% choosing the equilibrium strategy 42. Dominated strategies are chosen with frequencies between 5% and 25%. Most choices are far away from equilibrium.[4]

In the $p$-mean treatments with small player groups (Ho et al., in press, and Figs. 6.2, 6.3, and 6.4, $n = 3$ or 7), choices are widely scattered over the entire interval with a clear mode at the midpoint. The means in all these treatments are near the midpoint, which is either 50 or 150. Ho et al. (in press) found no

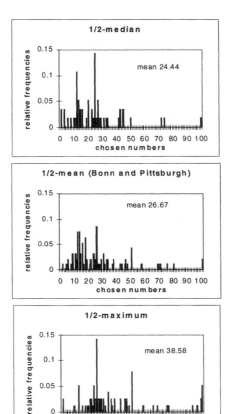

Fig. 6.5. Relative frequencies of first period choices, in large groups of players ($n$ = 13-18). Reprinted with permission from Duffy & Nagel (1997).

difference of first round behavior between experienced and inexperienced groups (subjects first played a game with $p > 1$ and then a game with $p < 1$, or vice versa). Therefore I pooled these data points into one figure.

In the remaining treatments there is much more concentration of choices in certain intervals. In the 0.7(median+18) treatment, about 85% of choices are between 40 and 50, with a mode at 48.[5] In the 0.8(median+18) treatment, 50% of the choices are between 50 and 70. The means of these two treatments are also near 50 (see Camerer & Ho, 1998, and Fig. 6.7). In the $p$-mean treatments with $n$

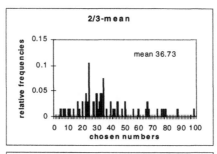

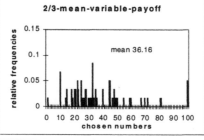

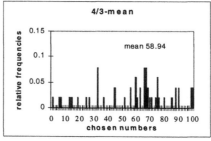

Fig. 6.6. Relative frequencies of first period choices, in large groups of players ($n$ = 13-18). Reprinted with permission from Nagel (1995).

between 13 and 18 (see Figs. 6.5 and 6.6), the peaks are at choices 15 and 25 in 1/2-mean/median games,[6] at 25 in the 1/2-maximum treatment (Duffy & Nagel, 1997), and at 25 and 35 in the 2/3-mean treatment (Nagel, 1995). In addition, there is concentration around 22 and 33 in the 2/3-mean variable payoff game. In the 4/3-mean game choices are more widely spread than in the other large player groups, however, with more than 1/3 of the choices falling between 60 and 70. The descriptive models explain these peaks and concentrations.

In all the large groups of players, the mean is further away from the midpoint

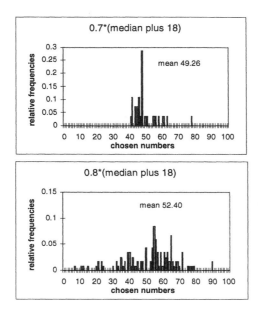

Fig. 6.7. Relative frequencies of first period choices in games with interior equilibria. Reprinted with permission from Camerer and Ho (1998).

and closer to the equilibrium than in the small groups; in the 2/3-mean game with $n = 15\text{-}18$ the mean is 36.73, whereas for $n = 7$ and $p = 0.7$ the mean is 46.07. The distributions of $p$-mean/median games with large groups can be ordered by the $p$-values; the smaller $p$, the smaller the means of the chosen numbers. Note that 1/2-mean and 1/2-median treatments have indistinguishable distributions, but the distributions of the 1/2-mean/median and 1/2-maximum treatments are significantly different. There is no difference between the 2/3-mean games with fixed payoff or variable payoff.

## Behavior Over Time

Figures 6.8, 6.9, and 6.10 show the evolution of the mean choices over time. In all treatments, there is a trend toward the (perfect) equilibrium. However, there are differences in speed of convergence between the different treatments.

Ho et al. (in press) reported that small groups ($n = 3$) converge slower than larger groups ($n = 7$). This can be confirmed by comparing convergence of 2/3-mean games ($n = 13$ to 18, Nagel, 1995) and 0.7-mean ($n = 7$). When $n = 7$, the

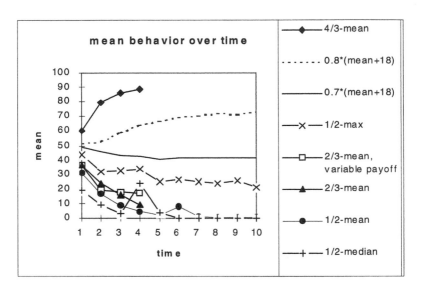

Fig. 6.8. Mean behavior over time in large groups and games with interior equilibira. Reprinted with permission from Camerer and Ho (1998), Duffy and Nagel (1997), and Nagel (1995).

mean is still above 20 in the fourth period (see Fig. 6.9, inexperienced players), whereas it is below 10 in the large group in that period (see Fig. 6.8). The downward trend in the 1/2-maximum game is as slow as in small groups (compare, e.g., 1/2-max with 0.7-mean, $n = 7$ or 3). In the 1/2-median treatment, there is some evidence that behavior converges faster than that in the 1/2-mean treatment (Duffy & Nagel, 1997). Thus, the smaller the influence of a single player on the order statistic, the faster the convergence to equilibrium.

The further $p$ is from 1, the faster the convergence (compare, for example, 2/3-mean and 1/2-mean in Fig. 6.8) and treatments with $p > 1$ converge faster than when $p < 1$; by the third period more than 50% choose the equilibrium when $p > 1$, whereas less than 5% do so when $p < 1$ (see Ho et al., in press; Nagel, 1995). One reason might be that equilibrium in games with $p > 1$ is reached within finitely many steps, whereas in games with $p < 1$ convergence takes infinite steps.

Note that although initial behavior in the 0.7(median+18) game is very close to the equilibrium of 42, convergence is much slower than in games with $p > 1$. Only in the 6th period do more than 50% choose 42. There are less than 20% of the choices that undershoot the equilibrium in any period. This is very different in the $p$(median+18) game. In the fifth period about 30% choose around the

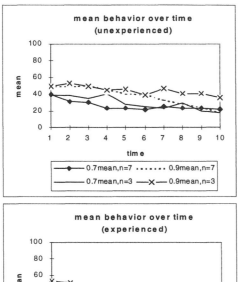

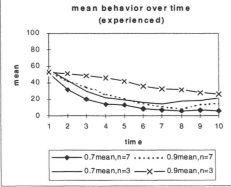

Fig. 6.9. Behavior over time in small groups and $p < 1$, separated by experienced and inexperienced players. Reprinted with permission from Ho et al. (in press).

equilibrium between 71-73 (and 10% higher); however, in the remaining periods choices higher than equilibrium increase from 25% to 60% in period 10.

A comparison of the 2/3-mean games (fixed prize and variable prize conditions) reveals a difference of choices that increases over time. Means in the variable treatment are significantly higher than in the fixed payoff treatment in the fourth period. To show the difference in individual behavior I present the transition behavior of these two treatments from period 1 to 2, 2 to 3, and 3 to 4 in Figs. 6.11 and 6.12. A cross represents the choices of a subject in period $t$ and in period $t + 1$. Although in periods 1, 2, and 3, there is no substantial difference with respect to decreases from period to period, the transition between period 3

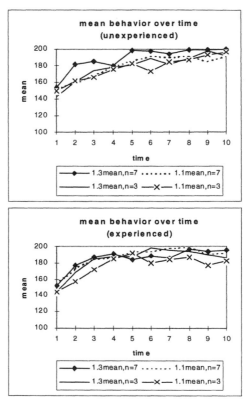

Fig. 6.10. Behavior over time in small groups and $p>1$, separated by experienced and inexperienced players. Reprinted with permission from Ho et al. (in press)

to 4 is quite different in these two treatments. Clearly, in 2/3-mean with fixed prize, players have learned to decrease their choices from period to period (almost all points are below the line in Fig. 6.12). However, in the 2/3-mean variable payoff treatment, 53% of the players increase their choices again. This resembles the beginning of a bubble (see Sunder, 1995). A comment by a subject might explain the high frequency of increases of choices: "I thought of choosing 100 to increase the winning prize, but then I hoped that somebody else would do so." She chose a higher number than the previous one but far from 100, "in order to have a high probability of winning." In the variable payoff treatment, a player who chooses a very high number, say 100, can be seen as an altruist (usually about 3% of the choices). If players believe that there are altruists in the group

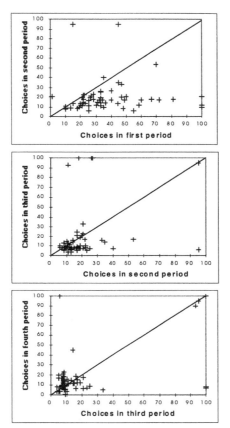

Fig. 6.11. Transition behavior in variable payoff treatment.

they will choose higher numbers and thus increase their expected payoff. At the same time, the altruist decreases his probability of winning. In the 2/3-mean treatment with fixed prize there are only about 1.5% of high choices (Nagel, 1995). Comments by the subjects indicate that they are annoyed about spoilers in the fixed payoff treatment (see also Ho et al, in press), but subjects did not complain about altruists in the variable payoff treatment.

Ho et al. (in press) tested and found that experienced players converge faster than inexperienced players (see Fig. 6.10, experienced vs. inexperienced treatments) whereas as mentioned earlier, in the first period there is no difference between experienced and inexperienced players.

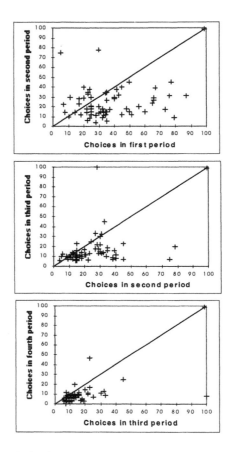

Fig. 6.12. Transition behavior in fixed payoff treatment.

The following section presents the models that were introduced to account for differences in behavior between the different treatments. In particular, it is interesting to understand why there is concentration around certain points or in certain intervals in the first period. Another important question is how subjects adjust their choices over time. This issue is addressed by the learning models studied.

# DESCRIPTIVE MODELS

In all research on the beauty contest game, special attention is devoted to the characterization of the first period choices. In general, in the first period, a player has no information about the behavior of the other players. He or she has to form expectations about choices of the others on a different basis than in subsequent periods and so he or she has to rely entirely on intuition and understanding of the game. In games where cooperation is sensible the player might ask whether he or she should cooperate, be fair, or contribute a lot without knowing whether the opponents also do so. In our game questions might be; should the player assume that others behave randomly, assume that others behave like himself or herself, are they less clever than the player, and how should he or she incorporate keywords like 2/3 times mean given in the instructions? These might be typical thoughts of a player in this game that were revealed as comments in written or nonwritten form during, or after, the experiments (Nagel, 1994, gave a sample of written comments). This kind of thinking could be called a reasoning process. Of course, even in subsequent periods a player does not have a complete picture of the thought processes of the others. The current discussion distinguishes between static reasoning models and adaptive learning models. Yet, as explained later, the two types of models are closely related. In particular, the suggested learning models often assume learning among different reasoning rules (see also Erev and Roth, chap. 4, this volume, for a discussion of the value of this approach).[7]

## Static Reasoning Models

**Levels of Iterated Dominance in the First Period**. The simplest method of organizing the data is to sort them by levels of iterated dominance. In a range from [0, 100] a choice belongs to level $k$ if it is in the interval $[100p^{k+1}, 100p^k]$ for $p < 1$, $k = 0, 1, \ldots$, and so on. For $p > 1$ and range [100, 200], a choice belongs to level $k$ if it is in $[100p^k, 100p^{k+1}]$ (see Ho et al., in press).[8] The results of Ho et al.'s (in press) analysis is that each $p$-mean game has the modal relative frequency of choices at very different levels of reasoning. For example, when $p = 0.9$, it is at level 6, whereas in the $p = 0.7$ game it is at level 1. However, why should one presume that with a change from 0.9 to 0.7, the level of reasoning would be so different? The reason is quite simple. As shown in the figures of first period choices for small groups, the modal frequency is around the midpoint of the interval. Thus, the level $k$ including 50 (or 150) should have the highest frequency. However, choosing the midpoint might not be related to any depth of reasoning, but rather to a focal point choice (Schelling, 1960). Nagel (1995) noted that testing the model $100p^k$ did not seem to organize the data set (4/3-mean, 2/3-mean, 1/2-mean) in a unifying way; this is attempted with the next model.

**Models of Iterated Best-Reply for the First Period.** In the large group – and the $p$(median + $c$) – treatments we showed that there was a concentration of choices around certain numbers. A variation of the model of iterated dominance that was proposed by Nagel (1995) and subsequently applied by Stahl (1996) and Duffy and Nagel (1997) helps to explain these patterns. In the first period a player searches for a reasonable mean (and similarly if the order statistic is the median, maximum) resulting from the chosen numbers, then gives the best reply to that mean, which is $p$ times the mean. If the player assumes that all players might do that, he or she chooses best-reply to that new number. The player might repeat this several times depending on whether he or she thinks that the others would also do so. Theoretically, the resulting numbers would be $rp^k$, where $r$ is a reference starting point and $k$ the iteration step or depth of reasoning, with discrete values 0, 1, 2, 3, . . ., and so forth. In the first period the reference point is assumed to be the midpoint of the entire interval, which can be derived as the expected mean or median of an assumed uniform distribution of choices over the interval [0, 100]. Because the reference point is not 100, the model is called an *iterated best-reply model* rather than iterated dominance model. Ho et al. (in press) tested the assumption of midpoint as the reference point for the Nagel (1995) data and concluded that 50 is a good approximation. For the maximum game, Duffy and Nagel (1997) assumed that the initial reference point was 100. From a cognitive point of view, this seems quite reasonable because the upper bound of the interval is 100 and the instructions hint to choose the number closest to 1/2 times the maximum.

In the mean game, a player using $k = 0$ (called step 0-rule) has essentially no understanding of the game (generally the player chooses 50 or a salient number, Schelling, 1960). A player using $k = 1$, gives best-reply to (uniform) random behavior of all players, believing that all others choose $k = 0$ and so on. A player believes that all other players choose one level lower than the level that the player chooses. Note that dominated strategies are excluded because a best-reply to a certain reference point that is different from the boundary of the interval precludes them.

The previous section shows that the period 1 data points concentrate in certain intervals. Is this concentration related to the numbers $50p^k$? To test this, choices around these theoretic numbers are grouped into step $k$. Nagel (1995), Stahl (1996), and Duffy and Nagel (1997) tested the model $50p^k$ and found that indeed there is concentration around these theoretical numbers and about 75% chose between levels 0 and 2 with modes at level 1 or 2. Less than 5% chose levels higher than level 3. The difference in the distribution between 1/2-maximum and 1/2-mean/median is explained by the different initial reference points and the same level of reasoning. Note also that for the 4/3-mean game and 0 as the lower bound there are no dominated choices. However, the $50(4/3)^k$ can account for the concentration of choices in the 60 to 70 interval. The iterated best-response model also accounts for the fact that the distributions can be ranked by the $p$-values. The $p$(median + 18) treatment can also be explained by this model. Level 0, 1, 2 players chose around 68, 54, and 58, respectively, when $p = 0.8$, which explains the high number of choices in the 50 to 70 interval; and around 68, 48, 46, when $p = 0.7$ which explains the concentration of choices between 40 and 50.

Note, that in the simple kind of best-reply, $50p^k$, one's own influence on the reference point is not incorporated. Ho et al. (in press), who experimented on small groups ($n = 3$ or $7$), based their model on the precise calculation of best reply assuming that all other players choose one level lower than oneself and incorporating player $i$'s influence on the average. For example a level 1 player who believes that all players but himself or herself choose 100 calculates

$$g_i^1 = \frac{p(100(n-1) + g_i^1)}{n} = 100\frac{p(n-1)}{n-p},\qquad(3)$$

or in general, level $k$ player calculates

$$g_i^k = \frac{p}{n-p}\sum g_i^{k-1}.\qquad(4)$$

$g^k$ is a chosen number classified by rule $k$ that lies in the interval $k$ with boundaries

$$\left[100\frac{p(n-1)}{n-p}\right]^{k+1} < g^k \le \left[100\frac{p(n-1)}{n-p}\right]^k.\qquad(5)$$

As in the previous model, they assume that a player believes that all other players choose one level lower than the level the player has chosen. They estimate the reference points rather than assuming them to be the midpoint of the entire interval. The estimated reference point is further away from the midpoint and the equilibrium with small groups than in large groups. The modal level is level 2 for infinite iteration games and level 1 for finite iteration games.

**Bayesian Model.** Stahl (in press) tested whether a more complicated step model can explain the data better. He introduced what he termed a noninteger step model. Stahl also added a type who plays a random strategy in every period. Higher reasoning players believe that there are types of players who use lower and different levels of reasoning. They best respond to a probability distribution over lower types; for example, 50% of the population are believed to be step-0 and 50% step-1 players and thus best-reply is a step-1.5 rule.[9] However, the assumption is still that nobody reasons further than himself or herself. This is similar to Stahl and Wilson (1995) who not only included step-0, step-1, and step-2 players but also Bayesian players. Stahl (in press) concluded that this type of reasoning does not explain the data in the beauty contest game in a better way than the discrete step model mentioned earlier. Written comments by the subjects in our lab experiments did not indicate any Bayesian thinking, that is, they did not mention best-response to a presumed probability distribution of types, whereas iterated best-response comments are rather common. However, some participants in the newspaper experiments (Bosch & Nagel, 1997a, 1997b; Selten & Nagel, 1998; and Thaler, 1997) provided comments of best-replies to subjective distributions.

## Adaptive Learning Models

The next section presents learning models that try to account for adjustment patterns over time. Behavior did not immediately jump to equilibrium, but converged rather smoothly in most treatments.

**Iterated Best-Response Models for Behavior Over Time**. Nagel (1995) and Duffy and Nagel (1997) classified the data over time according to their iterated best-response model as stated earlier. In a subsequent period, the new reference point is the mean, median, or maximum of the previous period, depending on the game. Numbers above the reference point $r$ are lumped into one category as outliers. Adjustment is based only on the previous period reference point. Step-1 and higher step players believe that everybody reasons one level lower than himself or herself. Step-0 players choose around the reference point of the previous period, step-1 around the best-reply number of the previous period. Such a step-1 player believes that the other players choose the same numbers as in the previous period. This can be called *Cournot behavior* (Cournot, 1838). Note that $r_{t-1}p^1$ is only an approximation of Cournot behavior and independent of $n$ because one's own influence on the reference points is not incorporated. Choices are classified into 6 categories: above reference point, step-0, step-1, step-2, step-3, and above rule 3.

Nagel (1995) interpreted the data set as indicating that there was no significant increase in depth of reasoning. That is, less than 50% apply steps higher than 2 over time. However, Stahl (1996) interpreted the data as strong evidence of increasing depth of reasoning. Duffy and Nagel (1997) showed that in the median game there is increasing depth of reasoning in the later periods (from round 8 onwards more than 50% choose levels 3 and higher) whereas this does not hold in the mean and maximum treatment. Table 6.2 shows the levels of reasoning for the 10-periods sessions of the 1/2-median/mean and maximum

**Table 6.2**
**Choice Classification According to Depth of Reasoning $k$ in 10-Round Sessions**

| | | | | | 1/2-Median Session | | | | | |
|---|---|---|---|---|---|---|---|---|---|---|
| Round | *1* | *2* | *3* | *4* | *5* | *6* | *7* | *8* | *9* | *10* |
| k>3 | 0 | 0 | 0 | 0.15 | 0.08 | 0 | 0.15 | 0.23 | <u>0.62</u> | <u>1.00</u> |
| k=3 | 0.08 | 0.08 | 0 | 0 | 0.08 | 0.08 | 0.31 | 0.31 | 0.23 | 0 |
| k=2 | 0.38 | 0.31 | <u>0.62</u> | <u>0.46</u> | <u>0.31</u> | <u>0.54</u> | <u>0.54</u> | <u>0.46</u> | 0.15 | 0 |
| k=1 | <u>0.54</u> | <u>0.38</u> | 0.31 | 0.15 | 0.08 | 0.15 | 0 | 0 | 0 | 0 |
| k=0 | 0 | 0.23 | 0.08 | 0 | 0.08 | 0.08 | 0 | 0 | 0 | 0 |
| k<0 | 0 | 0 | 0 | 0.23 | 0.38 | 0.15 | 0 | 0 | 0 | 0 |

| | | | | | 1/2-Mean Session | | | | | |
|---|---|---|---|---|---|---|---|---|---|---|
| Round | *1* | *2* | *3* | *4* | *5* | *6* | *7* | *8* | *9* | *10* |
| k>3 | 0 | 0 | 0 | 0 | 0.07 | 0 | 0.14 | 0.07 | 0.07 | 0 |
| k=3 | 0 | 0.14 | 0 | 0 | 0.07 | 0.14 | 0.29 | 0.14 | 0.14 | 0 |
| k=2 | 0.07 | 0.14 | 0.36 | 0.29 | 0.14 | <u>0.36</u> | <u>0.57</u> | <u>0.29</u> | <u>0.29</u> | <u>0.50</u> |
| k=1 | <u>0.71</u> | <u>0.57</u> | <u>0.43</u> | <u>0.57</u> | <u>0.71</u> | 0.29 | 0 | <u>0.29</u> | <u>0.29</u> | 0.29 |
| k=0 | 0.14 | 0 | 0.14 | 0 | 0 | 0.14 | 0 | 0.14 | 0 | 0 |
| k<0 | 0.07 | 0.14 | 0.07 | 0.14 | 0 | 0.07 | 0 | 0.07 | 0.21 | 0.21 |

| | | | | | 1/2-Maximum Session | | | | | |
|---|---|---|---|---|---|---|---|---|---|---|
| Round | *1* | *2* | *3* | *4* | *5* | *6* | *7* | *8* | *9* | *10* |
| k>3 | 0 | 0 | 0 | 0 | 0 | 0 | 0 | 0 | 0 | 0.07 |
| k=3 | 0.07 | 0.13 | 0 | 0 | 0 | 0 | 0 | 0 | 0 | 0.07 |
| k=2 | <u>0.40</u> | <u>0.53</u> | <u>0.40</u> | 0.13 | 0.07 | 0.27 | 0 | <u>0.73</u> | 0.07 | <u>0.80</u> |
| k=1 | 0.33 | 0.33 | <u>0.40</u> | <u>0.87</u> | <u>0.67</u> | <u>0.73</u> | <u>0.80</u> | 0.27 | <u>0.67</u> | 0.07 |
| k=0 | 0.20 | 0 | 0.07 | 0 | 0.20 | 0 | 0.13 | 0 | 0.07 | 0 |
| k<0 | 0 | 0 | 0.13 | 0 | 0.07 | 0 | 0.07 | 0 | 0.20 | 0 |

Note. Underlined numbers in table are modal frequencies. Reprinted with permission from Duffy & Nagel (1997).

treatments from Duffy and Nagel (1997). The higher levels of reasoning in the later rounds of the median game compared to the mean game explain why the mean game converged slower than the median game. For the maximum treatment, the maximum choice is the reference point and thus there is much slower convergence. Also, in small groups we observe slow convergence. There, however, this result is due to the behavior of a few players. Still, the vast majority chose below the reference point of the previous period; for example, in the 0.7-mean game with $n = 7$, only about 20% chose numbers higher than the mean in the previous period. In the variable payoff treatment, 45% of the players chose above the mean of the previous round in the fourth period. Thus, the mean does not further converge because almost half of the subjects do not choose lower numbers. The model $p$ times mean of previous period in that treatment does not seem to explain the behavior of many players.

Ho et al. (in press) extended their first period model. Players are assumed to take into account information of several previous periods (at most three periods). They assumed four rules were in operation. Rule 1 stated that players are assumed to choose from a normal distribution around the weighted sum of best-reply numbers of the previous periods. Rule 2 stated that players choose from a normal distribution of weighted average of best-reply to best-reply numbers of the previous periods, taking into account their own influence in the previous periods. Rules 3 and 4 are analogously constructed to rule 2. The simple best-reply formula to the choices of the opponents taking into account the own influence is

$$b(t) = \frac{p}{n-p} \sum g.(t-1), \qquad (6)$$

where $\Sigma g.(t\text{-}1)$ is the sum of the choices of the other players. This formula predicts faster convergence with smaller $n$, contrary to the behavior in the games. None of the models proposed here account for this disparity, which must be left for future work.

Ho et al. (in press) found that the information of the previous period has higher weight than that of 2 or 3 periods back. Furthermore, in games with $p < 1$ half of the players choose level 2 and the rest is evenly distributed between levels 1 and 3. In games with $p > 1$ level 1 and 2 players are equally likely. A similar results holds in the $p$(median + 18) games (see Camerer & Ho, 1998). The comparison of levels of experienced and inexperienced players explains why behavior in the latter converges faster; more players apply level 3 when they have gained experience in another $p$-game than inexperienced players.

**Learning Direction Theory.** The two best-reply models take into account the mean (median, maximum) result of a period and suppose that players might take various steps from these reference points. However, they do not deal with the question of how the number of steps are chosen given the observations of the previous periods. All data sets, except the median data set and experienced player treatments, indicate that the modal frequency of step of reasoning over time is mostly around step-2. In an attempt to explain why there is no strong evidence of increasing depth of reasoning over time, Nagel (1995) applied learning direction theory, a qualitative theory, introduced by Selten and Stoecker (1986). Duffy and Nagel (1997), Ho et al. (in press), and Stahl (1996) made further tests on that theory. The basic idea of learning direction theory is that a player considers in an ex post reasoning process whether he or she might have improved the payoff with another strategy, given the information of the previous periods results. If the player considers a change in the next period, the change should go into the direction of the supposed improving strategy. Selten and Buchta (chap. 5, this volume) use the analogy of a man shooting an arrow toward a tree. For example, if he aims too far to the right, in the next try he will aim more to the left.

The "tree" in our game is a moving target, the optimal number, that is $p$ times the mean, in the basic game. The choices of the players are categorized into three classes after each period:

1. Choices that were equal to the optimal number of the previous period (this class is not considered here because there are too few observations).
2. Choices that were lower than the optimal number of the previous period, that is, the player iterated too far.
3. Choices that were higher than the optimal number of the previous period, that is, the player did not iterate enough.

The basic question is whether players who have iterated too much behave differently than those who did not iterate enough. To answer this question, each choice in period $t$ was converted into an adjustment factor, a percentage-deviation from the previous period reference point, given by

$$a_i(t) = \frac{g_i(t)}{r(t-1)} \qquad (7)$$

where $r(t-1)$ is the previous period reference point, for example the mean of period $t-1$; the optimal adjustment factor is

$$a_{opt}(t) = p\,\frac{r(t)}{r(t-1)}, \qquad (8)$$

which is the best-reply of the previous period $t$ divided by the reference point of $t-1$. This optimal adjustment factor gives a measure how much one should have deviated optimally from one period to the next. According to learning direction theory, a player should decrease the adjustment factor in the next period if it was higher than the optimal adjustment factor in the previous period (he or she did not iterate enough) and should increase the adjustment factor in the next period if it was lower than the optimal adjustment factor (he or she iterated too much), both in the direction of the optimal adjustment factor. Each player's action can be easily classified as following or not following learning direction theory. Unchanged behavior is not considered in this analysis.

Choices of players that have been classified into categories with higher levels of reasoning than the optimal level will use lower levels and those in lower level classes will employ a higher level, but not necessarily the optimal one, of the previous period. Overshooting is also possible. Nagel (1995) and Stahl (1996) mentioned that the optimal level of reasoning was level 2 in most sessions and periods. That is why at least within the 4 or 10 periods observed, modal level remains largely within level 2. Stahl (1996) also showed that those players who employed a low level of reasoning in the first period will, on average, slowly converge to level 2 and those who have chosen higher levels than 2, go to level 2 on average.

Duffy and Nagel (1997) stated that in the median game more than 70% of the behavior can be explained by learning direction theory, similar to Nagel (1995); however, less than 50% is explained in the maximum game after the first few rounds. Here it might be that the previous period fundamental, $p$ times maximum, is not a good reference on which to rely, particularly if the maximum has fluctuated before. Thus, other considerations might explain behavior better than this theory. In the median game, on the other hand, the winning numbers are monotonically decreasing over time and thus observations from the previous period can be used more reliably for future actions.

Ho et al. (in press) estimated which of the two models, the iterated best-response model or learning direction theory, describes the data better. They parameterized learning direction theory, which has been stated as a qualitative theory. They found that the iterated best-response model was better than learning direction theory that explained only about 63% in the game with $p < 1$ and 54% in the game with $p > 1$. The reason for this lower explanatory ability might be similar to that articulated for the maximum game. With $n = 7$ or 3, the influence of a single player is rather large. Fluctuations of the mean are more likely so that there is no clear trend over time. However, learning direction theory should not be discarded. This theory and the iterated best-response model are not competing models but rather complementary models that should be combined. Furthermore, evidence of movement in the right direction by an *individual player* cannot be shown directly in the iterated best-reply models mentioned in the previous subsection.

**Rule Learning Model.** Stahl's (1996, in press) model integrates an iterative best-reply model similar to Nagel (1995) and the findings of direction learning theory in his learning model. Stahl (1996) combined the step-$k$ model ($k = 0, 1, .$ . ., and so forth) and a completely random rule with a modified law of effect or reinforcement model, related to Roth and Erev (1995). In Stahl (in press), the noninteger step-model is used. In addition to the random rule, a rule described as play random in every period is also added.

Here we review only Stahl (1996), since the noninteger step model does not explain the data better. In the first period each player has an initial probability distribution over step-0 to step-3 plus a completely random type, with highest probability on the step actually chosen and nonzero probabilities on the other rules. The latter assumption is needed because zero probability rules would never be chosen in later periods by a wide class of learning models. The initial probability distribution is estimated from the first round data.

The law of effect states that good performing rules are reinforced whereas bad performing rules should be less likely to be chosen in the future. Information of the past is discounted over time. In the simplest model of Roth and Erev (1995), the probability of a choice that has been picked in the previous period increases according to the payoff received for that choice. The probabilities of non-chosen strategies are adjusted only in the sense that the probabilities add up to one. Hence a choice that has not been selected by a player in the previous period cannot gain higher probability in the next period. (In a modified model Roth and Erev, 1995, assumed that the probabilities of the neighboring strategies of a chosen strategy also increased.)

Stahl (1996), on the other hand, updates probabilities of each possible rule depending on its past performance and the current performance with estimated weights[10] for the two measures. The performance of a rule depends on the likelihood of that rule winning in a period. Thus, even rules that have not been selected can be chosen with increasing probability in the next period. For example, if a player has chosen step-4, but step-2 was the best rule, then step-2 is reinforced, that is, the probability of choosing step-2 in the next period increases, whereas choosing step-4 decreases. The model predicts that, over time, behavior converges to the better rules and higher and higher rules should be chosen. The element in learning direction theory of looking for an improving strategy is successfully incorporated in the reinforcement model. This is done by increasing the probability of those rules that are seen to be better, although they have not been chosen. A parametric version of the qualitative learning direction theory performed significantly worse than the reinforcement model.

Note that with reinforcing choices instead of step-$k$ rules, the dynamics of the behavior in the game could not be picked up as well. Simulated convergence would be much smaller than actual convergence. That is why choices are converted into rules. The following model is similar to Stahl's model, however it reinforces choices.

**Experienced-Weighted Attraction Learning**. Camerer and Ho (in press) re-analyzed data sets of various experimental games, including the Ho et al. (in press) data set with what they called an experienced-weighted attraction (EWA) learning model. This model contained the reinforcement model and a class of belief-based models as special cases. The adjustment of the EWA model to the beauty contest game is similar to the model mentioned in the previous subsection. The main difference is that continuous choices are not converted into discrete steps. The initial distribution is assumed to be a beta distribution with parameters estimated from the data. Players update their probability distribution of strategies according to the payoff received by the actual choice in a period. But unchosen choices are reinforced if they lie around the optimal number, $p$ times mean of the previous period, which has been the winner or most likely the winner in the previous period. These are roughly the step-1 choices. The authors show that a choice reinforcement model that only reinforces the actual choice picked by a player in a period explains the convergence of the actual data much worse than does the model that allows for reinforcing best choices of a period. There is so far no comparison between Stahl's (1996) model and this model. It might be that a step model performs better because modal actual behavior is around level 2 rather than the winning number of the previous period. Steps could be easily build into EWA.

**Other Learning Models**. Stahl (1996) and Ho et al. (in press) test various other learning models that they reject in favor of their models. The most prominent rejected frequently mentioned in the economic literature are Bayesian learning models, fictitious play, and Cournot Dynamics.

## CONCLUSION

The experimental study of the beauty contest game clearly shows that behavior based on high levels of iterations has little descriptive value. At the same time, the experiments reveal convergence of choices toward the game theoretic solution over time.

The speed of convergence depends essentially on four factors; the $p$-value, the number of players, which is related to a player's influence on the target number, the method of awarding the winner, and also any experience with another beauty contest game.

The iterative best-response models, which were introduced to explain actual behavior, relate to the game-theoretic analysis, the iterative elimination of dominated strategies, an important strategic principle in game theory. The most important deviation from the game-theoretic reasoning is that most subjects do not engage in a high number of iteration steps. The level of reasoning does usually not go beyond level 3 as observed in many other studies. The starting point of the assumed thought process is often not the same as proposed by game theory, but instead it is the midpoint of a given interval. Introducing Bayesian players did not help explain the data better.

In all the research surveyed it is assumed that players think they are smarter (or reason more deeply ) than others. Ho et al (in press) gave a justification against a plausible criticism of that assumption. "While this is logically impossible, it is consistent with a large body of psychological evidence showing widespread overconfidence about relative ability (e.g., Lovallo & Camerer, in press)". Furthermore, one can argue that a player might think a (sufficient) majority plays one level lower than himself or herself and best responds to that. A slight deviation up or down from the resulting number might indicate that he believes that the rest is reasoning either less far or further than the majority. As one does not incorporate higher levels of reasoning, an assumed outlier can only be a low level player who, at the extreme, chooses farthest away from equilibrium. An evaluation of the extensive comments on the choices by participants of the *Expansion, Financial Times*, and *Spektrum des Wissensdaft* experiments (Bosch & Nagel, 1997a, 1997b; Selten & Nagel, 1998; Thaler, 1997) might give further understanding about the reasoning in the beauty contest games.

There are at least two features visible in the data that are unexplained by the models. First, none of the proposed learning models explain the dynamics dependent on the number of players. The smaller the number of players, the slower the convergence, contrary to iterative best-response models that take into account the influence of a considered player. The influence of the number of players is also not well understood in public good experiments where the number of players change the speed of convergence to the free-rider equilibrium in an unintuitive way: As $n$ increases, the average contribution level converges more slowly to the equilibrium (see Ledyard, 1995).

However, the reason why small groups in beauty contest games converge slower is quite simple. If there is a trend to the equilibrium, an outlier who wants to spoil the game has the greatest influence in a small player group or in the maximum game, by choosing a number far away from the equilibrium. Therefore the speed of convergence is impeded whereas in large player groups or the median game, this effect is much lower or even zero.

A second feature unexplained by our models is that when the winning number determines the payoff (variable payoff treatment) a similar phenomenon as in assets market is observed. Out of the blue, a large majority of subjects increase their choices (away from equilibrium) expecting or hoping that others also do so. Varying the payoffs in a similar way and playing longer games might be an interesting future study to connect more easily to other games with non-Pareto-optimal equilibria as in public good games or assets market experiments.

Much experimental research has focused on learning in games since the beginning of this decade. Here, two basic learning models have been extended and integrated. One is the reinforcement model of the old animal-learning literature that has been introduced to the experimental economic literature by Roth and Erev (1995). A major improvement in Stahl's (1996) model is that choices are converted into rules. Therefore the expectation of subjects that choices converge over time is easily incorporated into the learning process. Another stream of learning models that is often applied is the direction learning model introduced by Selten and Stoecker (1986). In the beauty contest studies this model was confronted with other learning models and outperformed. However, Stahl's (1996) and Camerer and Ho's (in press) models show the importance of the elements of learning direction theory, that ex post better replies should also be increasingly reinforced.

## ACKNOWLEDGMENTS

I would like to thank Antoni Bosch, Jordi Brandts, Antonio Cabrales, Colin Camerer, Gary Charness, Martin Dufwenberg, Ido Erev, Jane Marrinan, Albrecht Ritschl, Nick Vriend, and two anonymous referees for helpful discussions. Special thanks are due to Reinhard Selten for many clarifying discussions. I thank Colin Camerer and Teck-Hua Ho for providing their data set of beauty contest games for this research. I very much appreciated the support and thorough reading of the copy-editor and the editors for their help with this chapter.

## ENDNOTES

1. Moulin (1986) called the game "average game" and Nagel (1994, 1995) called it the "guessing game."
2. For two players choosing 0 is a dominant strategy.
3. Written comments are available on request.
4. Note, however, that subjects with training in game theory choose lower numbers than subject pools with a large number of untrained subjects. I ran the 2/3-mean, [0, 100] experiment before a talk with about 40 colleagues, advertising and playing it by e-mail. The winning number was 10, whereas in the same treatment mentioned in this study it is between 20 and 30. One of my colleagues, a strong believer in game theory, was disappointed by what she thought was a low level of reasoning by her colleagues. However, with her, 20% had chosen zero, the highest frequency so far observed in the first period!
5. Because there are no significant differences of behavior in the treatments with different payoffs, low fixed prize 7 and 28 and in the treatment with -\$2 to the losers, all data is aggregated in one figure (distinguishing either $p = .7$, $c = 18$-treatment, or $p = .8$, $c = 18$-treatment).
6. Because there are no differences between choices of Pitt-students and Bonn-students, these sessions are pooled.
7. In comparison with the economic learning literature, there are far fewer experimental studies that investigate reasoning in games or markets directly. The methods of obtaining insight into reasoning processes are various. Camerer, Johnson, Rymon, and Sen (1993) studied cognitive processes of subjects in three-round alternative offer bargaining game using a computer system called MouseLab. The information of the game is covered in boxes and can be selectively displayed if a box is touched by

the mouse. Selten, Mitzkewitz, and Uhlich (1997) applied the so-called strategy method (Selten, 1967) in a duopoly game experiment. This means that after some experience in playing the game, subjects have to specify a choice for each state possibly reached in the course of the game. So the experimenter obtains a more complete picture of player's thought process. Jacobson and Sadrieh (1996) ran video experiments on a two-player reciprocity game. Each player is represented by a group of three subjects that discusses which action to take. Each group sits in a different room and is constantly videotaped to collect arguments for their reasoning processes. Ball, Bazerman, and Caroll (1991) used verbal protocols to understand why subjects fail to avoid the winner's curse in bilateral negotiations with asymmetric information. Bewley (1995) used interviews to find out about reasons of rigidities of wages in labor markets. Although each method has obvious drawbacks, a conjunction of many of those studies provides useful insights into the reasoning of subjects (see also Nisbett & Wilson, 1977).

8. Remember that when $p > 1$ with lower bound of the interval equal to zero there are no dominated strategies, for example, in 4/3-mean game and interval [0, 100].
9. The idea of types of players was introduced into game theory with the influential research of Harsanyi (1967).
10. These weights determine how much past or current performance change the probability of a rule. Low weight on current performance means that a player does not much base updating on the best rule he or she could have chosen (slow learning). Low weight on past performance means that the past is strongly discounted.

# REFERENCES

Amershi, A., & Sunder, S. (1987). Failure of stock prices to discipline managers in a rational expectations economy. *Journal of Accounting Research*, *25*, 177-195.
Aumann, R. (1992). Irrationality in game theory. In P. Dasgupta, D. Gale, O. Hart, & E. Maskin (Eds.), *Economic analysis of markets and games* (pp. 214-227). Cambridge, MA: MIT Press.
Ball, S. B., Bazerman, M. H., & Caroll, J. S. (1991). An evaluation of learning in the bilateral winner's curse. *Organizational Behavior and Human Decision Processes*, *48*, 1-22.
Beard, R., & Beil, R. (1994). Do people rely on the self-interested maximization of others – an experimental test. *Management Science*, *40*, 252-262.
Bewley, T. (1995). A depressed labor market as explained by participants. *American Economic Review, Papers and Proceedings*, *85*, 250-254.
Binmore, K. (1987). Modeling rational players. *Economics and Philosophy*, *3*, 179-214.
Bosch, A., & Nagel, R. (1997a, June 16). El juego de adivinar el numero X: una explicacion y la proclamacion del vencedor [The game of guessing a number: An explanation and the announcement of the winner]. *Expansion*, 42-43.
Bosch, A. & Nagel, R. (1997b, June 30). Guess the number: Comparing the FT's and expansion's results. *Financial Times*, Mastering Finance section, 14.
Bosch, A., Nagel, R., & Satorra, A. (1998). *One, two, (three), infinity: Iterated reasoning in newspaper beauty contest experiments*. Universitat Pompeii Fabra, mimeograph.
Camerer, C. (1997). Progress in behavioral game theory. *Journal of Economic*

*Perspective, 11*, 167-188.

Camerer, C., Blecherman, B., & Goldstein, D. (1996). *Iterated dominance and learning in "electronic mail game" experiments.* Conference presentation at ESA.

Camerer, C., & Ho, T. (1998). *The effect of incentives in experimental p-beauty contest.* Caltech, mimeograph.

Camerer, C., & Ho, T. (in press). Experience-weighted attraction learning in games: A unifying approach. *Econometrica.*

Cournot, A. (1838). *Recherches sur les principes mathematiques de la theorie de richesses* [Researches into the mathematical principles of the theory of wealth]. (N. T. Bacon, Trans.). London: Haffner.

Duffy, J., & Nagel, R. (1997). On the robustness of behavior in experimental beauty contest games. *Economic Journal, 107*, 1684-1700.

Harsanyi, J. (1967). Games with incomplete information played by Bayesian players. *Management Science, 14*, 159-182, 320-334, 486-502.

Ho, T., Camerer, C., & Weigelt, K. (in press). Iterated dominance and iterated best-best response in experimental "p-beauty contests". *American Economic Review.*

Jacobson, E., & Sadrieh, A. (1996). *Experimental proof for the motivational importance of reciprocity.* University of Bonn, Germany, Discussion Paper B-386.

Keynes, J. M. (1936). *The general theory of interest, employment and money.* London: Macmillan.

Kreps, D., & Wilson, R. (1982). Reputation and imperfect information. *Journal of Economic Theory, 27*, 253-279.

Ledyard, J. (1995). Public goods: A survey of experimental research. In J. Kagel & A. E. Roth (Eds.), *Handbook of experimental economics* (pp. 111-194). Princeton, NJ: Princeton University Press.

Lovallo, D., & Camerer, C. (in press). Overconfidence and excess business entry: An experimental approach. *American Economic Review.*

McKelvey, R., & Palfrey, T. (1992). An experimental study of the centipede game. *Econometrica, 60*, 803-836.

Metha, J., Starmer, C., & Sudgen, R. (1994). The nature of salience: An experimental investigation of pure coordination games. *American Economic Review, 84*, 658-673.

Moulin, H. (1986). *Game theory for social sciences.* New York, NY: New York Press.

Nagel, R. (1994). *Reasoning and learning in guessing games and ultimatum games with incomplete information: An experimental study.* Unpublished dissertation, University of Bonn, Germany.

Nagel, R. (1995). Unraveling in guessing games: An experimental study. *American Economic Review, 85*, 1313-1326.

Nagel, R., & Tang, F.-F. (in press). An experimental study on the centipede game in normal form – an investigation on learning. *Journal of Mathematical Psychology.*

Nisbett, R. E., & Wilson, T. D. (1977). Telling more than we can know: Verbal reports on mental processes. *Psychological Review, 84*, 231-259.

Ochs, J. (1995). Coordination Problems. In J. Kagel & A. E. Roth (Eds.), *Handbook of experimental economics*, (pp. 195-252). Princeton, NJ: Princeton University Press.

Rapoport, A., & Amaldoss, W. (1996). *Competition for the development of a new product: Theoretical and experimental investigation.* Discussion paper, University of Arizona.

Roth, A. E., & Erev, I. (1995). Learning in extensive-form games: Experimental data and simple dynamic models in the intermediate term. *Games and Economic Behavior, 8*,

164-212.

Roth, A. E., & Xing, X. (1994). Jumping the gun: Imperfections and institutions related to the timing of market transactions. *American Economic Review, 84,* 992-1044.

Schelling, T. C. (1960). *The strategy of conflict.* Cambridge, MA: Harvard University Press.

Schotter, A., Weigelt, K., & Wilson, C. (1994). A laboratory investigation of multi-person rationality and presentation effects. *Games and Economic Behavior, 6,* 445-468.

Selten, R. (1967). Die Strategiemethode zur Erforschung des eingeschraenkt rationalen Verhaltens im Rahmen eines Oligopolexperiments. In H. Sauermann (Ed.), *Beitraege zur experimentellen Wirtschaftsforschung [The strategy method for analyzing bounded rational behavior in an oligopoly experiment],* (pp. 136-168). Tuebingen, Germany.

Selten, R. (1975). Reexamination of the perfectness concept for equilibrium points in extensive games. *International Journal of Game Theory, 4,* 25-55.

Selten, R. (1991). Anticipatory learning in two-person games. In R. Selten (Ed.), *Game equilibrium models I,* (pp. 98-154). New York, NY: Springer Verlag.

Selten, R., Mitzkewitz, M., & Uhlich, G. (1997). Duopoly strategies programmed by experienced players. *Econometrica, 65,* 517-555.

Selten, R., & Nagel, R. (1998). Das Zahlenwahlspiel – Hintergruende und Ergebnisse [The number choice game – Background and results]. *Spektrum der Wissenschaft* (German issue of Scientific American), Febr., 16-22.

Selten, R., & Stoecker, R. (1986). End behavior in sequences of finite prisoner's dilemma supergames: A learning theory approach. *Journal of Economic Behavior and Organization, 7,* 47-70.

Stahl, D. O. (1993). The evolution of smart players. *Games and Economic Behavior, 5,* 604-617.

Stahl, D. O. (1996). Rule learning in a guessing game. *Games and Economic Behavior, 16,* 303-330.

Stahl, D. O. (in press). Is step-k thinking an arbitrary modeling restriction or a fact of human nature? *Journal of Economic Behavior and Organization.*

Stahl, D. O., & Wilson, P. W. (1994). Experimental evidence on players' models of other players. *Journal of Economic Behavior and Organization, 25,* 309-327.

Stahl, D. O., & Wilson, P. W. (1995). On player's models of the players: Theory and experimental evidence. *Games and Economic Behavior, 10,* 218-254.

Sunder, S. (1995). Experimental asset markets: A survey. In J. Kagel, & A. E. Roth (Eds.), *Handbook of experimental economics,* (pp. 445-500). Princeton, NJ: Princeton University Press.

Thaler, R. (1997, June 16). Giving markets a human dimension. *Financial Times,* Mastering Finance section 6, 2-5.

van Huyck, J. B., Battalio, R. C., & Beil, R. O. (1990). Tacit coordination games, strategic uncertainty, and coordination failure. *American Economic Review, 80,* 234-248.

van Huyck, J. B., Wildenthal, J. M., & Battalio, R. C. (1996). *Tacit cooperation, strategic uncertainty, and coordination failure: Evidence from repeated dominance solvable games.* Texas A&M University, Economics Laboratory, Research Rep. No. 1.

# APPENDIX

## Instructions

<u>General</u>
You are taking part in an experiment in the economics of decision making. If you have any questions, please feel free to ask. You should have four response cards in front of you, each with a title: first, second, third, or fourth round. You should also have an "explanation sheet."

This experiment will consist of four rounds. The rules, described below, are valid for all four rounds and for all participants.

<u>The rules</u>
In each round you will be asked to choose a number between 0 and 100. Write the number you choose on the card of the corresponding round. At the end of each round all cards for that round will be collected, the numbers chosen will be written on the board, and the *median* will be determined. This will be done without identifying any participant. The winner of each round is the person who is closest to *1/2 times the median* of all chosen numbers for that round.

<u>What is the median</u>
The median is found by ranking all chosen numbers from lowest to highest, (or from highest to lowest) and picking out the middle number. For example if we have five numbers represented by the letters a, b, c, d, and e, and it is the case that a<b<c<d<e, then the middle number, c, is the median. Thus, the median is the number such that half of all numbers lie below it and half of all numbers lie above it.

Remember, however, that you want to choose a number that you believe will be closest to *1/2 times the median.*

<u>Payoffs</u>
1 participants will receive a $5 payment provided that they complete all four rounds of this experimental session. In addition, the winner of each round will get $20. If, in any round, there are several participants at an equal distance to *1/2 of the median*, the $20 prize will be divided among them. All payments will be made at the end of the session.

<u>Explanation Sheet</u>
Briefly describe your decision for each round on the explanation sheet.
ARE THERE ANY QUESTIONS BEFORE WE BEGIN?

# 7     Coordination in Market Entry Games

**Jack Ochs**
*University of Pittsburgh*

The theory of games addresses the question of how a group of individuals will interact when the best strategy for any one individual to take depends on the strategies pursued by others in the group. A list containing one strategy for each player in a game is called a *strategy profile*. Each possible play of that game by the group can be described by some profile. Nash (1950) proposed that when a group of individuals find themselves in a game situation they will eventually settle on a strategy profile (with its implied pattern of action) in which each individual's strategy yields that individual the highest payoff attainable, given the strategies being pursued by everyone else. A profile that has this mutual best response property is called a *Nash equilibrium*. The notion of such a profile being an equilibrium follows from the fact that once such a profile is found no individual has any incentive to change his or her strategy. Therefore, if a group of individuals had somehow adopted a Nash equilibrium profile then one would expect to observe the same strategy profile and its implied pattern of behavior being repeated whenever the same individuals found themselves in the same strategic situation.

For a well-defined game, the set of strategies available to every player and the payoffs associated with all possible strategy profiles are common knowledge. Finding the profiles that are Nash equilibria of a well-defined game is a pure mathematical exercise that does not require any empirical knowledge as to how people behave. To illustrate, consider the following game involving two players, Max and Erma. Each player has two possible strategies, labeled A and B, respectively. The players have never met and are placed in separate rooms. Each player must make a choice without prior communication with the other player and prior to knowing the choice of the other player. If both players choose A then both players receive $50. If both players choose B then both players receive $0. If Max chooses B and Erma chooses A then Max gets $100 and Erma gets -$50 (i.e., Erma loses $50). If Erma chooses B and Max chooses A then Erma gets $100 and Max gets -$50. After the choices are made Max and Erma are paid in private and never see one another. The theorist notes that if Erma were to play A then Max's best response would be B because $100 is more than $50; and if Erma were to play B then Max's best response would still be A because $0 is more than -$50. That is, for Max, strategy B is *a dominant strategy,* that is, a strategy that is a best response to all possible strategies of the other player. Furthermore, the theorist notes that the game is symmetrical and that, by the same logic for Erma, strategy B is her dominant strategy. Therefore, because a dominant strategy is, by definition, a best response to any possible strategy, the strategy profile (B,B) is the unique Nash equilibrium of this game. Indeed, because theorists like generality, theorists would immediately see that in the canonical version of this game in which the payoff function has the form:

| If the strategy profile is | and the payoff profile is |
|:---:|:---:|
| (A,A) | (W,W) |
| (B,A) | (X,Z) |
| (A,B) | (Z,X) |
| (B,B | (Y,Y) |

where $X > W > Y > Z$, then the unique Nash equilibrium is (B,B).

Notice that this is a game in which the Nash equilibrium gives both players strictly less than the could get if they both played A. This creates a dilemma. If the players could communicate ahead of time and make binding agreements they surely would agree to play A, not B. But, by assumption, such communication and commitment is not possible.[1] Because explicit agreements are impossible, if a game theorist is asked by someone how to play the game, the theorist will reply that if you have a dominant strategy you should play it. It might be bothersome to know that players who act on this advice will end up with less than they could conceivably get. But if they are strangers who are never to meet again, the theorist predicts that Max and Erma will be driven by the strategic nature of the situation to play the equilibrium profile.

For this class of games, the theory makes a precise prediction. Of course, many people may believe that the theory is wrong, that many individuals would behave cooperatively and be willing to take a chance, even with a stranger who will never be seen again, on getting the cooperative outcome (A,A) although this is not a Nash equilibrium. Indeed, precisely because there is a tension between the noncooperative equilibrium and the natural cooperative outcome, this game form known as the Prisoner's Dilemma (PD), and variants of it, have been subject to a very large number of experimental tests by both psychologists and economists.[2] I do not wish to discuss whether or not Nash equilibrium of this class of games is a good or a poor predictor of actual behavior in the situations that it characterizes. Rather, I only wish to note that the theory is potentially useful in these cases precisely because it makes a sharp, testable prediction.

However, many games have multiple Nash equilibria. These games call into question the very concept of a Nash equilibrium as a potentially satisfactory description of how such a game will actually be played. In these games even common knowledge that all players can identify the set of Nash equilibria provides no guidance to any player as to how to select a particular strategy. Consider, for example the "Divide the Dollar" game. In this game there are two players, A and B. Each player must call out an integer from 1 to 99. If they both call out the same integer, X, then A gets X cents and B gets 100-X cents. If they call out different integers then both get nothing. There are 99 Nash equilibria of this game. However, knowing this fact, and nothing else, will not allow the game theorist to give useful advice on how to play this game. The relevant information a player must have to select a "good" strategy is how other people are likely to play this game. This information is not contained in the structure of the game nor in considerations of rational play.

Sometimes, when a game has multiple Nash equilibria it is possible to appeal to purely a priori principles of rationality to distinguish among the equilibria. These principles are known as *refinements* in the theoretical literature. One such refinement that is applicable when the players move sequentially is called *subgame perfection*. The idea of this refinement is that each player writes down at the beginning of the game his or her strategy for the entire game. The strategy describes what the player will do at every point where that player is called on to make a decision. If the strategy profile of the players is a subgame perfect Nash equilibrium, then when the game reaches a point where a particular player must make a decision, given what has already transpired and given that the other players will continue to follow their preannounced strategies, it is optimal for this player to also continue following his or her preannounced strategy. In this way, the strategies that form a subgame perfect Nash equilibrium are not only mutual best responses to one another when they are announced – as required for a Nash equilibrium – but they are also *credible*, in that no player will have an incentive to deviate from the preannounced strategy as the game actually unfolds. The following variant of the Divide the Dollar game illustrates the distinction between Nash equilibria and subgame perfect Nash equilibria.

In this variant, known as the Ultimatum Game, one player is given the responsibility of announcing X first. Then, the second player, having heard X, announces either "Accept" or "Reject." Prior to the game actually being played, the second player could announce the strategy, "I will only accept if the first player chooses $X_0$." Taking this as the second player's strategy, the first player's best response is, "I will announce $X_0$." For each possible value of $X_0$ this pair of strategies constitute a Nash equilibrium. Therefore, the Ultimatum game has exactly the same set of Nash equilibria as the Divide the Dollar game. However, if the second mover adopted a strategy of this form it would not be credible because, if the first mover were to announce some number, X, such that $100 > X > X_0$, at the point where the second mover must actually decide, rejection would yield a payoff of 0 whereas acceptance of the offer would yield a positive payoff,

100-X. Because this is true for all X < 100, the only subgame perfect equilibrium (SPE) profile is one in which the first mover announces X = 99 and the second mover announces "accept."

A theorist might advise a player who moves first in the Ultimatum game to fully exploit the strategic advantage inherent in that position. There is, however, a large volume of experimental literature that demonstrates the folly of following such advice. People do not generally accept ultimatums that are extremely disadvantageous. Furthermore, this fact seems to be widely understood because only a small percentage of the demands made by first movers are extreme demands and only extreme demands get rejected. This is not to say that behavior is insensitive to strategic considerations, but rather that in bargaining games outcomes are not strictly determined by the structure of the games.[3]

Although the multiplicity of equilibria in the Divide the Dollar game poses a considerable challenge to game theorists, most people have little difficulty choosing a good strategy. In these games most people choose 50:50, which is a Nash equilibrium. Undoubtedly, considerations of fairness and symmetry play a role in making 50:50 a focal outcome for these games. However, there are many games with multiple equilibria where there are no external factors that serve to focus players' strategy selections on a particular pattern of play. In these games, the very usefulness of Nash equilibrium as an organizer of the data generated by play of the game is called into question. One such class of games are market entry games. In a market entry game each player selects one out of a common set of markets to enter. For at least one of the markets, the payoff to entering that market is a decreasing function of the number of entrants. This chapter reviews a variety of market entry game experiments.[4]

# MARKET ENTRY GAMES

The games used in these experiments share two characteristics in common. First, in all of these games the players have a common interest in having at least some of the players selecting different actions. Second, there is nothing in the structure of the game to differentiate one player from another. All players are symmetrical; they face exactly the same set of choices and the same payoff functions. Because they have a common interest in selecting different actions, they would like to have some external clues to determine how different players should act. But, because of the symmetry, and because the games involve more than two agents, the game does not offer any such clues. It is very unlikely, therefore, that a group of individuals who play one of these games only once would produce a pattern of choices that corresponds to a Nash equilibrium pattern. There are two questions of particular interest in the study of the actual play of such games. First, if individuals from the same population play the same game repeatedly, will a regular pattern of entry be observed and, if so, is that pattern consistent with a Nash equilibrium? Second, what are the properties of individual behavior that shape the observed aggregate entry pattern and what factors influence individual behavior?

The experiments reviewed differ in the following ways: First, in two of the experiments (Meyer, van Huyck, Battalio, & Saving, 1992; Ochs, 1990), the pattern of entry that would maximize the joint payoff of all of the players coincides with the distribution that would be generated by most, but not all, of the Nash equilibrium strategy profiles. However, in the other experiments that are reviewed, none of the Nash equilibrium profiles generate a distribution that maximizes the joint payoff to all of the players. Second, in one experiment (Ochs, 1990) there is a treatment in which a rotation scheme is used to assure that all subjects get experience with the same set of games but no set of subjects share a common history; in all of the other experiments all subjects share a common history. Third, in some of the experiments (Rapoport, 1995; Rapoport, Seale, Erev & Sundali, 1998; Sundali, Rapoport, & Seale, 1995) players have a market choice with a fixed payoff that is independent of the distribution of choices of market entry by the group as a whole, whereas in the other experiments a "safe" choice is not available. Finally, in Erev and Rapoport (1998), subjects get experience with repeated play of a single game that has one "safe" choice and one "risky" choice, whereas in the other experiments that use the same game form, subjects acquire experience with games of the same form but which vary with respect to the value of the "capacity" parameter in the "risky" market. Whether such variations produce systematic differences in behavior is a question to be addressed.

## Meyer, Van Huyck, Battalio, and Saving (1992)

In this experiment the same subjects play the same game repeatedly. This provides an opportunity for players who find themselves distributed over market locations in a way that corresponds to a Nash equilibrium profile to simply use the market choice they made that period as a precedent. If such a precedent is used then once an equilibrium distribution is achieved it will be sustained. Meyer et al. (1992) used this design in a market entry game in which there are only two pure strategies, termed enter market one and enter market two. Each market has the same payoff function in which the payment is a decreasing function of the number who enter the market. An even number of players participate so that any pattern of entry in which exactly N/2 entrants are in a given market corresponds to a Nash equilibrium. All of the equilibria in which exactly one half of the group is in each market also maximizes the joint payoff of all players. Therefore, the entire group of players cannot do better by allocating themselves over the markets in any other way. In addition to this large class of asymmetric equilibria in pure strategies, there is a symmetric equilibrium in which each player chooses the mixed strategy that gives a .5 probability weight to entering each market.

148                                    OCHS

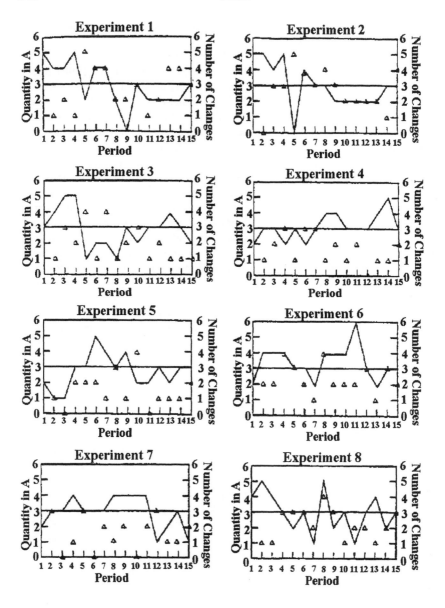

Fig. 7.1. Entry rates in the Meyer et al. (1992) entry game: Inexperienced
subjects . Source: Figure 2 in Meyer, et al. (1992). Reprinted with permission of
The University of Chicago Press.

This mixed strategy equilibrium does not maximize joint payoffs because with positive probability more people will enter one market than the other market. On the other hand, if people do randomize in their early experience then there is a positive probability that they will eventually experience a period in which they are perfectly coordinated. Therefore, the basic hypothesis that Meyer et al. (1992) wished to test was that regardless of what the process was that first led a group of individuals to a particular even distribution over the two markets, once such a distribution was attained it would serve as a precedent that determined all future entry choices. They ran 15 sessions with subjects who had no previous experience with the game. In each of these sessions an even distribution of entrants occurred several times, but no such distribution ever served as a precedent for the play of future stage games within the session.

Figure 7.1 displays the number of entrants in one of the two markets in eight sessions of this experiment. Equilibrium implies three entrants per period in this market and three entrants per period in the other market. The triangles indicate the number of individuals who switched markets. Notice that in most of these sessions subjects had several periods of experience with some individuals switching from one market to the other before they experienced a period in which the markets were perfectly balanced. And the first period in which the markets were balanced was always followed by at least one player switching markets within the next two periods. Therefore, the early experience of these subjects did nothing to instill in them a sense that if the markets were perfectly balanced the best course of action was to stay put.

Although Meyer et al. (1992) varied several different parameters across the sessions in their design, the most striking treatment effect is the difference they observed between experienced subjects and inexperienced subjects. In three out of the four sessions in which subjects who had experience in earlier sessions participated, perfect coordination was achieved in the very first period and in these sessions perfect coordination was observed over most of the periods in the session. However, the fourth group of experienced subjects did not start out perfectly coordinated and never did use any subsequent pattern of choices in which they were perfectly coordinated as a precedent for future play. This suggests that even a group of experienced subjects, who have had an opportunity to reflect on the advantages of perfect coordination, may only use a pattern of perfect coordination as a precedent if they happen to start out perfectly coordinated, but not otherwise. Tacit coordination requires that everyone believe that no one will switch markets if the group is currently properly divided between the markets. One interpretation of Meyer et al.'s (1992) findings is that such beliefs are both difficult to establish and easily broken.

## Ochs (1990)

Ochs (1990) provided another study of the behavior of small groups of subjects

Table 7.1
Experimental Design

| Experiment | Information Feedback | Payoff (success, failure) | Stock Distributions | Number of Subjects |
|---|---|---|---|---|
| **Block 2 – Low Turnover Markets** | | | | |
| 1 | Low | ($.25,0) | (6,1,1,1),(5,2,1,1), (4,3,1,1) | 27 |
| 2 | High | ($.25,0) | (6,1,1,1),(5,2,1,1), (4,3,1,1) | 27 |
| 5 | High | ($.25,0) | (6,1,1,1),(5,2,1,1), (4,3,1,1) | 27 |
| 11 | High | ($.25,0) | (6,2,1),(5,3,1),(3,3,3) | 27 |
| **Block 2 – Low Turnover Markets** | | | | |
| 3 | Low | ($.25,0) | (6,2,1),(3,3,3) | 18 |
| 4 | High | ($.25,0) | (6,2,1),(3,3,3) | 18 |
| 6 | High | ($.25,0) | (6,2,1),(3,3,3) | 9 |
| 7 | High | ($.50,0) | (6,2,1) | 9 |
| 8 | High | ($1.00,0) | (6,2,1) | 9 |
| 9 | High | ($1.00,0) | (3,3,3),(6,2,1),(1,2,6) | 9 |
| 10 | High | ($.50,-1.00) | (6,2,1),(3,3,3),(1,2,6), (2,1,6) | 9 |
| 12 | High | ($.25,0) | (6,1,1,1),(4,3,1,1), (5,2,1,1) | 27 |

Note. For ease of reference, markets with different stock distributions were also color coded as follows: (6,1,1,1) = Red, (5,2,1,1) = Blue, (4,3,1,1) = Yellow, (6,2,1) = Red, (5,3,1) = Blue, (3,3,3) = Yellow. Source: Ochs, 1990. Reprinted with permission of The University of Chicago Press.

who repeatedly play the same market entry game(s). This experiment is divided into two blocks. In one block (called "high turnover") all subjects played more than one market entry game. A session consisted of a sequence of rounds. In a given round a subject played only one market game. A rotation scheme was used to assign players to different market games from round to round so that no two subjects had the same sequence of assignments in a given session but all subjects had repeated experience with every game used in the session. In a second block (called "zero turnover") each individual in a given session was assigned to repeatedly play the same market entry game. In these zero turnover markets, therefore, subjects who were assigned to the same market shared a common experience. In all sessions, subjects had no prior experience in earlier sessions. The games used in these sessions had either three or four locations from which each subject had to make a choice. At each location, $i$, a fixed number of units of "stock", $R_i$, were posted. If $N_i$ of the subjects who were playing the game selected location $i$ then the probability of earning a fixed positive amount to a player who selected market $i$ was determined by the function:

$$P = \begin{cases} 1, & \text{if } N_i \leq R_i \\ 1 - [(N_i - R_i)/R_i], & \text{otherwise} \end{cases} \tag{1}$$

The sum over all locations of the posted stock was equal to the total number of subjects in the market game so that any distribution of individuals that exactly matched the distribution of stock yielded the maximum payoff/participant. The stock available at every location was publicly posted on a blackboard in full view of all of the subjects and the payoff function was common knowledge.

The upper portion of Table 7.1 describes the features of the sessions with high turnover. The lower portion of Table 7.1 describes the features of the design in the eight sessions in which the same subjects were repeatedly assigned to participate in the same market game. The low turnover sessions are discussed first.

There were several treatment variables in this design. The first variable was information feedback. In session 3, at the end of each round the identification numbers of those subjects who received a zero payoff for the period were publicly posted, but the actual distribution of location choices made that round was not posted. Therefore, all subjects could tell if the group achieved perfect coordination (no failures posted) but only an individual who was notified of his or her failure knew whether or not a particular location was oversubscribed that round. Session 4 differed from session 3 with regard to information feedback. At the end of each round in session 4 the actual distribution of choices made that round were publicly posted as well as the identification numbers of those who received a zero payoff for that round. A second treatment variable was permutation of the nine units of stock available in a given market over the locations in that market. Under the permutation treatment, at the beginning of each round the distribution of stock over the locations was publicly posted prior to the selection of locations by the subjects. For example, in the market with 3 locations labeled A, B, and C respectively, in one period the posted distribution among these locations would be (6,2,1) in the next period it would be (2,6,1) and in the next (1,2,6). In session 3 and in the first 16 periods of session 4 the distribution of stock over locations in the Red Market (a market that had 6 units posted at one location, 2 units at a second location, and 1 unit at a third location) was permuted from period to period. Session 6 was run under the same high information conditions as session 4, but there was no permutation of the

## Experiment 3 (6,2,1)

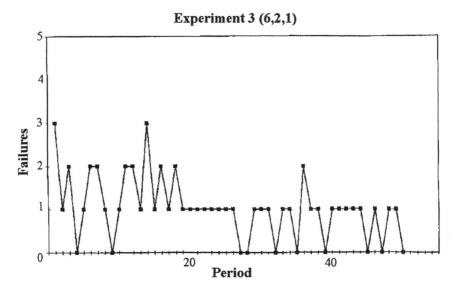

Fig. 7.2. Failure rates in the Red Market in session 3. Adapted from Table 2, Ochs (1990).

---

distribution of stock over locations from period to period. Figures 7.2, 7.3, 7.4, 7.5, and 7.6 display the pattern of failures for corresponding markets in these three sessions.[5]

A comparison of the failure rates in session 3 with those observed in session 4 indicates that the degree of coordination actually achieved is affected by the information feedback. The failure rates in both markets in session 3 in which there was no common knowledge of the oversubscribed markets are significantly higher than those observed in session 4 where there was common knowledge of the distribution of actual choices.[6] This suggests that individuals conditioned their strategy selection on the behavior of others and not merely on their own payoff history.

When the distribution of stock in a market is not permuted from round to round a higher degree of coordination is achieved than when such permutation takes place. This is reflected in the difference in failure rates between the Red and Yellow markets in both sessions 3 and 4. Although the only structural aspect of a market location that is payoff-relevant is the number of units of stock posted at that location, evidently it is easier to coordinate when individuals can focus on both a physical location (location A, B, or C) and a place in the distribution than

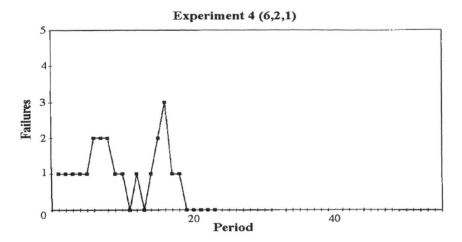

Fig. 7.3. Failure rates in the Red Market in session 4. Adapted from Table 2, Ochs (1990).

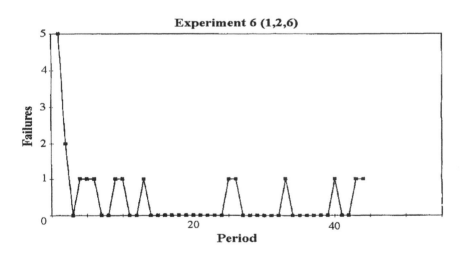

Fig. 7.4. Failure rates in the Red Market in session 6. Adapted from Table 2, Ochs (1990).

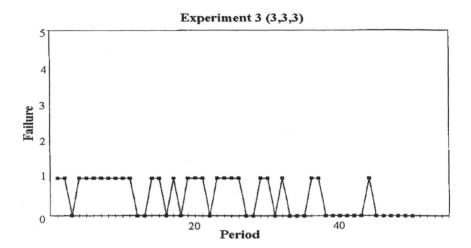

Fig. 7.5. Failure rates in the Yellow Market in session 3. Adapted from Table 2, Ochs (1990).

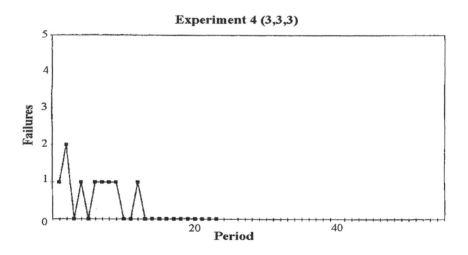

Fig. 7.6. Failure rates in the Yellow Market in session 4. Adapted from Table 2, Ochs (1990).

when repeated coordination requires selecting a location in the stock distribution, regardless of its physical location.

As in Meyer et al. (1992), any perfectly coordinated pattern of play in these zero turnover markets becoming an absorbing state is not observed. Instead, there are several episodes of perfect coordination during which everyone is making the same choice repeatedly. An episode is ended by someone moving and, although the group subsequently achieves another perfectly coordinated pattern of entry, the pattern of entry in one such episode is different from the pattern of entry observed in the last episode of perfect coordination. This episodic behavior indicates that it is difficult to build the mutual confidence that is necessary to sustain perfect coordination. Furthermore, such confidence once achieved may be too fragile to sustain external shocks.

Although sustained perfect coordination was not generally observed in the zero turnover markets, the degree of coordination achieved in these games was much higher than was achieved in the same games when there was a high rate of turnover from round to round in the membership of the group who played any given game. When the turnover rate is zero, most but not all agents persist in the selection of that location in which they had been successful in the past whereas those agents who were unsuccessful in the current round are likely to change location in the following round. This pattern of adaptation mitigates the seriousness of the coordination problem inherent in these market entry games. By contrast, when the turnover rate is high the behavior of the agents reflects the one-play nature of the game in which they find themselves. Table 7.2 displays the distributions of aggregate relative frequency of selection of location for each market in these high turnover games.

In a session three different markets operated simultaneously. Markets were distinguished by the distribution of stock over locations. Within a given market, in Experiments 1 and 2 the distribution of stock over locations was permuted from period to period. Thus, in Experiment 1, the first market always had one location at which 5 units of stock were posted, one location at which 2 units of stock were posted, and two locations at which 1 units of stock were posted. As Table 7.2 indicates, in Experiment 1 the location that had 5 units of stock posted drew between 56.6% and 68.9% of all choices in that session, whereas in Experiment 2 the location with 5 units of stock drew between 54.3% and 66.7% of all choices made in the first market. In Experiment 5, subjects rotated among markets, but there was no permutation of the stock distribution over locations within a market from period to period. In that session, the location with 5 units of stock drew 57.5% of all of the choices. Looking at the data, one can compare the percentage of choices drawn to the location with the largest volume of stock with the size of the stock at that location. The third market had only 4 units of stock at the location with the most stock, whereas the second market had 6 units

**Table 7.2**
**Aggregate Behavior in High Turnover Markets**

|  | **Equilibrium Probability Weights** |  |
|---|---|---|
| **Stock Distributions** | **Probability Weights*** | **Expectation of Success*** |
| (6,1,1,1) | (.835, .055, .055, .055) | .79 |
| (5,2,1,1) | (.683, .200, .0585, .0585) | .79 |
| (4,3,1,1) | (.517, .367, .058, .058) | .79 |
| (6,2,1) | (.783, .167, .05) | .83 |
| (5,3,1) | (.63, .32, .05) | .825 |
| (3,3,3) | (.333, .333, .333) | .818 |

**Actual Distribution of Choices**

**Experiment 1**

| | | |
|---|---|---|
| Stock Distribution | (  1,    1,    2,    5) | (  1,    1,    1,    6) |
| Freq. of choice | (.101,.111, .222,.566) | (.111,.111,.091,.687) |
| Stock Distribution | (  1,    1,    5,    2) | (  1,    1,    6,    1) |
| Freq. of choice | (.056,.078,.689,.177) | (.111,.067,.722,    1) |
| Stock Distribution | (  2,    5,    1,    1) | (  1,    6,    1,    1) |
| Freq. of choice | (.156,.644, .100,.100) | (.122,.756,.089,.033) |
| Stock Distribution | (  5,    2,    1,    1) | (  6,    1,    1,    1) |
| Freq. of choice | (.667,.192,.061,  .08) | (.657,.121,.101,.121) |
| | | |
| Stock Distribution | (  1,    1,    3,    4) | |
| Freq. of choice | (.101,.081,.323,.495) | |
| Stock Distribution | (  1,    1,    4,    3) | |
| Freq. of choice | (.089,.133,.467,.311) | |
| Stock Distribution | (  3,    4,    1,    1) | |
| Freq. of choice | (.444,.289,.167,.100) | |
| Stock Distribution | (  4,    3,    1,    1) | |
| Freq. of choice | (.485,.283,.141,.091) | |

**Experiment 2**

| | | |
|---|---|---|
| Stock Distribution | (  1,    1,    2,    5) | (  1,    1,    1,    6) |
| Freq. of choice | (.113,.087,.225,.575) | (.086,.099,.160,.655) |
| Stock Distribution | (  1,    1,    5,    2) | (  1,    1,    6,    1) |
| Freq. of choice | (.125,.056,.667,.152) | (.125,.125,.667,.683) |

| Stock Distribution | ( 2, | 5, | 1, | 1) | ( 1, | 6, | 1, | 1) |
|---|---|---|---|---|---|---|---|---|
| Freq. of choice | (.194, | .625, | .097, | .084) | (.111, | .764, | .042, | .083) |
| Stock Distribution | ( 5, | 2, | 1, | 1) | ( 6, | 1, | 1, | 1) |
| Freq. of choice | (.543, | .321, | .074, | .062) | (.716, | .098, | .088, | .098) |

| Stock Distribution | ( 1, | 1, | 3, | 4) |
|---|---|---|---|---|
| Freq. of choice | (.136, | .136, | .345, | .383) |
| Stock Distribution | ( 1, | 1, | 4, | 3) |
| Freq. of choice | (.097, | .083, | .569, | .251) |
| Stock Distribution | ( 3, | 4, | 1, | 1) |
| Freq. of choice | (.319, | .444, | .139, | .098) |
| Stock Distribution | ( 4, | 3, | 1, | 1) |

**Experiment 5**

| Stock Distribution | ( 2, | 5, | 1, | 1) | ( 1, | 1, | 6, | 1) |
|---|---|---|---|---|---|---|---|---|
| Freq. of choice | (.209, | .575, | .101, | .115) | (.101, | .105, | .712, | .082) |

| Stock Distribution | ( 1, | 3, | 1, | 4) |
|---|---|---|---|---|
| Freq. of choice | (.111, | .284, | .105, | .500) |

**Experiment 11**

| Stock Distribution | ( 6, | 2, | 1) | ( 5, | 3, | 1) |
|---|---|---|---|---|---|---|
| Freq. of choice | (.707, | .173, | .120) | (.549, | .340, | .111) |

| Stock Distribution | ( 3, | 3, | 3) |
|---|---|---|---|
| Freq. of choice | (.321, | .327, | .352) |

*Note.* Source: Table 4, Ochs, 1990. Reprinted with permission of The University of Chicago Press. * denotes approximation.

at the location with the most stock. As Table 7.2 shows, the location with the largest volume of stock posted consistently attracted the largest percentage of the choices and this percentage is positively related to the percentage of the market's stock that is available at that location. Indeed, the aggregate pattern of play is reasonably well characterized by the symmetric Nash equilibria of the various games that were played. This is reflected both in the closeness of the match between the aggregate distribution of choices over locations in the various markets and the distribution of the available stocks in these markets and in the properties of the time series on failure rates observed in these markets. Figure 7.7 displays the time series on failure rates from a representative high turnover market. The variance in the failure rate shows no time trend and is consistent

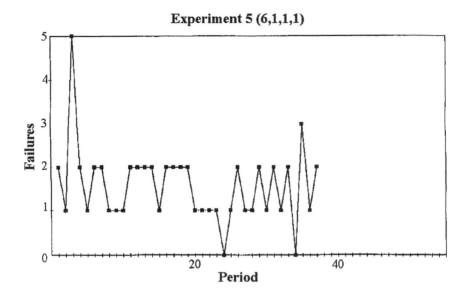

Fig. 7.7. Failure rates in the Red Market in session 5. Adapted from Table 2, Ochs (1990).

---

with the output from a stationary stochastic process.

The aggregate distributions of choices over locations in the high turnover markets fail to conform to the properties of a Nash equilibrium in mixed strategies in one respect. In every market, the location with the largest quantity of stock was selected with a smaller relative frequency than that predicted by the mixed-strategy Nash equilibrium. Consequently, subjects who consistently selected the location with the most stock would have had a higher expected payoff than the average subject. However, this strategy would have amounted to less than $.02/round additional profit relative to the payoff earned by a subject who placed the same probability weight on selecting any particular location as the relative frequency with which that location was chosen in the aggregate.

The relative frequency distributions that are observed in the aggregate in these high turnover markets are not an artifact of aggregation of subjects, each of whom were playing in a way that deviated significantly from the symmetric Nash equilibrium relative frequencies. Table 7.3 displays the pattern of choices by each of the 27 subjects who participated in Session 5 of this experiment.

Notice that for most subjects the rank order of frequency of choices over locations in the three markets is very highly correlated with the rank order of the available stock over the locations in those markets. That is, the pattern of choices

**Table 7.3**
**Individual Choices in High Turnover Session**

| Stock ID | Blue | | | | Red | | | | Yellow | | | |
|---|---|---|---|---|---|---|---|---|---|---|---|---|
| | 2 | 5 | 1 | 1 | 1 | 1 | 6 | 1 | 1 | 3 | 1 | 4 |
| | | Choices | | | | Choices | | | | Choices | | |
| 1 | 4 | 3 | 1 | 0 | 2 | 1 | 9 | 1 | 0 | 6 | 0 | 7 |
| 2 | 2 | 4 | 1 | 1 | 0 | 0 | 13 | 0 | 2 | 3 | 1 | 7 |
| 3 | 1 | 13 | 1 | 1 | 0 | 2 | 9 | 1 | 0 | 1 | 1 | 4 |
| 4 | 6 | 8 | 1 | 2 | 3 | 2 | 4 | 2 | 2 | 1 | 1 | 2 |
| 5 | 2 | 6 | 0 | 1 | 0 | 1 | 11 | 0 | 0 | 6 | 1 | 6 |
| 6 | 2 | 2 | 1 | 3 | 4 | 3 | 1 | 5 | 2 | 4 | 4 | 3 |
| 7 | 3 | 5 | 9 | 1 | 3 | 3 | 2 | 2 | 2 | 4 | 0 | 0 |
| 8 | 1 | 5 | 0 | 3 | 0 | 1 | 12 | 0 | 2 | 1 | 3 | 6 |
| 9 | 4 | 1 | 2 | 10 | 0 | 0 | 0 | 0 | 10 | 3 | 4 | 0 |
| 10 | 0 | 9 | 0 | 0 | 0 | 0 | 13 | 0 | 0 | 1 | 1 | 10 |
| 11 | 0 | 8 | 0 | 0 | 0 | 0 | 12 | 0 | 0 | 0 | 0 | 14 |
| 12 | 3 | 1 | 5 | 0 | 5 | 0 | 5 | 2 | 1 | 5 | 2 | 5 |
| 13 | 1 | 6 | 0 | 1 | 0 | 1 | 12 | 0 | 2 | 5 | 2 | 4 |
| 14 | 0 | 9 | 0 | 0 | 0 | 0 | 11 | 0 | 0 | 0 | 0 | 14 |
| 15 | 0 | 9 | 0 | 1 | 0 | 0 | 11 | 0 | 0 | 1 | 3 | 9 |
| 16 | 0 | 18 | 0 | 0 | 0 | 0 | 11 | 0 | 0 | 0 | 0 | 5 |
| 17 | 14 | 0 | 1 | 2 | 8 | 1 | 1 | 2 | 1 | 3 | 1 | 0 |
| 18 | 4 | 4 | 1 | 1 | 3 | 3 | 6 | 0 | 0 | 7 | 1 | 4 |
| 19 | 0 | 3 | 3 | 3 | 1 | 2 | 6 | 5 | 1 | 2 | 4 | 4 |
| 20 | 10 | 4 | 1 | 1 | 1 | 2 | 7 | 2 | 3 | 0 | 1 | 2 |
| 21 | 3 | 5 | 0 | 1 | 1 | 0 | 10 | 2 | 0 | 7 | 1 | 4 |
| 22 | 2 | 11 | 3 | 1 | 0 | 0 | 0 | 0 | 2 | 6 | 0 | 9 |
| 23 | 0 | 9 | 0 | 0 | 0 | 0 | 12 | 0 | 0 | 6 | 1 | 6 |
| 24 | 0 | 10 | 0 | 0 | 0 | 0 | 13 | 0 | 0 | 3 | 0 | 9 |
| 25 | 1 | 8 | 0 | 0 | 0 | 0 | 13 | 0 | 0 | 3 | 0 | 9 |
| 26 | 1 | 5 | 1 | 2 | 0 | 9 | 3 | 1 | 3 | 7 | 0 | 2 |
| 27 | 0 | 10 | 0 | 0 | 0 | 1 | 12 | 0 | 0 | 5 | 0 | 6 |

*Note.* Source: Ochs (1990).

made by most subjects is broadly consistent with individual play of mixed strategies that are sensitive to the distribution of stock across locations in a market. Nevertheless, there is substantial variation in the pattern of choices across subjects and this variation is inconsistent with the symmetric Nash equilibrium.

## Games With A Sure Payoff Strategy

Rapoport (1995), Rapoport, Erev, Seale, and Sundali (1998), and Sundali, Rapoport, and Seale (1995) reported a sequence of experiments that use a different market entry game that those used by either Meyer et al. (1992) or Ochs (1990). As in Meyer et al. (1992), in these experiments each of $N$ subjects must make a binary choice of the possibilities that we label Market A and Market B. Unlike the games used by Meyer et al. (1992) and Ochs (1990), in these games the payoff from making one of these two choices, say A, is a constant, $v$, whereas the payoff, $p$, to a player who makes the other choice, B, depends on the number of people, $e$, who make the same choice according to the function

$$p = k + r(c - e) \qquad (2)$$

where $r \geq 1$ and $0 < c < N$. When $v = k$, this payoff function implies two different aggregate distributions that can be supported by asymmetric Nash equilibria in pure strategies. If $N$-$c$ subjects choose A and the remaining $c$ subjects choose B then no individual can increase his or her payoff, conditional on the choices of the other $N$-1 subjects by changing his or her choice. This aggregate pattern yields equal payoff to all subjects, but requires different subjects to choose different pure strategies. The second aggregate distribution that can be supported as an asymmetric Nash equilibrium is when $N$-$(c$-1$)$ choose A and the remaining $c$-1 subjects select B. Given this pattern, the $c$-1 individuals who choose B earn more than those who select A but no one who chooses A can, given $c$-1 individuals have already selected B, get an increase in payoff by switching to B. In these games there is also a symmetric Nash equilibrium in mixed strategies where each subject enters Market B with probability = $(c$-1$)/(N$-1$)$. Not only are there some equilibria in which payoffs are unequal, but in this class of games the aggregate pattern of entry that maximizes the average payoff is not an equilibrium pattern. Instead, the pattern that maximizes average payoff requires one half of the equilibrium entry rate into Market B.

## Rapoport (1995)

Rapoport (1995) reported the results of an experiment using this class of market games in the following design. A group of 16 doctoral students, after being introduced to the basic concepts of game theory including the notion of a Nash equilibrium, were asked to participate in a simple market entry game experiment in which their earnings would be contingent on performance. The experiment consisted of the play of two blocks of 10 different market games. Each of the 10 games played within a block had a value of $c$ drawn at random and without replacement from the set of integers {3, 4, . . .,12}. The payoff for each game was $1 for choosing Market A (No entry) and $(1 + 2(c-e)) for choosing Market B. The games were played one at a time and the value of $c$ was not announced until the game corresponding to that $c$ was to be played. No information on individual or group outcomes was provided until the end of the entire sequence of 20 trials was completed. At the end of a session one of the trials was selected at random to determine the payment. Unlike most experiments, in this experiment subjects could lose money. Of course, a subject also had available a strategy that would guarantee positive earnings. However, the amount a subject won or lost if he or she chose to enter Market B in any game was not known to that subject until after the experimental session was over. Therefore, there was no possibility of the amount of money a subject earned or lost in prior periods having any influence on that subject's decision in subsequent games. Indeed, there was no possibility for any within-session learning in this design. Each game played within a session therefore constituted the play of a one-shot game. At the end of the first session the game randomly selected for payment had $c = 12$ and $e = 8$ so that all subjects earned a positive payoff and those who selected Market B earned $9.

Two weeks after the first session, the results of the session were reported to the group and they were asked if they wished to participate in a second session. Only 14 of the original 16 subjects were present and all 14 agreed to participate. In this session the game randomly chosen for payment had $c = 7$ and $e = 5$, so that once again all subjects received a positive cash payment. A week after this second session the results of that session were presented to and discussed with the participants. After a 2-week interval, the same subjects, who had been led to believe that no further sessions were planned, were asked to volunteer for a third session and all of the original 16 subjects participated.

Figure 7.8 displays the aggregate number of subjects who chose Market B as a function of $c$ by session and block.

Within a given session there is a strong similarity in entry rate patterns between blocks. This reflects the fact that most subjects made the same decision when a particular game (designated by the value of $c$) was played in the second block as they did when that game was played in the first block. This indicates that most subjects, facing a given value of $c$, did not use a randomization device (mixed strategies) in determining which market to enter when faced with a particular binary choice. Between sessions, subjects got information on the pattern of entry in prior sessions as well as their own individual earnings experience. Before participating in session 2, all subjects knew (could have observed) that in session 1 the number of entrants ($e$) in Market B was always less the capacity ($c$). This feedback apparently influenced individual behavior as the rate of selection/subject of Market B increased from just under 5/subject in session 1 to 9/subject in session 2 and the entry pattern much more closely matched capacity than in session 1. Indeed, in session 2, in 2 of the 20 trials entrants exceeded capacity and, in another 2, trial entrants just matched capacity.

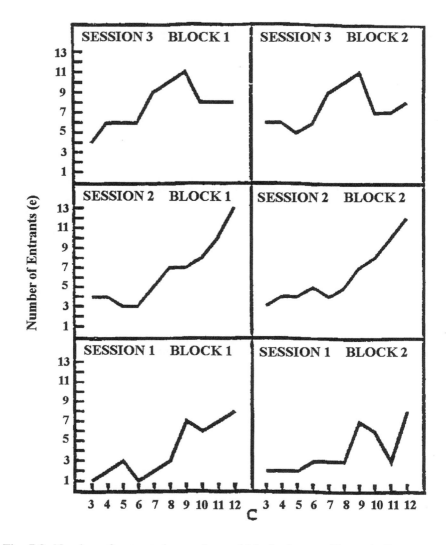

Fig. 7.8. Number of entrants by session and block. Source: Figure 1, Rapoport (1995). Reprinted with permission of Kluwer Academic Press.

Therefore, subjects entered session 3 knowing that entrants typically earned more than nonentrants, but also knowing that this was not true for all $c$. The entry rate/subject was only slightly higher in session 3 than in session 2 and rate of entry when $c$ exceeded 9 was much lower in session 3 than in session 2.

The aggregate pattern of behavior observed by Rapoport (1995) in this experiment is similar to that observed by Ochs (1990) in the high turnover markets. As in Ochs' (1990) study, there is a high correlation between the aggregate frequency with which a particular market is chosen and the capacity of that market. There was also considerable heterogeneity among individuals in their patterns of entry in both experiments. Finally, in both experiments, feedback on the pattern of choices influenced the degree of correlation between entry rate and capacity. There was, however, one significant difference in individual behavior between these two experiments. Most of the subjects in Ochs' (1990) experiment did not repeatedly make the same choice when placed in the same game, but most of the subjects in Rapoport (1995) did repeat the same choice when faced with the same game. Therefore, the correlation between the aggregate entry rate and market capacity in Rapoport's (1995) experiment is much more an artifact of aggregation that the correlation observed in the high turnover markets in Ochs' (1990) experiment.

## Sundali, Rapoport, and Seale (1995)

In the Rapoport (1995) experiment subjects received feedback between sessions, not after each trial. Furthermore, some of them might have had an opportunity to discuss the results and consider how they might play if they were ever to play again. This makes it difficult, in principle, to know how much of the increase in coordination observed from session to session is attributable to the feedback that was controlled. Sundali, Rapoport, and Seale (1995) reported another experiment using the same class of market games as those used in Rapoport (1995). This experiment is conducted under two different information conditions.

In the first condition, 20 subjects played 60 trials consisting of binary entry games of the same type as used in Rapoport (1995). Between trials there was no information feedback. The trials were divided into 6 blocks and within each block 10 market entry games, each with a different value for capacity, $c$, were presented. Within a given block, the order of presentation of the 10 games was determined by random draw without replacement. In the second condition, 3 groups, each consisting of 20 subjects played 100 trials, divided into 10 blocks. Within blocks the same 10 games, presented in random order, were played. Between trials individuals were given feedback on the number of entrants and were instructed that they could keep a written record of the capacity and the number of entrants for each trial. In a postsession questionnaire, 65% of the subjects reported keeping such records.

The degree of coordination achieved in the absence of information feedback was remarkably high. The correlation coefficient between the number of entrants and market capacity in the no information feedback condition, computed over all trials was .92. The range in this correlation coefficient across blocks was .91-.94. This aggregate behavior was achieved as a result of the heterogeneity of strategy choices among the subjects, rather than by the common adoption of mixed strategies in which entry probability reflected the ratio of capacity to the total number of subjects. Despite the high degree of coordination achieved without any information feedback, such feedback clearly raised the degree of coordination by influencing individual behavior. In the feedback condition, the correlation between capacity and entry rate increased from .86 in the first block of trials to .99 in every block thereafter. This reflects an observed pattern of adjustment in which the probability of entering a market with a given capacity was positively related to the difference between the market's capacity and the number of people who entered when the market had that capacity in prior rounds. This pattern was observed not only at the aggregate level, but was descriptive of the individual behavior of as many as 1/2 of all of the subjects in the experiment.

The combination of information feedback with a fixed group of subjects creates an environment that is conducive to adaptive behavior. The fact that the degree of coordination achieved in the Sundali et al. (1995) experiment is lower than that observed in the zero turnover condition in the Ochs (1990) experiment is possibly due to the fact that individuals played the same game once every 10 trials, on average in the Sundali et al. (1995) experiment whereas they played the same game every trial in the Ochs (1990) environment.

## Rapoport, Seale, Erev, and Sundali (1998)

Rapoport, Seale, Erev, and Sundali (1998) extended the design of the Sundali et al. (1995) experiment just discussed by comparing treatments in which the value of $v$, the payoff for not entering the market is both different from $k$ and either positive, as in the previous experiment, or negative. The Nash equilibrium entry rate is negatively related to the value of $v$.[7] Therefore, when $v$ is negative, the Nash equilibrium entry rate is greater than when $v$ is positive. When $v$ is negative individuals are faced with a decision to either enter a market in which their payoff is uncertain or to accept a loss with certainty. When $v$ is positive, the decision problem for individuals is framed within the context of selecting either a gamble or a sure thing with a positive payoff. Therefore, the use of $v$ as a treatment variable has an effect on the frame within which individuals view their decision problem. Rapoport et al. (1998) argued that "prospect theory would seem to imply that when $v > k > 0$, the observed frequency will be smaller than predicted by Nash equilibrium that assumes risk neutrality, and when $v < 0 < k$, the observed frequency of entrants will exceed the predicted frequency" (p. 121).

Rapoport et al. (1998) found that the aggregate rates of entry under both positive and negative values of $v$ were in close agreement with the rates predicted by Nash equilibrium. In both domains, observed entry rates exceeded predicted equilibrium rates when market capacity was small and were less than predicted equilibrium rates when market capacity was large. Rapoport et al. (1998) conjectured that

> One possible reason for the failure of the gain/loss distinction to affect coordination success is that the move from loss aversion as an *individual* choice principle to an *interactive* choice principle in our market entry game may be problematic (since) loss aversion is a property of preferences (while) on the interactive level it may, in addition, affect the beliefs players have about the preferences and subsequent behavior of others. (p. 139)

In the games used in Rapoport et al. (1998) and Sundali et al. (1995) there is a significant difference between the maximum possible per capita payoff and the per capita payoff associated with equilibrium entry rates. In both of these experiments, the players for each trial remained fixed over all trials in a session. This environment provided an opportunity for subjects to adapt their behavior over time and there is clear evidence that individuals did change their strategies with experience. Nevertheless, the pattern of individual adaptations did not lead the group to reduce entry rates below the Nash equilibrium rates, as would be required to increase per capita payoff. The large variability between subjects in entry behavior, together with the nonstationarity of individual behavior over blocks of trials implies that at the individual level, behavior was not consistent with the play of Nash equilibrium strategies. This leaves open the question, therefore, of how best to characterize individual learning behavior and why such individual adaptations tend to produce aggregate patterns of entry that are so consistent with those predicted by Nash equilibrium.

Rapoport et al. (1998) used a model of adaptive behavior introduced by Erev and Roth (1995) to characterize individual behavior observed in their experiment. They use the observed data to establish initial propensities for each subject and then run simulations using a fixed set of values for all other parameters in the Erev-Roth model, values that were found to provide best fits for observed behavior of many other subjects in many other experiments. The Erev-Roth model assumes that every player, $i$, has a set of $K$ pure strategies from which to choose. On trial teach subject selects one of these strategies, say $k$, with probability,

$$p_{ik}(t) = q_{ik}(t) / \sum q_{ij}(t) \qquad (3)$$

where $q_{ik}$ is the propensity of $i$ to select pure strategy $k$. Each individual's initial propensities,( $q_{i1}(0), \ldots, q_{iK}(0)$, are idiosyncratic, but all subjects are assumed to update their propensities by the same rule:

$$q_{ij}(t+1) = \max\left[\upsilon, (1-\phi)q_{ij}(t) + E_{ik}(j, R_t(x))\right] \qquad (4)$$

In the propensity updating function the parameter $\phi$ is a forgetting parameter that reduces the importance of past experience; $R$ is a mapping of payoffs into rewards and $E$ is a function that determines how the experience of receiving $R$ when playing strategy $k$ affects the propensity to play strategy $j$.

To allow for the reward or reinforcement from a given payoff to be influenced by its magnitude relative to some moving reference point, the reward function is written as

$$R_t(x) = x - \rho(t) \qquad (5)$$

where $\rho$ is the current reference point and the reference point is updated according to the rule

$$\rho(t+1) = \begin{cases} (1-w^+)\rho(t), & \text{if } x \geq \rho(t) \\ (1-w^-)\rho(t), & \text{otherwise} \end{cases} \qquad (6)$$

where $w^+$ and $w^-$ are weights assigned to positive and negative reinforcements relative to the current reference point.

The Erev-Roth model assumes that there is a natural ordering of strategies, so that any payoff from playing a particular strategy $k$ not only has an effect on reinforcement of the propensity to play strategy $k$ but also has an effect on the propensity to play "nearby" strategies $k-1$ and $k+1$. To apply this model, Rapoport et al. (1998) assumed that all strategies take the form of "cut-off" strategies in which strategy $k$ is "enter if $c$ is less than or equal to $k$, otherwise do not enter." Their rule is then to distribute the reinforcement weight from the payoff earned when strategy $j$ is played as follows:

$$E_{ik}(j, R(x)) = \begin{cases} R(x)(1-2\varepsilon) & \text{if } k = j \\ R(x)\varepsilon & \text{if } k = j \pm 1 \end{cases}. \qquad (7)$$

When the initial propensities are estimated from the initial round of play and then the subsequent play of agents simulated, the simulated pattern of entry conforms quite closely to the observed pattern of entry. That is, this adaptive learning model produces dynamics that tend to move the aggregate rate of entry into close conformity with the Nash equilibrium rates, while preserving heterogeneity of entry behavior among the simulated subjects. The only significant difference between the simulated patterns and the observed patterns of entry was that there was more heterogeneity among the entry patterns of the actual subjects than was observed among the simulated subjects. These simulations, together with the logit analyses of actual entry behavior strongly suggest that subjects who find themselves in an environment in which they repeatedly play the same set of market entry games do modify their behavior in response to their past experience. There is a stochastic component to their behavior but at the individual level that random component is not a reflection of any strategic thinking, as would be true if they were selecting a mixed strategy. The simulations further suggest that as long as there is a stochastic component to individual behavior, a group of individuals who follow adaptive learning dynamics that incorporate the law of effect and the power law of practice can generate behavioral patterns that display the kind of heterogeneity across symmetrically placed individuals that is consistent with Nash equilibrium at the aggregate level of observation.

## Erev and Rapoport (1998)

Notice that the Erev-Roth model makes no use of any information about the behavior of other subjects when updating propensities to follow various strategies. This implies that if individuals were behaving in the way that the model assumes, then they ought to behave in the same way in response to the same feedback on payoffs they receive, regardless of the character of the information they receive about the play of other people with whom they are playing. Indeed, individual behavior should, according to this model, be the same even if the individuals are completely unaware that they are playing a game, rather than facing an individual decision problem. In Erev and Rapoport (1998) this proposition is put to the test. In this experiment subjects played two market entry games of the same class of games used in the experiments of Rapoport et al. (1998) and Sundali et al. (1995). Subjects participated in groups of 12 members. Each subject participated in only one session. A session consisted of the play of 20 consecutive rounds of one game either $c = 4$ or $c = 8$, followed by 20 consecutive rounds of the second game. In this way, subjects received much more uninterrupted experience with a particular game than in the other experiments just described. A given session was conducted under one of three different information conditions.

There were 12 groups of 12 subjects, with 4 groups assigned to each information condition. In condition one no subject knew the payoff function and no subject knew what the other subjects had done on any round. In this condition, the only feedback the subject received was private information as to his or her payoff at the end of each round. In condition two, no subject knew the payoff function, but at the end of each round the payoffs for that round for each of the two possible actions were publicly announced. In condition three the payoff function for the game being played was common knowledge and at the end of each round the number of subjects who chose to enter and their payoff was publicly announced. If individuals play the market entry game as assumed in the Erev-Roth model then there should not be any systematic difference in play across these three information treatment conditions because the additional information contained in conditions two and three play no role in the description of adaptive learning in the basic Erev-Roth model. In particular, the updating of the reference point for a particular subject depends, in the Erev-Roth formulation described earlier, only on that subject's payoff for the action that subject took and is independent of information about the payoffs that were secured by subjects who took other actions. If, however, an individual who has information about the payoffs secured by actions other than the one he or she has pursued incorporates that information by updating the reference point, that is, by using the highest payoff received by anyone in a given round as the updating criterion, then the behavior observed under condition two will be different from that observed under condition one.

Erev and Rapoport (1998) find strong evidence that behavior is different in condition two from that exhibited under condition one. This shows that in at least some contexts, individual learning is a social phenomenon. The question of just what features of an environment determine whether individual learning is, or is not, sensitive to the experiences of others remains open.

Under conditions one and two subjects do not know the payoff function or the value of $c$. Therefore, each subject faces a pure decision problem. There is no room for strategic thinking under these two conditions. That is, there is no basis for a subject to condition his or her actions on beliefs formed about how other subjects are going to act. If there is adaptive behavior under conditions one and two, that adaptation must operate through payoffs directly, not through beliefs. In condition three, all subjects are aware that they are playing a game and know precisely what game they are playing. Therefore, if individual behavior in such games is mediated by a process of updating beliefs as to how others will behave and then acting on the basis of such beliefs, we might expect behavior in condition three to differ from behavior in condition two. Erev and Rapoport (1998) find no systematic differences between the play of individuals in condition three and condition two. In addition, they show that simulations using a variant of the Erev-Roth model that incorporates the highest payoff earned by the group into each individual's reference point function tracks the data quite well. Because there are a very large number of plausible ways to model the formation of expectations, it is not possible to reject the hypothesis that no such model would track the behavior of individuals in condition three better than the modified Erev-Roth model. Nonetheless, the results do show that simple probabilistic reinforcement learning models can provide a good approximation of aggregate behavior in this class of market entry games.

## CONCLUDING REMARKS

If game theory is viewed as a theory of social interaction and not merely a branch of pure mathematics then it must capture the important regularities of behavior that are observed when games of social interaction are played. In a market entry game all participants are in identical strategic positions. Yet, there are a multiplicity of Nash equilibria, all of which require that the group's membership be divided among different entry choices in a particular way. That without any central direction, people who face identical circumstances would not merely take different actions, but take them in a way that produces the proportions specified by all of the equilibria of that particular market entry game is quite unexpected. As Kahneman (1988) noted, "observing the regularity of behavior in these markets was a bewildering experience – to a psychologist it looked almost like magic" (p. 12).

This "magic" is one common feature of all of the market game experiments reviewed. Inexperienced groups of subjects, even in their earliest plays of a variety of market entry games, generate aggregate distributions of entry rates over market possibilities that conform rather closely to the aggregate distributions implied by the Nash equilibria of those games. A second common feature is that these aggregate distributions are not produced by Nash equilibrium profiles, that is, the individual behavior observed in all of these experiments is at variance with that implied by the best-response conditions of a Nash equilibrium. The fact that the *earliest* plays of such games should produce aggregate patterns so close to those implied by the Nash equilibria of these games cannot be given a game-theoretic explanation. Nor can this fact be accounted for by any other theory of which I am aware.

Less magical is the behavior of a group of subjects who repeatedly play the same market entry game (or the same set of such games). Repeated play allows for implicit coordination. In principle, implicit coordination could achieve the same per capita payoff as could be achieved by actual coordination of decisions through central assignment. This is not observed, even in those experiments where there exist Nash equilibria in pure strategies that yield maximal per capita payoff. That is, the play of these games reflects their noncooperative nature.

With experience, the aggregate distribution of play comes closer to that implied by the Nash equilibria of these games. However, behavior at the individual level does not come closer to that predicted by Nash equilibrium. Instead, as the experiment of Erev and Rapoport (1998) clearly demonstrates, the adaptive pattern of behavior observed in the same class of market entry games as were used in Rapoport (1995), Rapoport et al., (1998), and in Sundali et al. (1995), does not reflect any serious strategic thinking. Indeed, it is not clear that belief formation, as opposed to response to payoff experience, plays any role in the behavior of subjects in their experiment. A probabilistic model of adaptive behavior fits the data quite well. The pattern of behavior exhibited by inexperienced subjects in the Meyer et al. (1992) experiment may also be consistent with probabilistic reinforcement learning in that there was little evidence of long runs where no one switched markets.

One aspect of adaptive behavior that is revealed in these games is the role that information about the choices of other subjects play in shaping the behavior of any given subject. Both in the Erev and Rapoport (1998) study and in the zero turnover markets of Ochs (1990), there is clear evidence that an individual's choice behavior is influenced by information about the choices made by others. In the Erev and Rapoport (1998) experiment this influence can be characterized in terms of the adoption of a reference point that reflects the highest payoff secured by any subject in the group. Yet, the behavior exhibited in the zero turnover markets in the experiment reported in Ochs (1990) displayed a much greater frequency of zero failures and many fewer moves away from equilibrium rates of entry than were exhibited in those experiments conducted by Rapoport et al. (1998). Furthermore, whenever a group departed from zero failure and then returned to equilibrium, the locations selected by particular individuals tended to be different from the locations those individuals had been in when the market was last equilibrated. It is, in my view, more natural to interpret the data from that experiment as reflecting behavior that was supported by beliefs that other players would not change their choices rather than as reflecting purely probabilistic, reinforcement learning.[8]

In summary, a remarkable, but unexplained, feature of behavior in the variety of market entry games reviewed is the relatively high degree of correlation between aggregate entry rate and market capacity that is observed even when subjects have little or no prior experience with the game. This approximation to equilibrium at the aggregate level is improved as subjects acquire experience. The nature of the adaptations individuals make appears to be dependent on structural features of the game in ways that are not yet well understood. This makes market entry games a fascinating test bed for further study of learning processes.

# ENDNOTES

1. Game theorists assume that the rules regarding communication and commitment are crucial. They describe games where communication and the possibility of binding agreement exists as *cooperative games* and those where these possibilities do not exist as *noncooperative games*. The Nash equilibrium concept is assumed to apply only to noncooperative games.
2. It is important to note that if this game were played repeatedly, then each player's set of strategies would expand because a player could then condition his or her action in the $n$th repetition of the game on the history of the sequence of play up through game $n$-1. If the length of the sequence is indefinite, then other Nash equilibria, that produce a sequence of (A,A) repeatedly, are possible. For example, the strategy "Play A until I observe the other player selecting B then play B from that point onward" is a best response to itself in the game composed of an indefinite number of repetitions of the PD game. A strategy profile composed of this strategy for each player is, therefore, a Nash equilibrium of the indefinitely repeated game. As Roth (as quoted in

Kagel & Roth, 1995) noted, "the prisoner's dilemma has motivated literally hundreds of experiments . . . typical experiments . . . reported a level of cooperation (choice of A) . . . that was bounded well away from either zero or 100 percent. However, many experiments which were analyzed as one period games were in fact conducted on various kinds of repeated games" (pp. 26-27).

3. For a review of the experimental literature on ultimatum and other sequential bargaining games see Roth, "Bargaining Experiments," in Kagel and Roth (1995).

4. Economists have a great interest in games with multiple equilibria that may be ordered in terms of per capita payoff because they imply that an economy can get "stuck" in a poor state with self-confirming beliefs although a better equilibrium is possible. For example, low levels of production may be equilibrium phenomena and not merely transitory in an economy that could sustain a higher level of output. Also, high levels of unemployment may be associated with a kind of failure to achieve a market-clearing equilibrium because of the multiplicity of equilibria that exist in some models of decentralized exchange. For a review of related experimental literature on coordination problems see Ochs (1995).

5. The Yellow (3,3,3) Market in Experiment 6 behaved quite differently from the corresponding markets in Experiments 3 and 4. The reason for this is that one subject never chose the same location twice in succession. After the experimental session, this individual identified herself and explained her behavior by saying, "I just wanted to see what would happen." This suggested that the payoff amount may not have been sufficient to motivate subjects to "stay put" after the market cleared and led us to add sessions with higher differences in payoff between success and failure. Except for this one subject, we have no evidence of lack of payoff salience.

6. Comparison of the Red Markets should be limited to the first 16 periods in each session as there was a difference in permutation schemes in these markets subsequent to period 16 and this change may have influenced the ability to coordinate in the Red Market in session 4 after period 16. The lower failure rate observed in the Red Market in session 6, relative to that observed in the Red market in session 4, suggests that permutation of the distribution of the stock made coordination more difficult.

7. The symmetric mixed strategy equilibrium probability of entering is

$$P_e = \{r(c-1)+k-v\}/\{r(n-1)\} \tag{8}$$

and the equilibrium expected number of entrants is:

$$e = [n/(n-1)](c-1)+[n/(n-1)][(k-v)/r] \tag{9}$$

8. A simulation of the zero turnover market that was done by Erev using the Erev-Roth model produces significantly higher failure rates than was actually observed. This lends further credence to the claim that strategic thinking was playing a systematic role in that experiment.

# REFERENCES

Erev, I., & Rapoport, A. (1998). Coordination, "magic," and reinforcement learning in a market entry game. *Games and Economic Behavior, 23*, 146-175.

Erev, I., & Roth, A. (1995). *On the need for low rationality, cognitive game theory: Reinforcement learning in experimental games with unique mixed strategy equilibria.* Unpublished manuscript, The University of Pittsburgh.

Kagel, J., & Roth, A. (eds.). (1995). *The Handbook of experimental economics*, Princeton, NJ: Princeton University Press.

Kahneman, D. (1988). Psychological perspectives in experimental economics. In R. Tietz, W. Albers, & R. Seltin (Eds.), *Bounded rational behavior in experimental games and markets* (pp.11-18). Berlin: Springer-Verlag.

Meyer, D., Van Huyck, R., Battalio, R., & Saving, T. (1992). History's role in coordinating decentralized allocation decisions: Laboratory evidence on repeated binary allocation games. *Journal of Political Economy, 100*, 292-316.

Nash, J. F. Jr. (1950). Equilibrium points in n-person games. *Proceedings of the National Academy of Sciences, 36*, 48-49.

Ochs, J. (1990). The coordination problem in decentralized markets: An experiment. *Quarterly Journal of Economics, 105*, 545-559.

Ochs, J. (1995). Games with unique, mixed strategy equilibria: An experimental study. *Games and Economic Behavior, 10*, 202-217.

Rapoport, A. (1995). Individual strategies in a market-entry game. *Group Decision and Negotiation, 4*, 117-133.

Rapoport, A., Seale, D., Erev, I., & Sundali, J. (1998). Coordination success in market entry games: Tests of equilibrium and adaptive learning models. *Management Science*.

Sundali, J., Rapoport, A., & Seale, D. (1995). Coordination in market entry games with symmetric players. *Organizational Behavior and Human Decision Processes, 64*, 203-218.

# 8     Cheap Talk in a Large Group Coordination Game

**Darryl A. Seale**
*University of Alabama in Huntsville*

**James A. Sundali**
*University of Nevada*

In situations of strategic interdependence, cheap talk is a form of communication or signaling that is costless, nonbinding, nonverifiable, and payoff-irrelevant. In contrast to the recognized value of costly and credible communication (Ackerlof, 1970; Grossman, 1981; Kreps & Sobel, 1992; Milgrom & Roberts, 1982; Spence, 1974), the utility of cheap talk is less apparent.[1] Cheap talk imposes no cost or liability on its sender, therefore, it is possible to use it strategically. The fundamental tension in the study of cheap talk is whether players will use it strategically to transmit information.

Crawford and Sobel (1982) showed theoretically the informational value of cheap talk. They considered the case of sender-receiver games in which one player talks and another then takes a single action. They showed that if there is enough common interest between the two players, and that if the sender can signal something about his or her own type that leads the receiver to change his or her action, and that the subsequent outcomes improve for both players, then a costless signal may have value. For example, a retail store can post the hours that it is open and customers can trust that the store is being truthful because it is in the interest of the store to have customers know when it is open.

Farrell (1987, 1995) showed how cheap talk could help coordinate actions in simple two-person games. Consider Game A in Table 8.1. The pure strategy Nash equilibria are (Up, Left) and (Down, Right); (Up, Left) Pareto dominates (Down, Right). Imagine that Player 1 proposes, (Up, Left). Farrell argues that such a proposition will change both players subjective probabilities that (Up, Left) will be played and hence make it more likely that the players will choose this equilibrium. In this sense cheap talk can help prevent coordination failures, instances in which the most efficient equilibrium is not selected.

**Table 8.1**
**Two Person Coordination Games**

**Game A**

| Player 1 | Left | Right |
|---|---|---|
| | *Player 2* | |
| Up | 3, 3 | 0, 2 |
| Down | 2, 0 | 2, 2 |

**Game B**

| Player 1 | Left | Right |
|---|---|---|
| | *Player 2* | |
| Up | 4, 4 | 0, 3 |
| Down | 3, 0 | 2, 2 |

**Game C**

| Player 1 | Left | Right |
|---|---|---|
| | *Player 2* | |
| Up | 0, 0 | 1, 3 |
| Down | 3, 1 | 0, 0 |

It is presumed that cheap talk is valuable when players have a common incentive to coordinate their actions. Aumann (1990) argued that the existence of a common interest is very sensitive to the payoff structure of the game.

Consider Game B in Table 8.1. As in Game A, the pure strategy Nash equilibria are (Up, Left) and (Down, Right), and (Up, Left) Pareto dominates (Down, Right). It would seem that the players common interest is to coordinate on (Up, Left). But in this game each player has a strict preference over the opponent's strategy choice. In Game B it is unilaterally better for Player 1 (2) if Player 2 (1) moves left (up). Given this, Aumann argues that if Player 1 proposes (Up, Left) it is because he or she wants Player 2 to move left and not because he or she intends to move up. Aumann concludes that in such cases cheap talk will be used strategically and will not be effective in reducing coordination failures.

Several experiments have considered the effect of cheap talk in two-person coordination games. Cooper, DeJong, Forsythe, and Ross (1989) studied the combination of cheap talk and different communication structures in a one-shot, symmetric battle of the sexes game (e.g. Game C in Table 8.1). In these experiments a subject, prior to actual play, could issue a nonbinding statement concerning an intended course of action. Three communication structures were used: one-way one round, two-way one round, and two-way three rounds. This design varied whether one or both players issued signals and whether signals were exchanged only once or on multiple rounds. In the control group (no communication condition) the percentage of outcomes in equilibrium ex post was 48%. With one-way communication, 93% of row (column) players signaled Down (Right), and equilibrium was reached in 95% of all games. With two-way communication, an equilibrium was reached in 55% of all games; an equilibrium was reached in 80% of the games when the joint announcements constituted an equilibrium, but in only 39% of the games when the joint announcements were in disequilibrium. Multiple rounds of communication had a positive but minimal effect on coordination. Cooper et al. (1989) concluded that in the battle of the sexes game, where players' interests are opposed, one-way communication most effectively improves coordination.

Cooper, DeJong, Forsythe, and Ross (1992) conducted another set of experiments that considered the effect of cheap talk in coordination games with multiple, Pareto-ranked equilibria. They showed that two-way communication eliminated coordination failures whereas one-way communication did not. In comparing these results with those from the battle of the sexes experiments Cooper et al. (1992) wrote, "This suggests a general theme that may be worth pursuing: one-way communication is preferred in games of conflict, while two-way communication is needed to resolve coordination problems in games with strategic uncertainty" (p. 766).

Clark, Kay, and Sefton (1997) compared experimentally the effectiveness of two-way communication across different games. Specifically, they compared the effectiveness of cheap talk in games with payoff structures similar to those of Games A and B in Table 8.1. The similarity between these games is that the risk-dominant equilibrium is different from the Pareto-dominant equilibrium. Specifically, in both Games A and B, (Up, Left) is the Pareto-dominant equilibrium whereas (Down, Right) is the risk-dominant equilibrium. What this implies is that it is somewhat "riskier" for the players to reach (Up, Left) than it is to reach (Down, Right). The difference between the two games is that in Game B each player has a strict preference over the opponents' strategy choice.[2] Aumann (1990) suggested that cheap talk will be less effective in Game B where there is a strict preference than in Game A where there is no strict preference. While replicating the results of Cooper et al. (1992), Clark et al. (1997) found that two-way communication was significantly more effective in avoiding coordination failures in Game A than in Game B. They concluded that the results are consistent with Aumann's conjectures that players will use cheap talk in a strategic manner when it is in their interest to do so.

To summarize, in the domain of two-person coordination games the following propositions have support: (a) cheap talk can reduce coordination failures; (b) in games where players have conflicting interests, such as the battle of the sexes, one-way communication is effective in reducing coordination failures possibly because one player has the power to determine the focal point;

(c) in games where there is strategic uncertainty, players will tend toward the risk-dominant equilibrium unless there is bilateral communication that can effectively reduce the uncertainty and introduce trust; and (d) players will use cheap talk strategically if it is in their interest to do so.

This chapter experimentally assesses the effect of cheap talk in a large group coordination game. Whereas the aforementioned research has been limited to two-person coordination games, it is unknown whether these results will generalize beyond this domain of games. In the next section we introduce an $n$-person market entry game proposed by Rapoport (1995). After specifying the solution concepts and reviewing prior experimental research specific to this game, we outline how players could use cheap talk to optimally coordinate their actions. Because there is no prior research to suggest directly how cheap talk will operate in this multiplayer game, we recognize that our research is necessarily exploratory. Although one purpose of this research is to comment on the generalizability of the results from two-person games, our larger intent is to begin a program of research in which we systematically study the effect of communication in large groups. Specifically, we are interested in studying the effects of signal credibility, group size, feedback, and communication structure in large group coordination games.

The chapter is organized as follows. After discussing the market entry game and the potential effects of cheap talk in this environment, we present the design of a new experiment. The results are then presented and compared with prior experiments. We conclude with a discussion and suggestions for future research.

## THE N-PERSON MARKET ENTRY GAME

Inspired by experimental work of Kahneman (1988) and the theoretical work of Selten and Güth (1982) and Gary-Bobo (1990), Rapoport (1995) introduced a variant of the following game to a group of students in a graduate seminar at the University of North Carolina. Consider a group of $n$ symmetric players seated in a room where communication is forbidden. On each trial (period) $t$, $t = 1, 2, \ldots,$ T, a possibly different positive integer $c$ is publicly announced. The parameter $c$ is interpreted as the "known capacity of the market" $(1 \leq c \leq n)$. Once $c$ is announced, each player $i$ $(i \in N)$ must decide privately whether to enter $(\delta_i = 1)$ or stay out $(\delta_i = 0)$ of this market.

Individual payoffs are determined each period by the following formula:

$$H_i(\delta) = \begin{cases} v, & \text{if } \delta_i = 0 \\ k + r(c - e) & \text{if } \delta_i = 1 \end{cases} \quad (1)$$

where $H_i(\delta)$ is Player $i$'s payoff, given the vector of individual decisions for the period, $\delta = (\delta_1, \delta_2, \ldots, \delta_t)$, and $e$ $(0 \leq e \leq n)$ is the number of entrants. The parameters $v$, $k$, and $r$ are real valued constants that remain fixed throughout the game. Like the value of $c$, they are common knowledge.

This noncooperative $n$-person game is an iterated market entry game with symmetric players, complete information, binary actions, and zero entry costs in which the incentive to enter the market decreases linearly in the number of entrants. Each player has a choice between a certain payoff $v$ (which may be positive or negative) and an uncertain payoff which is linear function in the difference $c$ minus $e$.

It is easy to show that when $v = k$ the pure strategy Nash equilibrium prescribes $e = c$ or $e = (c - 1)$ entrants. The solution in pure strategies only prescribes the aggregate number of entrants; it is silent with regard to the prediction of individual decisions. Rapoport, Seale, Erev, and Sundali (1998) characterized the symmetric mixed strategy Nash equilibria. If $v = k + qr$, where $q$ is some integer, there are $nCm_e$ weak pure-strategy equilibria, each with $m_e$ entrants and $n - m_e$ nonentrants. In addition, there are $nCm_e - 1$ weak pure-strategy equilibria each with $m_e - 1$ entrants and $n - m_e + 1$ nonentrants, where $m_e = (rc + k - v) / r$. If $k = v$, the symmetric mixed strategy Nash equilibrium prescribes that each player enters with probability $p_e = (c - 1) / (n - 1)$, where the likelihood of entry increases with the value of $c$. If all players use the symmetric mixed-strategy equilibrium solution, then the expected number of entrants is simply $np_e$.

These equilibria are Pareto-deficient. The number of entrants that maximizes total group payoff ($e_p$) is the largest integer that is smaller or equal to $\lfloor (r(c + 1) + k - v) / 2r \rfloor$. A comparison of the pure strategy equilibria and the Pareto-optimal outcome shows that unless $c$ is very small, when $v = k$, $e_p$ is about half the value of $c$ (Rapoport et al., 1998). A similar analysis shows that if all players use the symmetric mixed-strategy equilibrium, then the Pareto-optimal outcome is reached when players enter with probability $p_p = p_e / 2$. Thus, to maximize total group payoff players must either coordinate on $e_p$, or all choose to enter the market with probability $p_p$.

The difference in payoffs between the pure strategy equilibria and the Pareto-optimal solutions can be substantial. Consider the market entry game with parameters $n = 20$, $r = 2$, $k = 1$, and $v = 1$. If $c = 8$, a pure strategy Nash equilibrium is reached when $e = 7$, or $e = 8$, and total group payoff is 34 or 20, respectively. With the Pareto-optimal number of entrants ($e_p = 4$), the total group payoff increases to 52. As $c$ increases, these results are even more striking. For example, when $c = 17$, equilibrium is achieved when $e = 16$, or $e = 17$, and total group payoff is 52 or 20, respectively. With the Pareto-optimal number of entrants ($e_p = 8$ or 9), total group payoff increases to 164. Clearly, payoffs can increase substantially if players use signals to successfully coordinate entry decisions in the direction of the Pareto-optimal outcomes. Although previous market entry games have shown that subjects do not coordinate actions toward Pareto-optimal outcomes, there is some evidence that signaling or cheap talk may have an effect. Farrell (1987) argued that cheap talk can achieve partial coordination among $n$ potential entrants into a natural monopoly industry where the payoffs are qualitatively like those in the battle of the sexes game. Farrell wrote

> Suppose that players' announced plans would, if actually played, constitute a Nash equilibrium. Then, we suggest, that equilibrium becomes focal. Moreover, if everyone expects such equilibria always to be followed once announced, then cheap talk can help coordinate behavior to produce asymmetric equilibria. (p. 35)

Although the environment in the present game is much more complicated than that of the battle of the sexes, it is not unreasonable to expect that cheap talk may, at times, help in coordinating on optimal outcomes.

To date there is published data from seven groups of 20 subjects, each participating in variants of the $n$-person simultaneous market entry game (Rapoport et al., 1998; Sundali, Rapoport, & Seale, 1995). Although there are substantial differences between these experiments in the payoff parameters, the general findings across the seven groups are quite consistent. First, there is rapid convergence to the pure strategy Nash equilibrium on the aggregate level and no evidence that subjects move away from this equilibrium over time in the direction of Pareto optimality. Second, there are substantial differences in individual strategies that do not diminish with time. Further, neither the pure nor the mixed-strategy equilibrium solution can account for the individual strategies. Finally, there is some evidence that behavior at the group level can be accounted for by an adaptive learning model developed by Roth and Erev (1995). Erev and Rapoport (1998) showed that this model has high descriptive power in Sundali et al. (1995) and Rapoport et al. (1998).

Given the consistent results noticed in past market entry experiments, combined with the opportunity to make and then review signaling decisions introduced in the present experiment, we examine several questions: Can signaling or cheap talk further improve coordination in the n-person simultaneous market entry game? Can signaling be used to move group outcomes in the direction of Pareto optimality? Can the act of making and then reviewing signaling decisions lessen the degree of individual differences noticed in previous experiments? And finally, will subjects signal their intentions honestly, or will they attempt to use signaling as a strategic device?

## DESIGN AND METHOD

Forty subjects, divided into two groups of $n = 20$, participated in the experiment. The subjects consisted of undergraduate and graduate students who responded to an advertisement in the school newspaper. The advertisement promised payoffs contingent on performance, from $5 to $50 for participation in a 2-hour computer controlled experiment in economic decision making.

The experiment was conducted at the Enterprise Room at the University of Arizona. This laboratory contains more than 20 networked microcomputers, separated by both built-in features and wide aisles. As subjects entered the laboratory they were seated at one of the workstations. Subjects were then asked to read a copy of instructions placed beside them. The instructions welcomed the subjects to the lab and informed them that if they made careful decisions they had an opportunity to earn a considerable sum of money, which would be paid to them in cash at the end of the experiment. After all subjects completed reading the instructions, one of the experimenters guided them through an example highlighting the requirements of the task and a sample payoff calculation. After subjects were given an opportunity to ask questions, the experiment began.

Each subject was then given an endowment of 20 francs (1 franc = $0.25) and advised that his or her earnings (losses) accumulated during the experiment would be added to (subtracted from) this endowment. The experiment lasted 50 trials, with each trial consisting of three steps. In the first step, the computer announced the capacity of the market ($c$) for the present trial, and subjects had an opportunity to signal their intention to enter the market, signal their intention to not enter the market, or signal no indication regarding their intention. Signals were costless, nonbinding, and not reported at the individual level. In the second step, after all of the subjects made their signaling decision, the computer displayed the aggregate results of signaling (i.e., the total number of subjects signaling enter, no enter, and no indication). Subjects were then prompted to estimate the total number of entrants for the current trial. A subject was paid $0.10 if the estimate was within 1 of the true number of entrants. In the third and final step of each trial, subjects were asked to make a binary decision – enter or not enter the market – based on the following payoff function:

$$H_i = \begin{cases} 1 & \text{if not enter} \\ 1 + 2(c - e) & \text{if enter} \end{cases} \qquad (2)$$

where $c$ is the capacity of the market and $e$ is the number of entrants in the present trial. Notice that subjects could guarantee themselves a positive payoff by not entering the market. The 50 trials were divided into 5 blocks of 10 trials each. In each block, the value of c was sampled without replacement from the set $\{1, 3, \ldots, 19\}$. To reduce the burden of computation, on each trial subjects were presented with a table that summarized payoffs for all possible number of entrants, given the current value of $c$.

After all subjects made their entry decision, the computer informed them of the number of entrants ($e$) for the trial, and their current and cumulative payoffs. When all subjects reviewed this feedback, the next trial began. Subjects were given paper and pencil to make notes or record any information they deemed important.

At the conclusion of the experiment each subject was asked to fill out a short questionnaire.[3] The subjects were then paid individually in cash, thanked, and dismissed from the lab. Each of the two sessions lasted approximately 2 hours. Average earnings were $20.73 in Group 1, and $24.19 in Group 2. Note that there was no between-group treatment. Conducting two groups provided additional data for individual and group level comparisons.

# RESULTS

The results are organized into three main sections. First, we briefly explore signaling behavior at the group level. Then, we examine the accuracy of subjects' estimates of market entry, given the aggregate signaling results. Finally, we investigate market entry decisions from both group and individual perspectives by characterizing: (a) convergence to equilibrium; (b) comparisons to the three baseline groups of Sundali et al. (1995); (c) the probability of market entry conditional on the relationship between entry signals and equilibrium; (d) the probability of market entry conditional on the subject's estimate of entry decisions relative to the market capacity; and (e) individual differences in entry signals, entry decisions, and consistency in signal-to-entry behavior.

To compare these results with prior research, we have chosen to use the three groups of Sundali et al. (1995) as a baseline. We believe it is appropriate to use these groups as our baseline because the only major differences in the design of these experiments was the introduction of signaling in the present study and that there were 100 trials (10 blocks) in Sundali et al. (1995) but only 50 trials (5 blocks) here. The fewer number of trials was due to the increased demands of the signaling and estimating aspects of the task.

## Signaling Results

Recall that after learning the value of $c$, subjects were required to make one of three signaling decisions. The mean number entry, no-entry, and no-indication signals by market capacity across both groups is shown in the area graph in Fig. 8.1. Entry signals are shown by the darkest shading on the bottom portion of the figure, no-entry signals by the next darkest shading in the middle of the figure, and no-indication signals by the lightly shaded area on the top portion of the figure. Across all values of $c$, subjects signaled their intention to enter the market 69% of the time, not enter 19%, and gave no indication the remaining 12%. This small but consistent number of no-indication signals is noticed for every value of $c$. Further, this figure shows that for every value of $c$ most subjects favored signaling their intention to enter the market. Although there was a positive and significant relationship ($F = 121.5$, p<.0001) between the number of entry signals and $c$, it is clear that for most values of $c$ the number of

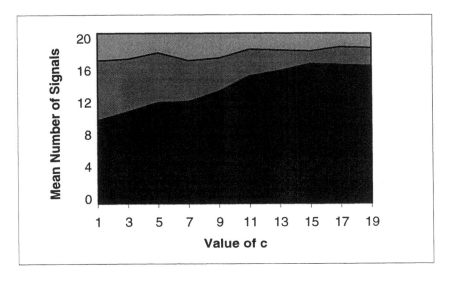

Fig. 8.1. Mean number of signals by type and value of $c$.

entry signals greatly exceeded the market capacity. For example, when the announced market capacity was 1 or 3, the mean number of entry signals was 9.8 and 10.8, respectively.

The number of entry signals by $c$ value and block are reported in Table 8.2. The shaded cells of the table indicate those trials where the number of entry signals are in equilibrium. This occurred on 12 trials; 4 trials in Group 1 and 8 trials in Group 2. Notice that half of these trials were when $c = 17$. Table 8.2 also reports the standard deviation (SD) of the number of entry signals across $c$, and the correlation between the number of entries and $c$ for each of the five blocks of trials. Consistent with the findings presented in Fig. 8.1, the correlations are high and significant. To test for group and block effects, we conducted a group by $c$ by block (2 X 10 X 5) ANOVA with block as a repeated measure. This analysis reveals significant main effects for both group ($F = 9.66$, $p = 0.0126$) and $c$ ($F = 10.89$, $p = 0.0007$), no main effect for block, and no interactions. The interpretation is straightforward: the number of entry signals increases in $c$ and Group 1 reports more entry signals than Group 2. In addition, there is no indication that the amount of entry signals changed over time; throughout the experiment subjects continued to exaggerate their entry signals at most values of $c$.

**Table 8.2**
**Number of Entry Signals by $c$ and Block**

**Group 1**

| $c$ | Block | | | | | *Total* | *Mean* | *Std.* |
|---|---|---|---|---|---|---|---|---|
|  | *1* | *2* | *3* | *4* | *5* | | | |
| 1 | 11 | 9 | 12 | 10 | 11 | 53 | 10.6 | 1.14 |
| 3 | 7 | 14 | 14 | 13 | 13 | 61 | 12.2 | 2.95 |
| 5 | 11 | 13 | 14 | 16 | 13 | 67 | 13.4 | 1.82 |
| 7 | 12 | 14 | 12 | 14 | 16 | 68 | 13.6 | 1.67 |
| 9 | 10 | 14 | 15 | 16 | 15 | 70 | 14.0 | 2.35 |
| 11 | 15 | 17 | 17 | 14 | 18 | 81 | 16.2 | 1.64 |
| 13 | 15 | 18 | 15 | 16 | 18 | 82 | 16.4 | 1.52 |
| 15 | 16 | 17 | 16 | 19 | 15 | 83 | 16.6 | 1.52 |
| 17 | 16 | 17 | 15 | 16 | 15 | 79 | 15.8 | 0.84 |
| 19 | 15 | 16 | 16 | 16 | 16 | 79 | 15.8 | 0.45 |
| Total | 128 | 149 | 146 | 150 | 150 | 723 | 144.6 | |
| Corr. | 0.83 | 0.81 | 0.71 | 0.72 | 0.65 | 0.89 | | |

**Group 2**

| $c$ | Block | | | | | *Total* | *Mean* | *Std.* |
|---|---|---|---|---|---|---|---|---|
|  | *1* | *2* | *3* | *4* | *5* | | | |
| 1 | 9 | 10 | 11 | 8 | 7 | 45 | 9.0 | 1.58 |
| 3 | 10 | 8 | 11 | 8 | 10 | 47 | 9.4 | 1.34 |
| 5 | 15 | 11 | 10 | 7 | 9 | 52 | 10.4 | 2.97 |
| 7 | 12 | 13 | 7 | 11 | 9 | 52 | 10.4 | 2.41 |
| 9 | 13 | 13 | 11 | 13 | 12 | 62 | 12.4 | 0.89 |
| 11 | 9 | 18 | 14 | 13 | 15 | 69 | 13.8 | 3.27 |
| 13 | 12 | 19 | 13 | 16 | 14 | 74 | 14.8 | 2.77 |
| 15 | 14 | 17 | 16 | 16 | 18 | 81 | 16.2 | 1.48 |
| 17 | 17 | 15 | 17 | 18 | 17 | 84 | 16.8 | 1.10 |
| 19 | 18 | 16 | 16 | 16 | 17 | 83 | 16.6 | 0.89 |
| Total | 129 | 140 | 126 | 126 | 128 | 649 | 129.8 | |
| Corr. | 0.71 | 0.79 | 0.80 | 0.94 | 0.94 | 0.98 | | |

## Estimates of Entry

We motivated subjects to accurately estimate the number of market entrants by paying them $0.10 if their estimate was within ±1 of the actual number of

**Table 8.3**
**Number of Accurate Estimates of Entry Decisions by *c* and Block.**

**Group 1**

| | Block | | | | | | | |
|---|---|---|---|---|---|---|---|---|
| c | *1* | *2* | *3* | *4* | *5* | *Total* | *Mean* | *Std.* |
| 1 | 8 | 15 | 15 | 19 | 12 | 69 | 13.8 | 4.09 |
| 3 | 3 | 0 | 14 | 12 | 11 | 40 | 8.0 | 6.12 |
| 5 | 5 | 11 | 5 | 5 | 15 | 41 | 8.2 | 4.60 |
| 7 | 10 | 1 | 13 | 10 | 12 | 46 | 9.2 | 4.76 |
| 9 | 11 | 7 | 7 | 0 | 11 | 36 | 7.2 | 4.49 |
| 11 | 8 | 10 | 0 | 0 | 4 | 22 | 4.4 | 4.56 |
| 13 | 13 | 2 | 1 | 7 | 5 | 28 | 5.6 | 4.77 |
| 15 | 8 | 3 | 7 | 1 | 14 | 33 | 6.6 | 5.03 |
| 17 | 16 | 17 | 8 | 5 | 17 | 63 | 12.6 | 5.68 |
| 19 | 11 | 14 | 20 | 17 | 17 | 79 | 15.8 | 3.42 |
| Total | 93 | 80 | 90 | 76 | 118 | 457 | 91.4 | |

**Group 2**

| | Block | | | | | | | |
|---|---|---|---|---|---|---|---|---|
| c | *1* | *2* | *3* | *4* | *5* | *Total* | *Mean* | *Std.* |
| 1 | 8 | 10 | 11 | 14 | 14 | 57 | 11.4 | 2.61 |
| 3 | 1 | 12 | 9 | 16 | 3 | 41 | 8.2 | 6.22 |
| 5 | 6 | 6 | 2 | 4 | 14 | 32 | 6.4 | 4.56 |
| 7 | 12 | 2 | 13 | 15 | 3 | 45 | 9.0 | 6.04 |
| 9 | 4 | 8 | 2 | 13 | 14 | 41 | 8.2 | 5.31 |
| 11 | 11 | 5 | 4 | 8 | 5 | 33 | 6.6 | 2.88 |
| 13 | 8 | 0 | 6 | 7 | 16 | 37 | 7.4 | 5.73 |
| 15 | 3 | 3 | 17 | 2 | 1 | 26 | 5.2 | 6.65 |
| 17 | 10 | 7 | 12 | 2 | 4 | 35 | 7.0 | 4.12 |
| 19 | 12 | 16 | 16 | 17 | 15 | 76 | 15.2 | 1.92 |
| Total | 75 | 69 | 92 | 98 | 89 | 423 | 84.6 | |

market entrants. The number of subjects that accurately estimated the total number of entrants by value of c and block, and the group mean and SD of these estimates across blocks are reported in Table 8.3. Across both groups, the subjects accurately (within ±1) estimated the number of market entrants approximately 44% of the time. A group by *c* by block (2 X 10 X 5) ANOVA with block as a repeated measure revealed a significant main effect for *c* ($F$ =

7.54, $p = 0.0030$), no main effects for group or block, and no interaction. The main effect for $c$ is easily seen in the mean number of accurate estimates, as more subjects were accurate at estimating the number of market entrants for small or large values of $c$ than for middle values of $c$.

## Market Entry Decisions

The number of market entry decisions by value of $c$ and block is reported in Table 8.4. For each block we report the total number of entries and the correlation between $c$ and $e$. For each value of c we report the total and mean number of entrants, and the SD of entrants. In each block the number of entrants is very highly correlated with $c$, ranging from 0.86 to 0.98. Across both groups the total number of entries per block varies from 94 to 107.

The shaded areas of the table indicate the trials where the number of entrants was in equilibrium. This occurred in 44 of the 100 trials. These trials tend to be distributed at low or high values of $c$, consistent with both previous results and theoretical predictions (Sundali et al., 1995). Of the remaining trials, 28 were within one entrant of the equilibrium prediction, and 12 were within two entrants. To test for differences between groups or over time, we conducted a group by $c$ by block (2 X 10 X 5) ANOVA with block as a repeated measure. This analysis revealed a significant main effect for c ($F = 84.29$, $p = 0.0001$), no main effects for group or block, and no interactions. It is interesting to note the discrepancy between the number of entry *signals* (Table 8.2) and the number of entry *decisions* (Table 8.4). Although signals were greatly exaggerated for low values of $c$, and underspecified for high values of $c$, entry decisions at the group level indicate rather successful levels of coordination.

## Comparisons to Sundali, Rapoport, and Seale

To compare these results with the baseline from Sundali et al. (1995) we proceeded as follows. First, we computed for each group the mean distance from the pure strategy Nash equilibrium by block. These data are displayed in Fig. 8.2. Although the Sundali et al. groups were conducted over 10 blocks of trials, the results are directly comparable to the SS groups through the first 5 blocks. The mean distance from equilibrium ranged form 2.5 to 0.4 across the five groups. In addition, there is no indication that the signaling groups performed better or worse than the baseline groups, or any indication that the mean deviation decreased with experience.

Our second comparison to the baseline study tracks the mean subject payoff by block (see Fig. 8.3). Because the payoff formulas between studies were identical, the results are directly comparable through the first 5 blocks. In equilibrium, [4] the payoff for entry equals the payoff for no entry ($v = 1$). This figure clearly shows that across all groups the mean subject payoff per block approaches $v = 1$. Again, there are no indications that the signaling groups

**Table 8.4**
**Number of Entry Decisions by $c$ and Block**

**Group 1**

| $c$ | Block 1 | 2 | 3 | 4 | 5 | Total | Mean | Std. |
|---|---|---|---|---|---|---|---|---|
| 1 | 0 | 1 | 1 | 1 | 0 | 3 | 0.6 | 0.55 |
| 3 | 2 | 8 | 4 | 4 | 5 | 23 | 4.6 | 2.19 |
| 5 | 5 | 6 | 8 | 3 | 6 | 28 | 5.6 | 1.82 |
| 7 | 7 | 3 | 7 | 6 | 8 | 31 | 6.2 | 1.92 |
| 9 | 11 | 12 | 9 | 14 | 8 | 54 | 10.8 | 2.39 |
| 11 | 12 | 11 | 7 | 18 | 9 | 57 | 11.4 | 4.16 |
| 13 | 13 | 9 | 17 | 15 | 11 | 65 | 13.0 | 3.16 |
| 15 | 12 | 17 | 13 | 11 | 16 | 69 | 13.8 | 2.59 |
| 17 | 17 | 17 | 15 | 15 | 17 | 81 | 16.2 | 1.10 |
| 19 | 19 | 19 | 18 | 18 | 19 | 93 | 18.6 | 0.55 |
| Total | 98 | 103 | 99 | 105 | 99 | 504 | 100.8 | |
| Corr. | 0.98 | 0.89 | 0.92 | 0.86 | 0.97 | 0.99 | | |

**Group 2**

| $c$ | Block 1 | 2 | 3 | 4 | 5 | Total | Mean | Std. |
|---|---|---|---|---|---|---|---|---|
| 1 | 2 | 1 | 3 | 1 | 1 | 8 | 1.6 | 0.89 |
| 3 | 2 | 3 | 5 | 3 | 1 | 14 | 2.8 | 1.48 |
| 5 | 6 | 4 | 8 | 3 | 5 | 26 | 5.2 | 1.92 |
| 7 | 8 | 10 | 8 | 7 | 9 | 42 | 8.4 | 1.14 |
| 9 | 13 | 11 | 7 | 9 | 10 | 50 | 10.0 | 2.24 |
| 11 | 12 | 10 | 14 | 10 | 9 | 55 | 11.0 | 2.00 |
| 13 | 12 | 8 | 12 | 11 | 13 | 56 | 11.2 | 1.92 |
| 15 | 10 | 13 | 15 | 18 | 12 | 68 | 13.6 | 3.05 |
| 17 | 19 | 15 | 16 | 19 | 15 | 84 | 16.8 | 2.05 |
| 19 | 18 | 19 | 19 | 19 | 19 | 94 | 18.8 | 0.45 |
| Total | 102 | 94 | 107 | 100 | 94 | 497 | 99.4 | |
| Corr. | 0.92 | 0.93 | 0.96 | 0.98 | 0.97 | 0.99 | | |

performed better or worse than the baseline groups, or any indications that the mean subject payoff changed over time. In addition, combining the results presented in Figs. 8.2 and 8.3 shows that there was no movement toward Pareto-optimal outcomes; such a movement would result in an increase in the mean distance measure (Fig. 8.2) and mean subject payoff (Fig. 8.3).

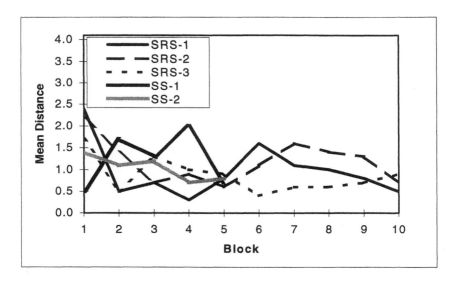

Fig. 8.2. Mean distance from equilibrium by block.

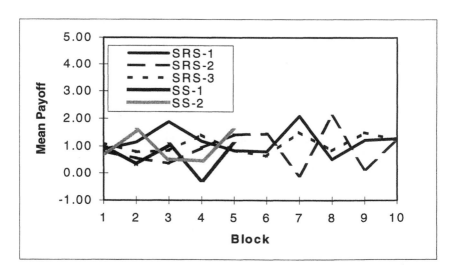

Fig. 8.3. Mean payoff by block.

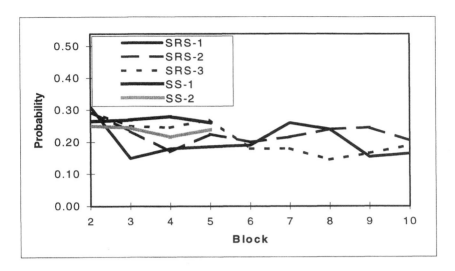

Fig. 8.4. Probability of alternation by block.

Our third comparison (see Fig. 8.4) to the baseline study tracks the probability of alternation by block. Using the method described by Rapoport (1995), an alternation is simply a change in a subjects' entry decision, for a given value of c, from one block to the next. Sundali et al. (1995) reported the probability that subjects altered their decisions from block 1 to block 2 at approximately 30%. From blocks 2 through 10 this probability averaged approximately 20%. Inspection of Fig. 8.4 reveals that the amount of alternation for the two signaling groups is well within this range. Across both groups the probability of alternation averaged 25%, reaching a high of 28% (Group 1, block 4) and a low of 22% (Group 2, block 4).

## Conditional Entry Decisions

The comparisons just discussed suggest that signaling had little or no discernible impact on group behavior. To further investigate the effects, if any, of signaling on market entry decisions, we considered two additional analyses. First, we examined the frequency of entry conditional on the relationship between the number of entry signals to equilibrium. Then, we examined the frequency of entry conditional on the relationship between the subject's estimate of the total number of entrants and market capacity. Table 8.5 shows the number of entry and no entry decisions conditional on the type of entry signal, and conditional on

**Table 8.5**

**Number of Entry and No Entry Decisions Conditional on Type of Entry Signal and Combined Entry Signals to Equilibrium**

| Decision \| Signal | Se < Eq. | Se = Eq. | Se > Eq. | Total |
|---|---|---|---|---|
| | **Entry Signals (Se) to Equilibrium** | | | |
| Entry \| entry signal | 188 | 145 | 489 | 822 |
| Entry \| no entry signal | 21 | 12 | 54 | 87 |
| Entry \| no signal | 19 | 18 | 55 | 92 |
| No entry \| entry signal | 10 | 34 | 506 | 550 |
| No entry \| no entry signal | 17 | 19 | 266 | 302 |
| No entry \| no signal | 5 | 12 | 130 | 147 |
| Total | 260 | 240 | 1500 | 2000 |

the combined entry signals to equilibrium. The rows of the table correspond to the six possible combinations of a binary entry decision and a ternary signaling decision. The columns coincide with the three possible outcomes between combined entry signals (Se) and the pure strategy Nash equilibrium; that is, the combined signals might be less than the equilibrium (Se < Eq), equal to equilibrium (Se = Eq), or greater than equilibrium (Se > Eq). As expected, entries in the table equal 2,000 (2 groups X 20 subjects X 50 trials). Consistent with our previous findings, subjects signaled their intention to enter the market on 1,372 (69%) occasions, not enter on 389 (19%) occasions and gave no indication on the remaining 239 (12%) times. Dividing the column totals by 20 (number of subjects per group) yields the number of trials where entry signals were less than, equal to, or greater than equilibrium. Entry signals were less than the equilibrium in 13 trials, in equilibrium in 12 trials, and exceeded the equilibrium in 75 trials.

Because the data in Table 8.5 are aggregated across subjects, we cannot determine reliably if the probability of entering the market given one's signal is independent of the combined entry signals to equilibrium outcome. To address the question we proceeded as follows. For each subject we computed the probability of entry by signal by the combined entry signals to equilibrium outcome. This produced a contingency table, similar to Table 8.5, for each subject. To facilitate interpretation and presentation, the individual contingency tables are not presented; the aggregate results are presented graphically in Fig. 8.5 and described here. The probability of entry given a signal to enter the market – labeled as P($e|Se$) – is depicted by the solid dark line; the probability of

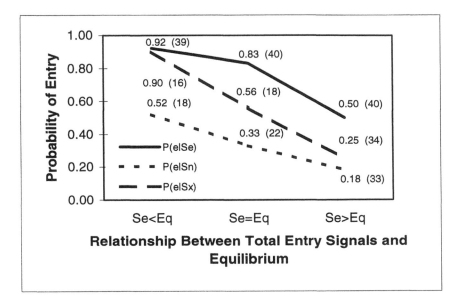

Fig. 8.5. Probability of entry given signal type – conditional on the relationship between total entry signal and $c$.

entry given a signal to not enter – labeled as P($e$|S$n$) – is illustrated by the long dashed line; and the probability of entry given a no indication signal – labeled as P($e$|S$x$) – is captured by the short dashed line. The numbers above each line report the aggregate probability, whereas the numbers in parentheses indicate the number of observations (subject data) used to compute the probabilities. A horizontal line would suggest that entry decisions, given entry signals, are not sensitive to the entry signals to equilibrium outcome; a line with a negative slope would indicate that the entry signals to equilibrium outcome has an expected effect on subsequent behavior. Notice that P($e$|S$e$) declines from 0.92 when S$e$ is less than the equilibrium number of entrants, to 0.83 when S$e$ is in equilibrium, and to 0.50 when S$e$ is greater than the equilibrium number of entrants. A paired $t$-test confirms that the probability of entry, conditional on entry signal, is greater when the number of entry signals is less than equilibrium, than when the number of entry signals equals equilibrium ($p = 0.0108$). Similarly, the probability of entry, given a signal to enter, is less when the number of entry signals exceed the equilibrium, than when the number of signals are in equilibrium ($p = 0.0000$). Comparable findings are noted for P($e$|S$n$), and P($e$|S$x$). In each case as the total number of entry signals

Table 8.6
**Number of Entry and No Entry Decisions Conditional on Relationship
Between Subject's Estimate of Entrants and Market Capacity.**

|  | Subject's Estimate vs. Market Capacity | | | |
|---|---|---|---|---|
| _Decision_ | _Est. < c_ | _Est. = c_ | _Est. > c_ | _Total_ |
| Entry | 428 | 348 | 225 | 1001 |
| No entry | 134 | 228 | 637 | 999 |
| Total | 562 | 576 | 862 | 2000 |
| Entry Probability | 0.76 | 0.60 | 0.26 | 0.50 |

approaches and then exceeds equilibrium, the probability of entry declines for each type of entry signal.[5]

Figure 8.5 highlights an additional comparison – the probability of entry given the relationship between total entry signals and equilibrium, conditional on a subject's type of entry signal. In other words, for example, given that $Se$ is less than the equilibrium, we are interested in comparing the probability of entry by the type of signal given. This answers the question "Are those that signal entry more likely to enter than those who either give no indication or signal no entry?" When $Se$ is less than the equilibrium number of entrants, subjects who signaled entry were more likely to enter ($p = 0.92$) than those who gave no indication ($p = 0.90$), or those who signaled no entry ($p = 0.52$). Similar findings are noted for $Se = $ Eq, and $Se > $ Eq. In each case subjects who signaled their intention to enter were more likely to enter than those who either gave no indication or signaled no entry. Taken together, Table 8.5 and Fig. 8.5, argue that signaling did have an impact on subsequent decision behavior. Although signaling did not move the group toward Pareto-optimal outcomes, reduce block-to-block alternations, or otherwise improve coordination, we have some evidence that signaling, when considered in relationship to equilibrium, was an important factor in entry/no-entry decisions.

In our final analysis of conditional entry decisions, we examined the frequency of entry and no-entry decisions, conditional on the relationship between estimated entrants and market capacity. That is, are subjects more (less) likely to enter when the value of $c$ is greater (less) that their estimate of the number of entrants. These data are reported in Table 8.6. The first column of the table indicates the type of entry decision; the next three columns report the frequencies of estimates that are less than, equal to, or greater than the value of $c$. The probability of entry, reported on the bottom row of the table, declines from 0.76 when subjects' estimates of entrants are less than $c$ (Est. $< c$), to 0.60 when estimates are equal to $c$ (Est. $= c$), to 0.26 when estimates exceed $c$ (Est. $> c$). Clearly, subjects entry decisions are fairly consistent with their estimates of the relationship between the number of entrants and value of $c$.

## Individual Differences

Our final discussion of results provides an analysis of individual subject data. To begin, we developed a profile for each subject that captures both signaling and entry behavior. These profiles are shown as individual bar charts on Figs. 8.6 to 8.9. Entry signals for each value of $c$ are shown as the lightly shaded bars. Entry decisions are depicted by the darker bars. The horizontal axis shows the values of $c$, whereas the vertical axis reports the frequency (0 to 5).

The header row at the top of each chart shows the subject number, followed by the number of individual entry signals (es), entry decisions (ed), and a measure of signal-to-decision consistency (sc). The average subject signaled entry 34 times, no entry 10 times, and gave no indication 6 times. The number of enter signals ranged from a low of 10 (S18) to a high of 49 (S16). One fourth of the subjects signaled enter in at least 88% of the trials, whereas half of the subjects signaled enter in at least 74% of the trials. Only six subjects signaled enter in less than 50% of the trials. Taken together, these findings clearly indicate that most subjects engaged in exaggerated signaling behavior.

Consonant with the baseline study, individual differences in entry decisions were conspicuous. Total entry decisions varied from 2 (S12) to 47 (S28) with $M = 25.03$ and $SD = 9.37$. The correlation between the total number of entry decisions and subject payoff was low and not statistically significant ($r = 0.04$, $p > 0.05$), indicating that subjects who entered frequently were neither more nor less likely to increase their payoffs. Patterns in these individual decision profiles yield no evidence that subjects used deterministic decision policies (i.e., cutoff policies) or mixed their strategies in approximate proportions as prescribed by the symmetric mixed strategy Nash equilibrium. A closer inspection of some decision profiles (e.g., S10, S13, S30) defy straightforward explanations.

SC reported in the header row above each individual plot, captures the percentage of trials where the subject's entry signal and entry decision were in agreement. A no-indication signal was considered in agreement with either entry decision. Signal-to-decision consistency averaged 68% ($SD = 0.18$), with a range from 16% (S12) to 96% (S28, S38, S15, S29). One fourth of the subjects were consistent in at least 80% of the trials, whereas half of the subjects were consistent in at least 68% of the trials. Five subjects were consistent in less than 50% of the trials. At first glance, these consistency measures appear rather high and at odds with the previous findings reporting exaggerated signaling yet general convergence to the equilibrium in the number of entry decisions. The reader is reminded that completely random play would, on average, yield consistency in the 50% range, and 12% of the time subjects gave no indication

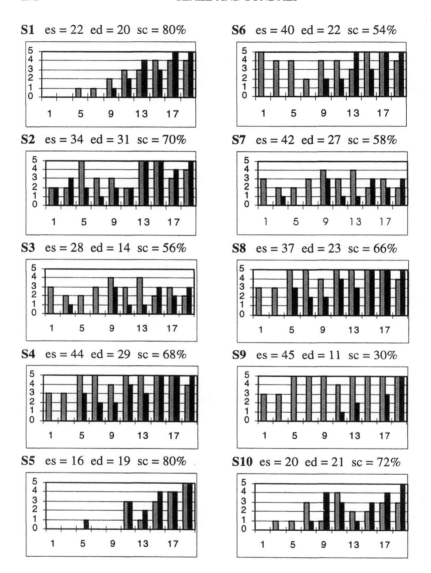

Fig. 8.6. Individual decision policies – subjects 1 to 10.

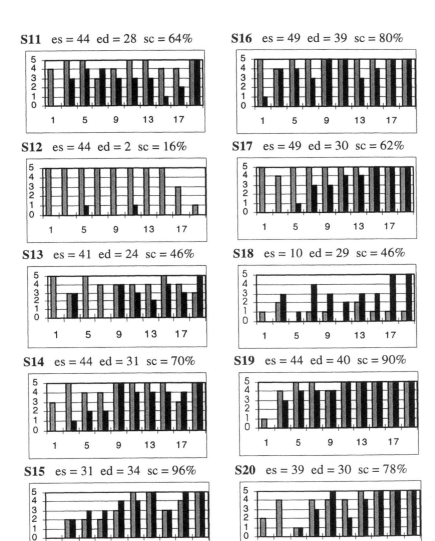

Fig. 8.7. Individual decision policies – subjects 11 to 20.

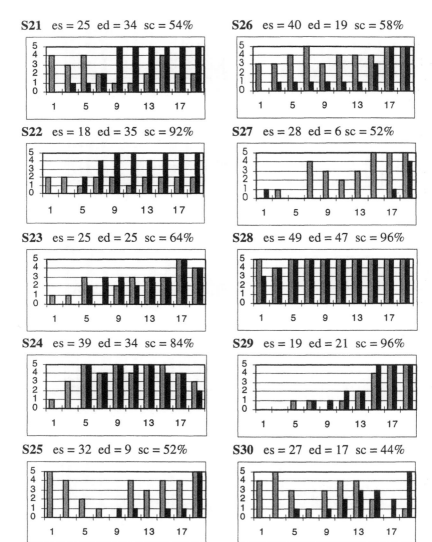

Fig. 8.8. Individual decision policies – subjects 21 to 30.

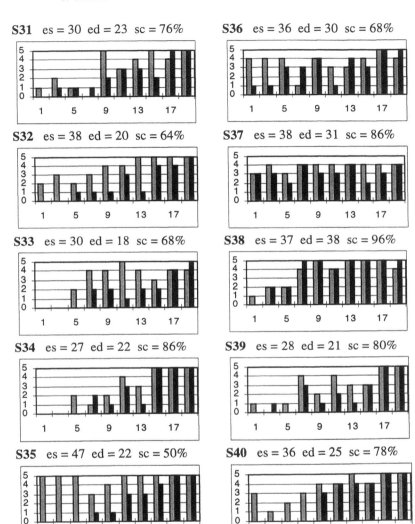

Fig. 8.9. Individual decision policies – subjects 31 to 40.

of their intention to the market. By definition, any decision following a no-indication signal was considered consistent.

## DISCUSSION

This chapter's contribution to the study of coordination in large groups is through examining the effects of costless, nonbinding signals in a simultaneous market entry game. We set out to address four principal questions. First, could this type of signaling further improve coordination? Although cheap talk has been shown to have value in simpler, two-person coordination games, our findings suggest that under the present experimental conditions it is of little or no value. Perhaps the main reason why signaling failed to improve coordination was the already high levels of coordination success achieved in previous studies. In the three other 20-person market entry groups used for comparison, and the two signaling groups reported in the present study, the correlations between $c$ and $e$, by block, ranged from 0.77 to 0.99. The average across all blocks was 0.92. Clearly, there was little room for much improvement.

The second question was whether or not cheap talk could be effective in moving group outcomes toward Pareto-optimal outcomes. Our results, which show no evidence of movement in this direction, deserve further discussion. Given that the total group payoff at the Pareto-optimal outcome is substantially more than total group payoff at the pure strategy Nash equilibria, a group has a strong incentive to coordinate actions. Efficient coordination requires that the there are approximately $c / 2$ entrants on each trial. Because binding agreements are not allowed, the group must tacitly agree on how to distribute the payoffs from such coordinated actions. There are many feasible arrangements. For example, some players might be the designated entrants when $c$ is large and others when $c$ is small, or, the group may attempt to distribute the rewards equally, which would require an entry rotation scheme.

Given the limited nature of the signals allowed in the present experiments, and the large size of the groups, tacit coordination on a Pareto outcome may have proved practically impossible for several reasons. First, it is very likely that subjects did not even recognize the existence of the Pareto-optimal outcome. Second, even if the existence of the Pareto-optimal outcome was known, there is no apparent mechanism available to share or rotate the rewards among group members. For the group as a whole to benefit, individuals must be willing to forego a high payoff in one round by not entering for their turn at a similar high payoff in another round. They must develop a tacit trust among the other group members using nonbinding signals, somehow agreeing in principal to share the rewards from underentry. Not only were the signals nonbinding, but there was no way to build or evaluate individual reputations. Additionally, given the level of signal exaggeration noticed in both groups, subjects learned quickly that, as a group, credibility of signal was at issue.

The third question we addressed concerned the degree of individual differences noted in previous studies. Specifically, we wondered whether or not giving subjects an opportunity to make and then review aggregate signal results might lessen the degree of individual differences. The individual data presented here confirm that signaling did little to lessen between-subject differences. As reported in previous market entry games, subjects' behavior varied not only in the frequency of entry, but in consistency and attraction for various market capacities. With the introduction of signaling, differences are also noticed in the nature and amount of signaling, accuracy in estimating the number of entrants, as well as the degree to which one's entry decision coincided with one's signaled intention. Thus, signaling did not seem to lower the degree of individual differences; it gave subjects additional dimensions on which to vary.

The final question we considered was whether subjects would signal honestly, or attempt to use signaling as a strategic device. Given that subjects failed to enter the market on 44% of the trials where they signaled their intention to do so, we concluded that a strong majority of subjects were signaling strategically. However, this is only part of the story. We also indicated that this behavior did not diminish with time, and although entry signaling was clearly exaggerated, subjects were able to make fairly accurate estimates of the number of entrants. In fact, these estimates indicated that, on average, subjects expected overentry on small values of $c$, and underentry on large values of $c$. Both of these expectations were supported in actual play.

Although signaling persisted at exaggerated levels throughout the course of the experiment, failed to move the group toward Pareto-optimal outcomes, and did little to reduce individual differences, we offered some evidence that it was not ignored. Combined signals, when considered in relationship to equilibrium, impacted subsequent decision behavior in an expected manner. When combined signals were less than the equilibrium, the probability of entry increased; when combined signals were greater than the equilibrium, the probability of entry declined. We also found that although signals were both "cheap" and anonymous, subjects were more likely than not to follow through with their signaled intention.

Although the apparent conclusion to draw from these results is that, in contrast to some of the findings in the domain of two-person coordination games, cheap talk is not an effective coordination mechanism in this game, we hesitate to draw this conclusion for several reasons. First, the studies of Cooper et al. (1989, 1992) showed that depending on the nature of the strategic interdependence, some communication structures are more effective than others at improving coordination. Specifically, their research suggested that as the level of strategic uncertainty increased so too must the complexity of the communication structure. Because our design employed a very basic communication structure in a game with much strategic uncertainty, it is possible that a more complex communication mechanism would enhance coordination in this game. Secondly, Aumann's (1990) argument and the results of Clark et al. (1997) suggest the effectiveness of cheap talk is diminished when a player has a strict preference over the opponent's strategy choice.

One possible explanation for subjects' persistence in signaling entry is that subjects who enter have a preference that other subjects do not enter. Thus, signaling entry is an attempt to reduce the probability that other entry will occur. But, if a subject does not enter then he or she is indifferent over the opponents' strategy choice. This suggests that a subject does not have a strict preference over the opponents' strategy choice (similar to Game A in Fig. 8.1). Why then does a subject who does not intend to enter signal enter? Obviously an entry signal imposes no cost, and the marginal gain is the possible reduction in the probability of other entry. But, collectively these individual actions impose a significant cost on group coordination and thus create a group coordination dilemma. Further investigation is necessary to determine if it is possible to reduce the high level of entry signaling.

There are several issues that subsequent experimental designs should consider and several directions that subsequent research could take. First, it would seem necessary to make subjects cognizant of the Pareto-optimal outcome in order for cheap talk to have a chance at improving coordination. This could be accomplished by simply reporting, either before or after the entry decision, the total group payoff contingent on $c$ and $e$. Second, one might also consider reporting the consistency in signaling and entry decisions at the individual level. This would allow for reputation building and evaluation among individual subjects. A decision maker could then consider not only the number of signaled entries, but the credibility of each signal as well. Although this might be cognitively demanding, the computer could be used to simplify presentation and record keeping. One direction subsequent research could take is to consider the effect of different communication structures. For example, it would be interesting to set the number of subjects allowed to signal each period equal to the market capacity. This would significantly reduce the amount of entry signals and also increase the possibility that the number of entry signals is a focal point. Another direction for future research would be to vary group size. A reduction in the group size from $n = 20$, to say, $n = 10$ may significantly reduce the amount of strategic uncertainty in the game and enhance the level coordination.

Another direction for this research would be to add credibility to the signals by imposing a cost. A subject could be charged for sending a signal, or for a failure to follow through on a signaled intention. Although this could be easily accommodated experimentally, if a cost is imposed then signals may no longer simply be cheap talk. Further theoretical work is necessary to examine this issue.

Finally, some of the results reported should be interpreted with caution. First, because of the size of the groups and the usual budgetary concerns, we were limited to running two 20-person groups. Statistical tests indicated that although there were between group differences in signaling behavior, there were no important differences in estimates of entry, or, more importantly, entry behavior. Thus, although signaling may have differed between groups, this had no effect on subsequent outcomes. In some sense this is added testimony to the power of the equilibrium predictions. Finally, we caution the reader in generalizing these signaling results to other coordination games or situations. We believe that the structure of the game matters a great deal. Simple changes in group size, payoff parameters, asymmetry, or order of play may result in entirely different findings.

## ACKNOWLEDGMENTS

This work was supported in part by the National Science Foundation grant No. SPR 9512724 "Coordination and Learning in Market Entry Games," awarded to Amnon Rapoport and Ken Koput. The authors would like to especially thank Amnon Rapoport for his untiring guidance and invaluable mentoring on this and many other research projects. Amnon has been an inspiration for us, showing us not only how to do scholarly research, but how to enjoy it as well.

## ENDNOTES

1. The research presented here is part of a continuing series of experimental studies on coordination in large groups (Erev & Rapoport, 1998; Rapoport, 1995; Rapoport, Seale, & Winter, 1997; Rapoport, Seale, Erev, & Sundali, 1998; Sundali, Rapoport, & Seale, 1995). This chapter specifically considers the effect of cheap talk in a large group coordination game. To our knowledge there in no research, either theoretical or experimental, that has directly considered the effect of cheap talk in the domain of large groups. All of the research on cheap talk has been limited to two-person coordination games.
2. In 2 x 2 games with two strong Nash equilibria, the pure strategy equilibrium with the greater Nash product is risk-dominant (Harsanyi & Selten, 1988; Straub, 1995). The Nash product of an equilibrium is the opportunity costs of each player unilaterally deviating from that equilibrium. For example, in Game A of Figure 1 the Nash product of Up/Left is $1 = (a_{11}-a_{21}) * (b_{11}-b_{12})$ and the Nash product of Down/Right is $4 = (a_{22}-a_{12}) * (b_{22}-b_{21})$.
3. Due to space limitations, questionnaire results, which were generally consistent with actual play, are not reported. A complete description of the questionnaire and results are available from the first author.
4. This holds for the mixed strategy equilibrium as well.
5. Additional statistical tests were not conducted as the number of observations used to compute individual probabilities were, in many cases, small.

## REFERENCES

Ackerlof, G. (1970). The market for lemons: Quality uncertainty and the market mechanism. *Quarterly Journal of Economics, 84*, 488-500.
Aumann, R. (1990). Nash equilibria are not self enforcing. In J. J. Gabszewicz, J. F. Richard, and L. Wolsey (Eds.), *Economic decision making: Games, econometrics and*

*optimisation (contributions in honour of Jacques Dreze)* (pp. 201-206). Amsterdam: Elsevier.

Clark, K., Kay, S., & Sefton, M. (1997). *When are Nash equilibria self enforcing? An experimental analysis.* Working Paper Series #97-04, University of Iowa, Iowa City, Iowa.

Cooper, R., DeJong, D., Forsythe, R., & Ross, T. (1989). Communication in the battle of the sexes: Some experimental results. *Rand Journal of Economics, 20,* 568-587.

Cooper, R., DeJong, D., Forsythe, R., & Ross, T. (1992). Communication in coordination games. *Quarterly Journal of Economics, 53,* 739-771.

Crawford, V., & Sobel, J. (1982). Strategic information transmission. *Econometrica, 50,* 1431-1451.

Erev, I., & Rapoport, A. (1998). Coordination, "magic," and reinforcement learning in a market entry game. *Games and Economic Behavior, 23,* 146-175.

Farrell, J. (1987). Cheap talk, coordination, and entry. *Rand Journal of Economics, 18,* 34-39.

Farrell, J. (1995). Talk is cheap. *American Economic Review, 85,* 186-190.

Gary-Bobo, R. (1990). On the existence of equilibrium points in a class of asymmetric market entry games. *Games and Economic Behavior, 2,* 239-246.

Grossman, S. (1981). The role of warranties and private disclosure about product quality. *Journal of Law and Economics, 24,* 461-483.

Harsanyi, J. C., & Selten, R. (1988). *A general theory of equilibrium selection in games.* Cambridge, MA: MIT Press.

Kahneman, D. (1988). Experimental economics: A psychological perspective. In R. Tietz, W. Albers, & R. Selten (Eds.), *Bounded rational behavior in experimental games and markets* (pp. 11-18). Berlin: Springer-Verlag.

Kreps, D., & Sobel, J. (1992). Signaling. In R. Aumann & S. Hart (Eds.) *Handbook of game theory with economic applications* (pp. 850-866). New York: Elsevier.

Milgrom, P., & Roberts, J. (1982). Limit pricing and entry under incomplete information. *Econometrica, 50,* 443-459.

Rapoport, A. (1995). Individual strategies in a market-entry game. *Group Decision and Negotiation, 4,* 117-133.

Rapoport, A., Seale, D., Erev, I., & Sundali, J. (1998). Equilibrium play in large group market entry games. *Management Science, 44,* 119-141.

Rapoport, A., Seale, D., Winter, E. (1997). *Coordination and learning behavior in large groups with asymmetric players.* Manuscript submitted for publication.

Roth, A., & Erev I. (1995). *On the need for low rationality, cognitive game theory: Reinforcement learning in experimental games with unique, mixed strategy equilibria.* Working Paper, University of Pittsburgh.

Selten, R., & Güth, W. (1982). Equilibrium point selection in a class of market entry games. In M. Diestler, E. Furst, & G. Schwadiauer (Eds.), *Games, economic dynamics, time series analysis* (pp. 101-116). Wien: Physica-Verlag.

Spence, A. M. (1974). *Market signaling.* Cambridge, MA: Harvard University Press.

Straub, P. (1995). Risk dominance and coordination failure in static games. *Quarterly Review of Economics and Finance, 35,* 339-363.

Sundali, J., Rapoport, A., & Seale, D. (1995). Coordination in market entry games with symmetric players. *Organizational Behavior And Human Decision Processes, 64,* 203-218.

# Part IV

## Bargaining, Fairness and Equity

# 9     Strong and Weak Equity Effects – Evidence, Significance, and Origins

## Gary E. Bolton
*Penn State University*

Among social scientists, the arguments and counterarguments that make up debates about fairness tend to reflect underlying attitudes toward altruism. Roughly, those who see behavior as basically self-interested tend to think that fairness is of little consequence, whereas those who are less certain of the self-interest paradigm, see in fairness an alternative motive for some behavior. The experiments I have been involved with over the past several years have led me to a different view. I suspect that people are basically self-interested (although I am open to being convinced otherwise), but I also see evidence that fairness is an important influence.

My position is practically untenable if analyzed using the definition of self-interest that dominates much of social science, particularly the field of economics. But if instead, we adopt the broader notion of self-interest used by biologists, then I think my position is on firm ground. To keep things straight I refer to the economic definition, self-interest in the sense of one's own consumption, as *narrow self-interest*. I refer to the definition used by biologists as *evolutionary self-interest*. The latter refers to the propagation of one's own genetic identity. Narrow self-interest no doubt plays a role in fulfilling evolutionary self-interest, but just as obviously other factors are involved. In this sense, evolutionary self-interest is the broader concept.

All the experiments I describe involve elementary bargaining games or closely related offshoots. Their appeal as research vehicles is their simplicity. Specifically, if we assume that people are motivated by narrow self-interest, then the behavior we expect to see in these games is very clear. The striking fact is that actual behavior differs substantially and systematically from that predicted. Because the ideas involved are so basic to so much thinking, figuring out why the theory fails for these simple laboratory games could provide pivotal insight into a broad spectrum of behavior.

Most of the experiments I describe involve testing one explanation for the data against another. Much of what I believe has been learned so far is

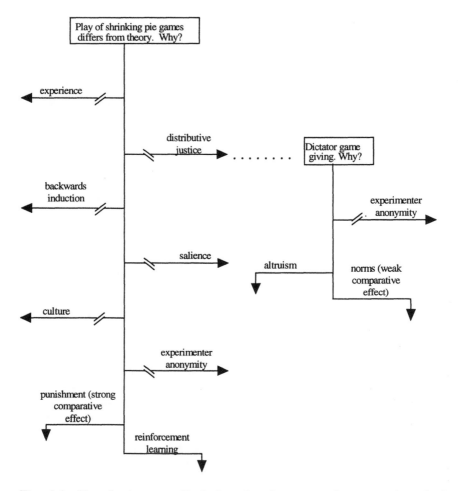

Fig. 9.1. Hypothesis trees. Each branch of a tree refers to a hypothesis addressing the question at the base. Cut branches refer to hypotheses for which there is strong evidence against.

summarized by the hypothesis trees displayed in Fig. 9.1. The figure also functions as an outline of this chapter. At the base of each tree is a question; each a version of "why does the theory fail?" customized to a specific family of games. Each tree branch represents a hypothesis that addresses the question at the tree base. Cut branches represent hypotheses for which there is strong evidence against. I emphasize that failure and success here are relative in nature.

None of the hypotheses can account for the behavior of each and every individual. Successful hypotheses are those that dominate in head-to-head tests on the data. Over time, new challengers have replaced the failures, and so over time, the trees have grown. The dotted line in the diagram indicates that the development of the smaller tree owes much to questions arising from the larger.

My work, much of it done with colleagues, represents only a small portion of either tree. But the work is representative in the sense that it addresses a variety of hypotheses arising at various stages in the trees' development. My colleagues and I owe much to the many people who have worked independently on various tree branches. I describe some of this work by way of placing our own in context, although this chapter is by no means a comprehensive survey (for that, see Roth, 1995). I am keenly aware that my views and interpretations of the progress are not shared by all. But then debate is the clearest symptom of the need for the work. To me, the most encouraging thing about experiments is the sense that the debate is progressing: there are hypotheses that were once forcefully put forward that no one with a knowledge of the evidence supports anymore. At one time or another the data has forced almost everyone, including myself, to modify their views. The new views tend to be more sophisticated and more encompassing, meaning the new debates and new experiments probe deeper. Whether this cycle of test and revision will ultimately converge on a generally accepted understanding remains to be seen. I think the process exhibits signs that it will converge – and soon.

The interpretation of the data that I defend here is that fairness mitigates the pursuit of narrow self-interest through two effects; I call these effects strong and weak equity to emphasize that the former has a relatively larger influence than does the latter. Roughly, the *strong effect* refers to a propensity to resist being treated unfairly. The *weak effect* refers to a propensity to treat others fairly. The evidence for these effects is not easily reconciled with altruism. A more promising line of explanation involves evolutionary self-interest. Some first steps in the direction of formalizing this argument have already been taken. I elaborate later, but the bare bones of it are this: The biological success of an individual is closely tied to group success. Appeals to mutual principles such as fairness allow the group to resolve (at least sometimes) conflicts in an efficient – and strategically sound – manner.

I think equity effects may be applicable to understanding various phenomena, including field negotiations. An appeal to fairness is an appeal to principle, and some field evidence suggests that establishing mutually agreeable principles is a key part of the negotiating process (e.g. Sebenius, 1984). By studying how fairness influences play in simple lab games, we may gain insight into how principle influences bargaining in the field. I try to give a sense of what the practical implications of these arguments might be by sketching an interpretation of the dispute cost hypothesis, often discussed in the field literature on bargaining.

# SHRINKING PIE BARGAINING GAMES: THE STRONG EQUITY EFFECT

The chronology of research on shrinking pie games provides an example of how experiments can clarify and resolve issues. Shrinking pie games usually involve two bargainers, a first mover and a second mover. Bargainers try to reach agreement on how to divide a pie, which is usually a fixed sum of money. The game is played in stages. In stage 1, the first mover proposes a division. If the second mover accepts, the pie is split accordingly; if the second mover rejects, the game goes to stage 2 and is played the same way as stage 1, but now with proposer and responder roles reversed. The game continues in this fashion until either an agreement is reached, or the last stage ends in disagreement; in the latter case, both bargainers finish with nothing. I refer to these games as shrinking pie because with each passing stage the pie shrinks by some predetermined amount. Bargainers thus have an incentive to find a settlement at the earliest possible stage.

The one-stage shrinking pie game has been investigated enough to have a special name: the ultimatum game. The standard theoretical analysis of the ultimatum game is known as perfect equilibrium, and it begins with the assumption that both bargainers are narrowly self-interested; each bargainer simply desires the largest possible slice of the pie. Given this assumption, the second mover should accept any positive amount because rejecting results in the lesser payoff of zero. The perfect equilibrium prediction, then, is that the first mover will offer no more than the smallest monetary unit allowed, keeping the rest for himself or herself; the second mover should accept.

Using college students as subjects, Güth, Schmittberger, and Schwarze (1982) performed an experiment on the ultimatum game. The study found behavior that differed strikingly from the theory. Agreements tended to be far from that predicted, with equal division playing a prominent role. Some games ended without an agreement. To explain their results, Güth et al. (1982) posited that bargainers choose in accordance with their sense of what I call "distributive justice." By this hypothesis, first movers make offers that they judge to be fair, and second movers turn down offers they judge to be unfair. So the distributive justice hypothesis implies that behavior is much less strategic than perfect equilibrium theory would lead us to believe.

Subsequent investigators employing their own designs reported findings that were not easily reconciled with Güth et al.'s (1982) results. Binmore, Shaked, and Sutton (1985) concluded that their two-stage shrinking pie game experiment provided qualified support for the theory. This is particularly striking because the reasoning necessary to the perfect equilibrium prediction for the two-stage game is somewhat more complex than the one-stage case. Hence Binmore et al.

(1985) were arguing in favor of a level of strategic sophistication that was even greater than that rejected by Güth et al. (1982). In the two-stage game, perfect equilibrium requires bargainers to do the equivalent of what is known as backwards induction. (This is technically necessary for perfect equilibrium in the ultimatum game too, but not so cognitively demanding as in the multistage games.) Bargainers must reason through stage 2 before making stage 1 decisions. To see what is involved, note that the second-stage game is equivalent to an ultimatum game in which the second mover is the proposer (and the pie is a discounted version of the stage 1 pie). If the game goes to stage 2, perfect equilibrium predicts that the second mover should get practically the entire stage 2 pie. Now back up to stage 1. In order to get the offer accepted, the first mover need offer no more than a slightly larger amount than the second mover can expect in stage 2. So by perfect equilibrium, the game should end in stage 1 with the second mover receiving an amount equal to about the value of the stage 2 pie.

The basis for Binmore et al.'s (1985) support for perfect equilibrium did not result directly from their experiment, but rather from a postexperiment questionnaire. In the experiment, subjects played the game once. Afterward second movers were asked what they would offer if they had the chance to play in the role of the first mover. Compared to offers in the experiment, the answers shifted significantly in the direction of perfect equilibrium. On this basis, Binmore et al. (1985) argued that experience appeared to be enough to turn "fairmen" into perfect equilibrium "gamesmen." Neelin, Sonnenschein, and Spiegel (1988) also found some support for the theory, but they qualified their conclusions, arguing that bargainers appear capable of looking ahead one stage but not much beyond that. Not everyone's claims were contrary to Güth et al (1982). Using an approximation to an infinite horizon shrinking pie game (perfect equilibrium was derived for this game by Rubinstein, 1982), Weg, Rapoport, and Felsenthal (1990) found results at odds with perfect equilibrium. In all, the extent to which people act in accord with the theory was mired in controversy.

The Ochs and Roth's (1989) study went a long way toward clarifying the matter. Ochs and Roth (1989) used a design that involved both two- and three-stage games, and they varied the discount factors across treatments. Previous studies used a single discount factor (although values varied *across* studies). Ochs and Roth (1989) used a full factor design, meaning all combinations of the manipulated factor values were considered. Bargainers were given experience with several games. Together, these features allowed Ochs and Roth (1989) to examine a wider variety of perfect equilibrium predictions than their predecessors. When viewed in isolation, a few of Ochs and Roth's (1989) cells appeared to verify the theory. But when all the cells were considered, the correspondence was no better than chance. Hence the Ochs and Roth (1989) experiment shows that if you look at just part of the picture you get an

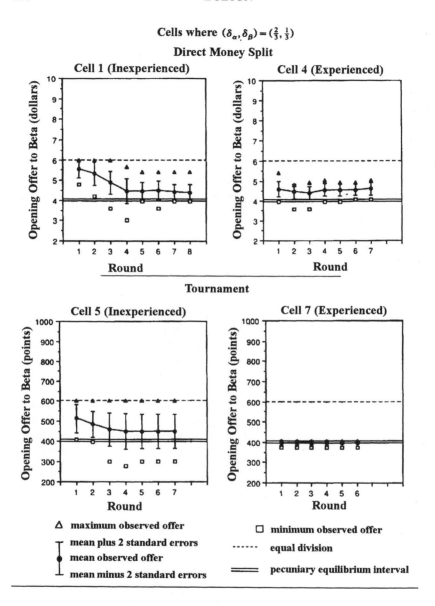

Fig. 9.2a. Mean observed opening offers. Cells where $(\delta_\alpha, \delta_\beta)$ = (2/3, 1/3). Reprinted with permission from Bolton (1991).

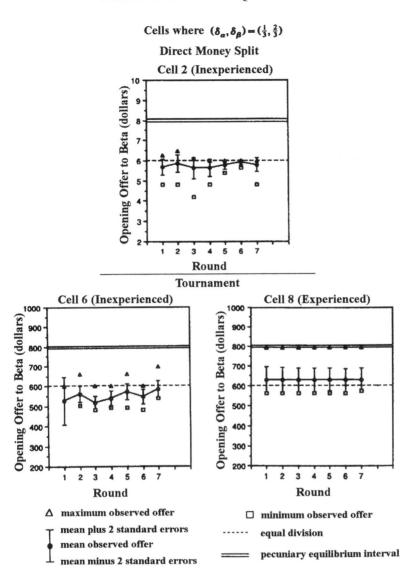

Fig. 9.2b. Mean observed opening offers. Cells where $(\delta_\alpha, \delta_\beta)$ = (1/3, 2/3). Reprinted with permission from Bolton (1991).

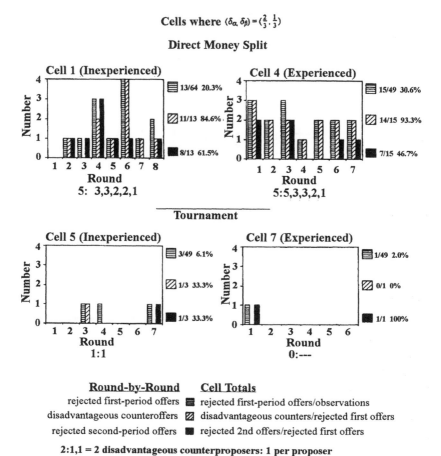

Fig. 9.3a. Summary of rejected offers. Cells where $(\delta_\alpha, \delta_\beta)$ = (2/3, 1/3). Reprinted with permission from Bolton (1991).

impression that is at odds with what you see when you look at the whole. And when you look at the whole, the theory is rejected.

As a graduate student, I helped Ochs and Roth (1989) run their experiment. The results captivated me. I began working on a theory as well as a new set of experiments to clarify the points that I thought needed addressing. My strategy was to first isolate the factors behind the standard theory's failure (Ochs and Roth had already accomplished much of this), and use these factors to construct

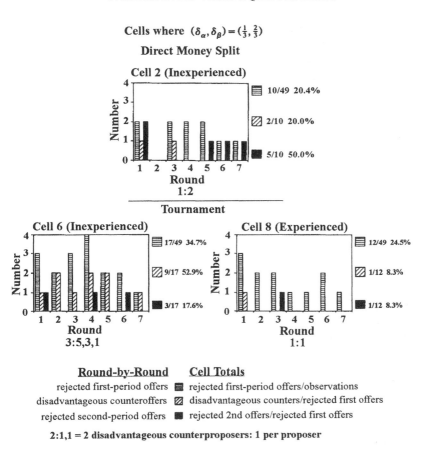

Fig. 9.3b. Summary of rejected offers. Cells where $(\delta_\alpha, \delta_\beta)$ = (1/3, 2/3). Reprinted with permission from Bolton (1991).

a new theory that could be validated through new tests. The study, Bolton (1991), is the subject of the rest of this section.

My experiment involved 10 cells, distinguishable by several factors. The direct money split cells involved standard two-stage shrinking pie games. The tournament cells involved the same game but with a modified payoff structure (I explain these cells later). In all cells, first movers, $\alpha$-players, played each second mover, each $\beta$-player, a single time in round-robin fashion. Pairings were anonymous and games were conducted through a computer interface. Most of the cells featured inexperienced subjects who had not participated in previous bargaining experiments. Two cells featured experienced subjects who were called back from the inexperienced cells. Subjects in the Ochs and Roth (1989) experiment gained experience through repeated play, but the exposure was limited (10 rounds). One could (and some did) argue that further experience was necessary to produce perfect equilibrium gamesmen. The experienced cells allowed me to look more carefully at the issue.

Cells were also distinguished by discount factors. I chose two different sets: $(\delta_\alpha, \delta_\beta) = (2/3, 1/3)$ and $(1/3, 2/3)$. When the game involves unequal discount factors, the bargainers see the pie shrink at different rates. I followed Ochs and Roth (1989) and had the bargainers negotiate over an intermediate commodity, 100 chips. In stage 1, each chip had a value of $0.12 to either bargainer. In stage 2, the values were $0.08 for the bargainer with the discount factor of one third and $0.04 for the one with two thirds. The perfect equilibrium for $(\delta_\alpha, \delta_\beta) = (2/3, 1/3)$ has the first mover getting two thirds of the chips and the second mover getting one third; the allocation proportions are reversed for the second set of factors, with the second mover now getting the larger share. So focusing on these two sets of discount factors allows us to examine two very different perfect equilibrium predictions.

The essential results of the experiment are reproduced here in Figs. 9.2 and 9.3. I focus first on the direct money split cells. Several patterns of behavior are evident. First, looking at Fig. 9.2, opening offers are generally different from those predicted by perfect equilibrium, particularly for cell 2, where the prediction is that the second mover gets two thirds of the pie. In fact, opening offers in all cells are biased in favor of the first mover. Second, deviation from perfect equilibrium is in all cases in the direction of the equal split. Third, looking at Fig. 9.3, a substantial proportion of opening offers are rejected, and a substantial proportion of these games then go on to end in disagreement.

There is a fourth pattern here that I believe is central. Fig. 9.3 lists the incidence of what Ochs and Roth (1989) called disadvantageous counteroffers, offers that give the proposer less money than the division rejected. From Fig. 9.3, a large percentage of counteroffers were disadvantageous. I believe that disadvantageous counteroffers are the key to understanding why perfect equilibrium theory fails – for two reasons. First, disadvantageous counteroffers immediately call into question the narrow self-interest postulate, an essential assumption of the theory. Second, disadvantageous counteroffers rule out many potential explanations for what we observe. For example, we might posit that bargainers prefer disagreement to accepting a meager offer; either because they find the offer insulting, or like so many American pennies, accepting is simply not worth the transaction cost involved. By this hypothesis, the only correction necessary to perfect equilibrium theory is that the threshold for disagreement must be changed from the smallest monetary unit to a somewhat higher level; one then simply performs the backwards induction using the new threshold. This argument, however, fails to explain disadvantageous counteroffers; if anything, it would seem to make them less likely: If you turn down a division because it has too little value, why would you then make an offer that gives you even less?

How about the experience hypothesis? The opening offers in cell 1 (see Fig. 9.2) were sufficiently close to theory to suggest that a little more experience might indeed produce perfect equilibrium behavior. I therefore called back some subjects, mostly from cell 1 and a few from cell 2 to play some more. The set-up for cell 4 was in all other respects the same as cell 1. Note from Fig. 9.2 that the average offers for the opening rounds of cell 4 are virtually identical to those in the final rounds of cell 1. Over the course of play in cell 4, average offers change little, but the standard deviations (SD) noticeably diminish. Rejections and disadvantageous counteroffers in cell 4 (Fig. 9.3) are quite similar to those in cell 1. In sum, play in cell 4 appears to represent a stable pattern – and one at odds with the perfect equilibrium forecast.

Still, we might posit that cell 4 gives subjects the wrong type of experience. Recall that Binmore et al. (1985) advanced their claims on the basis of what second movers said that they would do if given a chance to be first movers. Maybe the important thing about experience is not the amount but the type; maybe, in order to appreciate the strategic nature of the game, it is necessary to experience the game from both roles. To test this version of the experience hypothesis, I redid cell 1, this time rotating players between first and second mover roles. The results (reported in the research, but not in the figures here) were very similar to cell 1. Neither quantity nor type of experience appears to have much influence on the pattern of play.

The rest of the Bolton (1991) study was given over to describing the comparative model, a modification (not an abandonment) of the standard perfect equilibrium argument. When there is room for confusion, I refer to the standard perfect equilibrium as the pecuniary equilibrium, and the comparative model's perfect equilibrium as the comparative equilibrium.

The comparative model's sole innovation on the standard argument is to replace the narrow self-interest postulate with one that asserts that each bargainer evaluates the value of a proposal by two different yardsticks, one a pecuniary measure of the amount of money the proposal gives the bargainer, and the second a relative measure of the disparity in proposal shares. It is assumed that bargainers find pecuniary and relative payoffs to be substitutes. The explanation for disadvantageous counteroffers is immediate: A rejecting bargainer is trading away some pecuniary payoff for a chance at gaining some relative payoff.

Specifically, bargainer preferences over settlements are taken to be of the form:

$$u(x, i(x, z)) \qquad (1)$$

where $x$ is the pecuniary payoff to the bargainer, and $z$ the payoff to the partner.

The function $i$ provides a relative measure of the settlement; $i(x, z) = 1$ when $x = z = 0$, and otherwise $i(x, z) = x/z$. Utility, $u$, is assumed to be increasing in the pecuniary argument, and so long as $i < 1$, increasing in the relative argument; once $i > 1$, further increases in the relative argument neither contributes to nor detracts from $u$; so once a bargainer obtains parity, the only concern is with the pecuniary payoff. Note that these preferences do not imply any altruism. The bargainer is concerned with obtaining an outcome that is fair for self, and is willing to pay for it in the sense that he or she is sometimes willing to trade cash to obtain it. When I refer to the strong equity effect I am referring to this preference for having one's self treated fairly.

The comparative model is a theory of the strong equity effect. The model is solved using the same backwards induction applied to obtain the pecuniary equilibrium, but with the comparative utility function. Some predictions are consistent with pecuniary equilibrium: An increase in $\delta_\beta$ should increase the amount of money the second mover receives. Also, the amount the second mover receives should be greater when $(\delta_\alpha, \delta_\beta) = (1/3, 2/3)$ than when the discount factors are reversed. Other predictions are inconsistent with the pecuniary equilibrium: the value of $\delta_\alpha$ can effect the settlement. If $\delta_\beta \geq \frac{1}{2}$ then the second mover's share of the settlement will be less than what pecuniary equilibrium predicts. If $\delta_\beta < \frac{1}{2}$ then, as with pecuniary equilibrium, the second mover will receive less than half of the original pie, although the precise amount may differ. These predictions are in general accord with my experiment and the other shrinking pie studies I have discussed.

Of course the litmus test of a good theory is whether it can predict experiments that have not yet been run. To demonstrate that the comparative model could do so, I derived and tested two additional implications. One has to do with what happens when the second stage responder's options are restricted. I do not describe these predictions and results here because the experiment I discuss in the next section is similar in nature.

The second prediction has to do with an extension of the model to "tournament" payoffs. One of the interesting implications of relative payoff preferences is that behavior might be influenced by manipulating the group with whom subjects compare themselves. Consider again the two-stage shrinking pie game, but this time suppose that each bargainer's monetary payoff depends on how successful he or she is relative to other bargainers who have the same role. The amount a first (second) mover makes depends on how he or she does relative to other first (second) movers. The *tournament cells* paid bargainers in precisely this way, with separate but identical schedules for each role. The highest payoff went to the first (second) mover who made the highest total chips over the bargaining round-robin, the second highest payoff to the second highest total, and so on. In all other ways, tournaments were the same as the direct money split cells.

The tournament incentive scheme shifts the division of payoffs away from bargaining partner to bargaining counterparts. The way for a bargainer to gain the highest *relative* payoff among bargaining counterparts is to maximize earnings in each game; there should be no disadvantageous counteroffers. Because all bargainers will be doing the same, the pecuniary equilibrium should result. For tournaments, pecuniary and comparative equilibria are identical.

Figures 9.2 and 9.3 show that with experience, behavior for $(\delta_\alpha, \delta_\beta) = (2/3, 1/3)$ responds as predicted, with offers converging to equilibrium and offer rejections dramatically diminishing. With experience, behavior for $(\delta_\alpha, \delta_\beta) = (1/3, 2/3)$ moves in the predicted direction, but does not converge to equilibrium. So for these cells, the model's point predictions are sometimes, but not always, reliable. On the other hand, relative to the direct money cells, play of the tournaments always moves in the direction predicted. So at least in a comparative static sense, the theory predicts the data.

The comparative model modifies the narrow self-interest assumption but otherwise follows the perfect equilibrium solution technique. Two objections on principle have been raised to this approach. One is that anything can be explained by changing the utility functions. There is a straightforward rebuttal: Disadvantageous counteroffers stand in contradiction to narrow self-interest. To refuse to consider changing preferences is to refuse to entertain the possibility we are wrong in the face of contrary evidence. A second objection concerns basing a theory on something that is ultimately unobservable, in this case the trade-off between relative and pecuniary payoffs. Those who raise this objection worry that one will not be able to obtain falsifiable predictions from such a theory. But the analysis of the comparative model demonstrates that this is simply not so. There are many falsifiable predictions, several of which have now been derived and tested. Admittedly, the unobservable aspect makes for ambiguous predictions in some situations, and in other situations the falsifiable part of the prediction is qualitative not quantitative. (Camerer & Thaler, 1995, discuss the comparative model and contrast it to others.)

Another objection sometimes raised is to the notion that preferences for fairness are assumed fixed. This is ultimately an empirical question, and although at this time there is little data on the subject, it may be that preferences for fairness are not fixed. But the success of the theory suggests that positing fixed preferences is a reasonably accurate approximation, at least over relatively short periods of time.

Another implication of the comparative model is that the rejection thresholds of responders should vary with the size of the pie because this value has direct bearing on the measure of the relative payoff. One way to test this implication is to introduce incomplete information. In particular, if the responder knows only distributional information about the pie size, then we expect the rejection threshold to be strictly between the complete information threshold for the largest pie and that for the smallest pie. We also expect proposers, if they know the size of the pie and the limits of the responders information, to take advantage of large pies by making offers that are lower than they would if the pie size was known to responders. There are several studies of this type, including Kagel, Kim, and Moser (1996), Mitzkewitz and Nagel (1993), Rapoport, Sundali, and Potter (1992), and Straub and Murnighan (1992). All use the ultimatum game, and all find results generally consistent with the prediction.

## OTHER HYPOTHESES INCLUDING EXPERIMENTER ANONYMITY: FURTHER TESTS OF THE STRONG EFFECT

The evidence presented in the last section undercuts the experience hypothesis in favor of the strong equity effect. The evidence also undercuts the distributive justice hypothesis because it suggests that there is a strong strategic component to play of shrinking pie games. (In the next section, I discuss what I think is the clearest evidence on distributive justice.)

Another hypothesis has to do with whether people can properly do backwards induction. Johnson, Camerer, Sen, and Rymon (1996) suggested that they do not, whereas Harrison and McCabe (1992) suggested that they can learn. The issue is interesting because perfect equilibrium (pecuniary version) finds wide application. Two observations, however, imply that backwards induction by itself will be insufficient to account for shrinking pie games. First, perfect equilibrium fails even for the one-stage ultimatum game where the backwards induction is trivial. Second, the hypothesis is silent on why there are disadvantageous counteroffers, or why bargainers turn down nonzero offers in favor of a zero payoff. These observations limit the hypothesis' explanatory power, and also highlight another important point: all of the fundamental phenomena presented by shrinking pie games are present in the simplest case, the ultimatum game. To get at the base issues, you need not study the more complicated multistage games where issues like backwards induction may confound the analysis. In fact, most work on shrinking pie games done in recent years has focused on the ultimatum game.

*Culture* was another explanation put forward. Maybe the failure of the theory was an artifact of using college students as subjects, or of the limited number of countries where the experiment was performed. Roth, Prasnikar, Okuno-Fujiwara, and Zamir (1991) reported an ultimatum game experiment performed in four different countries. Although they found some effects, no country exhibited behavior consistent with the standard theory. Murnighan and Saxon (in press) have done ultimatum game experiments with young children, and Murnighan and Pillutla (1995) described (informal) ultimatum game experiments with business executives. Blount (1995) used University of Chicago MBA students. The theory fails in all of these groups.

Then there is *salience*, the hypothesis that the monetary incentives offered in these experiments are not sufficient to drive behavior. The most direct approach to testing salience is to increase the stakes. Hoffman, McCabe, and Smith (1993) did exactly this, comparing $10 ultimatum games to the same game played for $100. Measuring offers and settlements in terms of proportions, they found no statistical differences. The test, although satisfyingly direct, is inductive – we can never be sure whether a higher amount of money might change things. Another approach is to look for other games played for similar stakes that nevertheless produce results consistent with the theory. We then know it is not the amount of money per se that is responsible for the patterns in shrinking pie games. The best shot game, first studied by Harrison and Hirshleifer (1989) and then by Prasnikar and Roth (1992), provides precisely this sort of comparison. In best shot, the first mover chooses a contribution of tokens. After viewing this choice, the second mover makes a contribution. The maximum of the two determines the total cash to be divided; the larger the maximum, the larger the pie. The largest individual payoff, however, goes to the player who contributes the least. The perfect equilibrium allocation looks strikingly like that for the ultimatum game, with the second mover receiving much less than the first mover. Along the equilibrium path, the second mover has the opportunity to end the game with both players receiving nothing. Nevertheless, both best shot studies found that, after a few iterations, perfect equilibrium approaches 100%. Hence the size of the stakes alone is insufficient to predict perfect equilibrium; other factors must be at work.

Hoffman, McCabe, Shachat, and Smith (1994) put forward an altogether different type of hypothesis, one that accepts the notion that subjects are concerned about fairness – but goes on to posit that this concern is an artifact of a particular aspect of the lab environment. Hoffman et al. (1994) call this the *double blind hypothesis*. I prefer *anonymity hypothesis*. ("Double blind" has a different meaning in the context of medical experiments.) Anonymity between playing partners is the rule in experimental economics, and one that applies to all the experiments I have discussed. Experimental economists worry that nonanonymous play may introduce extraneous objectives among subjects, such as maintaining or bettering a social relationship. Hoffman et al. (1994) proposed that the same might apply between subjects and experimenter. Specifically, if subjects care about what the experimenter thinks of them, experimenter observation may inhibit self-interested behavior because subjects may worry that the experimenter will judge them "greedy."

The hypothesis is intriguing for a reason that goes beyond the study of the ultimatum game and perfect equilibrium. A reservation often expressed about experiments on people is that the behavior they produce may be distorted relative to field behavior. Although this reservation is often expressed in vague terms, experimenter observation seems to summarize much of what is intended. So testing the anonymity hypothesis provides evidence on a fundamental question about the use of experimental methods to study human behavior. Hoffman et al. (1994) presented data from a dictator game experiment to support the hypothesis. They found more self-interested behavior (in the narrow sense) when the game was played with experimenter-subject anonymity.

Rami Zwick and I set out to test the anonymity hypothesis for the ultimatum game. Doing so involved several intriguing design challenges. (Things are a bit more straightforward for the dictator game.) By definition, the test requires a treatment in which the experimenters are unable to attribute individual actions to individual subjects. This immediately rules out direct observation of the experiment, as well as direct payment of game earnings, because both imply revelation of subject actions to the experimenter. But once we give up direct observation, we risk giving up control of the experiment: How can we enforce the game rules? What about the moral hazard problem once there is no supervisor present to ensure that payments are consistent with outcomes? How can we retrieve the data if we observe neither play nor payments?

Many people's first impulse here is to suggest computers and secret ID's. It is instructive to see why such a scheme does not work. Computers do not dispense cash (at least not the ones we have access to), meaning that subjects would have to be paid by the experimenter or a conduit. Because the amount of money a person makes is a very big clue about his or her playing history, the experiment would not really be experimenter-subject anonymous. Another scheme would be to select a subject to administer the experiment. Although this may satisfy subject-experimenter anonymity, the experiment is no longer anonymous among subjects – we just replace one anonymity problem with another.

Our experiment, reported in Bolton and Zwick (1995), began with the simplified version of the ultimatum game, called *cardinal ultimatum*, illustrated in Fig. 9.4. The first mover chooses whether to play square (□) or triangle (Δ). Square corresponds to an offer of an equal split, and triangle corresponds to an offer of an unequal split favoring the first mover. The second mover chooses between accepting (*a*) or rejecting (*r*). When an offer is rejected, then as in the full ultimatum game, both bargainers receive nothing. The perfect (pecuniary) equilibrium for this game is much like that for the full game: bargainers should settle on the unequal division. The game also incorporates the behavioral friction we observe in the ultimatum game, in that the alternative to the perfect equilibrium is the symmetric division that bargainers in the full game are known to gravitate toward. The advantages of this simplified game become clear in a moment.

The experiment involved three cells. In the zero knowledge cell, bargainers played the Fig. 9.4 game with experimenter-subject anonymity. Here I give a brief synopsis of the procedure used to induce the anonymity: Each second mover was given four sealed boxes. Each box contained the cash equivalent for one of the outcomes exhibited in Fig. 9.1. One side of the box was labeled with a

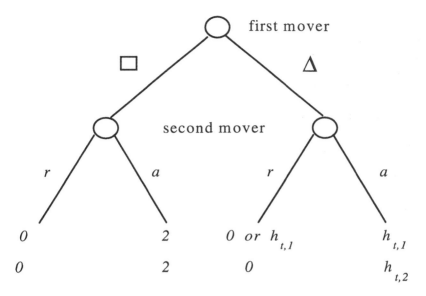

Fig. 9.4. Cardinal ultimatum and impunity games. Payoffs $h_{t,1} > h_{t,2} > 0$. In cardinal ultimatum, the first mover's payoff for the third node is 0; in impunity it is $h_{t,1}$.

description of its contents; the other side with either a square or triangle, depending on which action the first mover needed to take to reach the enclosed payoff. Each first mover was given two sealed, empty boxes, one labeled square and the other triangle. With the exception of labels, all boxes were identical.

The game proceeds as follows. The first mover indicates his or her choice by sending the corresponding box across a blind to the second mover. The second mover then selects a payoff box corresponding to the first mover's choice. For example, if the first mover sends the box labeled square, the second mover chooses between the equal split box and a no-payment box. The second mover unseals the chosen box, pockets his or her share, and sends the first mover's share back across the blind (in the case of a no-payment box, a no-payment card is sent back). The experimenter monitors the game at two points. On sending a box across the blind, the first mover must exhibit a second box, displayed geometric side down so that the experimenter cannot see which choice the first mover has made. This is to verify that only one box has been sent across the blind. On sending a payoff box back to the first mover, the second mover must exhibit four sealed boxes (three payoff boxes and the box sent by the first mover). This time, the geometric labels are up, with the content label down. If the second mover has followed the rules, all four boxes should be sealed and there should be two triangles and two squares. In this way, we verify that the rules have been followed without learning how individual subjects have played.

At the end of each game, all boxes are discarded into trash bins, one bin for first movers and another for second. The data is later reconstructed by going through the trash; open boxes indicating the path of play. Note that there is no deception here – we retrieve the aggregate distribution of play without being able to say which subject took which action. (Subjects in zero knowledge were not asked to provide receipts.)

The same procedure was followed in the cardinal ultimatum cell except that cards were substituted for boxes. Each card had labels identical to a corresponding box. Second movers cut the selected card in two, each half indicating the payoff. Card halves were redeemed at the end of the experiment; so in cardinal ultimatum, a subject had to present (explicitly reveal) the game actions to the experimenter. The third cell, the impunity cell, differed from the cardinal ultimatum cell in one detail: if the second mover rejected the unequal split, the first mover still received a share. This impunity game is illustrated in Fig. 9.4. The impunity cell was not experimenter-subject anonymous. The motivation for this cell was to test the punishment interpretation of the strong equity effect (imposing the disagreement outcome punishes the first mover for an unfair offer). According to the comparative model, removing the second mover's ability to resist the unequal outcome frees the first mover to make the more self-serving offer; we should see more pecuniary equilibria in the impunity cell than in the others.

Thus the experiment tests the anonymity hypothesis by comparing its explanatory power to the punishment hypothesis. Explanatory power is measured by success at predicting changes in (pecuniary) perfect equilibrium play. Anonymity predicts more perfect equilibria in the zero knowledge cell than in either the cardinal ultimatum or impunity cells; the later two are predicted to be the same. In contrast, the punishment hypothesis predicts the same amount of perfect equilibria in cardinal ultimatum and zero knowledge cells, but more in the impunity cell.

So far I have not said what unequal division was used. Actually, the division was rotated among several values. (Remember a lesson from Ochs and Roth: It may be necessary to collect data over a range of values to get a complete picture of the phenomenon.) The value of the unequal division was rotated through each trial of the game according to the following sequence:

$$\begin{pmatrix} h_{1t} \\ h_{2t} \end{pmatrix} = \begin{pmatrix} 3.8 \\ .2 \end{pmatrix} \begin{pmatrix} 3.4 \\ .6 \end{pmatrix} \begin{pmatrix} 3.0 \\ 1.0 \end{pmatrix} \begin{pmatrix} 2.6 \\ 1.4 \end{pmatrix} \begin{pmatrix} 2.2 \\ 1.8 \end{pmatrix}. \tag{2}$$

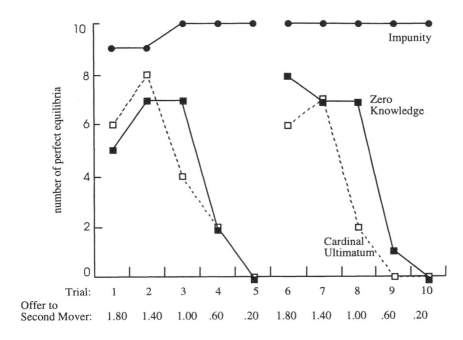

Fig. 9.5. Comparison of perfect equilibrium play. Reprinted with permission from Bolton and Zwick (1995).

---

To provide learning opportunity, the sequence was played twice. Bargaining pairings were rotated as in the experiment I described in the last section.

Use of the cardinal ultimatum game provides two advantages over the full game. First, without a reduction in possible offers, the experiment would not have been practically feasible: as it is, we had to fold, stuff, label and seal 720 boxes to run the zero knowledge cell. Second, and perhaps more important, cardinal ultimatum provides an unambiguous test benchmark. Specifically, the experiment measures the success of each hypothesis on the basis of ability to predict a shift (or lack of shift) in perfect equilibrium responses. If we were to allow many offers, there would be some ambiguity as to whether some observations were "close" to equilibrium. In cardinal ultimatum, the difference between perfect and nonperfect equilibrium play is clear-cut.

Figure 9.5 summarizes the main data resulting from the experiment. There is a dramatic increase in perfect equilibria in the impunity cell over cardinal ultimatum or zero knowledge. In contrast, whether there is any significant difference between the later two cells is unclear. Duncan Fong and I later analyzed the data using a Bayesian bioassay technique. Fong and Bolton (1997) concluded that given the assumptions of the Bayesian model, there is some statistical evidence that perfect equilibria are higher in zero knowledge than in cardinal ultimatum, but the difference is nevertheless very small.

I think there are three things to take away from this experiment. First, the explanatory power of the strong equity effect is confirmed – and strongly so. Second, there is little evidence that experimenter observation distorts subject behavior in any substantial way. Beyond the immediate implications for the ultimatum game, we have some reassurance about lab methodology. Third, and perhaps somewhat more subtle, note the contribution of formal game theory to the design. Game theory's precise language allows us to unambiguously define and modify the game structure – unambiguous, that is, with respect to the predictions made by anonymity and punishment hypotheses. Moreover, although standard perfect equilibrium is not an accurate predictor of behavior, it contributes a well-defined benchmark against which the other hypotheses can be measured. So while standard game theory predictions do not do well here, game theory's language and concepts provide a sharp context for testing a variety of ideas about behavior.


## DICTATOR GAMES: THE WEAK EQUITY EFFECT

Let us return for a moment to the distributive justice hypothesis. I think Forsythe, Horowitz, Savin, and Sefton (1994) provided the strongest evidence on this explanation. They compared first mover offers in an ultimatum game to those in a dictator game. The latter differs from ultimatum only in that the second mover cannot reject what the first mover offers. Although this is the sole difference, it is big. The dictator game is not really a game; the first mover unilaterally imposes a division of the pie. As such, the dictator game offers a relatively naked look at the distributive justice hypothesis (as well as at the narrow self-interest postulate). What Forsythe et al. (1994) found was that first mover offers were substantially more generous in the ultimatum game than in the dictator game. This is consistent with what we would expect from the strong equity effect – absent the rejection threat, first movers offer less. But it also contradicts the distributive justice interpretation of ultimatum game offers as primarily driven by a desire to do the fair thing.

That said, we have to be careful. Dictator offers in Forsythe et al.'s (1994) experiment were not negligible – a median of 25% of a $10 pie was given away. So while the experiment demonstrates that first mover generosity is not the driving force behind ultimatum game offers, it nevertheless uncovers a lot more generosity than is consistent with the narrow self-interest postulate (dictators should leave the game with all the money). Other dictator studies find similar

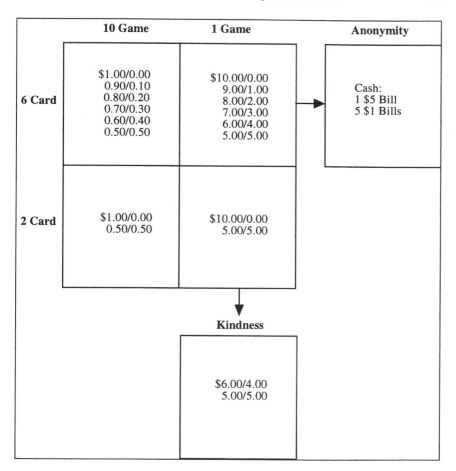

Fig. 9.6. Experimental design for the dictator study, from Bolton et al. (in press). The contents of each box represent the choice set available to Player A for each game played within the treatment. $x/y = Player A receives $x and Player B receives $y. Reprinted with permission from Bolton et al. (in press).

results (e.g., Kahneman, Knetsch, & Thaler, 1986). I mentioned that Hoffman et al. (1994) did a dictator experiment that was experimenter-subject anonymous. They had the dictators drop their unmarked contributions into a box, and then randomly distributed these among the recipients. They did the experiment twice, each time using somewhat different procedures. Although both versions exhibited lower levels of giving than the cell with experimenter observation, the percentage of contributing dictators never dropped below 30%.

So the propensity to leave money in the dictator game is robust. The strong equity effect, with its emphasis on the self-serving side of fairness, cannot explain this. What does? Is it altruism or something else? Also, note that impunity is a game very much like the dictator game. Yet in impunity there was virtually no generosity displayed beyond that mandated by the game. (See Fig. 9.5. Güth and Huck, 1997, replicated the basic pattern of play we observed in the impunity game.) How do we explain what appears to be a large behavioral disparity?

Bolton, Katok, and Zwick (in press) provided some clues. The initial experiment is represented by the 2 X 2 box in Fig. 9.6 (the other treatments represented were developed in response to the results from the initial design). Treatment variables were the number of division choices per game ("2Card" or "Card") and the number of games in which each subject participated ("10Game" or "1Game"). In the 1Game treatments, each game involved a $10 pie. In the 10Game treatments, each game involved a $1 pie. So in all treatments, a dictator split a total of $10.

The 1Game-6Card treatment was meant to provide a baseline replication of previous dictator game results. The other treatments were designed around two hypotheses about what might drive the difference between dictator and impunity studies. The I'm-no-saint hypothesis explains the difference in terms of the restriction impunity puts on impunity game choice. The first mover in dictator games can pretty much give any amount he or she pleases. Maybe, when faced with the kind of restricted choice impunity presents, the first mover systematically chooses to err in favor of himself or herself. Comparing 1Game-6Card to 1Game-2Card provides a direct test.

The experiment also tests the rational giving hypothesis, which begins with the observation that the impunity study involved repeated play whereas the dictator studies involved just one game. This explanation posits that the dictator's total contributions will be smaller in the 10Game treatments than in the 1Game treatments because of the free rider problem introduced when multiple contributors give to the same recipient. (In 10Game treatments, each dictator contributed to all recipients, whereas each dictator in 1Game was paired with one recipient.) Comparing 1Game-6Card to 10Game-6Card provides a direct test of the rational giving hypothesis. Comparing 10Game-2Card to the other three treatments tests for cross-effects; that is, we can check whether the two hypothesized effects tend to reinforce or cancel one another out or have some unanticipated effect. The 10Game-2Card treatment also represents a rudimentary attempt to replicate the impunity result; specifically, if the two hypotheses, either separately or in combination, explain the differences between dictator and impunity games, then we would expect 10Game-2Card to exhibit the same low levels of giving we observe in impunity.

The results from the initial experiment raised questions that led to two

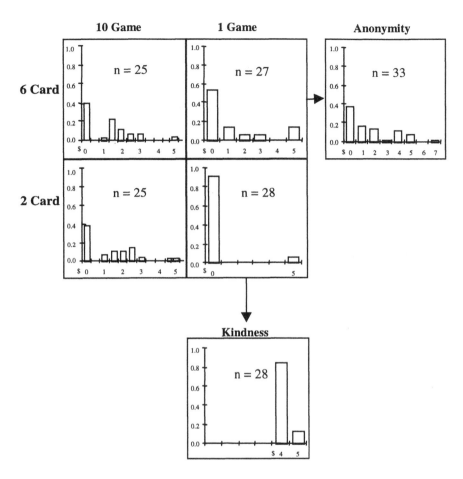

Fig. 9.7. Frequency of dictator giving by treatment, from Bolton et al. (in press). $n$ = number of observations within treatment. Reprinted with permission from Bolton et al. (in press).

additional treatments. The distributions of contributions we observed were not unlike what Hoffman et al. (1994) saw in their experimenter-subject anonymity treatments – but our treatments were not experimenter-subject anonymous. We therefore ran an anonymity treatment. The last treatment, kindness, differed from 1Game-2Card only in the values of the two choices presented to the dictator (see Fig. 9.6), and provides a second, alternative test of the I'm-no-saint hypothesis.

The main results of the experiment are of two types. The first type, the distribution of total contributions per dictator, appears in Fig. 9.7. The equivalent proportion of $5 contributions found in 1Game-6Card and 1Game-2Card supports the I'm-no-saint hypothesis. The kindness treatment provides further support. The rational giving hypothesis, however, finds no support because there is no significant difference between 6Card distributions.

We might be tempted to jump to the conclusion that the I'm-no-saint hypothesis explains the difference between dictator and impunity games. But there is something we learn from 10Game-2Card to give us pause. In fact, the pattern of giving observed in both 10Game treatments constitutes the second type of major evidence from the experiment. On reflection it is quite revealing: Most dictators in 10Game-2Cards give some recipients $.50 and some $0. The problem is that this contradicts the implicit assumption behind the I'm-no-saint hypothesis that dictators make the same division choice with respect to each recipient. An analysis of giving in 10Game-6Card adds still another twist to the story. Of the 13 dictators who gave a gift in 10Game-6Card, almost all appear to be distributing their gifts in a helter-skelter manner. The typical dictator gave a few relatively large gifts, as well as some small, and a few zero, gifts. All but one dictator passes a turning point test for randomization; in other words, the pattern of giving is practically indistinguishable from random.

This careless distribution of the gift is in sharp contrast to the selection of the total amount to give: the distributions of the total gift are statistically indistinguishable for 1Game-6Card, both 10Games, and anonymity treatments (Fig. 9.7). In the eyes of subjects, the game here is apparently the entire division task, not its 10 component parts. This is particularly remarkable because it implies that total gifts are independent of the number of recipients. Using a modified version of the dictator game, Selten and Ockenfels (1998) provided an even more dramatic demonstration of this "fixed sacrifice" phenomenon.

When applied at the level of the individual game, the I'm-no-saint hypothesis is insufficient to explain the pattern, or more correctly the lack of pattern that we observe in the 10Game treatments. But suppose instead, we posit that the I'm-no-saint hypothesis applies to how the dictator distributes the pie between self and group, disregarding whether the group is one or many. Now the pieces begin to fall into place. There is an immediate explanation for the difference between impunity and dictator: There is no real difference. In all the treatments of this experiment in which dictators were not otherwise constrained, only a few left appreciably more than 25% of the pie, the amount that first movers involuntarily contributed in the impunity game. When we abandon the notion that the dictator thinks of the task as a sequence of one-shot games, and instead focus on the total contribution, the results of the two experiments are quite consistent.

What is the motive for the gift giving? The behavior observed in this experiment, particularly the random aspect of it, is hard to reconcile with altruism. If altruism were the motive, we would expect a more systematic approach to gift distribution, something that squares with improving the welfare of others, such as giving the same amount to each recipient, or giving substantial gifts to some and none to others. But the helter-skelter distribution suggests that something besides welfare improvement (altruism) is on the mind of the donor (although I cannot claim that the evidence definitively rules altruism out).

What of the experiment-subject anonymity explanation for giving? The distribution for the anonymity treatment is no different than that for 1Game-6Card. Toward explaining the discrepancy with Hoffman et al. (1994), Bolton et al. (in press) provided a detailed comparison of the two experiments. We conclude that the fact that Hoffman et al. (1994) used somewhat different subject instructions for their anonymity and nonanonymity treatments is the most plausible explanation for why they find an effect and we do not. Hoffman et al. (1994) reported an experiment that includes experimenter anonymity treatments for which the instructions are carefully controlled. Although they do not report the $p$-values for the anonymity hypothesis (they test a different hypothesis involving more than the anonymity treatments), the graph in their paper shows that if there is a significant anonymity effect, it is very small.

One explanation for giving that fits the data is that dictators choose divisions according to rules of fairness. One observation that lends credence to this interpretation is that dictators rarely leave more than an equal share. In the research, we outline a hypothetical decision procedure. The data restricts the procedure in that it implies that the rule is independent of the number of recipients. I refer to the implied propensity for giving as the *weak equity effect*. It is "weak" in the sense that as the Forsythe et al. (1994) experiment shows, the strong effect dominates in a head-to-head test; the demand for relative money is greater than what is freely supplied. Our experiment demonstrates this dominance in a second way: the 1Game-2Card and kindness treatments show that when the dictator is constrained from giving precisely the amount he or she wishes, he or she has a strong tendency to err of the side of self-interest; dictators are most concerned with securing what they consider their fair share.

Methodological side note: As with most economics experiments, the design included no control for the gender composition of the subject samples. One might wonder whether some of our findings can be attributed to chance differences in gender. This boils down to asking whether there is some difference in gift giving across male and female dictators. Elena Katok and I reanalyzed the pooled data from the 10Game treatments and the 1Game-6Card treatment for signs of a gender effect. (For the remaining treatments, the gender of the subjects was either unknown or, in the case of the 1Game, 2Card treatments, the nature of the data was incomparable with the rest of the set.) We reported our results in Bolton and Katok (1995). As is evident from Fig. 9.8, we did not find any gender effect.

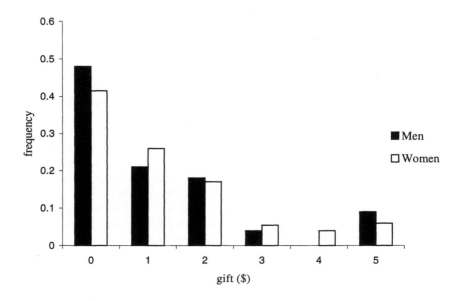

Fig. 9.8. Dictator giving by gender: total left for recipients. Reprinted with permission from Bolton and Katok (1995).

## FAIRMEN AS EVOLUTIONARY GAMESMEN: INTERPRETING THE DISPUTE COST HYPOTHESIS

I have argued that the key to understanding how people play these simple games is understanding their concern for fairness. But in the end, the reductionist in us all (including myself) would like an answer stated in terms of first principles. Caring about fairness is caring about relative comparisons. So why should people care about relative comparisons? Narrow self-interest, with its emphasis on the absolute level of consumption, has a hard time with this question. I have argued that the specific patterns of behavior we observe are difficult to reconcile with altruism. If, however, we take the perspective of evolutionary self-interest, there is an apparent (first pass) answer: evolution is a process of the stronger pushing out the weaker. Evolutionary self-interest, therefore, has a relative component that we might expect to be particularly pronounced among animals that depend on groups, such as people, for their success. Rules about what is fair and what is not may act to harmonize individual interests within the group. Worries about violations of fair distribution may reflect the concern that someone else is getting relatively more successful at one's own (biological) expense. de Waal (1996) argued that primitive versions of fairness concepts are found in animal societies, suggesting a deeply rooted biological purpose.

The fairman model analyzed in Bolton (1997) illustrates what I have in mind. The model provides an explanation for the observed attraction to equal division in the context of a symmetric bargaining game. That this attraction actually exists is borne out by the studies of Ashenfelter, Currie, Farber, and Spiegel (1992) and Bolton and Katok (in press). The attraction is plain in the bargaining games I have discussed too, but the asymmetric nature of these games pulls actual settlements away from equal division. The idea is to start by explaining the simpler symmetric case, where we know there will be a lot of equal division settlements. Maybe this will provide us with some clues as to the attraction to equal division in the more general setting.

The two-person bargaining game at the heart of the fairman model was first analyzed by Harsanyi (1977). I call it the *deadline game*. The game is divided into two stages. In stage 1, both bargainers simultaneously make a proposal of how to divide the bargaining pie. In stage 2, after viewing one another's proposal, the bargainers simultaneously choose either to stand on their own proposal (play $s$) or accept their partner's proposal (play $a$). If one bargainer plays $a$ and the other $s$, then the pie is divided in accord with the $s$-bargainer's proposal. If both play $s$, then the bargaining ends in disagreement, and each receives a payoff of $d \geq 0$. If both play $a$, then the division is the average of the two proposals.

Negotiations give bargainers the opportunity to probe for concessions. In the deadline game, each bargainer announces a stage 1 demand before making a final commitment in stage 2, providing a rudimentary opportunity to probe for a concession. I argue that a propensity to probe may be a key contributor to the stability of equal division settlements

The deadline game nicely illustrates the problems one runs into when one attempts to explain the special attraction of equal division starting from narrow self-interest. If we analyze the game assuming narrow self-interest, every possible settlement can be justified as a Nash equilibrium. Consider the division $(x, y)$. Suppose that both bargainers adopt the strategy to make this offer; and in stage 2 each plays $a$ as long as the other bargainer's proposal gives at least as much as does $(x, y)$, otherwise each plays $s$. This is a Nash equilibrium because given the strategy of one bargainer, the other can do no better than to follow what is prescribed. (With suitable adjustments to these strategies, every settlement can be justified as a perfect equilibrium as well.) There are even equilibria in which the game ends in disagreement with positive probability. In sum, standard equilibrium analysis says little about what we should expect to observe in the play of this game. Harsanyi (1977) adds some additional assumptions and finds a unique equilibrium involving risk dominance. But this solution implies we should observe diverse settlements across bargaining pairs.

But we don't – settlements cluster tightly about equal division.

The fairman model looks at the deadline game from the point of view of evolutionary self-interest. The bargaining pie is now interpreted as 100 fitness points. Bargainers are matched at random from a large pool. We look for an evolutionarily stable strategy (ESS), a strategy that when played by almost everyone prevents any new strategy from entering the population and doing at least as well. It can be shown that all ESS are symmetric Nash equilibria, but not vice versa, making ESS a more restrictive equilibrium concept – too restrictive in this case. It turns out that the deadline game has no ESS because there is no strategy that does uniquely best. In the language of evolutionary game theory, the strategies that do best admit drift mutations; for the fairman model, these are weak strategies that would eventually destabilize any would-be equilibrium. We can relax the ESS idea a bit by considering limit ESS (Selten, 1983), an ESS for a perturbed version of the game. We perturb the game by forcing all strategies to be played with some (small) positive probability. Intuitively, the perturbations imply a propensity to experiment or to make mistakes. This is enough to root out the drift strategies. In fact, in the context of the deadline game, the perturbations have a very nice interpretation.

The fairman model allows bargainers to match for play of the deadline game on the basis of a (possibly costly) signal, such as conforming to a custom. Those adopting a common signal negotiate exclusively among one another. Intuitively, it takes a group to implement a common division principle like equal division. Fitness provides the incentive for some groups to do so. A costly signal allows the innovators to keep obstructive nonconformers out. I emphasize that once nonconformers are out of the population, there is no need for a costly signal, and in equilibrium, no costly signal is used. A signal guarantees that the efficient innovators can get a start in the population. Once established, they no longer need it, nor is using one stable.

All equilibria in the fairman model have the same equilibrium path on which offering and accepting an equal split is done with maximum probability. To get the flavor of the result with a simple example, suppose bargainers choose from just three stage 1 proposals: *lion* (offer 25, keep 75), *fairman* (offer 50, keep 50), and *lamb* (offer 75, keep 25). For this special case of the model, there is a unique limit ESS (so not only is equilibrium path play unique, off-the-equilibrium path play is unique too). The equilibrium can be supported by a perturbed game in which all stage 1 and stage 2 strategies are played with minimum probability $\varepsilon >$ 0, save for the stage 1 strategy *lamb*, which is played with minimum probability $\varepsilon^2$. We are assuming that the propensity to experiment or make mistakes is skewed toward self-interest. All stage 2 subgames are therefore reached with some positive probability. It turns out that all limit ESS must be symmetric Nash equilibria in these subgames. The stage 2 subgames and the corresponding equilibria that support the unique limit ESS are enumerated in Table 9.1, where row and column state the stage 1 proposals (I assume that $\varepsilon$ is not very large).

**Table 9.1**
**Fairman Model - Stage 2 Equilibrium Play**

|            | _Lion_                                        | _Fairman_                          | _Lamb_                          |
| ---------- | --------------------------------------------- | ---------------------------------- | ------------------------------- |
| _Lamb_     | both play _a_ with max prob.                  | both play _a_ with max prob.       | both play _a_ with max prob.    |
| _Fairman_  | row plays _s_ and col. plays _a_ with max prob. | both play _a_ with max prob.     |                                 |
| _Lion_     | both play _s_ with prob. $\dfrac{25}{50\text{-}d}$ |                               |                                 |

The unique limit ESS, which I call FAIRMAN (all capitals to emphasize that it refers to the entire equilibrium strategy, not just the stage 1 offer) calls for the bargainer to propose fairman with maximum probability and then play stage 2 as prescribed by Table 9.1.

It is instructive to see how FAIRMAN keeps particular invaders out of the population. For example, consider a mutation of FAIRMAN that plays _lion_ in stage 1 with maximum probability, but plays the stage 2 strategy described in Table 9.1. The mathematics are rather messy, but the intuition is straightforward: relative to a _fairman_ proposal, _lion_ does not do well when partner plays either _fairman_ or _lion_; in both cases the increased probability of a disagreement from playing _lion_ outweighs any incremental payoff that might be gained from the more aggressive proposal. The only advantage proposing _lion_ has over proposing _fairman_ has to do with when partner proposes _lamb_ – but the FAIRMAN strategy proposes _lamb_ too rarely to compensate for the losses in the other cases. Hence the mutation does worse than FAIRMAN and cannot successfully invade. Likewise, consider a mutation that makes the same proposals in stage 1 as FAIRMAN, but plays _a_ with maximum probability when partner proposes _lion_. Because FAIRMAN occasionally plays _lion_, this mutation will find its weakness exploited, and although the mutation will have fewer disagreements when both bargaining parties propose _lion_, here it will do worse than FAIRMAN on average.

In sum, FAIRMAN's stability owes much to the fact that it resists more aggressive strategies and takes advantage of those that are open to exploitation. Put another way, the stability of FAIRMAN is supported by versions of both strong and weak equity effects. The strong effect is represented by the strategy's strong resistance to settling for less than 50% of the pie. The weak effect finds representation in that although FAIRMAN usually offers equal division, it does sometimes propose more aggressively (*lamb* is proposed far less often) and it does take advantage of *lamb*s who do not demand their own fair share.

The fairman model is also consistent with the dispute cost hypothesis, the hypothesis that the probability of dispute rises as the disagreement payoff, $d$, increases. We see in Table 9.1, that $d$ influences the probability of dispute in the case when both bargainers propose *lion*. In fact, the probability that both play $s$ increases with $d$. The usual intuition for the dispute cost hypothesis is different than what it is here. The usual intuition is associated with the view that bargaining disputes are due to incomplete information about one's bargaining partner; for example, incomplete information about how the partner values the pie. According to this view, bargainers convey their situation to their partner through their willingness to risk disagreement. There is no incomplete information in the fairman model. Instead, disagreements arise from the coordination failure that results when bargainers experiment or make mistakes. Lower dispute costs encourage bargainers to play more aggressively.

We have seen that incomplete information is not a necessary ingredient to bargaining disagreements in the lab. Reder and Neumann (1980) provided field evidence in favor of the dispute cost hypothesis in the context of repeated negotiations between the same bargaining parties. In addition, they offer an interpretation of bargaining and disputes that is very much in line with the view developed in the fairman model. Reder and Neumann (1980) reason that repeated bargaining allows bargainers to "learn about one another's behavior patterns during the bargaining process and develop conventions (protocols) to guide subsequent bargaining activity" (p. 868). Protocols are essentially coordination devices that cut the probability of dispute. In the fairman model, fairness – the propensity to split equally – functions as a rudimentary protocol.

Can we connect the approach of the comparative model, where fairness finds expression through the utility functions, to the fairman model approach? One very interesting method for linking models like these has been suggested by Güth and Yaari (1992) (also, see Huck & Oechssler, 1995). They propose an "indirect evolutionary approach," in which one uses evolutionary arguments to derive preferences, and then uses these preferences to predict play.

## SUMMARY WITH SOME REMARKS ON LEARNING AND APPLICATIONS

I have argued for a thesis that has three points. First, on the basis of laboratory evidence, fairness considerations mitigate the pursuit of narrow self-interest through strong and weak equity effects. The strong effect is most readily observed in experiments involving shrinking pie games. Here the disadvantaged bargainer's resistance to being treated unfairly appears to be the primary factor behind the behavior we observe. The weak effect is most readily observed in experiments involving the dictator game, where dictators leave money to recipients. The amounts left tend to be less than if the recipient had the option to punish the dictator by ending the game with a zero payoff for all. In this sense, the weak effect has a relatively smaller influence on narrow self-interest than does the strong effect.

Second, the evidence for these effects is not easily reconciled with altruism. Although dictators appear to give a great deal of consideration to the size of the total gift they will leave, they distribute the gift in a helter-skelter manner that seems inconsistent with concern for others' welfare. The fact that the size of the gift does not appear to change with the number of recipients also seems inconsistent with welfare improvement.

Third, evolutionary self-interest appears a promising explanation for these phenomena. Fairness is about relative comparisons. Evolution concerns the relatively weak being pushed out by the relatively strong. There would seem to be a canonical fit here. I described some of the first steps that have been taken in modeling these phenomena in this way.

Returning to the hypothesis trees in Fig. 9.1, note that fairness/punishment is not the only branch left uncut on the tree. The adaptive learning hypothesis attempts to explain ultimatum bargaining behavior in terms of an adaptive learning algorithm in which each bargainer modifies behavior in response to the payoff. Models of adaptive learning in experimental games are presented by Gale, Binmore, and Samuelson (1995) and Roth and Erev (1995). I believe that there is a learning component to these games, but at this time it is less certain whether learning is a prime factor. Learning models do not easily explain behavior in the dictator game. Research by Abbink, Bolton, Sadrieh, and Tang (1997) reported an experiment that compares the learning hypothesis to the strong equity effect hypothesis in an ultimatum game. Although the experiment does find some evidence of learning, learning is not sufficient to explain the phenomena explained by the strong equity effect. (Prasnikar, 1997, characterizes ultimatum game learning using a novel empirical method.)

I close with a comment on the practical implications of understanding fairness. I argued in the last section that understanding the coordinating role of protocols or principles may be the key to understanding negotiation behavior.

From this perspective, fairness is the rudimentary principle we observe in the simple bargaining games of the lab. Understanding how fairness considerations influence simple games may help us understand more complicated field phenomena, where the protocols and principles are no doubt more complex. Another promising set of applications has been explored by Ernst Fehr and his associates. For example, Fehr, Kirchsteiger, and Riedl (1993) studied how fairness influences labor market clearing.

## ACKNOWLEDGMENT

Many thanks to Werner Güth, Elena Katok, Rami Zwick, and an anonymous referee for comments on earlier versions of this chapter.

## REFERENCES

Abbink, K., Bolton, G. E., Sadrieh, A., & Tang, F.-F. (1996). *Adaptive learning versus punishment in ultimatum bargaining*. Unpublished manuscript, University of Bonn, Germany.

Ashenfelter, O., Currie, J., Farber, H. S., & Spiegel, M. (1992). An experimental comparison of dispute rates in alternative arbitration systems. *Econometrica, 60,* 1407-1433.

Binmore, K., Shaked, A. & Sutton, J. (1985). Testing noncooperative bargaining theory: A preliminary study. *American Economic Review, 75,* 1178-1180.

Blount, S. (1995). When social outcomes aren't fair: The effect of causal attributions on preferences. *Organizational Behavior and Human Decision Processes, 63,* 131-144.

Bolton, G. E. (1991). A comparative model of bargaining: Theory and evidence. *American Economic Review, 81,* 1096-1136.

Bolton, G. E. (1997). The rationality of splitting equally. *Journal of Economic Behavior and Organization, 32,* 365-381.

Bolton, G. E., & Katok, E. (1995). An experimental test for gender differences in beneficent behavior. *Economics Letters, 48,* 287-292.

Bolton, G. E., & Katok, E. (in press). Reinterpreting arbitration's narcotic effect: An experimental investigation of learning in repeated bargaining. *Games and Economic Behavior.*

Bolton, G. E., Katok, E., & Zwick, R. (in press). Dictator game giving: Rules of fairness versus acts of kindness. *International Journal of Game Theory.*

Bolton, G. E., & Zwick, R. (1995). Anonymity versus punishment in ultimatum bargaining. *Games and Economic Behavior, 10,* 95-121.

Camerer, C., & Thaler, R. H. (1995). Anomalies: Ultimatums, dictators and manners. *Journal of Economic Perspectives, 9,* 209-219.

de Waal, F. (1996). *Good natured: The origins of right and wrong in humans and other animals.* Cambridge, MA: Harvard University Press.

Fehr, E., Kirchsteiger, G., & Riedl, A. (1993). Does fairness prevent market clearing: An experimental investigation. *Quarterly Journal of Economics, 108,* 437-459.

Fong, D. K. H., & Bolton, G. E. (1997). Analyzing ultimatum bargaining: A Bayesian approach to the comparison of two potency curves under shape constraints. *Journal of Business and Economic Statistics, 15*, 335-344.

Forsythe, R., Horowitz, J., Savin, N. E., & Sefton, M. (1994). Fairness in simple bargaining experiments. *Games and Economic Behavior, 6*, 347-369.

Gale, J., Binmore, K. G., & Samuelson, L. (1995). Learning to be imperfect: The ultimatum game. *Games and Economic Behavior, 8*, 56-90.

Güth, W., & Huck, S. (1997). From ultimatum bargaining to dictatorship: An experimental study of four games varying in veto power. *Metroeconomica, 48*, 262-279.

Güth, W., & Yaari, M. (1992). An evolutionary approach to explain reciprocal behavior in a simple strategic game. In U. Witt (Ed.), *Explaining process and change – Approaches to evolutionary economics* (pp. 23-24). Ann Arbor, MI: University of Michigan Press.

Güth, W., Schmittberger, R., & Schwarze, B. (1982). An experimental analysis of ultimatum bargaining. *Journal of Economic Behavior and Organization, 3*, 368-388.

Harrison, G. W., & Hirshleifer, J. (1989). An experimental evaluation of weakest link/best shot models of public goods. *Journal of Political Economy, 97*, 201-225.

Harrison, G. W., & McCabe, K. A. (1992). Testing non-cooperative bargaining theory in experiments. In R. M. Isaac (Ed.), *Research in experimental economics Vol. 5* (pp. 137-169). Greenwich, CT: JAI Press.

Harsanyi, J. C. (1977). *Rational behavior and bargaining equilibrium in games and social situations.* Cambridge, England: Cambridge University Press.

Hoffman, E., McCabe, K., & Smith, V. (1993). On expectations and the monetary stakes in ultimatum bargaining games. *International Journal of Game Theory, 25*, 289-303.

Hoffman, E., McCabe, K., Shachat, K., & Smith, V. (1994). Preferences, property rights and anonymity in bargaining games. *Games and Economic Behavior, 7*, 346-380.

Huck, S., & Oechssler, J. (1995). *The indirect evolutionary approach to explaining fair allocations.* Mimeo, Humboldt University, Germany.

Johnson E. J., Camerer, C. F., Sen, S., & Rymon, T. (1996). *Limited computation and fairness in sequential bargaining.* Unpublished manuscript, Caltech.

Kagel, J. H., Kim, C., & Moser, D. (1996). Ultimatum games with asymmetric information and asymmetric payoffs. *Games and Economic Behavior, 13*, 100-110.

Kahneman, D., Knetsch, J. L., & Thaler, R. H. (1986). Fairness and the assumptions of economics. *Journal of Business, 59*, 285-299.

Mitzkewitz, M., & Nagel, R. (1993). Envy, greed and anticipation in ultimatum games with incomplete information. *International Journal of Game Theory, 22*, 171-198.

Murnighan, J. K., & Pillutla, M. M. (1995). Fairness versus self-interest: Asymmetric moral imperatives in ultimatum bargaining. In D. M. Messick & R. M. Kramer (Eds.), *Negotiation as a social process* (pp. 240-267). London: Sage.

Murnighan, J. K., & Saxon, M. (in press). Ultimatum bargaining by children and adults. *Journal of Economic Psychology.*

Neelin, J., Sonnenschein, H., & Spiegel, M. (1988). A further test of noncooperative game theory. *American Economic Review, 78*, 824-836.

Ochs, J., & Roth, A. E. (1989). An experimental study of sequential bargaining. *American Economic Review, 79*, 355-384.

Prasnikar, V. (1997). *Learning the decision rules in ultimatum games.* Unpublished manuscript, University of Pittsburgh.

Prasnikar, V., & Roth, A. E. (1992). Considerations of fairness and strategy:

Experimental data from sequential games. *Quarterly Journal of Economics, 107,* 865-888.

Rapoport, A., Sundali, J. A., & Potter, R. E. (1996). Ultimatums in two-person bargaining with one-sided uncertainty: Offer games. *International Journal of Game Theory, 25,* 475-494.

Reder, M. W., & Neumann, G. R. (1980). Conflict and contract: The case of strikes. *Journal of Political Economy, 88,* 867-886.

Roth, A. E. (1995). Bargaining experiments. In J. Kagel & A. E. Roth (Eds.), *Handbook of experimental economics* (pp. 253-348). Princeton, NJ: Princeton University Press.

Roth, A. E., & Erev, I. (1995). Learning in extensive-form games: Experimental data and simple dynamic models in the intermediate term. *Games and Economic Behavior, 8,* 164-212.

Roth, A. E., Prasnikar, V., Okuno-Fujiwara, M., & Zamir, S. (1991). Bargaining and market behavior in Jerusalem, Ljubljana, Pittsburgh, and Tokyo. *American Economic Review, 81,* 1068-1095.

Rubinstein, A. (1982). Perfect equilibrium in a bargaining model. *Econometrica, 50,* 97-109.

Sebenius, J. K. (1984). *Negotiating the law of the sea.* Cambridge, MA: Harvard University Press.

Selten, R. (1983). Evolutionary stability in extensive two-person games. *Mathematical Social Sciences, 5,* 269-363.

Selten, R., & Ockenfels, A. (1998). The experimental solidarity game. *Journal of Economic Behavior and Organization, 34,* 517-539.

Straub, P. G., & Murnighan, J. K. (1995). An experimental investigation of ultimatum games: Information, fairness, expectations, and lowest acceptable offers. *Journal of Economic Behavior and Organization, 27,* 345-364.

Weg, E., Rapoport, A., & Felsenthal, D. S. (1990). Two-person bargaining behavior in fixed discounting factors games with infinite horizon. *Games and Economic Behavior, 2,* 76-95.

# 10    On the Effects of the Pricing Rule in Auction and Fair Division Games – An Experimental Study

## Werner Güth
*Humboldt-University of Berlin*

The main goal of our experimental study is to investigate bidding behavior in a broader context than has previously been done (see e.g., Kagel, 1995). We examine both auctions and fair division games, which include situations where truth telling is optimal (in the second price sealed bid auction, see Vickrey, 1961) and where this desirable property is impossible (Güth, 1986). Experimental studies of auction games are numerous (see Kagel, 1995). However, we are not aware of any previous experimental study of bidding behavior in fair division games.

More specific goals are to explore whether behavior reacts at least qualitatively to changing institutions as predicted by normative theory and whether learning by beginners and education "improves" the adequacy of bidding behavior.

This chapter first describes the two pricing rules we use for auctions and fair division games, and the requirement that net trades are envy-free with respect to bids. The basic 2 x 2 experimental design is introduced (auctions vs. fair divisions and first price sealed bid vs. second-price sealed bid institutions) later. Although we do not expect our subjects to behave as if they were risk-neutral profit maximizers (see Cox, Smith, & Walker, 1982), we still expect them to reveal the qualitative types of behavior predicted by theory, that is, essentially avoiding misrepresentation (in second price sealed bid auctions), underbidding for the first price rule, and overbidding in the second price fair division game. We describe the main behavioral tendencies where we distinguish beginner and expert participants. After exploring qualitative learning the chapter concludes with a summary of our results and an outline of open problems.

# ENVY-FREE PRICING RULES AND GAME-THEORTIC SOLUTIONS

## Auctions

Consider a situation where a unique and indivisible commodity, for example, a unique piece of art, has to be sold to one of $n \geq 2$ bidders. The buyer is the bidder $i$ who receives the commodity. We impose the natural restriction that only the buyer pays for the commodity. [1] The rules of an auction have to specify for all bid vectors $b = (b_1, \ldots, b_n)$ the winner $w(b) \in \{1, \ldots, n\}$ and the price $p(b)$ that has to be paid. We require

> **Axiom** (Güth, 1986): According to his or her bid $b_i$ no bidder $i = 1, \ldots, n$ prefers another bidder's net trade to one's own.

For an auction we obtain the following condition:

$$
\text{or} \quad
\begin{aligned}
b_{w(b)} - p(b) &\geq 0 \geq b_i - p(b) \text{ for all } i \neq w(b) \\
b_{w(b)} &\geq p(b) \geq b_i \text{ for all } i \neq w(b)
\end{aligned}
\tag{1}
$$

This shows that the buyer $w(b)$ must be a highest bidder and that the price $p(b)$ cannot exceed the highest bid and cannot lie below the second highest bid. Envy-freeness is an ethical requirement that rules out arbitrary allocation results. Envy-free institutions are especially important when auction and fair division rules are used by public authorities.

## Fair Division Games

In fair division games there is no seller, the commodity is owned by the group of bidders who have to allocate it to one of its members. Situations like this result in case of an inheritance (a bidder is then an heir) or when terminating a joint venture. Notice, first of all, that the buyer will have to compensate the other bidders according to the envy-free axiom when all bids are positive. Furthermore, the axiom requires that this monetary compensation must be the same for all non-buyers.[2] Let $p(b)$ be $n$ times this monetary compensation. As before $w(b) \in \{1, \ldots, n\}$ is the buyer. The envy-free axiom requires

$$
\text{or} \quad
\begin{aligned}
b_{w(b)} - \{(n-1)/n\} \cdot p(b) &\geq \frac{p(b)}{n} \geq b_i - \{(n-1)/n\} \cdot p(b) \text{ for all } i \neq w(b) \\
b_{w(b)} &\geq p(b) \geq b_i \text{ for all } i \neq w(b)
\end{aligned}
$$

$$
\tag{2}
$$

Thus, again the buyer $w(b)$ has to be the highest bidder and the price $p(b)$ cannot exceed the highest bid $b_{w(b)}$ and cannot be less than the second highest bid max $\{b_j : j \neq w(b)\}$. The axiom therefore requires that the price $p(b)$ is equally distributed among all bidders. Although there are many possible pricing rules $p(b)$ satisfying the axiom, in our experiments we explore only the two extreme pricing rules consistent with the axiom, namely

$$\text{or} \quad \begin{array}{l} \text{(i)}: \ p(b) = b_{w(b)} \\ \text{(ii)}: \ p(b) = \max\{b_j : j \neq w(b)\} \end{array} \tag{3}$$

for all bid vectors $b = (b_1, \ldots, b_n)$. In case (i) we speak of the first price rule, and in case (ii) of the second price rule. A price rule does not yet define a well-specified game. For the case with multiple highest bids it is assumed that one of them is selected by an unbiased chance move (this would be implied by an intuitive anonymity axiom). Furthermore, we rely on the most simple $iid$ – private value case, that is, for each bidder $i$ the value $v_i \in [0,1]$ for the good is chosen independently and according to the uniform distribution, that is $v_i \sim U_i$ (0,1) for all $i$. Thus bidders know their own value and the distribution from which others' values are drawn.

## Equilibria

By adding the assumption that all highest bidders have an equal chance of buying in case of ties we have specified for all constellations of our 2 x 2 factorial design a well-defined game with incomplete information. In game theoretic studies of bidding behavior one usually assumes that true values $v_i$ can vary continuously. In an experimental study this is, however, impossible. Although the grid for true values is rather coarse – the unit interval [0,1] has been partitioned in only 10 equidistant intervals – we nevertheless use the solution for the uniform distribution over the unit interval [0,1] as a benchmark or standard of comparison when discussing our experimental results. According to Güth and van Damme (1985) the risk-neutral bidding behavior for our 2 x 2 experimental design is the one specified by Table 10.1. Table 10.2 describes how the expected price $E(p^*)$ and the conditional payoff expectations $E(v_i)$ of bidder $i$, whose true value is $v_i$, depends on the treatment, specified by our 2 x 2 factorial design.

The fact that the expected price in auctions does not depend on the price rule for risk-neutral bidders follows from well-known equivalence theorems. In fair division games the expected price is increased by $1/(n+1)^2$ when one substitutes the highest bid price rule by the second highest bid price rule. Because

**Table 10.1**
**The Solution for Uniform Beliefs on [0,1] and Risk Neutrality for the Four Game Versions**

| | Risk Neutral Equilibrium Bid Function | |
|---|---|---|
| **Pricing Rule** | *Auctions* | *Fair Division Games* |
| Price = highest bid | $\dfrac{n-1}{n} \cdot v_i$ | $\dfrac{n}{n+1} \cdot v_i$ |
| Price = 2nd highest bid | $v_i$ | $\dfrac{n}{n+1} v_i + \dfrac{1}{n+1}$ |

$\frac{n-1}{n+1} < \left(\frac{n}{n+1}\right)^2$ is always true, the expected price of fair division is always higher than in auctions. Notice, however, that the different prices in fair division do not imply different conditional payoff expectations $E(v_i)$.

The solution in Table 10.1 has been derived by assuming symmetry and monotonicity of bidding functions $b_i(v_i)$ for all bidders $i$. As shown by Plum (1992) these assumptions can be relaxed. Notice that symmetry and monotonicity imply that the buyer is always the bidder $i$ with the highest valuation $v_i$, that is, game theory predicts an efficient allocation.

In spite of this we expect to observe different levels of efficiency for the games of our 2 x 2 experimental design:

**Hypothesis A:** *Lack of efficiency*

(A.1): Efficiency will be lower in games employing the first price rule compared to games employing the second price rule.

(A.2): In games with the same pricing rule, efficiency will be lower for fair division games than for auctions.

Except when comparing the first price sealed bid auction with the second price fair division game, hypothesis A predicts different degrees of efficiency for our 2 x 2 experimental design, which, of course, contradicts the game theoretical predictions based on symmetry and monotonicity. The first price rule encourages underbidding. For nonrational bidders $i$, it is, however, difficult to coordinate the degree of underbidding as a function of $v_i$. For second price games this problem does not exist and justifies part A.1 of hypothesis A. Our reason for A.2 is simply the greater complexity of fair division games that should generate more variety in behavior and thereby decrease efficiency.

One may, of course, reject our implicit assumption of symmetry by allowing

**Table 10.2**
**The Expected Price $E(p^*)$ and the Conditional Expectations $E(v_i)$ for Uniform Beliefs on [0, 1] and Risk Neutrality for the Four Game Versions**

| Pricing Rule | Expected Price and Conditional Expectations for Risk Neutral Bidders | |
| --- | --- | --- |
| | *Auctions* | *Fair Division Games* |
| Price = highest bid | $E(p^*) = \dfrac{n-1}{n+1}$, $\qquad$ $E(v_i) = \dfrac{v_i^n}{n}$ | $E(p^*) = \left(\dfrac{n}{n+1}\right)^2$, $\qquad$ $E(v_i) = \dfrac{v_i^n}{n} + \dfrac{n-1}{n(n+1)}$ |
| Price = 2nd highest bid | $E(p^*) = \dfrac{n-1}{n+1}$, $\qquad$ $E(v_i) = \dfrac{v_i^n}{n}$ | $E(p^*) = \dfrac{n^2+1}{(n+1)^2}$, $\qquad$ $E(v_i) = \dfrac{v_i^n}{n} + \dfrac{n-1}{n(n+1)}$ |

for individual deviations from risk neutrality. We could have avoided easily this objection by employing the binary lottery-technique for rewarding subjects to guarantee risk neutrality. Here we did not do so because the evidence on the binary lottery technique is mixed (see e.g., Güth, van Damme, & Weber, 1993; Prasnikar, 1993; Rietz, 1993; Selten, Sadrieh & Abbink, 1996).

We do not expect subjects to play exactly as predicted by the optimal behavior in Table 10.1 particularly because these predictions neglect the discreteness of $v_i$ in our experiment. In the second price auction the solution $b_i(v_i)$ does not depend on this continuity assumption because it relies on dominance solvability. It also does not depend on beliefs and risk neutrality. Qualitative aspects of optimal bidding behavior in the three other games, which also are independent of discreteness, beliefs, and risk neutrality, are revealed by the weaker properties as:

(i): the games relying on the first price rule are overbidding proof, that is, strategies with $b_i(v_i) > v_i$ for some value $v_i$ are dominated.

(ii): the second price fair division game is underbidding proof, that is, strategies with $b_i(v_i) < v_i$ for some value $v_i$ are dominated.

To see why these properties are true assume for (i) a buyer $i$ who has bought at a price $p = b_i'(v_i) > v_i$. Clearly the player prefers a truthful bid $b_i(v_i) = v_i$ over $b_i'(v_i)$ regardless whether another bid $b_j$ with $b_i'(v_i) > b_j \geq v_i$ exists [$b_i(v_i) = v_i$ implies that $j$ would buy at the price $b_j$; in a fair division game $v_i - [(n-1) / n]$ $b_i'(v_i) < b_j / n$ is true] or not [$i$ would buy at the lower price $v_i$]. Similarly, assume for (ii) a bidder $i$ with $b_i''(v_i) < v_i$ whose bid is second highest and therefore determines the price in (ii). By bidding $b_i(v_i) = v_i$ the player would fare better regardless whether the highest bid $b_j$ satisfies $v_i \geq b_j > b_i''(v_i)$ [$b_i(v_i) = v_i$ implies that $i$ would buy at the price $b_j$ and receive $v_i - (n-1) / n \ b_j > b_i''(v_i) / n$] or not [due to $v_i / n > b_i''(v_i) / n$]. We expect these properties to be reflected in behavior.

**Hypothesis B:** *Misrepresentation of the true values*

(B.1): In the second price sealed bid auction the bids $b_i(v_i)$ will be more symmetrically distributed around $v_i$ than in the other three games.

(B.2): In the first price games (i.e., first price sealed bid auction and first price fair division game), we expect that bids on average will satisfy $b_i(v_i) < v_i$.

(B.3): In the second price fair division game we expect that bids on average will satisfy $b_i(v_i) > v_i$.

Our justification for hypothesis B is mainly the expectation that bidders will at least qualitatively react to changing institutions as predicted by (game) theory: Thus B.1 follows from the incentive compatibility of second price-auctions and B.2 from the underbidding incentives of first price games (see Table 10.1). Due to $v_i \leq 1$ one should expect overbidding for second price fair division games as stated in hypothesis B.3. We do not believe, however, that the degree of overbidding depends on $v_i$ as predicted by (game) theory. According to the game-theoretic solution, described in Table 10.1, one could also predict a qualitative difference in bidding behavior between the auction and the fair division game relying on the highest bid price rule:

(B.4): For the first price rule the bids $b_i(v_i)$ of fair division are higher than the corresponding bids $b_i(v_i)$ in auctions.

## EXPERIMENTAL PROCEDURE

The experiments were performed at Humboldt University of Berlin. The instructions (see Appendix A) and bidding form (see Appendix B) were all in English. A subject was first assigned by randomly distributing codes to one of the four game types of our 2 x 2 experimental design. The instructions for the four games only differed in one paragraph as well as in monetary value of one Experimental Currency Unit (ECU) which was DM 100 in auction games and

**Table 10.3**
**The Results for the Sophisticated Participants**

| Table Ref. | Game | Age | Gender | Field of Study | Deg. | Answer to Control Questions | | | |
|---|---|---|---|---|---|---|---|---|---|
| | | | | | | 1 | 2 | 3 | r/w |
| 1 | A.1 | 25 | f | econ. | mast. | 0 | -.2 | 0 | r |
| 2 | | 23 | m | econ. | mast. | 0 | -.2 | 0 | r |
| 3 | | - | m | econ. | mast. | 0 | -.2 | 0 | r |
| 4 | | 28 | m | math. | mast. | 0 | -.2 | 0 | r |
| 5 | A.2 | 25 | f | econ. | mast. | .0 | .1 | .0 | r |
| 6 | | 21 | m | math. | bach. | .0 | .1 | .0 | r |
| 7 | | 26 | m | econ. | mast. | .0 | .1 | .0 | r |
| 8 | | 27 | m | econ. | mast. | .0 | .1 | .0 | r |
| 9 | D.1 | 30 | m | econ. | mast. | .3 | .1 | .3 | r |
| 10 | | 29 | m | econ. | mast. | .3 | .1 | .3 | r |
| 11 | | 27 | m | econ. | mast. | 1.23 | .1 | 0 | w |
| 12 | | 26 | m | math. | mast. | .3 | .1 | .3 | r |
| 13 | D.2 | 24 | m | phys | bach. | .2 | .3 | .2 | r |
| 14 | | 27 | f | econ. | mast. | .2 | .3 | .2 | r |
| 15 | | 27 | m | math. | mast. | .2 | .3 | .2 | r |
| 16 | | 27 | m | | mast. | .2 | .3 | .2 | r |

f = female
m = male
BA = business administration
econ. = economics
math. = mathematics
phys = physics
A.1 = first price auction
A.2 = second price auction
D.1 = first price fair division
D.2 = second price fair division
bach./mast. = bachelor / master's degree
r/w = right / wrong answers of control questions

DM 20 in fair division games. These values have been chosen such that $E(v_i = ½)$ is the same for all four games what implies that one ECU in fair division games corresponds to one fifth of one ECU in auction games.

To check whether the instructions were carefully read and completely understood all subjects had to answer the control questions (see Appendix C).

**Table 10.4**
**The Results for the Sophisticated Participants**

| Table Ref. | Bids $b_i$ $(v_i)$ for $v_i =$ | | | | | | | | | | |
|---|---|---|---|---|---|---|---|---|---|---|---|
|  | .0 | .1 | .2 | .3 | .4 | .5 | .6 | .7 | .8 | .9 | 1.0 |
| 1 | .0 | .1 | .2 | .3 | .4 | .5 | .5 | .5 | .5 | .5 | .5 |
| 2 | .0 | .08 | .16 | .25 | .32 | .4 | .48 | .5 | .52 | .55 | .6 |
| 3 | .0 | .1 | .1 | .2 | .3 | .4 | .4 | .6 | .7 | .8 | .8 |
| 4 | .0 | .0 | .1 | .3 | .4 | .5 | .5 | .6 | .7 | .8 | .9 |
| 5 | .0 | .1 | .2 | .3 | .4 | .5 | .6 | .7 | .8 | .9 | 1.0 |
| 6 | .0 | .1 | .2 | .3 | .4 | .5 | .6 | .7 | .8 | .9 | 1.0 |
| 7 | .0 | .1 | .2 | .3 | .4 | .5 | .6 | .7 | .8 | .9 | 1.0 |
| 8 | .0 | .2 | .3 | .4 | .5 | .6 | .7 | .8 | .9 | 1. | 1.0 |
| 9 | .0 | .0 | .0 | .0 | .0 | .05 | .1 | .1 | .1 | .2 | .2 |
| 10 | .0 | .1 | .2 | .3 | .4 | .5 | .6 | .7 | .8 | .9 | 1.0 |
| 11 | .0 | .1 | .3 | .4 | .5 | .6 | .7 | .8 | .9 | 1. | 1.1 |
| 12 | .0 | .09 | .19 | .29 | .39 | .49 | .59 | .69 | .79 | .89 | .99 |
| 13 | .0 | .1 | .2 | .3 | .4 | .5 | .6 | .7 | .8 | .9 | 1.0 |
| 14 | .0 | .1 | .2 | .5 | .6 | .8 | 1.0 | 1.0 | 1.2 | 1.3 | 1.5 |
| 15 | .0 | .1 | .2 | .3 | .4 | .5 | .6 | .7 | .8 | .9 | 1.0 |
| 16 | .0 | .1 | .2 | .3 | .4 | .5 | .6 | .7 | .8 | .9 | 1.0 |

This form was distributed after answering questions privately and collected immediately after its completion. The control questions are, of course, slightly more demanding for fair division than for auction games.

In addition to the four different game variants, as described by Table 10.1, we have distinguished two different groups of participants. Some of our participants were highly educated (awaiting or having completed their master's examination). We refer to them as "experts." The other participants had not even passed their bachelor examination in economics and are called "beginners." Whereas experts played the respective game just once, beginners where given some opportunity to learn: After playing the game once, beginners received feedback about the outcome, then played the game again with new partners.

When allowing beginners to gain experience, the group of subjects was partitioned to subgroups of six subjects. In each round these six subjects were allocated randomly into two subgroups with three subjects each, the three bidders in the game. What we guaranteed was only that the same three bidders will not compete again. Thus repeated game effects in the sense of reputation formation were not completely excluded. Each subgroup with six subjects qualifies as an independent observation even in the second round. This is,

**Table 10.5**
**The Results for the Beginners**

| Table Ref. | Game | Age | Gender | Field of Study | Deg. | Answer to Control Questions | | | |
|---|---|---|---|---|---|---|---|---|---|
| | | | | | | 1 | 2 | 3 | r/w |
| 1 | | 20 | f | BA | no | .1 | .2 | -0.2 | w |
| 2 | | 25 | m | BA | no | 0 | 0 | .2 | w |
| 3 | | 21 | m | BA | mast. | 0 | -.2 | 0 | r |
| 4 | | 21 | m | BA | no | 0 | -.2 | 0 | r |
| 5 | A.1 | 21 | m | BA | bach. | -.1 | -.2 | 0.2 | w |
| 6 | | 28 | m | econ.ped | no | -1 | .2 | .2 | w |
| 7 | | 22 | m | BA | no | 0 | -.2 | 0 | r |
| 8 | | 23 | f | math. | no | 0 | -.2 | 0 | r |
| 9 | | 23 | m | BA | no | -.1 | -.2 | .2 | w |
| 10 | | 22 | m | - | no | 0 | .1 | 0 | r |
| 11 | | 21 | m | geogr. | bach. | 0 | .1 | 0 | r |
| 12 | | 25 | f | econ.ped | bach. | 0 | 0 | 0 | w |
| 13 | A.2 | 20 | m | BA | no | 0 | .1 | 0 | r |
| 14 | | 20 | f | BA | no | 0 | .3 | 0 | w |
| 15 | | 22 | m | BA | no | .1 | .2 | -.2 | w |
| 16 | | - | f | econ. | no | 0 | .1 | 0 | r |
| 17 | | 23 | f | econ. | no | .3 | .1 | .3 | r |
| 18 | | 24 | f | econ. | no | .13 | .1 | .2 | w |
| 19 | D.1 | 23 | m | econ. | no | 1/3 | 1/10 | 1/3 | w |
| 20 | | 29 | f | - | - | - | - | - | - |
| 21 | | 19 | m | BA | no | - | .1 | .4 | w |
| 22 | | - | m | econ. | no | .04 | .1 | .4 | w |
| 23 | | 20 | m | econ. | no | .3 | .3 | .3 | w |
| 24 | | 24 | f | geogr. | bach. | .3 | .1 | .3 | w |
| 25 | | 22 | m | BA | bach. | 1/3 | 1/10 | 1/3 | w |
| 26 | D.2 | 22 | m | BA | no | .2 | .3 | .2 | r |
| 27 | | 29 | m | BA | no | - | .1 | - | w |
| 28 | | 24 | m | BA | no | -.3 | .1 | .2 | w |
| 29 | | 21 | m | - | - | -.3 | .6 | .6 | w |

ped. = pedagogics
no = no degree
geogr. = geography
BA = business administration

however, not the only reason why we do not provide statistical tests of some of the hypotheses by assuming that all plays are independent. As demonstrated

**Table 10.6**
**The Results for the Beginners**

| Table Ref. | **First Bids $b_i(v_i)$ for $v_i =$** | | | | | | | | | | |
|---|---|---|---|---|---|---|---|---|---|---|---|
| | **.0** | **.1** | **.2** | **.3** | **.4** | **.5** | **.6** | **.7** | **.8** | **.9** | **1** |
| 1 | .1 | 1.0 | .1 | .2 | .3 | .4 | .5 | .6 | .7 | .8 | 0 |
| 2 | 0 | .05 | .11 | .19 | .23 | .31 | .41 | .41 | .52 | .53 | .61 |
| 3 | 0 | .1 | .1 | .2 | .4 | .4 | .5 | .6 | .8 | .8 | .9 |
| 4 | 0 | .06 | .16 | .23 | .3 | .37 | .51 | .57 | .73 | .71 | .88 |
| 5 | 0 | .08 | .17 | .25 | .32 | .40 | .50 | .53 | .60 | .67 | .79 |
| 6 | 0 | .07 | .17 | .26 | .34 | .47 | .57 | .63 | .69 | .82 | .87 |
| 7 | 0 | .05 | .15 | .25 | .35 | .45 | .5 | .6 | .7 | .7 | .7 |
| 8 | 0 | .05 | .16 | .22 | .23 | .4 | .5 | .56 | .61 | .8 | .8 |
| 9 | 0 | .1 | .15 | .25 | .35 | .45 | .55 | .65 | .75 | .89 | .95 |
| 10 | 0 | .10 | .20 | .30 | .40 | .50 | .60 | .70 | .80 | .90 | 1 |
| 11 | 1 | 0 | .1 | .2 | .3 | .4 | .5 | .6 | .7 | .8 | .9 |
| 12 | 0 | .02 | .11 | .19 | .27 | .31 | .48 | .51 | .7 | .75 | .84 |
| 13 | 0 | .1 | .2 | .3 | .4 | .5 | .6 | .7 | .8 | .9 | 1 |
| 14 | .9 | 1 | .7 | .8 | 0 | .1 | .4 | .6 | .2 | .5 | .3 |
| 15 | 0 | .06 | .12 | .2 | .23 | .32 | .5 | .55 | .7 | .6 | .66 |
| 16 | 0 | .1 | .2 | .3 | .4 | .5 | .6 | .7 | .8 | .9 | 1 |
| 17 | 0 | .1 | .2 | .2 | .3 | .4 | .5 | .7 | .7 | .8 | .8 |
| 18 | 0 | .1 | .1 | .2 | .3 | .4 | .4 | .4 | .5 | .6 | .7 |
| 19 | 0 | .1 | .2 | .3 | .4 | .5 | .6 | .7 | .8 | .8 | .9 |
| 20 | 0 | - | .23 | .32 | .41 | - | .5 | .6 | 0 | 0 | 0 |
| 21 | .2 | .4 | .1 | .5 | .3 | .7 | .8 | .6 | .9 | 0 | 1 |
| 22 | 0 | .06 | .1 | .2 | .3 | .33 | .41 | .47 | .57 | .61 | .7 |
| 23 | 0 | .06 | .14 | .22 | .29 | .36 | .43 | .5 | .57 | .64 | .74 |
| 24 | 0 | 0 | .1 | .2 | .3 | .4 | .5 | .6 | .6 | .7 | .9 |
| 25 | 0 | .1 | .2 | .3 | .4 | .5 | .6 | .6 | .8 | .8 | .9 |
| 26 | 0 | 0 | 0 | 0 | .1 | .2 | .3 | .4 | .5 | .6 | .7 |
| 27 | .03 | .13 | .23 | .33 | .43 | .53 | .63 | .73 | .83 | .93 | 1.03 |
| 28 | 0 | .1 | .2 | .3 | .4 | .5 | .6 | .7 | .8 | .9 | 1 |
| 29 | 0 | .03 | .07 | .1 | .13 | .17 | .2 | .23 | .27 | .3 | .79 |

later, many beginner participants had great difficulties comprehending the instructions for an abstract sealed bid game. Tests based on such decision data are hardly reasonable.

As required by the strategy method participants $i$ had to specify simultaneously their bids $b_i(v_i)$ for all possible values $v_i$. After collecting all bid vectors the individual values $v_i$ were chosen randomly according to the uniform distribution. We then determined the highest bidder and the price that had to be paid. Participants $i$ learned their chosen value $v_i$ and what they have earned. Only

**Table 10.7**
**The Results for the Beginners**

| Table Ref. | Second Bids $b_i(v_i)$ for $v_i =$ | | | | | | | | | | |
|---|---|---|---|---|---|---|---|---|---|---|---|
| | *.0* | *.1* | *.2* | *.3* | *.4* | *.5* | *.6* | *.7* | *.8* | *.9* | *1* |
| 1 | 0 | .9 | .1 | .2 | .3 | .4 | .5 | .6 | .7 | .8 | .1 |
| 2 | 0 | .05 | .11 | .21 | .31 | .41 | .51 | .61 | .71 | .81 | .91 |
| 3 | 0 | .1 | .1 | .1 | .2 | .3 | .4 | .5 | .6 | .7 | .8 |
| 4 | 0 | .05 | .12 | .22 | .3 | .31 | .51 | .52 | .62 | .81 | .9 |
| 5 | 0 | .08 | .18 | .27 | .34 | .42 | .54 | .57 | .62 | .69 | .81 |
| 6 | .48 | .62 | .71 | .39 | .52 | .67 | .64 | .68 | .59 | .43 | .57 |
| 7 | 0 | .05 | .15 | .25 | .35 | .45 | .5 | .6 | .61 | .65 | .7 |
| 8 | 0 | .05 | .15 | .28 | .38 | .48 | .55 | .68 | .75 | .88 | .95 |
| 9 | 0 | .1 | .2 | .3 | .39 | .49 | .59 | .66 | .79 | .89 | .99 |
| 10 | 0 | .05 | .15 | .25 | .32 | .42 | .50 | .60 | .70 | .80 | .9 |
| 11 | 0 | .2 | .1 | .3 | .7 | .5 | .4 | .6 | .9 | .8 | 1 |
| 12 | 0 | .05 | .13 | .21 | .38 | .41 | .54 | .61 | .51 | .61 | .72 |
| 13 | 0 | .1 | .2 | .3 | .4 | .5 | .6 | .7 | .8 | .9 | 1 |
| 14 | .9 | 1 | .8 | .7 | .5 | .6 | .4 | .1 | .2 | .3 | 0 |
| 15 | 0 | .06 | .13 | .20 | .26 | .34 | .60 | .70 | .80 | .60 | .66 |
| 16 | 0 | .1 | .2 | .3 | .4 | .5 | .6 | .7 | .8 | .9 | 1 |
| 17 | 0 | 0 | .1 | .1 | .2 | .3 | .4 | .5 | .6 | .7 | .7 |
| 18 | 0 | .05 | .1 | .2 | .3 | .4 | .5 | .6 | .7 | .8 | .8 |
| 19 | 0 | 0 | 0 | .2 | .2 | .5 | .6 | .5 | .8 | .9 | 1 |
| 20 | | | | | | | | | | | |
| 21 | .1 | 0 | .2 | .3 | .5 | .4 | .7 | .6 | .8 | 1 | .9 |
| 22 | 0 | .07 | .13 | 0 | 0 | 0 | 0 | 0 | 0 | 0 | 0 |
| 23 | 0 | .05 | .15 | .22 | .29 | .38 | .45 | .52 | .58 | .67 | .75 |
| 24 | 0 | .1 | .2 | .3 | .4 | .5 | .6 | .7 | .8 | .9 | 1 |
| 25 | 0 | 0 | 0 | 0 | .1 | .2 | .3 | .4 | .5 | .6 | .7 |
| 26 | .2 | .3 | .4 | .5 | .6 | .7 | .8 | .9 | 1 | 1.1 | 1.2 |
| 27 | .04 | .14 | .24 | .34 | .44 | .54 | .64 | .74 | .84 | .94 | 1.01 |
| 28 | 0 | .08 | .16 | .24 | .32 | .40 | .48 | .56 | .64 | .72 | .80 |
| 29 | 0 | 0 | .2 | .2 | .2 | .2 | .2 | .2 | .2 | .2 | .2 |

beginner participants repeated the game once (with at least one new partner).

## EXPERIMENTAL RESULTS

The results of the 16 expert participants are listed in Tables 10.3 and 10.4. Only one of them answered the control questions incorrectly and all 16 strategies elicited are weakly monotonic, that is, $b_i(\bar{v}_i) \geq b_i(\underline{v}_i)$ whenever $\bar{v}_i > \underline{v}_i$. We thus never observed low bids for high values as Selten and Buchta (chap. 5, this volume) who also relied on the strategy method in an auction context.[3]

For the beginners the results are listed in the same way in Tables 10.5, 10.6, and 10.7 with the only difference that one has to distinguish between first and second bids $b_i(v_i)$ because the experiment was repeated once. The dramatic effect of further education is revealed by Table 10.8 with the right ($r$) and wrong ($w$) answers of the control questions. Games A.1 & A.2, respectively, denote the first (second) price auction. Games D.1 & D.2, respectively, denote the first (second) price fair division game. Whereas the proportion of correct answers by sophisticated bidders was with 15/16 extremely high, it is with 10/29 frustratingly low for beginners.

As expected, the proportion of monotonic bidding functions among beginners is lower for fair division games than for auction games.

From Table 10.9 one can see that this poor understanding is reflected by a considerable proportion (14 of 58) of nonmonotonic strategies. Because the number of such strategies increased from 6 to 8 from the first to the second trial, it seems that learning does not improve decision quality. None of the 10 beginners who answered the control questions correctly (see Table 10.8), chose a nonmonotonic bidding strategy.

There are too few markets to test our Lack of Efficiency hypothesis A. We therefore suggest to count simply the number of weak potential inefficiencies in the sense of $b_i(v_i) \geq b_j(v_j)$ in spite of $v_i < v_j$ for two different bidders $i$ and $j$ and of strict ones in the sense of $b_i(v_i) > b_j(v_j)$ for $v_i < v_j$. Notice that one bidder can cause many such potential inefficiencies.

Due to the many rather inadequate strategies by beginners we rely only on expert participants when evaluating hypothesis A (see Table 10.10). There are certainly more strict inefficiencies in fair division games than in auctions, as predicted by hypothesis A.2. However, contrary to hypothesis A.1 at least in fair division games there are fewer strict inefficiencies in first price than in second price games.

To test hypothesis B on strategic misrepresentation, we first look at the results in Table 10.11 where we counted the truthful bidding strategies $b_i(v_i) = v_i$ for all $v_i$. Although the proportion of truthful bidding strategies is highest for game A.2, where this is the optimal behavior, truthful bidding is also observed in game D.2. Truthful bidding is the modal behavior of expert bidders not only in game A.2, but also in both fair division games. Hypothesis B.1 is only partly supported. Second price auctions involve more truthful bidding than first price auctions.

The data are consistent with hypothesis B.2 for beginners only. Taking into account the difficulties of some participants to understand the rules,[4] especially of fair division games (see Table 10.8), one can conclude that the underbidding incentives of the first price rule were reasonably understood.

**Table 10.8**
**The Right and Wrong Answers of Control Questions by Beginners**

| Type of Answer | Game | | | |
|---|---|---|---|---|
| | *A.1* | *A.2* | *D.1* | *D.2* |
| Right | 4 | 4 | 1 | 1 |
| Wrong | 5 | 3 | 4 (5) | 5 (6) |

Note. Brackets give numbers of those who answered wrongly or not at all.

**Table 10.9**
**Weakly Monotonic and Nonmonotonic Strategies of Beginners**

| Type of Strategy | Game | | | | | | | |
|---|---|---|---|---|---|---|---|---|
| | *A.1* | | *A.2* | | *D.1* | | *D.2* | |
| | *1st* | *2nd* | *1st* | *2nd* | *1st* | *2nd* | *1st* | *2nd* |
| Weakly Monotonic | 8 | 7 | 5 | 5 | 4 | 2 | 6 | 7 |
| Nonmonotonic | 1 | 2 | 2 | 2 | 2 | 4 | 1 | 0 |

Hypothesis B.3, which predicts overbidding in game D.2, is only weakly confirmed: Only one of four expert participants and one of seven beginners submitted bids of more than their true value. Hypothesis B.4 is consistent with the behavior of expert bidders who all underbid in the auction game A.1 and never underbid in the fair division game D.1.

# THE PREDICTIONS OF QUALITATIVE LEARNING

Although we do not expect participants to choose as predicted by the normative solution, they may nevertheless improve their behavior over time in the light of their earlier experiences. According to qualitative or directional learning (see,

**Table 10.10**
**Weak and Strict Potential Inefficiencies for Expert Participants**

| Potential Inefficiencies | Game | | | |
|---|---|---|---|---|
|  | _A.1_ | _A.2_ | _D.1_ | _D.2_ |
| Weak | 20 | 28 | 25 | 21 |
| Strict | 8 | 0 | 17 | 21 |

for instance, Selten & Buchta, chap. 5, this volume), after receiving some feedback, a participant will question whether the decision could have been better or not, and adjust decision behavior in the direction of the better choice. For the case at hand these conclusions depend, of course, on the game model.

For a first price auction a bidder, who did not buy, will increase the bid when the price was below the true value. In more formal notation this can be described by

$$b^t\left(v^t\right) \le p^t < v^t \Rightarrow \Delta b^{t+1}\left(v^t\right) = b^{t+1}\left(v^t\right) - b^t\left(v^t\right) > 0 . \tag{4}$$

Here $v^t$ is the realized true value in period $t$ and $b^t(v^t)$ the corresponding bid in $t$, $p^t$ the price in $t$ and $b^{t+1}(v^t)$ the bid for the value $v^t$ in the next period $t+1$. In the same way one derives qualitative improvements or directions for adjusting behavior for a buyer as well as for nonbuyers and buyers for the three other game models (see the nonbuyer and buyer row of Table 10.12).

Of course, the situations described for nonbuyers and buyers in the first four rows of Table 10.12 are not exhaustive – they exclude, for instance, situations with $b^t(v^t) = v^t$ for nonbuyers: In auctions there is nothing to be learned if the bid $b^t(v^t) = v^t$ led to nonbuying. The same applies to fair division games relying on the highest bid-price. Increasing one's bid $b^t(v^t)$ above $v^t$ in fair division games with the second price rule does not change the result as long as $b^t(v^t) \le p^t$. Increasing one's bid above $p^t$ is, furthermore, no sure improvement because it could result in buying at a too high price.

The second to last line of Table 10.12, which uses only beginners' data, [5] simply lists the number of applicable cases out of the total number of observations meaning that the situation fell into one of the four categories. In the last line one can find how many of the applicable cases confirmed to the theory of directional learning as it has been specified. In general, at least half of the applicable cases confirmed to theory. An exceptional high hit rate was achieved for the first price auction where all eight applicable cases did not contradict the

**Table 10.11**
**Frequencies of Truthful Bidding Strategies $b_i(v_i) = v_i$ for Sophisticated Bidders and Beginners**

| | Expert bidders | | | | Beginners | | | |
| --- | --- | --- | --- | --- | --- | --- | --- | --- |
| | Game | | | | Game | | | |
| Strategy | A.1 | A.2 | D.1 | D.2 | A.1 | A.2 | D.1 | D.2 |
| Truthful | 0 | 3 | 2 | 3 | 0 | 5 | 0 | 2 |
| Nontruthful | 4 | 1 | 2 | 1 | 18 | 9 | 12 | 12 |

**Table 10.12**
**The Evidence of Qualitative Learning (Beginners Only)**

| Trader | Situation | Game A.1 1st Price Auction | A.2 2nd Price Auction | D.1 1st Price Fair Division | D.2 2nd Price Fair Division |
| --- | --- | --- | --- | --- | --- |
| Non buyer | $b^t(v^t) \le p^t < v$ $b^t(v^t) < v^t \le p$ | $\Delta b^{t+1}(v^t) > 0$ $\Delta b^{t+1}(v^t) \ge 0$ | $\Delta b^{t+1}(v^t) > 0$ $\Delta b^{t+1}(v^t) \ge 0$ | $\Delta b^{t+1}(v^t) > 0$ $\Delta b^{t+1}(v^t) > 0$ | $\Delta b^{t+1}(v^t) > 0$ $\Delta b^{t+1}(v^t) > 0$ |
| Buyer | $b^t(v^t) \ge p^t > v$ $v^t \ge b^t(v^t) \ge p$ | $\Delta b^{t+1}(v^t) < 0$ $\Delta b^{t+1}(v^t) \le 0$ | $\Delta b^{t+1}(v^t) < 0$ $\Delta b^{t+1}(v^t) \le 0$ | $\Delta b^{t+1}(v^t) < 0$ $\Delta b^{t+1}(v^t) \le 0$ | $\Delta b^{t+1}(v^t) < 0$ $\Delta b^{t+1}(v^t) \ge 0$ |
| Number of applicable cases | | 8 of 9 | 5 of 7 | 4 of 5 | 3 of 7 |
| Hit rate | | 8 of 8 | 3 of 5 | 2 of 4 | 2 of 3 |

predictions of directional learning.

## SOME (PRELIMINARY?) CONCLUSIONS

Our study demonstrates the dramatic consequences of further education as measured by our simple control questions and the observation of weakly monotonic bids. In our view, it is not education as such, but the selection bias of advanced courses that caused the fundamental differences in understanding of instructions. In general, it seems fair to say that expert bidders reveal similar qualitative aspects as optimal bidders.

What can one conclude from the behavior of beginners who poorly understood the instructions? Here we have relied on the theory of directional learning applied by Selten and Buchta (chap. 5, this volume) to first price auctions. For this game it also helps to organize the data here (all eight applicable cases confirmed the theory, see Table 10.12). But for the three other games the results on learning are more ambiguous.

Of course, one could hope to gain better results even from beginners by relying on computerized experiments[6] with many repetitions like Selten and Buchta (chap. 5, this volume). Because they have concentrated on the first price auction where the theory works without many repetitions, it remains an open problem whether a similar number of repetitions will work for the other three games.

In case of sophisticated participants the interesting question seems to be whether the decision behavior, which confirms to theory, is caused by education itself (e.g., by some basic understanding of game theory) or by the selection bias of advanced courses requiring considerable analytic thinking. With respect to beginners further pen-and-paper experiments with too few opportunities for directional learning appeared useless. Further experiments with beginners should offer similar learning opportunities as Selten and Buchta (chap. 5, this volume). This, of course, means that such experiments must be computerized. Notice, however, that this may have the drawback of inducing variety seeking, for example, in the sense of "going for the big money" by bidding low when the true value is very high (see Selten & Buchta, chap. 5, this volume).

## ACKNOWLEDGMENTS

I gratefully acknowledge the discussions with Peter Bohm and Joakim Sonnegard and the very helpful comments by Rami Zwick and two anonymous referees. I want to thank Amnon Rapoport for many inspirations and also thank him and Maya for their friendship and hospitality.

# ENDNOTES

1. This excludes so-called "all pay auctions" although they can be studied in the same way as "only the buyer pays auctions" (see, for instance, Amann and Leininger, 1995).
2. If not, some nonbuyers would envy each other.
3. This, of course, could be an artifact of their experimental design, for example, their ingenious method of eliciting piecewise linear bid functions for continuously varying true values $v_i$. More likely, in our view, is that participants in the Selten and Buchta experiment strive for the big profit because they play the game very often and want to try something new, that is, by playing risky because it could yield a large profit. The assumption of constant risk aversion is often imposed in economic models, but is hardly supported by facts. As in their consumption attitudes and in risky matters, people are looking for variety, for example, by buying insurance and lottery tickets at the same time.
4. In view of the poor understanding of the rules by beginners, especially of the fair division game D.1 (see Table 10.11), we refrain from comparing the amount of underbidding in the two games A.1 and D.1 by beginners. Any such attempt would be mainly measuring the quantities of inadequate decision making.
5. Because expert participants did not repeat the game, their learning cannot be tested.
6. Future research will concentrate on computerized experiments in which participants confront all four game situations repeatedly with at least partly changing partners (Güth, Ivanova, Königstein, & Strobel, 1998).

# REFERENCES

Amann, E., & Leininger, W. (1995). Expected revenue of all-pay and first price sealed-bid auctions with affiliated signals. *Journal of Economics, 61*, 273- 279.

Cox, J., Smith, V. L. & Walker, J. M. (1982). Theory and behavior of single object auctions. In V. L. Smith (Ed.), *Research in experimental economics.* Greenwich, CT: JAI Press.

Güth, W. (1986): Auctions, public tenders, and fair division games: An axiomatic approach, *Mathematical Social Sciences, 11*, 283 - 294.

Güth, W., & van Damme, E. (1986). A comparison of pricing rules for auctions and fair division games. *Social Choice and Welfare, 3*, 177-198.

Güth, W., van Damme, E., & Weber, M. (1993). *The normative and behavioral concept of risk aversion – An experimental study.* Working Paper, University of Tilburg.

Güth, W., Ivanova, R., Königstein, M., & Strobel, M. (1998). *Learning to bid – An experimental study of bid function adjustments in auctions and fair division games.* Working Paper, Humboldt University, Berlin.

Kagel, J. H. (1995). Auctions: A survey of experimental research. In J. H. Kagel & A. E. Roch (Eds.), *The Handbook of Experimental Economics* (pp.501-585). Princeton, NJ: Princeton University Press.

Plum, M. (1992). Characterization and computation of Nash-equilibria for auctions with incomplete information. *International Journal of Game Theory, 20*, 393 - 418.

Prasnikar, V. (1993). Binary lotteries in experimental economics. *Unpublished doctoral dissertation*, University of Pittsburgh.

Rietz, T. A. (1993). Implementing and testing risk-preference-induction mechanisms in experimental sealed-bid auctions. *Journal of Risk and Uncertainty, 7*, 199 - 213.

Selten, R., Sadrieh, A., & Abbink, K. (1996). Money does not induce risk neutral behavior, but binary lotteries do even worse. *Discussion Paper No. B-343*, Sonderforschungsbereich 303, University of Bonn.

Vickrey, W. (1961). Counterspeculation, auctions, and competitive sealed tenders. *Journal of Finance, 16*, 8-37.

# APPENDIX A: INSTRUCTIONS

Please read these instructions carefully. After reading these instructions and trying to understand them you can ask questions privately if necessary. Please, indicate this by raising your hand. But do not speak aloud!

In the experiment you - let us call you 'bidder $i$' - can buy a fictitious indivisible commodity from us whose only value for you consists in reselling it to us at your personal reselling value $v_i$. This value $v_i$ can assume the following levels:

$$0.0 \text{ or } 0.1 \text{ or } 0.2, ..., 0.9 \text{ or } 1.0$$

which are all shares of one ECU (Experimental Currency Unit where ECU $1.0 = $ DM ?) and where all the eleven values of $v_i$ are equally likely.

Since you will not know your value $v_i$ when trying to buy the commodity, you will have to determine a bid $b_i (v_i)$ for all eleven (11) values of $v_i$. There are two other participants who are confronted with the same instructions as you, and who also are interested in buying the commodity. When all three of you have chosen their bids $b_i (v_i)$, we have three vectors of bids

$$(b_i (0), b_i (0.1), ..., b_i (0.9), b_i (1.0))$$

Since the three reselling prices of the three bidders $i$ are determined independently according to the same random device (all $v_i$'s are equally likely), they will rarely be the same.

For the three bid vectors the result will be determined as follows:

First we randomly and independently determine for all the three bidders $i$ the reselling values $v_i$ (all $v_i$'s are equally likely) and look at the corresponding bids $b_i (v_i)$. Of course, the bidder $i$, whose bid $b_i (v_i)$ is highest, buys the commodity. In case of more than one highest bidder each of them has an equal chance to buy the commodity. We refer to the highest bidder as the buyer.

**Important!**
The price which the buyer has to pay is the highest bid, i.e., his own bid. The buyer resells the commodity at the price $v_i$ and thus earns a profit of $v_i - b_i (v_i)$. The two remaining bidders receive 0-payments, i.e., they do not win or lose money.

Please, notice that your payment can become negative only if you overbid your reselling price $v_i$ in the sense of $b_i (v_i) > v_i$. Thus you can avoid a monetary loss by avoiding overbidding. It is up to you, of course, what you decide to do. You should, however, be aware that we collect losses (you would have to pay) as we pay out gains (you collect money).

**Important!**

The price which the buyer has to pay is the second highest bid, i.e., the price is lower than his own bid if he is the only highest bidder. Let's call this price $p_2$. The buyer $i$ resells the commodity at the price $v_i$ and thus earns a profit of $v_i$ - $p_2$. The two remaining bidders receive 0-payments, i.e., they do not win or lose money.

Please, notice that your payment can become negative only if you overbid your reselling price $v_i$ in the sense of $b_i(v_i) > v_i$. Thus you can avoid a monetary loss by avoiding overbidding. It is up to you, of course, what you decide to do. You should, however, be aware that we collect losses (you would have to pay) as we pay out gains (you collect money).

**Important!**
The price which the buyer has to pay is the highest bid, i.e., his own bid. The price has to be equally divided among all the three bidders. The buyer $i$ resells the commodity at the price $v_i$ and thus earns a profit of

$$v_i - b_i(v_i) + 1/3 \cdot b_i(v_i) = v_i - 2/3 \cdot b_i(v_i)$$

whereas the two remaining bidders receive $b_i(v_i)/3$ each.

Please, notice that your payment can become negative only if you overbid your reselling price $v_i$ in the sense of $b_i(v_i) > v_i$. Thus you can avoid a monetary loss by avoiding overbidding. It is up to you, of course, what you decide to do. You should, however, be aware that we collect losses (you would have to pay) as we pay out gains (you collect money).

**Important!**
The price which the buyer has to pay is the highest bid of the two other bidders, i.e., the price is lower than his own bid if he is the only highest bidder. Let's call this price $p_2$. This price has to be equally divided among all the three bidders. The buyer $i$ resells the commodity at the price $v_i$ and thus earns a profit of

$$v_i - p_2 + 1/3 \cdot p_2 = v_i - 2/3 \cdot p_2$$

whereas the two remaining bidders receive $p_2/3$ each.

Please, notice that your payment can become negative only if you overbid your reselling price $v_i$ in the sense of $b_i(v_i) > v_i$. Thus you can avoid a monetary loss by avoiding overbidding. It is up to you, of course, what you decide to do. You should, however, be aware that we collect losses (you would have to pay) as we pay out gains (you collect money).

# APPENDIX B

<u>Bidding Form</u>                                         Code No.........................

Please, notice that your reselling value may be (as shares of one ECU = Experimental Currency Unit = DM ?)

$$0.0, 0.1, 0.2, 0.3, 0.4, 0.5, 0.6, 0.7, 0.8, 0.9, 1.0$$

and that all these values are equally likely. You therefore must choose a bid for all these values. If you do not specify a bid for each of these values, we unfortunately will have to exclude you from the experiment.

If my reselling value is 0.0, I bid ...............................................

If my reselling value is 0.1, I bid ...............................................

If my reselling value is 0.2, I bid ...............................................

If my reselling value is 0.3, I bid ...............................................

If my reselling value is 0.4, I bid ...............................................

If my reselling value is 0.5, I bid ...............................................

If my reselling value is 0.6, I bid ...............................................

If my reselling value is 0.7, I bid ...............................................

If my reselling value is 0.8, I bid ...............................................

If my reselling value is 0.9, I bid ...............................................

If my reselling value is 1.0, I bid ...............................................


(you must fill in a bid in each of the 11 rows!)

# APPENDIX C

<u>Preexperimental Questionnaire</u>                    Code No ...........................

Before the experiment starts we kindly ask you to answer a few personal questions and to calculate for a simple example the monetary profits (as shares of one ECU) of all three bidders 1,2, and 3. These answers do not influence what you will finally gain, but they have to be answered completely.

Assume that the chosen reselling values $v_1$, $v_2$, $v_3$ for bidders 1, 2, and 3 are $v_1 = 0.3$, $v_2 = 0.7$, and $v_3 = 0.8$ and that the bids of 1, 2, and 3 for these values are $b_1$ (0.3) = 0.4, $b_2$ (0.7) = 0.9, and $b_3$ (0.8) = 0.6. Please, calculate the monetary profits for all three bidders:

- Bidder 1 with $v_1 = 0.3$ gets:     ...........................
- Bidder 2 with $v_2 = 0.7$ gets:     ...........................
- Bidder 3 with $v_3 = 0.8$ gets:     ...........................

Gender:                 □ female □ male

Age:                    I am ......... years old.

Field of study:         I study / have studied
          ....................................................

          ....................................................

Academic degree:
bachelor (Vordiplom)                    □ Yes          □ No
masters (Diplom o.ä.)                   □ Yes          □ No
doctoral degree (Doktortitel)           □ Yes          □ No

Nationality:                    ......................................

# 11     Infinite Horizon Bargaining Games: Theory and Experiments

## Eythan Weg
*Indiana University*

## Rami Zwick
*Hong Kong University of Science and Technology*

This chapter attempts to dismantle the myth that modeling bargaining as an infinite horizon bargaining process is too complex to merit experimentation by providing a simplified approach to the solution of the games underlying this process. In addition, a very rich menu for experimentation with external opportunities and risks is provided. A finite horizon model would be much more cumbersome and *artificial*. The solution of infinite games is approached through a very natural strategic game form built from the original bargaining tree. A distinguished subset of its Nash equilibria are identified for many cases (met in practice) with subgame perfect solutions of the tree. This approach exposes the fact that infinite horizon reasoning relies on a very weak form of backward induction, as opposed to the complete and lengthy induction necessary for finite games.

Although promising, the experimental work surveyed provides only weak and equivocal support for rational behavior. The need arises for further abstraction of the bargaining process for a better fit with the phenomena investigated, a procedure recommended by Rubinstein (1991) in the wider context of game theory in practice.

## PURE BARGAINING

How is a valuable object, jointly owned by two parties, shared? This question epitomizes a fundamental question of economics. It encompasses the boundedness of a resource that must be shared if it is to be useful at all.

Two general approaches have been pursued. The axiomatic, with Nash (1950) its most well-known representative, and the procedural, best represented by Rubinstein (1982). The axiomatic method specifies certain desiderata that a bargaining ruling should satisfy. In the best case, these are also sufficient to specify a solution to the problem. This method refrains from promulgating a procedure by which the bargaining outcome is to be attained. Therefore, it is robust regarding changes in the bargaining conditions. The procedural approach specifies exactly how the bargaining is to take place. In this way, it is less dependent on axioms that lack unanimous endorsement. Ideally, as Nash hoped for, a bargaining procedure could be found to justify an axiomatic approach to bargaining. Although this idea has been pursued nothing convincing seems to appear.[1]

It was Rubinstein (1982), equipped with the then new concept of the *subgame*[2] *perfect equilibrium* (SPE) rationality developed by Selten (1975), who was able to exploit what seemed to many to be a natural bargaining scenario. It is this bargaining approach that is explored in this chapter.

Consider a unit (the pie) jointly owned by two people who can enjoy any part of it as described by their respective continuously increasing utility function $u_i$. Rubinstein considers an atomic building block of bargaining and iterates it as follows. One player suggests a demand $x$ of the pie with the rest offered to the other player. If the latter agrees, the bargaining terminates with the demand accepted. Otherwise, the discrete bargaining clock ticks one period forward and the players swap their roles and start all over again. This continues until the white smoke of agreement is detected.

This description fits perfectly into the standard paradigm of games in extensive form, which, after Selten's innovation, could be solved in a more refined manner than provided by the approach endorsed by Von-Neumann, who saw such games in their folded normal (or strategic) form. Thus, instead of looking for Nash equilibria, which are guaranteed to exist, one looks for a subset of these equilibria that survives after eliminating all those that fail to remain in equilibrium for at least one subgame.[3] The principal beauty of Rubinstein's result is that this set is not empty under a very mild requirement regarding the effects of time: the utility of $x$ consumed at time $t$ is given by $u_i(x)\delta_i^t$, where $0 \leq \delta_i \leq 1$.[4]

To introduce SPE in a very transparent approach (good at least for the periodic structure of bargaining we have in mind), we consider the *fold* of the given bargaining game. This is a two-person strategic game defined as follows. Let

$$X_i(x_j) = \{0 \leq x \leq 1 | u_j(1-x) \geq u_j(x_j)\delta_j\} \qquad (1)$$

be player $i$'s strategy set depending on player $j$'s strategy $x_j$. The strategy set of each player depends on the strategy chosen by the other. Thus a player's choice of strategy is restricted by the other's choice, with the simple interpretation that in the extensive bargaining game what one offers the other $(1-x)$, must not be lower in utility than the expected utility from the latter's planned action. This interpretation might be characterized as mutual individual rationality. But it is not sufficient to specify any action. For example, the strategy 0 is mutually rational with every strategy of the other player. It is clear that these sets are nonempty, closed, and convex. We define formally the utility of a strategy combination $(x_1, x_2)$ to player $i$ as $u_i(x_i)$. A Nash equilibrium of the fold game is a point $(x_1, x_2) \in X_1(x_2) \times X_2(x_1)$ such that for all $x \in X_i(x_j)$ we have $u_i(x) \leq u_i(x_i)$.

It is clear that the Nash equilibria of the fold game are given by the solutions of the set

$$u_1(1-x_2) \geq \delta_1 u_1(x_1)$$
$$u_2(1-x_1) \geq \delta_2 u_2(x_2) \tag{2}$$

where at least one of these inequalities is satisfied as an equality. It should be intuitively clear that not all Nash equilibria of the fold game are supported in the extensive game by a subgame Nash equilibrium. This distinguished set is characterized as the solutions of Eq. 2 satisfied as equalities. One can view the choice of strategy sets as satisfying a necessary condition for subgame perfectness.

For the immediate experimental applications we assume that $u(x) = x$ or $u(x) = \exp(x)$. One can easily see that for the first case

$$x_1 = \frac{1-\delta_2}{1-\delta_1\delta_2} \tag{3}$$

and for the second

$$x_1 = \begin{cases} 1 & \text{if } \delta_1 > \delta_2 \\ -\log\delta_2 & \text{if } \delta_2 > \delta_1 \\ [-\log\delta_1, 1] & \text{otherwise.} \end{cases} \tag{4}$$

The value of $x_2$ is then calculated by substitution.

We refer to the first type of time utility interaction as *geometric depreciation* and to the second as *arithmetic depreciation*.[5] This distinction is not mutually exclusive. It has more to do with the framing of the space-time preference structure than with anything else. Geometric depreciation with risk-neutral utilities, however, is directly comparable with the arithmetic case.

## Duality

There are situations where the need arises to share a painful or an aversive joint object. Examples are the joint losses of a failed partnership or the division of a shared investment. In such cases, each of the parties attempts to *minimize* his or her share in the joint aversive property that we call, for simplicity, *deficit*. In contrast, the thing desired would be termed joint *surplus*. It will be efficient if the same theory could be applied to both cases. The following *duality* principle shows that this is indeed the case. It serves as a dictionary for the translation of bargaining problems over deficit into bargaining problems over surplus, and vice-versa.

Assume that a timed loss can be measured by the product of an increasing nonnegative function $l$ and a power of $\gamma > 1$. Thus the total loss of a share $x$ at time $t$ is $l(x)\gamma^t$.[6] Then

$$l(x)\gamma^t \leq l(y)\gamma^s \tag{5}$$

iff

$$\frac{1}{l(1-x')}(\frac{1}{\gamma})^t \geq \frac{1}{l(1-y')}(\frac{1}{\gamma})^s \tag{6}$$

where $x = 1 - x'$ and $y = 1 - y'$. If we set $\frac{1}{l(1-x')} = u(x')$, and $\frac{1}{\gamma} = \delta < 1$, we see that to solve a deficit problem amounts to solving a surplus problem and applying the appropriate transformation. Thus we have the following duality:

**Theorem (The Dictionary).** *Every deficit bargaining situation* $D = (l_1, \gamma_1, l_2, \gamma_2)$ *has a dual surplus problem* $S = (u_1 = \frac{1}{l_1(1-(\cdot))}, \delta_1 = \frac{1}{\gamma_1}, u_2 = \frac{1}{(l_2(1-(\cdot)))}, \delta_2 = \frac{1}{\gamma_2})$ *and vice-versa. Moreover,* $x$ *is a rational share to party 1 in* $D$ *if and only if* $1 - x$ *is a share to party 1 in* $S$.

Note that the proof has nothing to do with the bargaining procedure from which the particular solution is derived. Thus, the duality principle can be applied to any bargaining solution where time affects utility in the manner assumed by the theorem.

**Corollary.** *When* $l_i(x) = x$, *party 1's share is*

$$\frac{1 - \gamma_1}{1 - \gamma_1 \gamma_2}. \tag{7}$$

The proof is immediate by invoking the dictionary with Eq. 3.
**Example.** For the risk-neutral (identity) loss functions with $\gamma_i = 10/9$, party 1's share is $9/19$.

We consider another special case:

**Corollary.** *Let the loss functions be* $l_i(x) = \exp(x)$. *Then party 1's cost share is*

$$x_1 = \begin{cases} \{0\} & if\ \gamma_1 < \gamma_2 \\ \{1 - \log(\gamma_2)\} & if\ \gamma_1 > \gamma_2 \\ [0, 1 - \log(\gamma_1)] & if\ \gamma_1 = \gamma_2. \end{cases} \tag{8}$$

*Proof.* This follows immediately from the dictionary and Eq. 4.
**Example.** Consider an arithmetic depreciation bargaining on a deficit, with bargaining costs of $\log(\gamma_1) = c_1 = 0.2$ and $\log(\gamma_2) = c_2 = 0.1$. The last corollary shows that Player 1's share in the deficit is 0.9.

Again, although the duality principle depends only on the separability of the time and space components of the preference structure, the formulas derived by these corollaries *do* depend on the bargaining procedure and on the rationality concept prescribed — SPE.

## SHARING A PIE IN PRACTICE

Several experiments were carried out to test a variety of the hypotheses implied by the solution of the bargaining problem. Some employed arithmetic depreciation (also referred to as fixed cost), some geometric depreciation (also referred to as discount rate) and some even proposed alternative rejection procedures. This section reviews the outcomes of these experiments.

## Arithmetic Depreciation

The very first experiment implementing the Rubinstein procedure with a fixed cost ($c = -\log(\delta)$) per period was conducted by Rapoport, Weg, and Felsenthal (1990). This experiment is divided into two studies that differ only by the levels of the fixed costs of the bargaining periods. In each step of this experiment, an initial group of students is subdivided randomly into pairs and each pair is engaged in a division of a pie of 30 Israeli Shekels according to the Rubinstein regime. In order to end each bargaining within reason, bargaining is allowed to continue for at least eight periods but no more than 13 periods. The exact cutoff is randomly chosen within this interval but subjects were not privy to this rule. The logistics of running concurrent bargaining games and stepping through the several games that each member of the group of subjects is engaged in during a given experimental session are governed by a computer program running under a time sharing system.

In both parts of the experiment, three power relationships between the players were conceived: $S$ ($c_1 < c_2$), $W$ ($c_1 > c_2$), and $E$ ($c_1 = c_2$). The $c_i$ are members of $\{0.1, 2.5\}$ for the first study and of $\{0.2, 3.0\}$ for the second. A maximal cost within these respective sets is taken for condition $E$.

Figure 11.1 presents the data as reflected by last period demands by Player 1 (first mover) in the last iteration of each play.[7] Under condition $S$, Player 1 is expected to demand (in the first period) 30 Shekels in either of the studies and under condition $W$, 2.5 Shekels in Study 1 and 3.0 Shekels in Study 2. This assumes that the bargaining terminates immediately, but if not, it repeatedly starts a new subgame of type $S$ or type $W$ and because 2.5 or 3.0 are small compared to 30.00 we do not expect to find much of a difference if we look at last period demands.[8] The raw data is particularly impressive as extreme demands by and offers to the strong players are not buried in the averages. Averages, in this case, are not particularly appropriate because boundary outcomes are predicted whereas statistics based on typical values normally assume deviations on *either* side, that is, demands are expected to fall beyond the boundary.

The second study (Weg & Zwick, 1991), which followed a similar design to the Rapoport et al.'s studies investigated the robustness of the rational solution under an isomorphic transformation provided by the duality principle discussed earlier. Specifically, it defines an apparently different arithmetic depreciation bargaining where a better outcome is measured by how small it is. That is, a bargainer minimizes losses instead of maximizes gains. Formally, the disutility of $x$ at time $t$ is measured by $x + tc$ where $c > 0$. In a previous section we have shown that the problem is identical to the maximization of share under the utility $1 - x - tc$. Thus the experiment provides for a comparison between playing dual surplus and deficit games. Weg and Zwick (1991) compared bargaining over losses to bargaining over gains by the same subjects (within subject design) with pies of \$15 and costs set of $\{0.05, 1.25\}$. Condition $E$ studied by Rapoport et al. was not investigated due to the expected uninformative outcomes of such a condition. Fig-

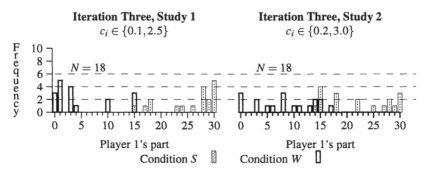

Fig. 11.1. Last period demands.

ure 11.2 presents the raw data for the second (and last) iteration, where payoffs for deficit bargaining are normalized by the duality transformation $1 - x$ which allows comparisons on equal footing with surplus games.

Three conclusions can be drawn from these experiments:

1. Strong parties obtain in general what is predicted by subgame perfect rationality.
2. It is hard to tell the difference between bargaining over losses and bargaining over gains.
3. Weak Player 1s (first movers) cannot in general improve their lot by decree: The game moves on to a subgame where the strong player usually sets the "price". The outcomes are invariant with regard to the position of the strong party except that a strong second party tends to get his or her share later than expected.

What makes the arithmetic depreciation preference structure attractive is the clear-cut extreme predictions it implies. We explore some interesting applications of this structure and now turn to a relatively more complex prediction derived from the Rubinstein paradigm.

## Geometric Depreciation

According to Eq. 3, Player 1's demand is a continuous and nonconstant function of the discounting parameters. Can one expect human subjects to attend to the type of influence these parameters have on the predicted (subgame perfect) demands? Equation 4, which is applicable to arithmetic devaluation, is immensely simpler although discontinuous. It is (two-valued) constant almost everywhere. And, moreover, the domain of constancy is a union of two connected regions. Therefore, assuming only rough sensitivity to parameter values by subjects, it stands to reason that rational but perhaps cognitively limited players would ad-

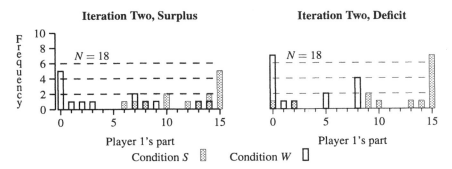

Fig. 11.2. Final demands by Player 1. Seven data points (of plays ended prematurely) are not shown.

here more closely to subgame perfect rationality in an arithmetic depreciating environment than in a geometric one.[9]

Much research reports on experiments where the identity utility is depreciated geometrically over time. Weg, Rapoport, and Felsenthal (1990) attempted to test rationality in a purely Rubinstein, alternating offer bargaining. Bargainers in this paradigm have no other option but to come to an agreement in finite time even though time is not formally limited, though no infinite paths are superior to any other path. Thus, bargainers have a strong incentive not to pursue such paths.

Two independent studies, which are replications of each other in every way except for the quotient values (discount rates), are reported. In either study the pie is 60.00 Shekels. In the first study the discounts are relatively mild and specify three conditions: $(\delta_1, \delta_2)$ is either $(0.90, 0.17)$, or $(0.50, 0.90)$, or $(0.67, 0.67)$. The second study experiments with steeper rates — $(0.50, 0.17)$, $(0.17, 0.50)$, or $(0.17, 0.17)$. Table 11.1 shows the general trends.

The pattern seems to support the conclusion that strong players 1 are only able to extract *at best* half pies, and weak players 1 signal their intention to compensate for their steeper devaluation.[10] Note that these findings are in distinct contradiction to rationality because they fail to account for the cost of time in many ways:

1. A breakdown of monotonicity (in the right direction) with quotient values. For example, if we denote by $x(\alpha, \beta)$ the payoff to player 1 for game parameters $(\alpha, \beta)$, then for $\delta_1 < \delta_2$ we must have $x(\delta_1, \delta_1) > x(\delta_2, \delta_2)$. In fact, for these cases bargainers split pies in half, which is approximately correct only for extremely high quotients, that is, when time is negligible.

2. Symmetrization of players' positions. In theory, time is valuable and therefore $x(\delta_1, \delta_2) \neq 1 - x(\delta_2, \delta_1)$, or putting it differently, in general bargaining is not symmetric with respect to time. Unfortunately, this is not reflected in the data. Regardless of position, players' payoffs depend solely on their time

**Table 11.1**
**Mean First and Final Shares to Player 1 in Studies 1 and 2**

| Iteration | $\delta_1 > \delta_2$ | $\delta_1 = \delta_2$ | $\delta_1 < \delta_2$ | $\delta_1 > \delta_2$ | $\delta_1 = \delta_2$ | $\delta_1 < \delta_2$ |
|---|---|---|---|---|---|---|
| | **Study 1** | | | | | |
| | **First Offers** | | | **Final Offers** | | |
| 1 | 29.4 | 31.6 | 36.4 | 27.1 | 30.5 | 36.0 |
| 2 | 30.6 | 31.1 | 36.9 | 27.6 | 30.7 | 36.4 |
| 3 | 30.1 | 31.0 | 36.0 | 24.4 | 31.0 | 36.5 |
| | **Study 2** | | | | | |
| 1 | 29.5 | 33.0 | 42.8 | 22.4 | 31.8 | 40.3 |
| 2 | 28.6 | 34.3 | 43.3 | 23.2 | 32.5 | 42.1 |
| 3 | 19.2 | 36.1 | 46.1 | 23.1 | 34.3 | 43.6 |

devaluation.

## A Prelude to Optional Game Termination

One of the more interesting applications of arithmetic depreciation bargaining is the assessment of the prevalence of fairness considerations in economic situations (Kahneman, Knetsch, & Thaler, 1986). Güth, Schmittberger, and Schwarze (1982) initiated a long line of ultimatum studies where one person proposes a "take it or leave it" offer regarding the division of a pie. Thus, one player proposes $x$ and the other either accepts it, in which case the game terminates with the proposed outcome, or rejects it where the status quo (normalized to 0) is obtained. This study showed that most proposers would share the pie evenly, in apparent support of fairness considerations, and further, positive offers are rejected in contradiction to rational behavior. Rejection of any part of the pie is an admission that obtaining nothing, in this game, is preferred to consuming a positive part of it, which is normally untrue in the context of individual choice. The problem with the ultimatum game as a tool in the investigation of fairness in economic settings is that it does not have an appropriate control game. Thus, it is not a priori clear whether the proposer is mitigated by a fear of rejection or by a consideration of fairness.[11] We shall now show how the arithmetic cost structure lends itself to several types of tests of the fairness issue. For this we need to dwell a little more on the theory of division problems with so-called outside options.

## BASIC OUTSIDE OPTIONS

Rubinstein's alternating offer paradigm is considered as atomic or pure bargaining. There are several directions one can take with the aim of expanding the atomic form. Here we consider one such extension. In a later section, we provide a broader generalization of this route.

In atomic bargaining, players find satisfaction only through an agreement. But this is possible only in a fully deterministic world. Because bargaining proceeds through steps in time, it is conceivable that the intentions of the players may not be fulfilled and/or some new opportunities may arise.

We introduce a new move that results in the realization of the status quo. Thus a player may opt to quit the bargaining on receipt of any offer. Of course, the termination of bargaining without an agreement should lead to some payoffs. If bargaining is to take place, we shall impose some restrictions on these payoffs. A natural rough requirement is that the sum of these payoffs in pie units is no greater than the pie. For otherwise, one party may not have enough incentive to bargain at all.

Sutton (1986) suggested a generalization of this idea. Consider a random event $E$ that may follow a rejection of an offer with a given, and commonly known probability, $p$. Sutton suggests two interpretations for the occurrence of $E$:

$V$. In the *voluntary* interpretation the rejecting player ($i$) has the option to consume an outside value of $s_i$. In this case the other player consumes an outside value and the bargaining terminates. If the rejecting player chooses not to consume the outside value, the bargaining clock moves one unit forward and a new demand (normally by the rejecting player) is considered.[12]

$F$. In the *forced* interpretation, the occurrence of $E$ signifies the necessity to terminate the bargaining with each player consuming his or her outside values $s_i$. The clock does not tick.

If $E$ does not occur, the bargaining clock simply ticks a unit. We refer to a player as an F-player or a V-player depending on the interpretation of the event $E$ that may follow his or her rejection of an offer.

Note that the notion of outside options is orthogonal to the bargaining procedure and that, in fact, only the Rubinstein procedure has been given experimental treatment in non-cooperative bargaining.

### Forced Termination

Consider two F-players characterized by the probability $p$ of being terminated with outside status-quo payoff $s_i$. How should they play? We imitate the approach we have taken earlier by defining an appropriate fold game. We derive subgame perfectness from the following principles:

*Interperiod Rationality*. An offer will not be accepted if it dictates less utility

than what one offers oneself. This will be translated into a specific operationalization, depending on the bargaining environment. Equation 2 is specific to pure Rubinstein bargaining. For an FF bargaining environment, this
is translated to $u_i(1 - x_j) \geq (1 - p)\delta_i u_i(x_i) + p u_i(s_i)$ for $i \neq j$. The right-
hand term in this inequality is the *expected prospect* of a rejection to the
rejecting player. This assumes, as is currently all too common, that players
obey expected utility. In principle, other utility theories can be grafted as
long as they are made to be common knowledge. Thus we set the strategy
set for player $j$,

$$X_j(x_i) = \{0 \leq x \leq 1 | u_i(1 - x) \geq (1 - p)\delta_i u_i(x_i) + p u_i(s_i)\} \qquad (9)$$

and the formal utility for the strategy combination $(x_1, x_2)$ to player $i$ is
$u_i(x_i)$.

*Interperson Rationality.* Again we look for the Nash equilibria for the fold
game.

To make the fold game playable, the strategy sets need to be nonempty for
all values of their argument. One sees by inspection of the definitions that this
condition depends on the probability $p$ and the outside values $s_i$. We define the
*present value* to player $i$ of a promise to share $x$ one period later to be

$$PV_i(x, p) = u_i^{-1}((1 - p)\delta_i u_i(x) + p u_i(s_i)) \qquad (10)$$

where for an increasing function $f$, $f^{-1}(x) = \inf\{y | f(y) \geq x\}$.[13] We say "promise"
because its fulfillment depends on the occurrence of a random event $E$ whose
probability is $p$. Now we assume that $s_i$ is such that $PV_i(x, p) \leq 1$, which makes
the strategy sets non-empty. This is true automatically, for example, when $s_i \leq 1$.
As above, the Nash equilibria of the fold game are of interest. They exist
because the equations

$$1 - x_2 = PV_1(x_1, p)$$
$$1 - x_1 = PV_2(x_2, p) \qquad (11)$$

are equivalent to the equation

$$x_1 = 1 - PV_2(1 - PV_1(x_1, p), p). \qquad (12)$$

Because the $PV_i$ maps the unit interval continuously into itself, this equation must
have a solution by elementary considerations.

Now $(x_1, x_2)$ is supported by SPE if and only if two conditions are satisfied:

$$PV_1(1 - x_2, p) + PV_2(x_2) \leq 1 \qquad (13)$$

and

$$PV_2(1 - x_1, p) + PV_1(x_1) \leq 1. \qquad (14)$$

For example, suppose player 1 demands more then $x_1$. Then it is rejected by player 2's plan, and the utility of a promise of $1 - x_2$ one period later is $u_1(PV_1(1 - x_2, p)) \leq u_1(1 - PV_2(x_2, p)) = u_1(x_1)$ (we use both mutual consistency (Eq. 13) and the fact that $(x_1, x_2)$ is a solution of Eq. 11). Hence player 1's deviation is not profitable in the extensive game! If Player 2 accepts $x > x_1$ then he does not gain because: $u_2(1 - x) < u_1(1 - x_2) = u_2(PV_2(x_2))$ by Eq. 11.

A sufficient condition for Eq. 13 and 14 is $s_i \leq x_i$. This follows from

**Lemma** (*PV$_i$*). $PV_i(x, p) \leq \max(s_i, x)$.

The proof is a simple observation.

**Corollary.** $PV_1(1 - x_2, p) \leq \max\{s_1, 1 - x_2\} = \max\{s_1, PV_1(x_1, p)\} \leq \max\{s_1, x_1\} = x_1 = 1 - PV_2(x_2, p)$.

This chain of inequalities is justified by appeal to Eq. 11 and the lemma which results in Eq. 13.

**Example.** Here is a case where Eq. 13 and 14 are not satisfied. Suppose the utilities are identities, $s_i = 0.9$, $p = 0.9$ and $\delta_i = 0.1$. Then Eq. 11 reduces to:

$$1 - x_2 = 0.01x_1 + 0.81$$
$$1 - x_1 = 0.01x_2 + 0.81. \tag{15}$$

Then $x_1 = x_2 = 0.188119$ but when player 1 demands, say $0.20 > x_1$, it is rejected and he or she is "promised" a little-valued future amount of $1 - 0.188119$ but its present value is much higher (due to the relatively high probability of receiving immediately 0.9), so a deviation is profitable. Hence $(x_1, x_2)$ cannot be subgame perfect. This is the intuition. Plugging in the proper values in Eq. 13 and 14 shows that the conditions are not fulfilled.

## Voluntary Termination

The same logic we applied to forced termination can be applied to voluntary termination with $PV_i(x, p) = PV_i^V(x) = u_i^{-1}((1 - p)\delta_i u_i(x) + p \max(\delta_i u_i(x), u_i(s_i)))$. If we denote the definition of present value for F-player by $PV_i^F$ we see immediately that $PV_i^V \geq PV_i^F$. Therefore, the intuition that *ceteris paribus*, being under a voluntary regime is advantageous to being under a forced regime is justified by inspecting the equation determining the partitions. In making this statement we imply that the logic can be applied to heterogenous players (F and V).

Note that lemma $PV_i$ with its immediate consequence still holds and for future use we also record the following

**Theorem** (VV inequalities). *Suppose the players are risk averse and zero at zero ($u_i$ are concave and $u_i(0) = 0$). Then for a VV bargaining where*

$$\delta_2 u_2(1 - s_1) \geq u_2(s_2) \tag{16}$$

*and*

$$\delta_1 u_1 (1 - s_2) \geq u_1 (s_1) \tag{17}$$

*we have:*

$$s_1 \leq 1 - \delta_2 (1 - s_1) \leq x_1 \leq 1 - s_2$$
$$s_2 \leq 1 - \delta_1 (1 - s_2) \leq x_2 \leq 1 - s_1. \tag{18}$$

Note that the conclusion implies that $(x_1, x_2)$ is supported by an SPE strategy combination.

*Proof.* Note that

$$1 - x_2 \geq PV_1(x_1, p) = u_1^{-1}((1 - p) \max(\delta_1 u(x_1), u_1(s_1)) + p u_1(s_1)) \geq \atop u_1^{-1}(u_1(s_1)) = s_1. \tag{19}$$

Hence we obtain the second inequality of the second assertion of the theorem. Similarly, we obtain the corresponding inequality of the first assertion.

It follows from what we have just proved and the monotonicity of $PV_i$ with respect to the first variable that $PV_2(x_2, p) \leq PV_2(1 - s_1, p)$.

Now

$$PV_2(1 - s_1, p) = u_2^{-1}((1 - p) \max(\delta_2 u_2(1 - s_1), u_2(s_2)) + p u_2(s_2)) \leq \atop u_2^{-1}(\delta_2 u_2(1 - s_1)) \leq u_2^{-1}(u_2(\delta_2(1 - s_1))) \leq \delta_2(1 - s_1), \tag{20}$$

which follows because of risk aversion and Eq. 16.

Therefore, by Eq. 11

$$x_1 = 1 - PV_2(x_2, p) \geq 1 - PV_2(1 - s_1, p) \geq 1 - \delta_2(1 - s_1). \tag{21}$$

*Note:* The conditions on the utilities required by the theorem are satisfied for the identity utilities, which make the theorem useful in experimental work.

## Arithmetic Depreciation with Outside Options

We return now to the experimental setting. Weg and Zwick (1994) and Zwick and Weg (1996) experimented with exponential utilities and side options. Their general setup is especially simple. The probability of access to an outside value is always 1 and it is voluntary for each of the players. Thus outside options are always present when an offer is considered by a recipient. What makes the predicted outcomes especially simple is the choice of fundamental utilities for money — $u_i(x) = \exp(x)$. The solution for the fixed points is simple.

We use Eq. 11 with the proper understanding that $PV_i(x, 1) = PV_i^V(x, 1)$. We see that Eq. 11 is equivalent to

$$x_2 = 1 - \max(x_1 - c_1, s_1) \tag{22}$$

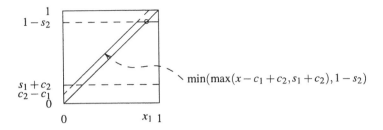

Fig. 11.3. Arithmetic depreciation, $c_1 < c_2$.

and

$$x_1 = 1 - \max(x_2 - c_2, s_2), \qquad (23)$$

where $c_i = -\log(\delta_i) \geq 0$. It is only in the special case of $p_i = 1$ that we can represent the utility in logarithmic form, thereby the arithmetic depreciation of the identity utility by the fixed cost $c_i$. This is in fact the terminology used by Weg and Zwick (1994).

The fixed-point equation is easily shown to be

$$\min(\max(x - c_1 + c_2, s_1 + c_2), 1 - s_2) = x. \qquad (24)$$

To make the solution of the bargaining problem a little more interesting, we assume that $s_1 + s_2 + \max(c_1, c_2) < 1$. This condition implies mutual consistency of the solution, as required. Now the predicted payoff to Player 1 is

$$x_1 \begin{cases} 1 - s_2 & \text{if } c_1 < c_2 \\ s_1 + c_2 & \text{if } c_1 > c_2 \\ [s_1 + c_2, 1 - s_2] & \text{if } c_1 = c_2. \end{cases} \qquad (25)$$

Figure 11.3 shows the graphic solution. A simple way to conceive this result is given by this rule: *Every bargainer claims his or her outside option and bargains over what's left* (without outside options). This rule has a significant heuristic value. It fact, it corresponds to individual rationality, which is well known in the theory of games in characteristic function form. Every solution concept suggested for that domain satisfies this requirement.

The main purpose of using exponential utilities with fixed discount rates (or what amount to the same thing, identity utilities with fixed costs of depreciation) is to present fairness considerations in a different light. It is particularly suitable for experimentation because as we have seen, the bargaining scene is very simple and must be understood that way, given the "good" behavior under the nonoutside option regime (Rapoport et al., 1990; Weg & Zwick, 1991).

Although the standard economic method employs the ultimatum game that was popularized by Güth (see Güth & Tietz, 1990), Weg and Zwick (1994) opted for an alternative. Recall that an ultimatum is a single period game and therefore using the standard temporal accounting where the present is never discounted, discounts are irrelevant and bargaining is reduced to a single offer that Player 2 is entitled to either accept or reject. In the latter case, the game ends with some predefined status quo. Normally the ultimatum is normalized to have outside options equal to zero. It is obvious that rational offers should amount to nothing (assuming a continuous pie). What Güth et al. (1982) found is that most offers settle on the midpoint of the pie. Their interpretation is that Player 1 normally shows a taste for fairness. This interpretation was given additional support by Kahneman et al. (1986) who, for that purpose, invented the dictator game, an ultimatum where Player 2 is relegated to merely an observer. But naturally, the fairness interpretation attributed to Player 1 was contested with the alternative, which attributes asymmetric fairness component to Player 2's utility. This is postulated to be evident to Player 1 who is as greedy as can be and merely optimizes payoffs by reducing the risk that a small offer might be rejected. Supporters of this alternative hypothesis explain Kahneman, Knetsch, & Thaler's (1986) generous dictators as merely desirous of the experimenter's good will, and therefore imply that dictator experiments are likely to produce artifactual results.[14]

Weg and Zwick (1994) considered arithmetic depreciation a complementary if not better arena to test for fairness. Consider first the analog to the standard dictator given by a bargaining game without outside options and where $c_1 < c_2$. The predicted payoff allocates the whole pie to Player 1 in the first period. Thus the outcome is the same as predicted for the dictator game (as well as the ultimatum game), but without allowing for early termination. Player 1 is the omnipotent player who can, if he or she so chooses, deviate from the rational dictum and offer symmetric allocations. Next, consider the analog to the ultimatum game. Here we take the arithmetic depreciation again but with the provision of outside options of *zero* to each of the players. Again the predicted allocation is the same as in the dictator analog, except that now Player 2 has the same option as Player 2 in the ultimatum game — refuse a small offer by opting out to obtain even a smaller payoff of zero. Because Player 1 in the dictator analog was found to be a highly greedy player, unaffected by his or her appearance to the experimenters (Rapoport et al., 1990; Weg & Zwick, 1991), any mitigation of demands in the ultimatum analogs is attributed to the fear that Player 2 will act on a threat of quitting. This expected behavior was in fact tested by Weg and Zwick (1994). Figure 11.4 is a conceptual schema of the various games and their interrelationships.

This experiment is concerned with the division of pies of $20.00, with a cost set of $\{0.1, 2.00\}$. Some bargaining games allow for opting out with zero payoffs and some do not. Although the bargaining is conceived as unlimited in time, in practice, a game is terminated if the negotiation reaches the fourteenth period, which in fact occurred only twice in 216 plays. The experiment has a $2 \times 2 \times 3$

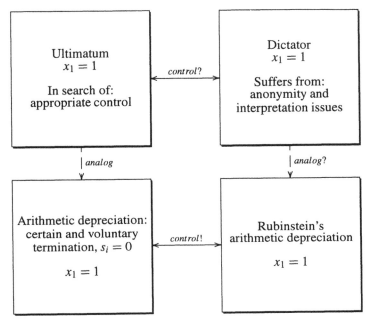

Fig. 11.4. Schematic relationships among games in the search for fairness.

factorial structure consisting of game type (with or without outside option), costs pattern ($c_1 < c_2$ or $c_1 > c_2$), and iteration (whether the first mover holds this role for the first, second, or third time). The last two factors are of the within-subject type, which means that during a single session, subjects play only one of the game types. For our purposes here, our main interest lies with the condition $c_1 < c_2$.

Figure 11.5 presents the frequency distribution of the last offers to the strong player (the one with the smaller cost) in the first and third (last) iteration by game type (with access to null outside options and without). Some summary statistics for this experiment are shown in Table 11.2.

Although the cost-based weaker player seldom exercises the option to opt out (3 times out of 108 games), the mere availability of this option is sufficient to deter the cost-based strong player from high demands. Thus, the main hypothesis that sharing in competitive environments is less affected by fairness considerations than by the threat of lost opportunities is supported, but the extreme greed shown by Rapoport et al. (1990) and Weg and Zwick (1991) failed to materialize in this experiment. A possible explanation for this discrepancy is suggested later. Nonetheless, the principal contribution of this setup is in providing an economic test bed to the hypothesis. In particular, any behavior in a dictator setup is inherently confounded. It is analogous to a boxing match with one contestant fighting

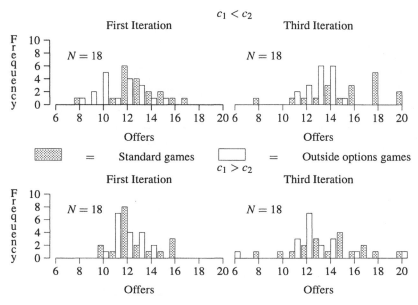

Fig. 11.5. Last period offers to the strong player.

with his arms tied down. [15]

## Geometric Depreciation With Outside Options

Several studies were conducted under a richer format than the original Rubinstein's paradigm with several intentions in mind. Some like Binmore, Shaked, and Sutton (1989) and Binmore, Morgan, Shaked, and Sutton (1991) were motivated perhaps to demonstrate the sensitivity of subjects to the structure of bargaining. Bargaining outcomes in these studies depend on the precise specification of the available moves. Thus, Nash's (1950) bargaining solution, which is derived from axioms, would not be applicable predictor for the bargaining procedures employed in these studies.

On the other hand, Zwick, Rapoport, & Howard's (1992) experiment was guided by the formal similarity between discounting and the probability of continuation of the bargaining. And finally, Weg, Zwick, and Rapoport (1996) and Kahn and Murnighan (1993) explored the applicability of rational bargaining with outside options under somewhat less focal predictions. In fact, their games, especially Kahn and Murnighan's, might be described as games in a reasonably general position. Nonetheless, as we shall see, they all carry a significant heuristic as to the relative power of the players, and thus provide clues to reasonable behavior.

**Table 11.2**
**Upper Quartiles of First and Final Offers to the Strong Player (Proportions)**

| Iteration | Costs Pattern | Game Type | First Period | Final Period |
|-----------|---------------|-----------|--------------|--------------|
| 1 | $c_1 < c_2$ | No Quit | 0.80 | 0.70 |
|   |             | Quit    | 0.70 | 0.62 |
|   | $c_1 > c_2$ | No Quit | 0.60 | 0.70 |
|   |             | Quit    | 0.60 | 0.61 |
| 2 | $c_1 < c_2$ | No Quit | 0.80 | 0.75 |
|   |             | Quit    | 0.70 | 0.67 |
|   | $c_1 > c_2$ | No Quit | 0.70 | 0.70 |
|   |             | Quit    | 0.60 | 0.65 |
| 3 | $c_1 < c_2$ | No Quit | 0.90 | 0.90 |
|   |             | Quit    | 0.70 | 0.70 |
|   | $c_1 > c_2$ | No Quit | 0.75 | 0.80 |
|   |             | Quit    | 0.60 | 0.70 |

Note. pie 20, $c_i \in \{0.1, 2.0\}$

**Deal Me Out (DMO).** Binmore et al. (1989) set out to show that the conventional wisdom of evenly sharing the leftover after accounting for outside options (obtained if bargaining fails to reach an agreement) is not always a reliable predictor of behavior. For this they exploit the $VV$ bargaining procedure with $s_1 = 0$, $s_2 = \{0, \frac{2}{7}, \frac{4}{7}\}$ with identities as utilities. Note that the conditions for theorem $VV$ *inequalities* are satisfied in this case and therefore solutions for Eq. 11 are subgame perfect. They hold regardless of probabilities and discounting quotients! Conventional wisdom would lead us to predict that player 1's share will be $\frac{1+s_1-s_2}{2}$. This is reasonable, perhaps, if one does not specify the negotiation procedure. But applying Eq. 11 we see that the Nash equation is reduced to

$$x_2 = 1 - \max(\delta_1 x_1, s_1) \tag{26}$$

and

$$x_1 = 1 - \max(\delta_2 x_2, s_2). \tag{27}$$

Hence, by substitutions we need to solve the fixed points for

$$1 - \max(\delta_2(1 - \max(\delta_1 x, s_1)), s_2). \tag{28}$$

Simplification shows that we need to solve

$$\min(\max(1 - \delta_2 + \delta_2\delta_1 x, 1 - \delta_2(1 - s_1)), 1 - s_2) = x. \tag{29}$$

We assume that $\delta_i(1 - s_j) \geq s_i$ . From this we conclude that bargaining would continue as usual if and only if

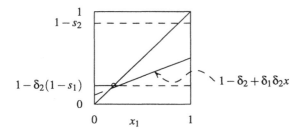

Fig. 11.6. Extreme case of VV solution.

$$1 - \delta_2(1 - s_1) \leq \frac{1 - \delta_2}{1 - \delta_1\delta_2} \leq 1 - s_2 \qquad \text{(See Fig. 11.6).} \qquad (30)$$

Consequently, player 2 does not bargain if bargaining results in an offer of less then $s_2$ and player 1 demands $1 - \delta_2(1 - s_1)$ if bargaining results in a smaller payoff. Bargaining here means that players act as if outside options are not available (or they are zero). Otherwise, outside options are too small to make an effect. Note that we have met this situation in a different guise: arithmetic depreciation with outside options.

By choosing a common discount quotient of 0.9 and $p = 1$, Binmore et al. (1989) made the expected bargaining outcome (without outside options) be $0.526 = \frac{1}{1+0.9} \approx 0.5$. They provide experimental evidence that for the two smaller values of $s_2$, there is a noticeable concentration of offers at about this point, whereas when $s_2$ is larger than half, the concentration is shifted to about $\frac{3}{7}$ (see Fig. 11.7). This is exactly what is expected when the bargaining procedure, which proceeds in a very well-specified manner, is taken into consideration. Note that the conventional Nash solution is predicted to result in significant increases in payoff to Player 2 (for the nonnull outside options), which is not the empirical case. We come back to this explanation later.

**Forced Termination.**  In an attempt to partially replicate Weg et al. (1990) without the possible drawback of finite implementation of an infinite game, Zwick et al. (1992) substituted probabilities of termination (or rather of continuation) for discount quotients. Their design can be viewed as an $FF$ bargaining with no time devaluation but with probability $p > 0$ and $s_1 = s_2 = 0$. Thus, the problem of termination is built into the design. Using Eq. 11 we see that

$$1 - x_i = (1 - p)x_j. \qquad (31)$$

By setting $\delta = 1 - p$ we see that in the bargaining problem with forced termination

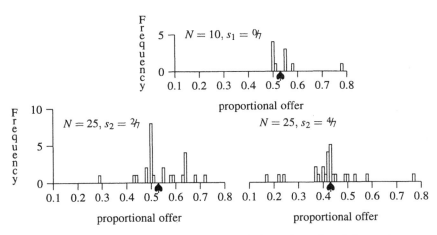

Fig. 11.7. First period demand by player 1. A ♠ marks rational demand.

the probability of continuation can formally be seen as the discount quotient, and therefore rational behavior is predicted by the same formulas as given by the corresponding discount version (Eq. 3). Zwick et al. (1992) experimented with these values of $p$: $5/6$, $1/3$, and $1/10$ and \$30 pies. Their results are presented in Fig. 11.8 and can be simply summarized by a dictum: equal split (plus a correction favoring the first mover). They follow a similar pattern found in Weg et al. (1990). Note that for high values of $p$ we have an approximate ultimatum, and in this light, fairness considerations might be in force. We discuss possible interpretations of this deviation later.

**Split the Difference (STD) vs. DMO — Procedural Implementation.** Binmore et al. (1991) can be viewed as an extension of both Binmore et al. (1989) and Zwick et al. (1992). First recall that DMO can be stated as "allocate your opponent a side option unless he or she can do better by bargaining." Binmore et al. (1989) showed that the bargaining part can be given a precise meaning, as in Rubinstein bargaining with having always accessible outside options that are not taken. But the outside option idea is more versatile.

Note that with the Rubinstein's bargaining paradigm, players can be made symmetric only at the limit point, when time is irrelevant. (Of course, at that point the rational outcome of the equal split fails to be unique.) Now, the next step is to ask whether one can obtain by bargaining (in the limit) an equal split, after status quo values ($s_1$ and $s_2$) are paid; that is, Player $i$ is paid $\frac{1+s_i-s_j}{2}$. We recall that formally we can take discounts to be interpreted as probability of continuation with $s_i = 0$. Therefore, when $p_i \to 0$ the players share the pie equally. Zwick et al. (1992) experimented with this framework except that their probabilities are never

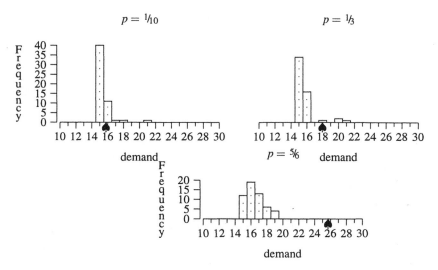

Fig. 11.8. First period demand during last. A ♠ marks rational partition.

close enough to zero. This intuition leads to the prediction that, quite generally, rational payoffs for a nonzero outside option game under an $FF$ regime are split the difference, when $p$ is small enough. This is shown more formally in the next two paragraphs.

Assume that $s_1 + s_2 < 1$, $\delta_i = 1$, and utilities are identities. According to Eq. 11

$$x_2 = 1 - ((1 - p)x_1 + ps_1) \tag{32}$$

and

$$x_1 = 1 - ((1 - p)x_2 + ps_2). \tag{33}$$

Therefore

$$x_1 = \frac{p(1 - s_2) + (1 - p)ps_1}{1 - (1 - p)(1 - p)}. \tag{34}$$

Multiplying the above by $1 = \frac{(1/p)}{(1/p)}$ for $p \neq 0$ we see

$$x_1 = \frac{1 + s_1(1 - p) - s_2}{2 - p}. \tag{35}$$

Taking the limit $p \to 0$ we obtain STD payoffs: each player gets an outside option plus half the remaining interval. Thus, STD as conventional wisdom can be approximated by procedural bargaining. Note that $x_i \geq s_i$ for a small enough $p$. Thus according to the corollary to lemma $PV_i$, the solution to Eq. 11 is in fact supported by SPE.

**Table 11.3**
**The Design of Binmore et. al (1991) Study**

|      | High — $s_2 = 0.64$ | | | Low — $s_2 = 0.36$ | |
|------|:----:|:----:|----|:----:|:----:|
|      | $\delta$ | $p$ | | $\delta$ | $p$ |
| $VV$ | 0.9 | 1 | $VV$ | 0.9 | 1 |
| $FF$ | 1 | 0.1 | $FF$ | 1 | 0.1 |

Does it work in practice? An affirmative answer is the essential claim of Binmore, Morgan, Shaked, & Sutton's (1991) research. They arrange for the play of four types of games, all sharing a common impatience coefficient (discount quotients interpreted as risk values or vice versa), which are classified as shown in Table 11.3 (outside values are normalized to unit pies).

The outside option to Player 1, $s_1$, is negligible and set to 0.04 for all games. Pies are £5 sterling apiece. As common with equal parameter games, pies and outside options shrink over time whenever impatience is a discount quotient. The main findings can be detected in Fig. 11.9. Referring to Player 2's high outside option condition, Binmore et al. (1991) wrote:

> It is not surprising that 50 : 50 does not do well when player 2 can get 64% without the consent of his partner, but it is instructive that S-T-D predicts *very much better* than D-M-O in forced breakdown games, while D-M-O predicts *better* than S-T-D in optional breakdown games. (p. 304; italics added)

Unfortunately, this beautiful result is not replicated so well when Player 2's outside option is low.[16] Note also that STD, when outside options are zero, is also equal split. Zwick et al. (1992) showed that equal splits are typical *regardless* of the probability of access to the outside option.[17] Thus, the finding of splitting differences in the limiting case of $FF$ games might reflect a general tendency to ignore the effects of time. The fact that DMO is not seen in $FF$ games is obviously due to the very meaning of voluntary exit (which is not available), and the fact that the forced probability of exiting is behaviorally irrelevant! But theoretically, STD depends on low probabilities and Binmore, Morgan, Shaked, & Sutton's (1991) satisfaction over their subjects' good behavior is perhaps not completely justified.

**Outside Options — Middle Range Cases.**   Two other studies followed the path pioneered by Binmore and his associates in the studies just reported.

The research by Weg et al. (1996) is a direct descendant of Binmore et al. (1991). It compares playing $VV$ games to playing $FF$ games where probabilities of access to outside options are *not* boundary values — $p \in \{0.2, 0.8\}$. These events are realized by the spin of an actual wheel of fortune shown to the bargainers. It allows, therefore, the testing of the prevalence of STD where the normative

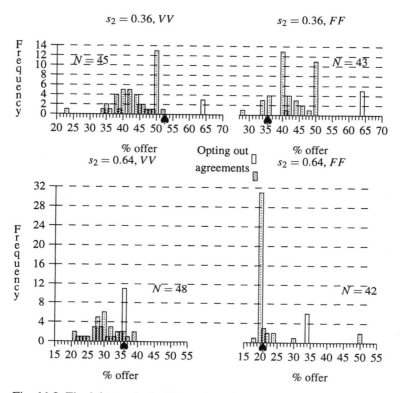

Fig. 11.9. Final demands for Player 1. A ♠ marks rational demand.

point of view forbids it. Subjects paticipated in both types of games in the the same session. The paradigm is a shrinking pie where all pies start with a relatively large sum of $30.00. Because the shrinking rate is uniformly set to 0.9, games might extend slightly but meaningfully longer in time without dealing with negligible pies. Only Player 1 has a nonzero outside option — one of $\{3, 12, 24\}$ in dollars.[18] Probablities and outside option values do not vary within an experimental session.

Figure 11.10 presents the frequency distribution of first period demand by the main parameters of the experiment. The fact that, for the more interesting parameters, average splits do not support theoretical predictions is perhaps understandable. The best one can say about the results is that first period demands are in general monotonic with the rational demands. Also, general qualitative predictions that players 2 in FF games are worse off than their counterparts in $VV$ is borne out. But again, rational outcomes are almost never attained and actual mean

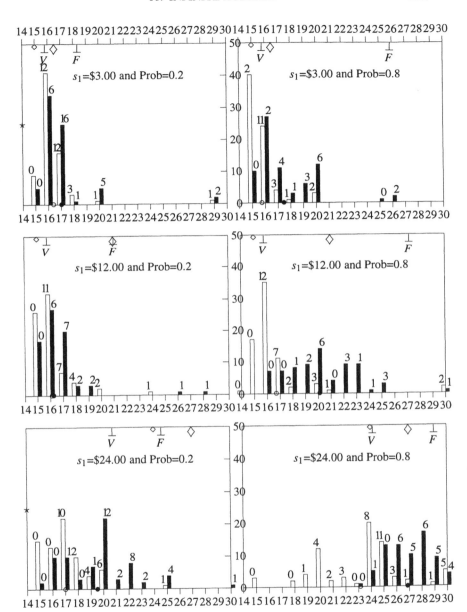

Fig. 11.10. Frequency distribution of first period demands by side value, probability and game type. $\perp_V \Rightarrow SPE$ for $VV$, $\perp_F \Rightarrow SPE$ for $FF$, $\Diamond \Rightarrow$ S-T-D, and $\diamond \Rightarrow$ D-M-O. $\blacksquare \Rightarrow FF$, $\square \Rightarrow VV$. Numbers are rejection counts. A $\star \Rightarrow$ uncounted point of less then 14 in a $VV$ game. $\bullet \Rightarrow FF$ mean demand. $\circ \Rightarrow VV$ mean demand.

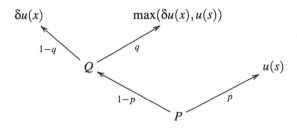

Fig. 11.11. A tree diagram of bargaining termination rules.

---

behavior is very conservative. The effects of time (or probabilities of termination) are underestimated.

**Mixed Options.**   The research by Kahn and Murnighan (1993) presented an experiment with mixed features of voluntary and forced termination in a single game.   In order to provide an appropriate framework for this experiment, we present a general framework that encompasses all bargaining procedures we have discussed so far under a single paradigm. In fact, there are two such (inconsistent) extensions that happen to coincide in the special case of Kahn and Murnighan.

***Extension A.***   When a player receives an offer it may be accepted or rejected. In the former case, the game ends as usual. Otherwise, the game continues as follows.  There are two stochastically independent events $P$ and $Q$. If $P$ occurs, the game terminates immediately with each player consuming an outside option. Otherwise, if $Q$ occurs then the player may announce the immediate termination of bargaining with each of the players consuming an outside option or opt to counterpropose in the next bargaining period.  If $Q$ fails to occur, the player counterproposes in the next period.

There are two extreme cases that we have already treated. Assume that $P$ is the impossible event. Then, obviously, we have a voluntary option depending on the occurrence of $Q$. If $Q$ is the impossible event then we have a forced termination depending on the occurrence of $Q$. Figure 11.11 depicts the situation with labels attached to the terminal nodes describing the utility of reaching these nodes.

Consider now the standard Rubinstein bargaining tree. To each rejection branch one attaches the tree diagram to obtain the bargaining tree for a general bargaining game with outside options.

In this manner we have unified the existing bargaining schemes into a cube whose dimensions are $F$, $V$, and $D$. A point in the cube and a point in the unit interval[19] is a choice of parameters $p$, $q$, $\delta$, and $s$, respectively, which with the

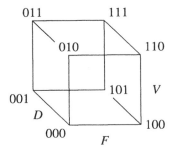

Fig. 11.12. The bargaining regime cube.

addition of a utility $u$ defines a bargaining player. A choice of two such quintets, $P^i = (\delta_i, p_i, q_i, s_i, u_i)$, and an order between them defines a bargaining game (See Fig. 11.12), denoted by the signature $(P^1, P^2)$. This unification facilitates a comparison of plays of bargaining games characterized, perhaps, by slightly different parameters. This is so because the games generated in this way map continuously into the predicted payoffs to Player 1.[20] In this manner we see that the $FF$ games and $VV$ games are not separate entities, as could have been assumed, but rather members of a larger family of hybrid games characterized by events that are peculiar to each of the bargainers.

To solve this type of game we need our standard technique in which we have to define only the appropriate *present value* functions. But these are simple extensions to the voluntary and forced termination paradigms:

$$PV_i^{P,Q}(x, p_i, q_i) = PV_i(x, p_i, q_i) = u_i^{-1}((1 - p_i)(1 - q_i)x + \\ (1 - p_i)q_i \max(u_i(x), u(s_i)) + pu_i(s_i)) \tag{36}$$

that are continuous when $u_i$ are. Again we fold the extensive game and focus on its Nash equilibria that satisfy Eq. 11. Now the conditions in Eq. 13 and 14 look as follows:

$$PV_1(1 - x_2, p_2, q_2) + PV_2(x_2, p_2, q_2) \leq 1 \tag{37}$$

and

$$PV_2(1 - x_1, p_1, q_1) + PV_1(x_1, p_1, q_1) \leq 1 \tag{38}$$

for any solution $(x_1, x_2)$ of Eq. 11. And we note the indices. Player $i$ would not demand more than $x_i$, the solution of Eq. 11, if and only if Eq. 37 and Eq. 38 are satisfied and the expectation from a "promise" of $(1 - x_j)$ depends on $j$'s probabilities! Lemma $PV$ as well as its corollary still holds in this extended case. Thus, when $x_i \geq s_i$ for a solution $(x_1, x_2)$ of Eq. 11, the latter must be supported by SPE.

*Extension B.*    There is no reason to arrange the events $P$ and $Q$ in this order. Their reversal results in a gamble with, in general, different expected utility. One case in which the two schemes coincide is the case where the event $Q$ is the sure event.

For then

$$PV(x, p, 1) = u^{-1}(\max((1 - p)\delta u(x) + p_i u(s), u(s)))$$  (39)

under scheme-A, and

$$PV(x, p, q) = u^{-1}(q(\max(u(s), (1 - p)\delta u(x)) + pu(s)) + $$
$$(1 - q)((1 - p)\delta u(x) + pu(s)))$$  (40)

under scheme-B. A substitution for $q = 1$ in the latter gives the result.

Very interesting cases arise by the choice of extreme values for some parameters and among those is the case where $q_i = 1$ and $0 < p_i < 1$, which was explored by Kahn and Murnighan (1993). The only asymmetry allowed among the players is reflected by the outside options ratio the experimenters choose — $\infty$, which means that only one player has a nonzero outside option. In a sense, their experiment is one of several natural continuations of the other experiments reported. The novelty lies in the mixing of voluntary outside options weighted by a certain risk (high or low) of forced termination.

Kahn and Murnighan (1993) opted for games of scheme-B semantics with common termination probability $p$, common voluntary exit probability $q = 1$, and a common discount quotient $\delta$. One player has zero outside option and the other may opt for 0.1 or 0.9 of the pie in any given game. These options are available (in two different games) in both orders to Player 1 and 2, respectively. The games are implemented by the shrinking pie method and information exchange between players is by human messengers. Random events are realized by coin tossing or chip drawing. All game pies are $10 at the start of the negotiation. In addition to these parameters, other game parameters are all elements from the product of these sets: $F = \{0.05, 0.5\}$ for probabilities of forced terminations, and $D = \{1, 0.8\}$ for discount quotients.

Two last remarks regarding the design are in order. First, when Player 1 has a nonzero outside option, he or she may leave the bargaining before even giving an offer. Second, because the zero outside option is not normatively effective, the experimenters have opted to express it by not allowing any voluntary opting to its owner. This makes the framing of bargaining a bit more natural.[21] In the language of this research, the probability $q$ could in fact be any value.

Table 11.4[22] presents the subgame perfect prediction and mean first period offers for the various combination cells of the experiment. Admittedly, the table is complex. But a glance at Fig. 11.13 reveals almost all the reader may need to know. It plots the mean first-period demand on the predicted SPE demand. Note that subgame perfectness is rare, and that subjects overdemand when SPE

**Table 11.4**
**Mean First Period Demand (Slanted) and SPE (Upright)**

|       |      |      | $q = 0$ |        | $q = 1$ |        |
|-------|------|------|---------|--------|---------|--------|
| $p$   | $\delta$ | $s$ | Rich   | Poor   | Rich    | Poor   |
| 0.05  | 1    | 0.1  | *0.6500* | *0.6500* | *0.5600* | *0.6200* |
|       |      |      | 0.5615  | 0.4615 | 0.5615  | 0.4615 |
|       |      | 0.9  | *0.8500* | *0.6200* | *0.9200* | *0.2500* |
|       |      |      | 0.9513  | 0.0513 | 0.9513  | 0.0513 |
|       | 0.8  | 0.1  | *0.5700* | *0.5500* | *0.5700* | *0.6300* |
|       |      |      | 0.5772  | 0.5563 | 0.5772  | 0.5563 |
|       |      | 0.9  | *0.5700* | *0.5100* | *0.8400* | *0.2500* |
|       |      |      | 0.6491  | 0.4616 | 0.9240  | 0.1000 |
| 0.5   | 1    | 0.1  | *0.5300* | *0.6300* | *0.5600* | *0.6400* |
|       |      |      | 0.7000  | 0.6000 | 0.7000  | 0.6000 |
|       |      | 0.9  | *0.8100* | *0.4800* | *0.9300* | *0.3000* |
|       |      |      | 0.9667  | 0.0667 | 0.9667  | 0.0667 |
|       | 0.8  | 0.1  | *0.5900* | *0.5900* | *0.6200* | *0.6100* |
|       |      |      | 0.7381  | 0.6548 | 0.7381  | 0.6548 |
|       |      | 0.9  | *0.8500* | *0.4900* | *0.9100* | *0.2900* |
|       |      |      | 0.9286  | 0.1786 | 0.9600  | 0.1000 |

Note. SPE's are significant to at least three digits (the minimum necessary to distinguish between the cells) and observed means are rounded to two digits. The rich player is the one with $s > 0$. Columns classify first movers.

indicates small values, underdemand on high SPE values, and are insensitive in the middle range.[23] It is also misleading to quote the Pearson correlation coefficient of 0.86 here. With the range of predicted values as it is, very approximate behavior is sufficient to induce this artifact.

**Abstract Vs. Potential Outside Options.**   "To accept or not to accept" is the fundamental question for one of the parties at any given period and, of course, by implication, "what an is acceptable demand" to the other. Naturally, it depends on the available alternatives. But what are they? In Rubinstein's formulation, the single option is to initialize the bargaining at the next period. The outside options

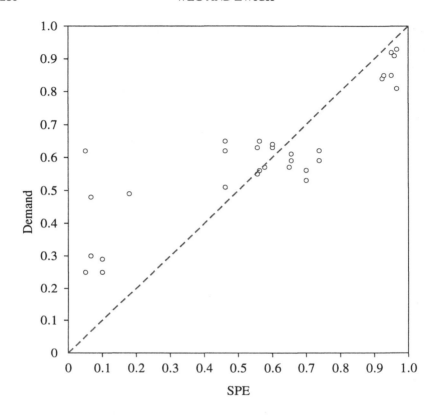

Fig. 11.13. Observed mean first period demand on subgame perfect predictions.

add certain other alternatives to the list. These alternatives should be looked at as encapsulations of certain situations that are expected to net a present utility.

We have seen some more or less reasonable bargaining behavior when such outside options are present (Binmore et al., 1989, 1991; Kahn & Murnighan, 1993; Weg et al., 1996). Zwick, Rapoport, and Weg (1996) tested the hypothesis originally made in Weg et al. (1996) that "correct" behavior does not necessarily reflect the centrality of SPE rationality in players' considerations, but is rather due to marginal cues provided in these studies, which in turn narrow the acceptable outcomes significantly. For example, consider Kahn & Murnighan's (1993) games where one player's outside option nets 90% of the pie. Any demand, under many experimental conditions, cannot be too far from the rational demand.

For another example, consider the bargaining problem with signature $(P^1, P^2)$

where $P^1 = (1, 0.1, 0, 0.64, 1)$ and $P^2 = (1, 0.1, 0, 0, 1)$ investigated by Binmore et al. (1991). This is an $FF$ game with 0.64 outside option to Player 2 and a relatively small probability of the game terminating after any given rejection. Thus, the cost of rejection to the receiving party is rather small. Therefore, the players are made almost *symmetric* with respect to the remaining pie after Player 2 is immediately paid the outside option. Therefore, STD is expected. Of course, for the normative theory to result in a unique prediction, some uncertainty with respect to continuation is necessary and this happens to coincide with the idea that in case of insufficient reason, one tends to argue for the equalizing of treatments. However, when one stays away from the limit cases, either because the discount quotients are steep or because the probability of termination is high, bargaining is greatly affected by time.

We know from Zwick et al. (1992), Weg et al. (1990), and Kahn and Murnighan (1993) that people are highly conservative and lack an appreciation for these effects. Weg et al. (1996) conjectured that when outside options are given in their unencapsulated form, for example, as outside bargaining options, their effects would be washed away. To test this hypothesis, Zwick et al. (1996) considered a game $\Lambda$ defined recursively as $\Lambda = (P^1, P^2)$ where $P^1 = (\delta, 0, 1, \Lambda, 1)$ and $P^2 = (\delta, 0, 1, 0, 1)$.[24] That is, although Player 2 has a voluntary outside option valued at 0, Player 1 is entitled to opt out to play a bargaining game of the same type with another player. The semantics given to this game are as follows. There are three players, one seller and two buyers. The seller sells a product valued by the seller at \$0 and to each of the buyers at \$10. The selling price and price saving are discounted by $\delta$ for every participant. The bargaining starts with the seller offering a price to a buyer of choice. The buyer may accept and the bargaining terminates, opt out and receive nothing while the seller starts the same game with the other buyer (the bargaining clock *does* tick), or reject the offer in order to make a counteroffer to the seller in the next period. The seller then can accept immediately, opt to restart the bargaining with the other buyer at the next period by making him or her a price offer, or reject and make a counteroffer to the same buyer in the next period.

What should reasonable bargainers do? Of course, the outside options are irrelevant! For the buyers an outside option is certainly a nongaining advantage and therefore might as well be ignored. And the seller must be indifferent between either of the buyers and therefore expects to obtain the same as when playing against a single buyer. Therefore, reasonable people are not impressed by the enriched situation. The price is set by the logic of a 2-person Rubinstein paradigm — $\frac{1}{1+\delta}$ to the seller and the rest to one of the buyers.[25]

But the data tell a different, nonetheless familiar story (recall Weg & Zwick, 1994). We do not cover the full design of Zwick et al. (1996) here. They compared standard Rubinstein's bargaining to bargaining under the bargaining rule defined by $\Lambda$ with two between-subject discount quotients: ⅙ and ⅔. The observed first period prices when the seller has the option to switch buyers are sig-

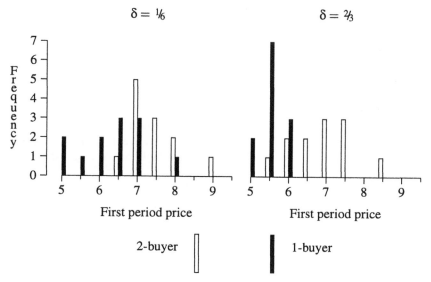

Fig. 11.14. Mean first period prices.

---

nificantly higher than when he or she does not, contrary to normative expectations (Fig. 11.14). Further, demands in the 1-buyer game are not predicted by rational behavior (note the distinctly modest demands for $\delta = \frac{1}{6}$). This aspect is a replication of Weg, Rapoport, & Felsenthal's (1990) results.

## DISCUSSION

Our conclusions are rather simple, although yet very tentative: People are reasonable within their cognitive limitations and moral constraints. This does not mean that they behave rationally according to point specifications. No one expects them to. Rather, people respond to changing bargaining conditions, in general, in the right directions. This is clear, for example, by recalling that:

i. Voluntarily terminated Player 2 is in general more powerful than a forcibly terminated Player 2 with the same time and utility preferences (Weg et al., 1996).

ii. Under well-chosen parameters, DMO is observed under voluntary termination and STD under forced termination (Binmore et al., 1989, 1991). We also observe the limitation of those rules (Kahn & Murnighan, 1993). The mental accounting for this is the same as for the previous item.

iii. Arithmetic depreciation is, sometimes, understood and acted on very accurately (Rapoport et al., 1990; Weg & Zwick, 1991).

But these rules are easily foiled by well-chosen red herrings. Thus, ultimatum-like game situations attenuate demands (Weg & Zwick, 1994) and implementing outside options as actual bargaining bolsters them (Zwick et al., 1996). In both cases, some seemingly strategic options take center stage in human bargaining behavior.

And finally, there is a cue whose effects can increase or diminish strategic accuracy depending on well-specified circumstances as follows. Nothing, of course, changes in the preference structure of a Rubinstein bargaining game when time is taken into account from the very first period.[26] This rule was adopted by Rapoport et al. (1990) and Weg and Zwick (1991), but the customary rule was followed by Weg and Zwick (1994) in an arithmetic depreciation bargaining game. More extreme demands were found with the immediate depreciation rule. It appears that the advantage of the strong player (particularly when moving first) is more easily seen when the effects of delays in coming into an agreement are immediate. On the other hand, Weg et al. (1990) showed that this immediate depreciation has quite a different effect when implemented geometrically. Subjects seem to solve the equation $x_1\delta_1 = (1 - x_1)\delta_2$ and thus appropriate the pie in proportion to their counterpart's discount quotient. This implies that when discounts are equal, equal split prevails regardless of time effects. We conclude further that the idyllic prescription given by the DMO rule is behaviorally borne out only when the discount quotients are high (when rational and behavioral focal predictions are approximately the same), and can be totally fallacious otherwise. We just have to consider equal but steep time effects. In this case, when Player 2's outside options are high but less than half, he or she may still obtain half the pie unjustifiably. This is because the Rubinstein bargaining partition, which predicts a low share to player 2, is invariably missed. The neglect of strategic advantage on the part of subjects also can be seen when it is derived from risk (Kahn & Murnighan, 1993; Zwick et al., 1992). But in these cases, the argument is slightly weaker due to unaccounted (by experimenters) effects of risk nonneutrality.

What story can we whip up (for the data is rather scarce) from these successes and failures of rationality? Bargaining is a group problem-solving activity with well-specified rules of communication and message content. And, like any other problem solving, it relies on meaningful and reliable clues. Out of the clues people create the story and even set the goals (such as wealth, wealth mitigated by fairness) that they want to achieve. Of course, bargainers are not clones of each other, and therefore the scenarios they build independently of each other are not necessarily compatible, although they often are.

## Bargaining Time

The essence of the theoretical success of the noncooperative approach to bargaining rests not on utility, linear or not, but on the diminishing usefulness of any gain over time.[27] This is clear intuitively, and can be seen by two unknowns when the discount quotients are 1, and therefore provides no clue for adequate action. When time of agreement makes a difference, players need to realize what an adequate proposal is.

In the case of a finite horizon, it is very tempting to try to reach it. This leads to the following calculation, which is shown only for the simplest case: the discounts are the same and the utilities are identities. The proper demand for a game of order 0 (which ends after a single demand) is $a_0 = 1$, and the proper demand for a game of order $n$ is $a_n = 1 - \delta a_{n-1}$. The problem boils down to the solution of this recursive definition. Reaching for the horizon means backward induction.[28] Everyone knows what $a_0$ is, unless perhaps fairness is at issue. But, very quickly, the recursive step goes out of behavioral tune (Neelin, Sonnenschein, & Spiegel, 1988; Ochs & Roth, 1989). In fact, this approach, which may seem attractive, is very cumbersome and seems cognitively intractable for subjects. Learning is expected to be difficult (in fact, a never-ending problem) because of its linear dependence on game order.

The infinite horizon case has two immediate benefits. First, because there is no definite end to the bargaining, the fairness issue derived from last mover advantage, as is known from ultimatum plays, vanishes. This can be seen by imitating the procedure taken in Endnote 28. Assuming that $0 \leq a_0 = b \leq 1$, the payoff to player 1 for a game of order $n$ is $\sum_{0 \leq i < n-1} (-\delta)^i + b(-\delta)^n$. Taking the limit as $n \to \infty$ shows that fairness considerations due to end game effect do not appear to be an issue.

Second, the infinite horizon invites a different approach,[29] which often works but can easily be made to fail. If the present is *not* discounted, there is a strong incentive to ignore differential effects of bargaining delays. If no delays are wanted and the infinite regress is unpalatable, what seems more likely than an equal share? This is the common case, except for a small commission taken by the bargainer who is the proposer. It must be noted that this is the behavior of naïve subjects, who, after a few practice plays, are made to play a few games for real. We have no knowledge at all of what the effect of saturated behavior is.

What if the pie is depreciated immediately and perhaps even at different rates? Again, subjects are guided by manageable tools. If the frame is discount quotients, then equal net share seems appealing. But even this solution may tax communication channels. It relies on both players realizing the reason for such an odd offer, especially when a strong player is to receive it.[30] Failure to coordinate in this manner is the reason for the prevalence of the focal equal split.

The arithmetic frame has a different effect in this case. Recall that the rescaling of the exponential utility structure also provides for a different and much more meaningful consequence of delay in that utility may be reflected in actual loss, penetrating out the pie limits. For this reason, perhaps, many subjects tend to settle on extreme demands very quickly, but only when loss takes its toll immediately.

## Outside Options

The introduction of outside options has resulted in some of the best support that subgame perfectness has received in the area of bargaining under geometric depreciation. This might seem surprising given the counterrational behavior under pure bargaining. Nonetheless, we give our interpretation — an interpretation that underscores the need to understand the precise mechanisms governing *pure* bargaining.

The relative success in playing outside option games lies in the clear understanding of the immediate impact of the access to those options.

It is cognitively trivial to realize (because it lies at the very core of what an outside option is and is thus understood at the instructional level) that the larger the outside option one has access to, the larger the piece of the pie it is reasonable to expect under any given conditions. In a sense, the introduction of an immediate outside option brings the game close to a single period game.

When a player is in a forced termination state $(F)$, the higher the probability of termination the closer the payoff to the outside option. This may not be the case if the outside option is low enough to raise fairness restraints.

When a player has the option to terminate the game voluntarily, the outside option provides a certain protection against the otherwise inferior bargaining position. Obviously, the larger the probability of access, the better this protection.

We think that this type of simple deduction, which follows directly from the instructions, drives the results obtained in bargaining experiments with side options. This will be true to a large degree regardless of the precise bargaining procedure. But there is more to the bargaining that can be derived only from the specific nature of the discounted alternating procedure. For example, consider the nature of the protection provided by the voluntary position. In order for this to be compatible with rational behavior, it is required that the players are bargaining rational. For example, under pure bargaining with discounts $(\delta_1, \delta_2) = (0.7, 0.9)$, Player 2 is offered about 73% of the pie through bargaining. If the voluntary outside option is 20%, he or she rejects anything smaller than this value (73%) because of the bargaining advantage. However, if the equal share rule prevails, then even a 50–50 split is reasonable and even attractive. In fact, this behavior seems pretty likely, albeit irrational. Consider now the same parameters except that the game is made into a single period game with Player 2 having an outside option of 50%. In this case, the subgame perfect demand is 50%, which deals Player 2 out. These examples serve to show that estimating the usefulness of an outside option depends on the underlying prevailing bargaining rationality. DMO behavior is thus fortuitous. Its beauty relies more on its mathematical elegance than on its behavioral reality.

## Final Remarks

In the abstract to his paper on the interpretation of game theory, Rubinstein (1991) wrote:

> It is argued that a good model in game theory has to be realistic in the sense that it provides a model for the *perception* of real life social phenomena. It should incorporate a description of the relevant factors involved, as perceived by the decision makers. These need not necessarily represent the physical rules of the world. It is not meant to be isomorphic with respect to "reality" but rather with respect to our perception of regular phenomena in reality. (p. 909)

In experimental economics, we often create the "realities" to be tested. It seems that our subjects insist on telling a story different from SPE. Do they perceive a different reality than intended? As we have already pointed out, one step in the abstraction process in the area of bargaining was taken by Rubinstein (1982) himself in his research. The essential step was the freeing of bargaining models from an irrelevant restriction — the finite horizon. Nonetheless, an inherent asymmetry between the players derived from the discrete and ordered procedure is still left — a vestige of technical requirements. These might be overcome by considering the discount quotient — $\delta$, as cumulative over infinitely small subintervals of the unit of time. This is another method of abstraction, although it is not in the formal rule of the game. In that case, the payoff to player 1 in pure bargaining becomes

$$\lim_{x \to 0} \frac{1 - \delta_2^x}{1 - (\delta_1 \delta_2)^x} = \frac{\log \delta_2}{\log \delta_1 + \log \delta_2}. \tag{44}$$

It follows that the order in the alternating procedure loses its significance, for the partition is independent of it. Similarly, one may operate on Eq. 35 in the same manner[31] and obtain the STD rule, regardless of the probability of access per unit of time. In this way, one may argue for the Zwick et al. (1992) results of equal split when the probability of access is far from 0.

The main difficulty, of course, is that the limit process has no implementation.[32] How would subjects be forced to consider smaller intervals of time if their actions are unitized by the experimenter? One may think of the limit process taking the role of an axiom. But then we fall back to square one, started with the Nash axiomatic method. We are inclined to believe that another step in the process of abstraction starting with Rubinstein is needed. As we have heuristically indicated, a procedural symmetrization of players is required to achieve predictions that better accommodate subjects' behavior.

## ACKNOWLEDGMENTS

We are grateful to Gary Bolton, Ido Erev, and Jack Ochs for their useful suggestions on an earlier version of this chapter.

**ENDNOTES**

1. Harsanyi (1977), for example shows that a certain Zeuthen's process for bargaining does lead to Nash's bargaining solution. But it seems that the required procedure is quite cumbersome for practical application. Nash provided his own suggestion, which rests on a technical selection criterion among the many Nash equilibria of a certain demand game.

2. For our needs, a subgame is to a game as a subtree is to a tree.

3. There are at least two general problems in applying Nash equilibria to our case. First, the Nash equilibrium lacks predictive value. There are simply too many of them. In fact every partition is supported by a Nash strategy. Second, it ignores the depth that is inherent in a tree structure, which is related to the first problem. The fact that acting out a strategy in a tree game unfolds over time is responsible for eliminating incredible moves.

4. Consider a general representation of preference over space-time given by the utility $U(x,t)$, which is continuous, increasing in the first variable and decreasing in the second. Assume that $U(x,t) - U(x,s) = k(t-s)$ for $k < 0$. Then $U(x,t) = U(x,0) + kt$. Thus the preference relation is represented by $u(x)\delta^t$ where $u(x) = \exp(U(x,0))$ and $\delta = \exp(k)$. The assumptions permitting this representation are acceptable to us and therefore we limit our discussion to the bargaining procedure and its impact on behavior.

5. This is because the logarithmic transformation that allows for a simple linear representation of utilities over time, because $\exp(x)\delta^s \geq \exp(y)\delta^t$ is equivalent to $x - cs \geq y - ct$ where $c = -log(\delta)$. Although the original representation is useful for a more compact theoretical treatment, the logarithmic representation is particularly convenient for experimentation.

6. Similar to the way compounded interest is treated.

7. Condition $E$ is not reported here due to the fairly consistent equal split behavior found.

8. But quite generally, unbounded horizon bargaining games are isomorphic to infinitely many of their subgames. Raw data of last offers show convergent behavior that quite often reveals how closely subjects play the original game.

9. We do not expect, however, that all fixed-cost predictions would be verified. Note, for example, that the expected shares are contingent only on the ordinal relationship between delay costs rather than on actual quantitative levels. Rapoport et al. (1990) and Weg and Zwick (1991) experimented with highly separable parametric values. This is understandable given that an initial test of a theory tends to be done under rather "promising" conditions. However, Zwick and Chen (1997) demonstrated that cost values do indeed affect agreements in a significant way.

10. The experiment discounts from the very first period!

11. This is not exactly the case. One comparison was indeed proposed: the dictator game (Kahneman et al., 1986), which is discussed later.

12. Exactly when the clock ticks makes a difference computationally, but conceptually it has little significance.

13. The function $f^{-1}$ is everywhere defined and non-decreasing. Note that $f$ can in general obtain infinite values, but it is irrelevant in our application. It is continuous if it is not infinite (regardless of whether $f$ is).

14. For an ardent attempt to differentiate fairness from greed, and thus to disprove Kah-

neman, Knetsch, & Thaler's (1986) conclusions, see Hoffman, McCabe, Shachat, and Smith (1994) who by careful experimentation argued for selfish dictators. A later attempt by Hoffman, McCabe, and Smith (1996) to replicate their earlier results under improved experimental control has not been completely successful.

15. Another, perhaps more successful, control game to the classical ultimatum, may be found in Bolton and Zwick (1995) where single period bargaining is suggested. Player 1 may choose between a 50/50 split and, without risk, a more extreme partition. A rejection by Player 2 does not affect Player 1's share. The main difference between this game and the dictator analog is that Player 2's acquiescence is not required to implement Player 1's desire. This could be desirable, depending on one's point of view.

16. Binmore, Morgan, Shaked, & Sutton's (1991) attempt to clarify this point through the removal of attractive focal points by changing the denomination of the pie is less than a complete success.

17. Recall that STD is expected only at the limit.

18. Having Player 1 possess the meaningful outside option makes the games more complex than Binmore et al. (1989) and Binmore et al. (1991) due to the need to account for Player 1's opportunities being devalued one period after the commencement of play.

19. We separate the dimensions in this way for the lack of visible four dimensional boxes.

20. For simplicity, this portrayal assumes identity utilities, denoted by 1.

21. Binmore et al. (1989) opted for a similar framing when a player has a voluntary outside option of zero. That this simplification may be behaviorally unwarranted was noted by Weg and Zwick (1994).

22. The authors are thankful to Lawrence Kahn and Keith Murnighan for furnishing the data for this table.

23. By looking at the table one sees that split-the-difference fails for extreme predicted allocations. For $q = 1$, very weak bargainers ignore the realities altogether.

24. For this special case we shall assume that outside options are consumed a period later than the usual convention.

25. In reality, neither buyer has an option to leave the bargaining. In this way, the apparent disparity between the buyers and the seller is made larger.

26. Thus, the utility of $x$ at time $t$ is $u(x)\delta^{t+1}$ for $t = 0, 1, \ldots$, instead of the usual, $u(x)\delta^t$.

27. The stationarity requirement is reviewing Equation 2, which is reduced to a single equation with more technical.

28. Another way is the paper and pencil approach. Let

$$\phi(x) = \sum_{n \geq 0} a_n x^n \tag{41}$$

be a power series with coefficients, $a_n$, being the payoffs to Player 1 in Ståhl bargaining games of order $n$ and

$$\psi(x) = \sum_{n \geq 0} x^n. \tag{42}$$

Then we see that $(\psi(x) - \delta\phi(x))x + 1 = \phi(x)$ and therefore

$$\phi(x) = \frac{x\psi(x)+1}{1+\delta x} = \frac{\psi(x)}{1+\delta x}. \tag{43}$$

It follows that $a_n = \sum_{n \geq i \geq 0}(-\delta)^i$.

29. Entertaining delays just induces games of the same type, and the "horizon" remains as far away as it normally is.
30. Therefore, this rule is often adopted by weak proposers.
31. That is, by considering

$$\frac{1 + (1 - p)^x s_1 - s_2}{2 - \omega(p, x)} \qquad (45)$$

as $x \to 0$ where the function $\omega(p, x) \to 0$ as $x \to 0$.
32. Limit process is a common manner of *definition* in certain areas of mathematics. Take, for example, the concept of area. But this is precisely what it is: a definition, which is not appropriate in the case we are discussing.

## REFERENCES

Binmore, K., Shaked, A., & Sutton, J. (1989). An outside option experiment. *Quarterly Journal of Economics, 104*, 753–770.

Binmore, K., Morgan, P., Shaked, A., & Sutton, J. (1991). Do people exploit their bargaining power? An experimental study. *Games and Economic Behavior, 3*, 295–322.

Bolton, G. E. & Zwick, R. (1995). Anonymity versus punishment in ultimatum bargaining. *Games and Economic Behavior, 10*, 95–121.

Güth, W. & Tietz, R. (1990). Ultimatum bargaining behavior: A survey and comparison of experimental results. *Journal of Economic Psychology, 11*, 417–449.

Güth, W., Schmittberger, R., & Schwarze, B. (1982). An experimental analysis of ultimatum games. *Journal of Economic Behavior and Organization, 3*, 367–388.

Harsanyi, J. C. (1977). *Rational Behavior and Bargaining Equilibrium in Games and Social Situations*. Cambridge: Cambridge University Press.

Hoffman, E., McCabe, K. K., Shachat, K., & Smith, V. (1994). Preference, property rights, and anonymity in bargaining games. *Games and Economic Behavior, 7*, 346–380.

Hoffman, E., McCabe, K. K., & Smith, V. (1996). Social distant and other-regarding behavior in dictator games. *American Economic Review, 96*, 653–660.

Kahn, L. M. & Murnighan, J. K. (1993). A general experiment on bargaining in demand games with outside options. *American Economic Review, 83*, 1260–1280.

Kahneman, D., Knetsch, J. L., & Thaler, R. H. (1986). Fairness and the assumptions of economics. *Journal of Business, 59*, S285 – S300.

Nash, J. F. (1950). The bargaining problem. *Econometrica, 18*, 155–162.

Neelin, J., Sonnenschein, H., & Spiegel, M. (1988). A further test of noncooperative bargaining theory. *American Economic Review, 78*, 824–836.

Ochs, J. & Roth, A. E. (1989). An experimental study of sequential bargaining. *American Economic Review, 79*, 355–384.

Rapoport, A., Weg, E., & Felsenthal, D. (1990). Effects of fixed costs in two-person sequential bargaining. *Theory and Decision, 28*, 47–71.

Rubinstein, A. (1982). Perfect equilibrium in a bargaining model. *Econometrica, 50*, 97–109.

Rubinstein, A. (1991). Comments on the interpretation of game theory. *Econometrica, 59*, 909–924.

Selten, R. (1975). Reexamination of the perfectness concept for equilibrium points in extensive games. *Econometrica, 4*, 25–55.

Sutton, J. (1986). Non-cooperative bargaining theory: An introduction. *Review of Economic Studies*, *53*, 709–724.

Weg, E. & Zwick, R. (1991). On the robustness of perfect equilibrium in fixed cost sequential bargaining under isomorphic transformation. *Economics Letters*, *36*, 21–24.

Weg, E. & Zwick, R. (1994). Toward a settlement of the fairness question in sequential bargaining games. *Journal of Economic Behavior and Organization*, *24*, 19–34.

Weg, E., Rapoport, A., & Felsenthal, D. (1990). Two-person bargaining behavior in fixed discounting factors games with infinite horizon. *Games and Economic Behavior*, *2*, 76–95.

Weg, E., Zwick, R., & Rapoport, A. (1996). Bargaining in uncertain environments: A systematic distortion of perfect equilibrium demands. *Games and Economic Behavior*, *14*, 260–286.

Zwick, R. & Chen, X.-P. (1997). *What price for fairness? A bargaining study*. Working Paper 97.088, The Hong Kong University of Science and Technology, Department of Marketing.

Zwick, R. & Weg, E. (1996). *An experimental study of buyer-seller negotiation: self interest versus other regarding behavior*. Working Paper 96.070, The Hong Kong University of Science and Technology, Department of Marketing.

Zwick, R., Rapoport, A., & Howard, J. C. (1992). Two-person sequential bargaining behavior with exogenous breakdown. *Theory and Decision*, *32*, 241–268.

Zwick, R., Rapoport, A., & Weg, E. (1996). *A breakdown of Invariance: the case of two vs. three-person sequential bargaining*. Working Paper 96.070, The Hong Kong University of Science and Technology, Department of Marketing.

# Part V

# Social Dilemmas and Coordination

## Collaboration and Coordination

# 12    Reciprocation and Learning in the Intergroup Prisoner's Dilemma Game

Harel Goren
Gary Bornstein
*The Hebrew University of Jerusalem*

Intergroup conflicts (e.g., elections, wars, labor management disputes) are often associated with conflicts of interests within the competing groups as well. The fundamental intragroup conflict stems from the fact that the payoffs associated with the outcome of the intergroup conflict (e.g., political influence, territory, higher wages) are public goods that are equally available to all the members of a group, regardless of whether they contributed to the group's effort. Thus, although the group as a whole gains from winning the competition and acquiring these goods, rational and selfish group members who free ride (e.g., by declining to vote, fight, or stand on a picket line) gain more.

The problem of public goods provision that arises in intergroup conflict is fundamentally different from that studied in the traditional single-group case. In the case of a single group, the level of contribution needed for the public good to be provided is either fixed (van de Kragt, Orbell, & Dawes, 1983) or determined by a random move of nature (Messick, Allison, & Samuelson, 1988; Suleiman & Rapoport, 1988), and the group, as a collective, has simply to maximize its payoff, or its expected payoff, respectively. In contrast, the production function in intergroup conflict is determined by comparing the levels of contribution of the two groups. The existence of a second group whose choices also affect the outcome requires strategic considerations that cannot be reduced to simple maximization problems, and, depending on the game's payoff structure, the groups may decide to cooperate, to compete, or to strike some balance between cooperation and competition (Colman, 1982).

Obviously, if this problem of collective action is to be properly investigated, the intragroup and intergroup levels of conflict must be considered simultaneously. Traditional game paradigms are too restrictive for this purpose. Two-person games treat the competing groups as unitary players, thereby overlooking conflicts of interest within the groups (Allison, 1971; Brams, 1975; Snidal, 1986). *N*-person games ignore the conflict of interests between the groups.

# THE INTERGROUP PRISONER'S DILEMMA (IPD) GAME

Following the work of Palfrey and Rosenthal (1983) on voting behavior, we model intergroup conflict as a team game involving two groups, or teams of players. Each player chooses how much to contribute toward his or her team effort. Contribution is assumed to be costly. Payoff to a player is a monotonically increasing function of the total contribution made by members of his or her own team and a monotonically decreasing function of the total contribution made by members of the opposing team. Net of cost, all players on the same team receive the same payoff. A simplified team game where each player makes a binary choice between a costly and a noncostly action (contributing or not contributing) is called a *participation game*.

This chapter focuses on one such participation game, called the Intergroup Prisoner's Dilemma (IPD) game (Bornstein, 1992). The IPD game is structured so that a prisoner's dilemma game (PDG) is created both between and within the competing teams. In the present experiment the IPD game was operationalized as a six-person game in normal form, described as follows. The set of players is partitioned into two teams of three players each. Each player receives an endowment of $e$ points at the beginning of the game and has to decide whether to contribute this endowment. After decisions are made, payoffs are allocated to each player based on the difference between the number of contributors on his or her team and the number of contributors on the opposing team. Formally, the strategy set of Player $i$ is $\{0,1\}$, where 1 stands for contribution ($C$) and 0 stands for no contribution ($NC$). Given a strategy combination $(\sigma_1,\ldots,\sigma_6)$, the payoff for $i$ is determined according to the following expression:

$$h_i(\sigma) = \alpha\left(\sum_{j\in A(i)}\sigma_j - \sum_{j\in N/A(i)}\sigma_j\right) + 3\alpha + e(1-\sigma_i) \tag{1}$$

where $N$ is the set of players and $A(i)$ is the group to which $i$ belongs, $\alpha > 0$ is the players' incremental payoff for each additional contribution by an ingroup member, and $e > 0$ is the initial endowment given to each individual (the cost of contribution). We impose that $\alpha < e < 3\alpha$. Given the first inequality ($\alpha < e$), playing 0 (not contributing) is the dominating strategy for each player. This is because independently of the strategies of the remaining players, contributing increases a player's reward by $\alpha$ but costs $e$, hence reducing the net payoff by $e - \alpha > 0$. Given the second inequality ($e < 3\alpha$), the dominant joint strategy for each team is to have all of its members contribute. This is because regardless of the actions taken by the other team, each player's contribution increases the total

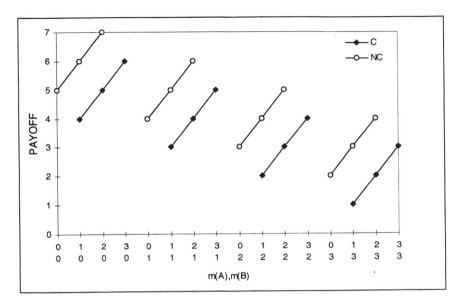

Fig. 12.1. Individual payoff structure of the IPD game. $m(A)$ = number of contributors in group A, $i$'s Ingroup; $m(B)$ = number of contributors in group B, $i$'s Outgroup; $C$ = contribution; $NC$ = non-contribution.

team payoff by $3\alpha - e > 0$.[1] Hence, by our conditions on $\alpha$ and $e$, the intragroup game defined for each team by fixing a joint strategy for the other team is a three-person PDG. Although the dominant strategy for each team is to have all of its members contribute, both teams are better off when none of their members contribute. This is because when all players contribute, each gets $3\alpha$, whereas, when none contribute, each gets $3\alpha+e$. The conflict between the two teams is thus a two-person PDG. A graphic representation of the IPD game with the payoff parameters used in the present study appears in Fig. 12.1. Figure 12.1 displays the payoff to Player $i$ as a function of the player's decision to contribute ($C$) or to avoid contribution ($NC$); $m(A)$ is the number of contributors in group A, $i$'s ingroup, whereas $m(B)$ is the number of contributors in group B, $i$'s outgroup.

The purpose of this study was to investigate the dynamics of repeated play in the IPD game. In particular, the study focused on two processes that are possible in an iterated game. The first process is *learning*. An iterated game provides players with an opportunity to learn the structure of the game and adapt their behavior accordingly. The dynamic context of a repeated game thus provides a different, and perhaps more realistic, justification for the theory of equilibrium without assuming strategic rationality (e.g., Harley, 1981; Maynard Smith, 1984; Selten, 1991). Instead, it assumes that simple trial-and-error adaptation to success and failure can steer players in the direction of the game-theoretic equilibrium (Boyd & Richerson, 1985).

The second process is *reciprocation*; in an iterated game, behavior can depend on the earlier choices of other players. As a result, behavior which may be regarded as irrational in a one-shot game may be rational when the game is repeated. The game theoretical formulation of an infinitely repeated interaction is given by the "folk theorem," which states that every feasible and individually rational payoff vector is sustained by some Nash equilibrium of the game. In a finitely repeated game with incomplete information about the length of the horizon (as is the case in our experiment), the set of Nash equilibria is also much larger than that in the one-shot game (e.g., Neyman, 1995). In the IPD game this means that defection by all players is no longer the unique Nash equilibrium. In particular, the efficient outcome within each team (i.e., contribution by all team members) can be sustained as an equilibrium of the repeated game by using strategies of within-team reciprocal cooperation.

Another equilibrium in the repeated IPD game involves reciprocation between teams. By making their contribution decisions contingent on the decisions of outgroup members, the players can bring about the Pareto-efficient outcome in which no one contributes and each player receives $3\alpha+e$ on each round. However, because this outcome is also the equilibrium of the one-shot IPD game, the effect of between-team reciprocation on contribution behavior is difficult to disentangle from that of learning.

In a recent experiment, Bornstein, Winter, and Goren (1996) found that the tendency to cooperate in the IPD game decreases with time, which suggests that the effect of learning is perhaps more decisive than that of within-group reciprocation. Their experiment, however, involved a fairly small number of repetitions (40) and therefore could not rule out the possibility that some reciprocation would have evolved if the game had lasted longer. As found in earlier experiments on the iterated two-person PDG (Guttman, 1986; Radlow, 1965; Rapoport & Chammah, 1965), subjects first learn the payoff structure of the one-shot (constituent) game, treating the behavior of the other player(s) as invariant. It takes subjects much longer to realize that the behavior of the others may be contingent on their own behavior. The result is a U-shaped trend--a decrease in contribution rates at the beginning of the game and then a rise or a recovery as players start reciprocating. The present experiment involved a longer interaction, allowing enough time for the (potential) upward-sloping part of the U-shaped function to appear.

The IPD game was played under three matching protocols. In the fixed-matching condition, team composition and matching between teams was constant throughout the entire game. This condition replicates the Bornstein et al. (1996) study, with the possibility of both within- and between-team reciprocation. In the fixed-ingroup condition, team composition was constant, but on each round the teams were paired randomly for an IPD competition. This condition allows reciprocation within teams, but makes reciprocation between teams impossible, or at least unlikely. Finally, in the mixed-matching condition, the subjects were randomly assigned to teams at the beginning of each round. This protocol hinders any form of effective reciprocation among the players. Of course, all three matching protocols provide subjects with the opportunity to learn the structure of the constituent (one-shot) IPD game.

## EXPERIMENTAL PROCEDURE

The subjects were 120 undergraduate students at the Hebrew University of Jerusalem with no previous experience with the task. Subjects participated in the experiment in groups of 12. When they arrived at the lab the subjects were seated in separate cubicles facing a personal computer, and were given verbal and written instructions concerning the rules and payoffs of the game. The instructions were phrased in terms of the individual's payoffs as a function of his or her own decision to contribute or not and the decisions made by the other players. The payoffs were summarized in a table that was available to the subjects throughout the experiment (see Appendix). Subjects were not instructed to maximize their earnings, and no reference to cooperation or defection was made. Subjects were given a quiz to test their understanding of the game, and the instructions were repeated until the experimenter was convinced that all the subjects understood the payoff rules. Subjects were also told that to ensure the confidentiality of their decisions they would receive their payment in sealed envelopes and leave the laboratory one at a time with no opportunity to meet the other participants.

Subjects played 150 rounds of the IPD game (with $\alpha = 1$ point and $e = 2$ points) under three matching protocols. In the fixed-matching condition, the 12 subjects were divided into four three-person teams, and the same two teams competed against each other in all 150 rounds (iterations). In the fixed-ingroup condition, the 12 participants were also divided into three-person teams, but on each round pairs of teams were matched randomly for an IPD competition. In the mixed condition, the 12 subjects were randomly divided into teams at the beginning of each round and matched randomly with another randomly composed team. The matching protocol was fully explained to the participants. Following each round, subjects received feedback concerning: (a) the number of ingroup contributors in that round, (b) the number of outgroup contributors, (c) the number of points they had earned on that round, and (d) their cumulative earnings. The number of rounds to be played was not made known.[2]

Following the last round, the points were added up by the computer and cashed in at the rate of one Israeli Shekel (IS) for fifteen points (1 IS was equal to $0.40 at the time the experiment took place, and the average subject earned IS

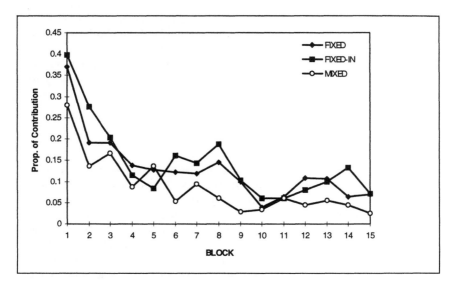

Fig. 12.2. Proportion of contributions per block in the three matching conditions: Experimental results.

34.8, or about $14). Subjects were then debriefed on the rationale and purpose of the study, and were paid and dismissed individually.

## RESULTS

### Contribution Rates

The 150 rounds were divided into 15 blocks of 10 rounds each, and the mean proportion of contributions per block was calculated. These means appear in Fig. 12.2. For the purpose of statistical analysis, the data was further divided into three segments of five blocks (or 50 rounds) each. As seen in Fig. 12.2, the trends in contribution rates during these three time segments were quite different. In the first segment contribution declined monotonically, in the second it increased and then decreased again, and in the final segment it remained quite low and relatively flat. Because there was little variation in contribution behavior in the last 5 blocks, we analyzed only the first and second segments (blocks 1 to 5 and 6 to 10, respectively).[3] The two segments were analyzed separately because, given the different trends described earlier, analyzing them together might have obscured the effect of time (i.e., block) on behavior.

An additional issue that had to be addressed when analyzing these data involved potential dependencies among players in the different matching conditions. We addressed this problem by analyzing the data with ANOVAs that included random nested factors that corresponded to the sources of the possible dependencies (Neter, Wasserman, & Kutner, 1990). In the fixed condition, where individuals interacted repeatedly with the same ingroup and outgroup players, we included the three-person team and the six-person group (consisting of members of both teams) as nested factors in the analysis (the three-person team factor was nested within the six-person group factor, which, in turn, was nested within the fixed-matching condition). In the fixed-ingroup condition, where ingroup members interacted repeatedly but the outgroup changed from one iteration to the other, we included the three-person team as a nested factor. In the mixed condition, where the dependency between the players was minimal, we did not include any nested factors in the analysis.

Thus, the ANOVAs included the factors of matching condition, block, and their interaction, and the just-mentioned nested factors and their interactions with block. We chose to conduct such an analysis because it offers a way of examining the main effects and their interaction while controlling for possible dependencies among players, which are captured by the nested factors. Moreover, examining the effects of the nested factors themselves is also important because it helps to detect dependencies in contribution behavior among repeatedly matched players, resulting from the employment of reciprocal strategies. Note that contribution level and reciprocation are not necessarily correlated. For example, reciprocation among ingroup members can facilitate contribution in the IPD game if the initial level of contribution is sufficiently high, but it can also hinder contribution if the initial willingness to contribute is too low. First, we present the results concerning the effects of matching condition and block. The ANOVA performed on the first time segment (the first 50 rounds, or five blocks) shows a significant main effect of block [$F_{(4, 4.2)} = 27.99$, $p < .05$].[4] The effects of matching condition and the interaction of condition with block were insignificant, indicating that the effect of time (or iteration) was essentially the same in the three matching conditions. As can be seen in Fig. 12.2, contribution rates generally decreased as the game progressed. In the first block, subjects contributed at a rate of 28% in the mixed condition, 40% in the fixed-ingroup condition and 37% in the fixed condition. (In the very first round these rates were 42%, 58% and 53%, in the mixed, fixed-ingroups, and fixed conditions, respectively. An analysis of the contrast between the mixed condition and the fixed and fixed-ingroup conditions indicated that the level of contribution in the first block was significantly lower in the mixed condition than in the other two [$t_{(117)} = 2.11$, $p < .05$].) In block 5 the contribution rates declined to 13.6%, 8.3%, and 12.8%, respectively. Similar results were obtained in the ANOVA performed on the second time segment; contribution rates continued to decline regardless of the matching condition (in block 10, contribution rates reached a level of 3.3% in the mixed condition, 6.0% in the fixed-ingroup condition and 3.8% in the fixed condition). Despite

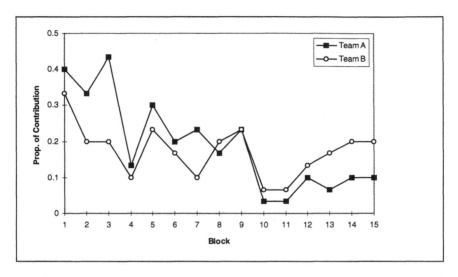

Fig. 12.3. Proportion of contributions per block in two matched teams in the fixed condition.

this decline, the main effect of block was not statistically significant in this time segment [$F_{(4,3.97)}$ = 5.43, $p$ = .07]. The effects of matching condition and the interaction of condition with block were also insignificant.

Next we report the results for the nested factors, namely, the three-person team membership and the six-person group membership. The ANOVA conducted on the first time segment (first 50 rounds) shows a significant effect of the six-person group membership [$F_{(5,18.18)}$ = 3.9, $p$ < .05], but a nonsignificant interaction of group membership with block. The effect of the three-person team membership was insignificant. However, the interaction of team membership with block was significant [$F_{(84,364)}$ = 1.69, $p$ < .05]. The analysis of the second time segment (blocks 6 to 10) reveals similar results, namely, a significant effect for the six-person group membership [$F_{(5,11.55)}$ = 5.35, $p$ < .01] and a significant interaction of the three-person team membership with block [$F_{(84,364)}$ = 2.42, $p$ < .01].

Obviously, the significant effect for the six-person group membership applies only to the fixed-matching condition. This effect means that subjects from different six-person groups differed in their level of contribution (i.e., there was a dependency in contribution levels between participants in the same six-person group). It follows that the level of contribution in each three-person team depended, at least to some extent, on the level of contribution in the other matched team. This dependency is illustrated in Fig. 12.3, which plots the contribution rates of two matched teams in one of the sessions in the fixed

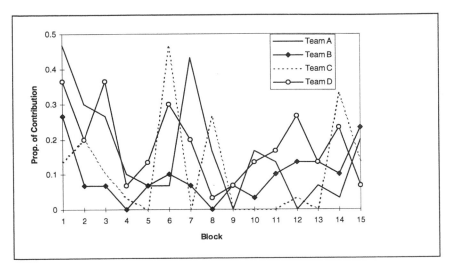

Fig. 12.4. Proportion of contributions per block in four teams in a session of the fixed-ingroup condition.

condition.

The significant interaction of the three-person team factor with block means that subjects in different three-person teams exhibited different changes of contribution levels over time (i.e., there was a dependency in contribution level changes over time between members of three-person teams). This effect, however, can stem from either the fixed condition (where it was nested within six-person group factor) or the fixed-ingroup condition (or, of course, both). Analyses performed on each of these two conditions separately suggest that the primary source of this interaction is the dependency among team members in the fixed-ingroup condition. In the fixed-ingroup condition the interaction between team membership and block is significant [in the first 5-block segment $F_{(60,128)} = 2.01$, $p < 0.01$, in the second segment $F_{(60,128)} = 2.01$, $p < 0.01$], whereas in the fixed condition the effects of the three-person team membership (both main effect and interaction with block) are insignificant.

To illustrate the interaction between team membership and block, Fig. 12.4 displays the contribution levels of four (three-person) teams in one session of the fixed-ingroup condition. We again see a general decline in contribution rates over time. However, this decline is not smooth. Rather, it contains intermediate periods in which contribution actually increased. The fact that these peaks in contribution level occurred at different times for different teams means that members of the same team changed their behavior in a fashion that was

Table 12.1

**Proportion of Players' Contribution on Round *t* as a Function of the Number of Ingroup Contributors on Round *t-1* in the Three Matching Conditions**

| | # of Ingroup Contributors in *t-1* | | | |
|---|---|---|---|---|
| | *0* | *1* | *2* | *Total Proportion of Contribution* |
| *Condition* | | | | |
| Fixed | 0.112 (n = 4114) | 0.174 (n = 1094) | 0.212 (n = 156) | 0.128 |
| Fixed-Ingroup | 0.113 (n = 5312) | 0.219 (n = 1596) | 0.279 (n = 244) | 0.142 |
| Mixed | 0.075 (n = 4492) | 0.133 (n = 804) | 0.177 (n = 68) | 0.085 |
| Mean proportion (unweighted) | 0.100 | 0.175 | 0.222 | |

correlated with the other members of their team and uncorrelated with other teams, hence the significant interaction.

To summarize, the analysis of the nested factors indicates that time-correlated changes in contribution behavior exist within teams in the fixed-ingroup condition and between teams (or within the six-person superordinate group) in the fixed condition. These contingencies, however, did not result in marked differences in contribution levels. When the nested factors are controlled, the main effect of matching condition and the interaction of condition with block are nonsignificant. Thus, although the general effect of repetition is to reduce the level of contribution in the IPD game, this effect seems to be independent of the particular matching protocol used.

## Reciprocation

In the following section we examine the contingencies among the players' decisions. Specifically, we look at the relation between an individual's decision to contribute in a particular round and the decisions made by the other ingroup and outgroup players in the previous round. First, we cross-tabulated each participant's decision to contribute or not in round *t* (*t* = 2 to 150) with the

**Table 12.2**
**Proportion of Players' Contribution on Round $t$ as a Function of the Number of Outgroup Contributors on Round $t-1$ in the Three Matching Conditions**

| | # of Outgroup Contributors in $t-1$ | | | | Total Prop. of Cont. |
|---|---|---|---|---|---|
| | _0_ | _1_ | _2_ | _3_ | |
| _Condition_ | | | | | |
| Fixed | 0.086 | 0.191 | 0.302 | 0.431 | 0.128 |
| | ($n = 3672$) | ($n = 1326$) | ($n = 315$) | ($n = 51$) | |
| Fixed-Ingroup | 0.106 | 0.184 | 0.277 | 0.439 | 0.142 |
| | ($n = 4692$) | ($n = 1860$) | ($n = 534$) | ($n = 66$) | |
| Mixed | 0.064 | 0.146 | 0.214 | 0.200 | 0.085 |
| | ($n = 4143$) | ($n = 1047$) | ($n = 159$) | ($n = 15$) | |
| Mean proportion (unweighted) | 0.085 | 0.174 | 0.264 | 0.357 | |

number of contributors in the team in round $t-1$. In the mixed condition, where the composition of the ingroup changed from one round to the next, we examined the choice behavior of the two players who had belonged to Player $i$'s team in round $t-1$. These data, aggregated across all subjects and rounds, appear in Table 12.1.

As can be seen in the table, the likelihood of contribution in round $t$ increased as more ingroup members contributed in the previous round. Although this is true for all matching conditions, this dependency is higher in the fixed-ingroup condition than in the fixed and mixed conditions. To test whether this difference is significant, we computed the correlation (phi) between each subject's decision to contribute in round $t$ and the decisions made by the other ingroup members in round $t-1$. Specifically, this variable took on a value of 0 if there were no other contributors in the ingroup, and a value of 1 if there was at least one other contributor.[5] The average correlation was 0.11 in the mixed condition, 0.19 in the fixed-ingroup condition, and 0.11 in the fixed condition. The differences among the three correlations are not statistically significant

$[F_{(2,109)} = 2.86, p = .062]$. However, the contrast between the fixed-ingroup and the mixed conditions is significant $[t_{(109)} = 2.04, p < .05]$.

Next, we performed a similar analysis correlating each player's contribution decision at time t with the decision made by the outgroup members at time $t$-1. Again, for the mixed and fixed-ingroup conditions we analyzed the behavior of the actual outgroup players at time $t$-1. These data, aggregated across all subjects and rounds, are summarized in Table 12.2.

The results presented in Table 12.2 indicate that, in all three matching conditions, the decision of whether or not to contribute at time $t$ was contingent on the level of outgroup contribution at time $t$-1. We computed the correlation (phi) between each subject's decision to contribute at round $t$ and the decisions made by the outgroup members on the previous round (again only two categories were used: 0 if there were no outgroup contributors and 1 if there was at least one contributor). The mean correlations were 0.16 in the mixed condition, 0.17 in the fixed-ingroup condition, and 0.20 in the fixed condition. Although the higher correlation in the fixed condition is consistent with the notion that between-team reciprocation played a larger role in this condition than in the other two, the difference is not statistically significant.

Additional analysis, using a different correlation coefficient (gamma), computed on the full range of others' contribution (0 to 2 for the ingroup, 0 to 3 for the outgroup), yielded results similar to those just described. Analysis of the correlations (Pearson's $r$) between the subject's number of contributions in each 5-round block and the number of ingroup and outgroup contributions in the previous block yielded results that were even weaker.

# DISCUSSION

Our main finding is that subjects became more likely to defect as they gained more experience with the task. Because defection is the equilibrium strategy in the constituent IPD game, it is natural to ask whether this trend can be accounted for by a simple learning principle. One such principle is the law of effect (Thorndike, 1898), which states that choices which have led to good outcomes in the past are more likely to be repeated in the future.

To examine this possibility, we conducted computer simulations in which we applied the law of effect, as formulated by Roth and Erev (1995), to the IPD game. The Roth and Erev learning model assumes that Player $i$, when deciding how to act, considers the two pure strategies: contribution $(C)$ and noncontribution $(D)$. At time $t = 1$ (before any experience with the task has been acquired) Player $i$ has some initial propensity to play each of these two strategies. The propensity to select a particular strategy, say strategy $C$, at time $t = 1$ is denoted by $q_{iC}(1)$. If Player $i$ plays strategy $C$ at time $t$ and receives a payoff of $x$, then the propensity to play $C$ is updated by setting $q_{iC}(t+1) = q_{iC}(t) + x$, whereas for the other strategy, $D$, the update is described by $q_{iD}(t+1) = q_{iD}(t)$.

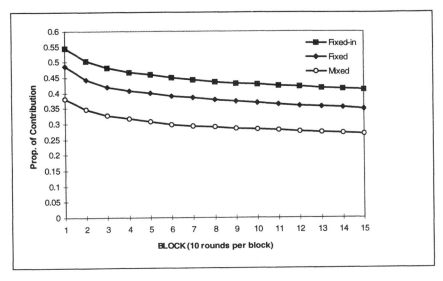

Fig. 12.5. Proportion of contributions per block in the three matching conditions: Simulated results.

The probability $p_{iC}(t)$ that Player $i$ will play strategy $C$ at time t is $p_{iC}(t)$ $=q_{iC}(t)/q_{iC}(t)+q_{iD}(t)$, the ratio of the propensity to play $C$ divided by the sum of the propensities to play each of the two strategies. Thus, the probability of playing strategy $C$ increases the more successful that strategy has been on previous rounds.

In performing the simulations we assumed that at $t = 1$ all players in the same matching condition have the same initial propensity to cooperate. In setting these initial propensities we considered two factors: the ratio $q_{iC}(1)/q_{iD}(1)$ of the propensities to play strategy $C$ and $D$, which determines the probability that $C$ will be played at time $t = 1$; and the sum of the initial propensities for the two strategies $C$ and $D$, $S(1) = q_{iC}(1)+q_{iD}(1)$. This second factor can be thought of as the *strength* of the initial propensities. When the value of $S(1)$ is large, the initial propensities are strong and learning is relatively slow. When the value of $S(1)$ is small, the initial propensities are weak and adaptation occurs more quickly. We set $S(1) = 10$ and calculated the ratio $q_{iC}(1)/q_{iD}(1)$ for the fixed, fixed-ingroup, and mixed conditions from the observed choices in the first round in each condition. The initial propensities for the computer simulations were set at 5.28 and 4.72 (for $C$ and $D$, respectively) in the fixed condition, 5.83 and 4.17 in the fixed-ingroup condition, and 4.17 and 5.83 in the mixed condition.

For each matching condition we ran 50 simulations. The mean contribution rates in these simulations is presented in Fig. 12.5. As can be seen in the figure, contribution rates among the simulated subjects decreased monotonically over time, and most of this decrease occurred in the early stages (the first 20 or so rounds) of the game. Although none of our experimental groups corresponded exactly to this pattern, the results of the mixed-matching condition seem to be the closest. This is primarily because the fixed and fixed-ingroup conditions contained intermediate increases in contribution rates that are not predicted by the learning model.

To conclude, our results suggest that the main process that occurs during repeated interaction in the IPD game is that of learning. There was also some evidence that subjects attempted, when possible, to reciprocate with other ingroup as well as outgroup members. These attempts, however, had little effect on contribution decisions. In particular, within-team reciprocation was largely unsuccessful in sustaining long-term contribution.

## ACKNOWLEDGMENTS

This research was supported by grants from the Israel Foundations Trustees (1994-1996) and the Israel Science Foundation (1994-1997). We wish to thank Abdolkarim Sadrieh, Klaus Abbink and Bernd Irlenbusch, of the Laboratory for Experimental Economics at the University of Bonn, Germany, for devising and programming the software for this experiment; and Ronit Nirel and Malka Gorfine of the Department of Statistics at the Hebrew University of Jerusalem for their help in data analysis.

## APPENDIX

Subjects were told that each player had to decide whether to keep the 2 points endowment or "invest" it. The number of investors in the two teams would be counted and a bonus would be given to each member of a team depending on the difference between the number of ingroup and outgroup contributors. If all members of Team A contribute, and no members of Team B contribute, members of Team A receive a bonus of 6 points whereas those in Team B receive no bonus. If there are two more contributors in Team A than in Team B, each member of Team A receives a bonus of 5 points, whereas each member of Team B receives 1 point. If Team A has one more contributor than Team B, each member of Team A receives 4 points, whereas each member of Team B receives 2. Finally, in case of a tie (an equal number of contributors in both teams), each member of both teams receives a reward of 3 points. In addition to the bonus, each player keeps the endowment if he or she does not invest it. The payoffs are summarized in Table 12.3.

## ENDNOTES

1.  The constant $+3\alpha$ is included to guarantee positive payoffs to the subjects.

**Table 12.3**
**Payoffs in the Experiment**

| | More investors in your group | | | | More investors in other group | | |
|---|---|---|---|---|---|---|---|
| Ingroup-Outgroup | 3 | 2 | 1 | 0 | -1 | -2 | -3 |
| You Invest | 6 | 5 | 4 | 3 | 2 | 1 | - |
| You do not Invest | - | 7 | 6 | 5 | 4 | 3 | 2 |

2.  Subjects decisions and all feedback information was handled by a computer program that used the RatImage toolbox (Abbink & Sadrieh, 1995).
3.  A large proportion of the participants defected consistently on the last 50 rounds of the game. In the mixed and fixed conditions more than half of the participants did not contribute at all (20 of the 36 subjects in each condition), and in the fixed-ingroup condition this rate was more than 30% (15 of the 48 participants defected on all 50 rounds). Analyzing these data by an ANOVA is problematic since the assumption of normal (or at least symmetric) distribution is violated.
4.  All the reported $F$ values were calculated using the Greenhouse-Geisser adjustment.
5.  It would be misleading to compute a single measure of correlation for each condition because this would overlook individual differences in using reciprocal strategies. For instance, there were a few subjects who did not contribute throughout the entire game. These subjects might have an effect on a general measure of correlation although they clearly did not reciprocate.

# REFERENCES

Abbink, K., & Sadrieh, A. (1995). *RatImage: Research assistance toolbox for computer-aided human behavior experiments.* University of Bonn, Discussion paper No. B-325.
Allison, G. (1971). *Essence of decision: Explaining the Cuban missile crisis.* Boston: Little, Brown.
Bornstein, G. (1992). The free rider problem in intergroup conflicts over step-level and continuous public goods. *Journal of Personality and Social Psychology, 62,* 597-606.
Bornstein, G., Winter, E., & Goren, H. (1996). Experimental study of repeated team games. *European Journal of Political Economy, 12,* 629-639.
Boyd, R., & Richerson, P. I. (1985). *Culture and the evolutionary process.* Chicago: University of Chicago Press.
Brams, S. (1975) *Game theory and politics: International relations games.* New York: The Free Press.
Colman, A. (1982). *Game theory and experimental games: The study of strategic interaction.* Oxford, England: Pergamon Press.

Guttman, J. M. (1986). Matching behavior and collective action: Some experimental evidence. *Journal of Economic Behavior and Organization, 7,* 171-198.

Harley, C. B. (1981). Learning the evolutionary stable strategy. *Journal of Theoretical Biology, 89,* 611-633.

Maynard Smith, J. (1984). Game theory and evolution of behavior. *Behavioral and Brain Sciences, 7,* 95-125.

Messick, D., Allison, S., & Samuelson, C. (1988). Framing and communication effects on group members' responses to environmental and social uncertainty. In S. Maital (Ed.). *Applied behavioral economics,* (Vol. 2, pp. 677-700). New York: New York University Press.

Neter, J., Wasserman, W., & Kutner, M. H. (1990). *Applied linear statistical models: Regression, analysis of variance, and experimental design* (3rd ed.). Boston: IRWIN.

Neyman, A. (1995). *Cooperation in the repeated Prisoner's Dilemma when the number of stages is not commonly known.* Discussion Paper No. 65., The Center for Rationality and Interactive Decision Theory, The Hebrew University of Jerusalem.

Palfrey, T. R., & Rosenthal, H. (1983). A strategic calculus of voting. *Public Choice, 41,* 7-53.

Radlow, R. (1965). An experimental study of cooperation in the Prisoner's Dilemma game. *Journal of Conflict Resolution, 9,* 221-227.

Rapoport, A., & Chammah, A. M. (1965). *Prisoner's dilemma: A study in conflict and cooperation.* Ann Arbor, MI: University of Michigan Press.

Roth, A., & Erev, I. (1995). Learning in extensive-form games: Experimental data and simple dynamic models in the intermediate term. *Games and Economic Behavior, 8,* 164-212.

Selten, R. (1991). Evolution, learning, and economic behavior. *Games and Economic Behavior, 3,* 3-24.

Snidal, D. (1986). The game theory of international politics. In K. Oye (Ed.), *Cooperation under anarchy,* (pp. 25-57). Princeton, NJ: Princeton University Press.

Suleiman, R., & Rapoport, A. (1988). Environmental and social uncertainty in single-trial resource dilemmas. *Acta Psychologica, 68,* 99-112.

Thorndike, E. L. (1898). *Animal intelligence: An experimental study of the associative processes in animals.* Psychological Monographs, 2.

van de Kragt, A. J. C., Orbell, J. M., & Dawes, R. M. (1983). The minimal contributing set as a solution to public goods problems. *American Political Science Review, 77,* 112-122.

# 13    Reciprocity and Cooperation in Social Dilemmas: Review and Future Directions

**Samuel S. Komorita**
*University of Illinois at Urbana-Champaign*

**Craig D. Parks**
*Washington State University*

One of the most intriguing questions involving social dilemma research is how we can promote mutual cooperation among members of a group. The importance of this question was recognized by Luce and Raiffa (1957), who argued that in the repeated play prisoner's dilemma game (PDG), mutual cooperation maximizes long-run payoffs. However, in reviewing the voluminous social science literature on the prisoner's dilemma (PD), Axelrod (1980a) concluded that no one had really addressed the question of *how* to bring about mutual cooperation. He argued that laboratory researchers had focused exclusively on description of the choice patterns of naive, inexperienced subjects; that field researchers examined real PDG-type situations that changed too slowly to provide reliable data on strategy; and that simulation theorists used PDG variants that designed away the dilemma aspect of the situation. "To learn more about how to choose effectively in an iterated Prisoner's Dilemma," Axelrod wrote, "a new approach is needed" (p. 6). This chapter summarizes the results of Axelrod's new approach and the empirical studies and computer simulations that it spurred. We also present some important follow-up questions that have yet to be addressed.

## AXELROD'S SIMULATIONS

Axelrod's new approach to the question of effective choice in PD was to solicit choice strategies from people who were familiar with the logic of PDG. He then

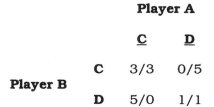

Fig. 13.1. Payoff matrix used in Axelrod's simulations.

pitted these strategies against each other in a computer tournament. Each strategy's objective was to finish the tournament with more total points than any other strategy. Winning or losing any one particular contest was irrelevant; the emphasis was on performance across all types of situations. In addition to 14 entries (from faculty members in psychology, sociology, mathematics, economics, and political science), he included a purely random strategy, for a total of 15 strategies. All possible pairs of strategies (including the strategy playing against itself) played 200-trial, two-player PDGs, with the matrix shown in Fig. 13.1. He conducted five rounds of the tournament in order to obtain stable point totals. The winning strategy, submitted by Anatol Rapoport, was a reciprocal strategy, tit-for-tat (TFT), which cooperates on the first trial, and thereafter chooses what the opponent chose on the previous trial.

In his discussion of the tournament, Axelrod (1980a) pointed out that it was easy to derive strategies that could have outgained TFT in the 15-strategy environment. This led him to raise concerns about the generality of the results; hence, he conducted a second, more extensive tournament (Axelrod, 1980b). He again solicited entries from knowledgeable parties, but this time Axelrod provided the parties with the results from the first tournament, including a discussion of strategies that would have beaten TFT had they been part of the contest. For this second tournament, Axelrod received 62 entries, and a random strategy was again included. The payoff matrix from the first tournament was used, and five rounds were again conducted, but the length of a contest was no longer fixed at 200 trials. Rather, a distribution of contest lengths was created for the probability = .00346 that the contest would end on any given move, and five lengths (one for each round) were selected at random from this distribution. As a result, the five rounds contained contests of 63, 77, 151, 156, and 308 trials, for a mean contest length of 151 trials. The winner was again TFT.

The two tournaments provided strong support for the notion that reciprocation is a very effective choice strategy in PD. However, Axelrod (1980b) was careful to point out that there is no single strategy that is "best" irrespective of the situation. The obvious question is, what factors account for TFT's success? Axelrod (1984) argued that there are four important factors.

## Lack of Envy

Reciprocation is based on personal success, not on how well one is doing when compared to one's opponent. In fact, it is impossible for TFT to ever win a contest because TFT is never the first to defect, which is necessary to gain an advantage over the other person. Beating one's opponent requires exploitation (i.e., choosing D when the other has chosen C). Axelrod argued that people will not tolerate being exploited, and eventually the pattern of choices will fall into the mutually destructive D-D cell.

## "Niceness"

TFT is a "nice" strategy in that it is never the first to defect, and as such is likely to lead players into the desirable C-C cell. The importance of niceness was very clear in Axelrod's data. In his first tournament, the eight highest point totals were achieved by nice strategies; in the second, the seven highest totals, and 14 of the top 15. Axelrod qualified the importance of niceness, however, by suggesting that it is better to be "not nice" (i.e., defect first) if one does not anticipate any future interactions with the opponent.

## Provocability and Forgiveness

TFT immediately reciprocates any change in the opponent's behavior. This demonstrates that TFT will not tolerate a defection (by switching from C to D after the opponent does so), but will forgive a defection (by switching from D to C after the opponent does so). This conveys to the opponent that TFT cannot be consistently exploited, but will engage in mutual cooperation even after it has been exploited.

## Clarity

Finally, TFT is an easy strategy to use and to perceive. The former is important if we want to encourage others to adopt TFT, and the latter is important in situations in which there can be no communication between players, assuming that we want our opponent to understand exactly what we are doing. The opponent can track the choices made under a reciprocal strategy, and fairly quickly realize that he or she is being imitated.

Axelrod's work had an immediate impact in many areas of science. His general summary of the simulations (Axelrod & Hamilton, 1981) won the Newcomb Cleveland award from the American Academy for the Advancement of Science for the best paper published in *Science* in 1981. By 1993, the work had been cited in over 200 scientific publications across a wide range of disciplines (see Axelrod & D'Ambrosio, 1994). One element of that impact was to stimulate considerable debate about the role of reciprocation in nature. Basically, the debate centers around the evolutionary stability of reciprocity, with some theorists (e.g., Boyd & Lorberbaum, 1987) arguing that no species that behaves purely reciprocally can survive in the long run, whereas others (e.g., Swistak, 1989) argue that such species can thrive.

Of more interest to us is that researchers began empirically testing Axelrod's assertions, and conducting further simulations designed to test the limits of TFT's effectiveness. In the remaining sections of this chapter, we focus on the effectiveness of reciprocal strategies on facilitating cooperation among group members, not only in the two-person PDG but in the *n*-person social dilemma. The concept of reciprocity is of interest in a variety of disciplines (philosophy, religion, social sciences), and to narrow the scope of our review, we restrict ourselves to the empirical (especially experimental) research on the effects of reciprocity.

# EXPERIMENTAL RESEARCH ON RECIPROCITY

There are some early laboratory studies on the effects of TFT (e.g., Oskamp, 1971; Wilson, 1971). Patchen (1987) presented an extensive summary of this earlier research, as well as a summary of the effectiveness of several variants of TFT. Despite this extensive research on the effects of TFT, there are few direct tests of Axelrod's hypotheses. This chapter focuses on some empirical studies that we conducted to test Axelrod's hypotheses.

The empirical research that has been conducted has employed the same general laboratory paradigm. Groups of subjects are told that they will be playing a number of trials of a dilemma-type game with some of the others in the room. They are separated and do not know exactly who the opponents are; they are not allowed to talk with the other members at any time, and the exact number of trials of the game is left unspecified. Typically, every point that is earned is converted to something valuable at the end of the game (prizes, tickets in a cash lottery, etc.). This paradigm is doubly beneficial in that it is efficient – the typical four-person group will complete one trial every minute – and it is credible. As is shown, in most of our experiments subjects are actually pitted against programmed strategies. The number of subjects who reported being suspicious of the deception (on postsession questionnaires) was always very small; typically nobody reported such suspicion.

In our first study (Komorita, Hilty, & Parks, 1991) we addressed three of Axelrod's principles: provocability/forgiveness, niceness, and clarity. Specifically, we wanted to know (a) how important it is to *immediately* punish or forgive a defection; (b) how important niceness is, and (c) whether subjects would accurately perceive the use of TFT (strategy of imitation). We ran two studies of two-person games. Each subject competed against a programmed strategy that was constructed from two independent variables: Reciprocation of

**Table 13.1**
**Sample Choice Patterns for Programmed Strategies with Immediate and Delayed Reciprocation**

|  | Trial | | | | | | | |
|---|---|---|---|---|---|---|---|---|
|  | **1** | **2** | **3** | **4** | **5** | **6** | **7** | **8** |
| **Subject choices** | C | C | D | C | D | D | D | D |
| **Strategy choices:** | | | | | | | | |
|    **C, D immediate** | C | C | C | D | C | D | D | D |
|    **C delayed** | C | C | C | D | D | D | D | D |
|    **D delayed** | C | C | C | C | C | C | D | D |
|    **C, D delayed** | C | C | C | C | D | C | D | D |

Note. When there was a conflict between delayed reciprocation of one choice and immediate reciprocation of another, immediate reciprocation was given priority.

a cooperative choice (immediate or one-trial delay), and reciprocation of defection (immediate or one-trial delay). In the first study, every strategy was "nice" in that it cooperated until provoked into defection by the subject; in the second, we manipulated niceness by having some strategies begin with a D choice. Table 13.1 presents some sample choice patterns for each of the four possible nice strategies. In the C-delayed and D-delayed conditions, it was possible for the manipulations to prescribe conflicting choices for the same trial. In such situations, the prescription for immediate reciprocation was given priority.

Three major findings emerged from these studies. First, we found that immediate reciprocation of a C choice induced greater rates of cooperation than did immediate reciprocation of a D choice. This finding supports Axelrod's contention, but is in contrast to work by Bixenstein and Gaebelein (1971), who obtained high rates of cooperation by delaying reciprocation of both C and D choices. The most likely explanation for this discrepancy is that reciprocation was probabilistic in Bixenstein and Gaeblein's study (i.e., eventual reciprocation of a specific choice was not guaranteed), whereas in our study it was deterministic – choices were *always* reciprocated. Second, strategies that began with a D choice induced greater cooperation over time than did nice strategies. This result is counterintuitive; the most likely explanation is that not nice TFT immediately conveys the impression that it is tough and cannot be exploited. Finally, we found that only about 25% of all subjects who played against a standard TFT strategy (immediate reciprocation of both cooperation and defection) correctly identified it as a reciprocal strategy. We also asked subjects to predict their opponent's choice before the start of every trial, and we found that subjects in the standard TFT condition were no more accurate than subjects in the other three conditions. Assuming that clear strategies are predictable, these two pieces of evidence seem to indicate that clarity is not as prominent a feature of TFT as Axelrod thought. However, there was no correlation between accuracy of prediction and rate of cooperation, suggesting that clarity is not very important in inducing cooperation.

Our next goal (Komorita, Parks, & Hulbert, 1992) was to test the effectiveness of TFT in the *n*-person case. We ran three experiments using groups of three, five, and nine persons. We found that with increasing group size, the use of TFT by any one group member becomes less effective in inducing others to cooperate. As group size increases, the number of members who use TFT must also grow. This is probably because, as group size increases, it becomes more difficult to recognize that one is being reciprocated. In the three-person groups, 38% of subjects correctly recognized that they were being reciprocated; in the five-person groups, the rate was 25%; in nine-person groups, 14%. We also asked subjects to predict the choices of others before the start of each trial, and found that subjects who played against TFT strategies were no more accurate than subjects who played in intact groups. These data support our previous argument that TFT is not as clear as was originally thought. Also consistent with Komorita et al. (1991) was the fact that we found no connection between accuracy and rate of cooperation; this supports our contention that accuracy is not necessary for inducing cooperation. Within the three- and five-person studies, we also compared intact groups against groups consisting of one subject and two or four programmed strategies. In both cases, we found that the intact groups had significantly lower rates of cooperation than did the groups with programmed strategies. This is an interesting point to which we return later.

Our next study (Komorita, Chan, & Parks, 1993) further explored the effects of group size, and potential interactions with the reward structure of the dilemma. In a large group, it is difficult to use TFT because it is hard to track the behavior of any one specific group member. A more user-friendly strategy would be one that reciprocates not the choice of just one group member, as in TFT, but rather the group as a whole. That is, one could decide to cooperate only if a certain number of other group members cooperated on the previous trial.

Thus, we designed two types of strategies: a "soft" strategy, that cooperates if just a few (less than a majority) of others do so, and a "tough" strategy, that cooperates only after a majority of others have done so. We also varied the strength of the temptation to defect in the payoff matrices by using matrices with high and low temptation. We used both five- and eight-person groups. In both groups, we found that tough strategies induced greater rates of cooperation than did soft strategies. This is probably because the soft strategies created an exploitative environment, in that they cooperated when just a few others had done so, and subjects took advantage of this. However, it was also the case that neither tough nor soft strategies induced much cooperation when the temptation to defect was high. This suggests that reciprocation is not effective at overriding substantial temptation, an important limitation of reciprocal strategies.

We have expanded on the notion of reciprocation of subsets of members, rather than of just one person, by devising the group-based reciprocal strategy (GBRS). The logic of a GBRS is that one cooperates only after a certain number of others have cooperated on the previous trial. We have conducted a series of computer simulations of 100-person groups, and have found that a GBRS that cooperates only after 75% of all others have cooperated induces the greatest rates of cooperation (Parks & Komorita, 1997). These findings, of course, need empirical confirmation, but in a large-group setting, the effectiveness of reciprocating groups of people, rather than just one person, seems promising.

Although the brunt of our work has focused on group size, we have investigated other factors that may moderate the effectiveness of reciprocal strategies. For example, in a study of reciprocity across cultures, we were able to replicate the effect of immediate reciprocation of a cooperative choice when the subjects were from an individualistic culture (United States); however, when the subjects were from a highly collectivistic culture (South Vietnam), immediate reciprocation of cooperation was not important (Parks & Vu, 1994). This suggests that TFT may be less effective (or necessary) in cultures in which the group is emphasized, a possibility that has yet to be tested. We have also tested TFT in a two-person asymmetric game and, consistent with Komorita et al. (1993), we found that the effectiveness of TFT was highly dependent on the opponent's payoff structure (Parks & Scamahorn, 1997).

## POST-AXELROD COMPUTER SIMULATIONS

Axelrod's tournaments encouraged other researchers to conduct further computer simulations of TFT in various environments. The results of these simulations shed light on both the generality and limitations of TFT, and suggest many interesting empirical questions, some of which are beyond the scope of this review. (The interested reader can find a complete summary in Komorita & Parks, 1995.) Considerable attention has been paid to TFT's performance in a noisy social dilemma, in which actions have a chance of being misperceived (Bendor, 1987, 1993; Bendor, Kramer, & Stout, 1991; Fudenberg & Maskin, 1990; Lomborg, 1996; Molander, 1985; Mueller, 1987; Wu & Axelrod, 1995; Young & Foster, 1991). Such a misperception could sabotage TFT because if a TFT user misperceives cooperation as defection, he or she will end up responding to cooperation with defection, which could cause the opponent to retaliate, and so on. All of these studies have shown that TFT does not perform very well (i.e., does not accumulate a very substantial point total) in a noisy environment. However, the authors differ in regards to what behavioral strategy will work best. Some have argued that a slight modification of TFT, under which one would make an occasional, unconditionally cooperative choice, is most effective (Bendor et al. 1991; Molander, 1985), but others suggest moving away from a reciprocal strategy and adopting a type of "lapsed saint" approach, under which one cooperates until the other defects, at which point one switches to complete defection (Mueller, 1987). Wu and Axelrod (1995) argued that the particular strategy to use is dependent on the extent to which others have adapted to the noise: The less well-adapted the others are, the more forgiving one should be of misperceptions.

A number of simulations have pitted TFT against strategies that did not appear in either of Axelrod's tournaments. A strategy called Pavlov, which "learns" to cooperate via rewards and punishments that change its probability of cooperation on the next trial, has been shown to outgain TFT (Kraines & Kraines, 1989, 1993, 1995),[1] as have strategies that seek to maximize expected utility (Marinoff, 1992). In addition, Messick and Liebrand (1995) proposed an affective TFT rule called "win-cooperate, lose-defect," under which one cooperates if the payoff on the previous trial was at least as good as the average of one's neighbors' payoffs; if it is not, one defects. This rule seems to invoke high rates of cooperation.

Finally, the effectiveness of TFT in games with an expanded range of choices has been tested. To (1988) conducted simulations using two-person games in which each player had five choice options available, the choices differing by the degree of cooperation they represented. In such a situation, To found the highest gaining strategy to be a subtler version of TFT, under which a defecting choice was reciprocated with a defection that was one degree less severe than the opponent's choice.

Each of these areas of simulation poses many interesting questions for the behavioral researcher. Given the ease with which behaviors can be misinterpreted, it would be very interesting to collect some empirical data on TFT and noise. Similarly, the role of learning in cooperation has been understudied. We have suggested elsewhere that learning principles are important in strategic behavior (Komorita et al., 1991), and some researchers have begun to investigate learning and cooperation (Bornstein, Erev, & Goren, 1994), but much more can be done. Finally, there seems to be almost no research on TFT in expanded-choice games. This is potentially a very fruitful line of inquiry, as research on behavior in such games has revealed patterns of behavior that differ considerably from that seen in two-choice games (e.g., Insko, Schopler, Hoyle, Dardis, & Graetz, 1990).

# FUTURE DIRECTIONS FOR EMPIRICAL RESEARCH

We are slowly gaining insight into the effectiveness and limitations of reciprocation as a means of inducing others to cooperate. Specifically, we have learned that one of Axelrod's original recommendations is very important – one should immediately reciprocate a cooperative choice. However, it is less crucial that some of his other recommendations be adopted. Specifically, to induce high rates of cooperation, one need not be nice, immediately reciprocate a defection, or clearly convey one's strategy. We know nothing about the importance of his final recommendation – do not be envious – and we discuss this lack of data later. We have also learned that TFT's success is limited to very small groups, and in larger groups, reciprocating a subset of individuals may be a better strategy. However, there remain a number of basic questions that have not been addressed by researchers. To conclude our review of reciprocity, we present a few of these questions that we consider to be especially important.

## How Does TFT Arise in Groups?

Perhaps the most important question is how reciprocity emerges in real groups. In all of the studies that we have reviewed, TFT was introduced by means of a programmed strategy. But what happens in intact groups of people? Although no study has directly addressed this question, both Komorita et al. (1992) and Bornstein et al. (1994) included intact groups in their studies, and neither research team found choice behavior in those groups to resemble what would be observed if some members were using TFT. In fact, Komorita et al. made a direct statistical comparison of the rates of cooperation in three-person intact groups and groups consisting of one subject and two TFT strategies. They found that the intact groups had a significantly lower rate of cooperation (27%) than the human strategies groups (49%). It seems, then, that TFT does not spontaneously arise within groups. There are two possible explanations for why not. First, TFT may not appear in intact groups because no group members are cognizant of TFT as a possible behavioral strategy. Secondly, it may be that some group members are aware of TFT, but refrain from acting reciprocally. We address each of these possibilities in turn.

First, it may be the case that few group members are aware of reciprocation. Empirical data suggest that this is a very plausible explanation. In our work, we have asked subjects to describe on post hoc questionnaires on what basis they made their choices during the game. We have consistently found 75%-80% of the subjects reporting that they either largely chose the competitive choice, or chose randomly. We never had more than 10% of the subjects report basing their choices on the choices of others. Hence, it is very likely that, in real groups, few members even know what reciprocation is. In these situations, the task is to introduce reciprocity into the group. How can this be done? There is a long-term answer to this question that has been discussed by both Axelrod (1984) and Komorita et al. (1991), namely, socialize children into the ways of reciprocation. But what do we do in the short term, for groups that exist right now? There seems to be no research that can answer this question, although other areas of social dilemma research might hold some clues. For example, some research suggests that cooperation can be enhanced by educating people about the nature of a social dilemma before they actually engage in the dilemma (Mio, Thompson, & Givens, 1993; Stern, 1976). Perhaps reciprocity could be introduced into a group simply by educating group members about the benefits of reciprocity.

Alternately, it is plausible that some group members know about reciprocity, but do not use it. Why might this be? One possible explanation may be related to feelings of low self-efficacy: How can one single reciprocator make a difference in such a large group of people (cf. Kerr, 1989)? Many members may be willing to cooperate if others would do so also. If this is true (and it should be noted that there is very little data on this), then the task becomes one of encouraging others on the use of reciprocity. There are several ways in which this might be accomplished. First, one might have group members communicate with each other, so that those who know of reciprocity can inform others on how it works and why it should be used. Communication of a planned behavioral strategy has been found to enhance cooperation (Hulbert, Mead, & Komorita, 1997; Lindskold, 1978; Parks, Henager, & Scamahorn, 1996), and perhaps the ability to tell others about reciprocation may encourage group members to use it. When communication is possible, one variant of this approach is to ask members to make a *pledge*. A pledge may be defined as an informal poll of group members regarding their preference or intention to contribute to a common good (cooperate). The results of studies by Chen and Komorita (1994) and Chen (1996) indicate that a pledge – provided members are required to make a partial commitment to the pledge – significantly enhances cooperation rates in an iterated social dilemma. One explanation for the effectiveness of a pledge is that it allows members who make a pledge to communicate their intention to cooperate; subsequently, other nonpledge members reciprocate the cooperative intentions of the pledge members.

Another means of encouraging others to use reciprocity is to take a "strength in numbers" approach and organize into a coalition. Then, the coalition can approach the remaining group members and induce them into joining the coalition. The coalitional approach to cooperative induction was suggested by Schelling quite some time ago (1973, 1978), but there seems to be no direct evidence, and only scant indirect evidence (Komorita et al., 1993) that it will work with reciprocation.

## Effects of Envy

The one aspect of Axelrod's (1984) recommendations that has not yet been tested is his advice not to be envious of the other's outcomes. This is a simple recommendation if one is creating an algorithm, but among humans envy could easily be a factor that underlies behavior in social dilemmas. How long will a person continue to reciprocate if they realize that the opponent is outgaining him or her? The reason one should not be envious is because reciprocation will produce a greater average payoff in the long run than any other tested strategy. The payoffs from any one interaction are irrelevant. But it has been hypothesized that actors in social dilemmas typically begin with a short-run perspective (Yamagishi, 1986), so it is plausible that users of reciprocity will be ignorant of the long-term benefits of the strategy. Further, research on relative deprivation clearly shows that when people evaluate outcomes, they do so not in an absolute sense, but rather in terms of how those outcomes compare to what others have received (Mark & Folger, 1984). Recall that reciprocity can never beat another strategy in any one contest because it is never the first to defect. Thus, it may well be the case that people will avoid using reciprocity because *in the short run*, it appears to be suboptimal – it never wins. Arguing for the long-term benefits of reciprocity should be ineffective, given the relative deprivation research. If our reasoning is valid, then it would represent an important constraint on implementing reciprocity in real groups. Our argument would suggest that reciprocity will only be adopted by group members who have a long-term, absolute-gain focus.

This hypothesis is consistent with the results of a study by Hulbert et al. (1997). Subjects in a six-person social dilemma were led to believe that some members would be allowed to send written messages to other members. The effects of different types of preprogrammed messages were assessed, including a reciprocal message that stated, "If most of you cooperate, I will cooperate on the next trial." Reciprocal messages enhanced cooperative behavior, but its effectiveness was attenuated (decreased cooperation) if subjects believed they could exploit such behavior. Note that in the *n*-person social dilemma, it is possible to exploit a subset of members who use a reciprocal strategy, whereas in the two-person PDG, the reciprocal TFT strategy cannot be exploited. Thus, this is another important constraint on the effectiveness of reciprocal strategies.

## Reciprocity in Continuous- and Sequential-Choice Dilemmas

The empirical research on TFT to date has concerned itself with dichotomous-choice dilemmas: One either cooperates or defects. But many real-life social dilemmas involve a range of choices. The decision to contribute to a charity involves not just a decision to give, but also a decision regarding how much to give. How could we apply reciprocity to such a continuous-choice situation? On the face of it, there is an easy solution: Reduce the situation to one of dichotomous choice. That is, one might pick a target of reciprocation, and decide, "If she contributes, I will contribute the same amount. Otherwise, I will give nothing." There are many situations, however, in which such an approach is impractical. What if the target gives something that we cannot give? We are forced to give nothing. Alternately, one might decide to reciprocate only the action itself – "I will give if she gives" – and then make a decision regarding the size of the contribution independent of how the target behaves. The danger of this approach is that it may impact upon the clarity of TFT. If I give $100, and I observe that someone else gave $20, did that person reciprocate me or not? Of course, our studies have shown that clarity is not important for inducing cooperation in the dichotomous-choice situation, but behavior in continuous-choice dilemmas seems to be quite different from behavior in dichotomous-choice games (Suleiman & Rapoport, 1992); thus, it would be unwise to assume that clarity is irrelevant in the continuous-choice dilemma.

Extending the social dilemma to the continuous case also suggests that some bargaining games may be interpreted as a social dilemma. Consider two bargainers, a buyer and a seller, who are both faced with a situation in which reaching agreement yields a far better outcome than not reaching agreement. Concessions must be made to reach an agreement, but the bargainer who makes larger concessions will receive a much smaller payoff than the other bargainer. Thus, making a concession represents a cooperative response, whereas remaining firm represents a defection. Various strategies of inducing concessions have been investigated (Pruitt, 1981). As in PDG, a strategy of reciprocating concessions (TFT) has been found to be most effective in inducing concessions and reaching a cooperative agreement (Komorita & Esser, 1975).

Another choice mechanism that one often encounters in the real world involves sequential action. Under this procedure, group members do not all act at the same time, but rather some members act before others do (e.g., Erev & Rapoport, 1990; Rapoport, Budescu, & Suleiman, 1993). It would be valuable to study reciprocity under sequential contribution mechanisms because the reciprocity could occur on the same trial; for example, I could decide to imitate the actions of the others who have just made their choices. It is plausible that the clarity of TFT under sequential choice would be at a maximum, as would the impact of both provocability and forgiveness.

Finally, social dilemma research is being taken in an important new direction with the recognition that social dilemmas are present in organizations (e.g., Kramer, 1991). Research has only just begun to trickle in on organizational dilemmas, but the study of reciprocity in these dilemmas seems appropriate and important, for many reasons. First, reciprocity is thought to be a key influence on many facets of organizational behavior, like prosocial organizational behavior (Brief & Motowidlo, 1986) or successful leader-subordinate relations

(Albrecht & Halsey, 1992), so it is very reasonable to expect that it will also play a role in the resolution of organizational dilemmas. Second, industrial/organizational psychologists are calling for more research on interpersonal relations in organizations (Campion, Medsker, & Higgs, 1993; see also Guzzo & Shea, 1992), so the need is clearly there. Finally, the study of reciprocity in organizational dilemmas affords dilemma researchers the opportunity to move beyond the laboratory into more applied research settings, a type of research that is seriously lacking in the dilemma field (Komorita & Parks, 1996).

## CONCLUSION

An interesting body of work is arising around the question of whether reciprocity is effective in inducing cooperation in mixed-motive situations. At present, there are far too many variables that have not been adequately addressed to draw any firm conclusions; nonetheless, there is considerable evidence to suggest that reciprocal strategies are generally quite effective. The study of reciprocity is important for two reasons. First, it is an approach that can easily be implemented in the real world. In fact, some elements of reciprocity have long been part of the socialization process for at least some individuals: be forgiving; do not be envious; do unto others as you would have them do unto you (the Golden Rule). Second, the idea of reciprocity as a fundamental basis of human behavior remains a powerful one. The notion of an internal "norm of reciprocity" (e.g., Gouldner, 1960), which suggests that humans have an innate tendency to reciprocate, has persisted in the social sciences for many years, despite fundamental questions being raised about how the norm develops in the first place (Ellis, 1971). Our focus has been on the issue of whether these tenets actually influence behavior. The question of how the principles of reciprocity can be taught to, and reinforced in, others is a separate one, but it is the logical next step once we have a better understanding of the constraints, strengths, and weaknesses of reciprocal strategies.

## ENDNOTE

1. Nowak and Sigmund (1993) also proposed a strategy called "Pavlov." Their Pavlov is simply a win-stay, lose-change rule (cf. Kelley, Thibaut, Radloff, & Mundy, 1962), under which one repeats a choice if one received the reward or temptation payoff on the previous trial, or switches if the punishment or sucker payoff was received. Wu and Axelrod (1995) showed that win-stay, lose-change is an ineffective strategy for dealing with noise. The reader should be careful to distinguish between the Kraines-Kraines and Nowak-Sigmund uses of the name "Pavlov."

328 KOMORITA AND PARKS

# REFERENCES

Albrecht, T. L., & Halsey, J. (1992). Mutual support in mixed-status relationships. *Journal of Social and Personal Relationships, 9*, 237-252.

Axelrod, R. (1980a). Effective choice in the prisoner's dilemma. *Journal of Conflict Resolution, 24*, 3-26.

Axelrod, R. (1980b). More effective choice in the prisoner's dilemma. *Journal of Conflict Resolution, 24*, 379-404.

Axelrod, R. (1984). *The evolution of cooperation.* New York: Basic Books.

Axelrod, R., & D'Ambrosio, L. (1994). *Annotated bibliography on The evolution of cooperation.* Unpublished manuscript, University of Michigan.

Axelrod, R., & Hamilton, W. D. (1981). The evolution of cooperation. *Science, 211*, 1390-1396.

Bendor, J. (1987). In good times and bad: Reciprocity in an uncertain world. *American Journal of Political Science, 31*, 531-558.

Bendor, J. (1993). Uncertainty and the evolution of cooperation. *Journal of Conflict Resolution, 37*, 709-734.

Bendor, J., Kramer, R. M., & Stout, S. (1991). When in doubt: Cooperation in a noisy prisoner's dilemma. *Journal of Conflict Resolution, 35*, 691-719.

Bixenstein, V. W., & Gaebelein, J. W. (1971). Strategies of "real" opponents in eliciting cooperative choice in a prisoner's dilemma game. *Journal of Conflict Resolution, 15*, 157-166.

Bornstein, G., Erev, I., & Goren, H. (1994). The effect of repeated play in the IPG and IPD team games. *Journal of Conflict Resolution, 38*, 690-707.

Boyd, R., & Lorberbaum, J. P. (1987). No pure strategy is evolutionarily stable in the prisoner's dilemma game. *Nature, 327*, 58-59.

Brief, A. P., & Motowidlo, S. J. (1986). Prosocial organizational behaviors. *Academy of Management Review, 11*, 710-725.

Campion, M. A., Medsker, G. J., & Higgs, A. C. (1993). Relations between work group characteristics and effectiveness: Implications for designing effective work teams. *Personnel Psychology, 46*, 823-850.

Chen, X. P. (1996). The group-based binding pledge as a solution to public goods problems. *Organizational Behavior and Human Decision Processes, 66*, 192-202.

Chen, X. P., & Komorita, S. S. (1994). The effects of communication and commitment in a public goods social dilemma. *Organizational Behavior and Human Decision Processes, 60*, 367-386.

Ellis, D. P. (1971). The Hobbesian problem of order: A critical appraisal of the normative solution. *American Sociological Review, 36*, 692-702.

Erev, I., & Rapoport, A. (1990). Provision of step-level public goods: The sequential contribution mechanism. *Journal of Conflict Resolution, 34*, 401-425.

Fudenberg, D., & Maskin, E. S. (1990). Evolution and cooperation in noisy repeated games. *American Economic Review, 80*, 274-279.

Gouldner, A. W. (1960). The norm of reciprocity: A preliminary statement. *American Sociological Review, 25*, 161-179.

Guzzo, R. A., & Shea, G. P. (1992). Group performance and intergroup relations in organizations. In M. D. Dunnette & L. M. Hough (Eds.), *Handbook of industrial and organizational psychology* (Vol. 3, pp. 269-313). Palo Alto, CA: Consulting Psychologists Press.

Hulbert, L. G., Mead, A. D., & Komorita, S. S. (1997). *Reciprocity and communication in social dilemmas.* Manuscript submitted for publication.

Insko, C. A., Schopler, J., Hoyle, R. H., Dardis, G. J., & Graetz, K. A. (1990). Individual-group discontinuity as a function of fear and greed. *Journal of Personality and Social Psychology, 58,* 68-79.

Kelley, H. H., Thibaut, J. W., Radloff, R., & Mundy, D. (1962). The development of cooperation in the "minimal social situation." *Psychological Monographs, 76,* whole no. 538.

Kerr, N. L. (1989). Illusions of efficacy: The effects of group size on perceived efficacy in social dilemmas. *Journal of Experimental Social Psychology, 25,* 287-313.

Komorita, S. S., Chan, D. K. S., & Parks, C. D. (1993). The effects of reward structure and reciprocity in social dilemmas. *Journal of Experimental Social Psychology, 29,* 252-267.

Komorita, S. S., & Esser, J. K. (1975). Frequency of reciprocated concessions in bargaining. *Journal of Personality and Social Psychology, 32,* 699-705.

Komorita, S. S., Hilty, J. A., & Parks, C. D. (1991). Reciprocity and cooperation in social dilemmas. *Journal of Conflict Resolution, 35,* 494-518.

Komorita, S. S., & Parks, C. D. (1995). Interpersonal relations: Mixed-motive interaction. *Annual Review of Psychology, 46,* 183-207.

Komorita, S. S., & Parks, C. D. (1996). *Social dilemmas.* Boulder, CO: Westview Press.

Komorita, S. S., Parks, C. D., & Hulbert, L. G. (1992). Reciprocity and the induction of cooperation in social dilemmas. *Journal of Personality and Social Psychology, 62,* 607-617.

Kraines, D., & Kraines, V. (1989). Pavlov and the prisoner's dilemma. *Theory and Decision, 26,* 47-79.

Kraines, D., & Kraines, V. (1993). Learning to cope with Pavlov: An adaptive strategy for the prisoner's dilemma with noise. *Theory and Decision, 35,* 107-150.

Kraines, D., & Kraines, V. (1995). Evolution of learning among Pavlov strategies in a competitive environment. *Journal of Conflict Resolution, 39,* 439-466.

Kramer, R. M. (1991). Intergroup relations and organizational dilemmas: The role of categorization processes. *Research on Organizational Behavior, 13,* 191-228.

Lindskold, S. (1978). Trust development, the GRIT proposal, and the effects of conciliatory acts on conflict and cooperation. *Psychological Bulletin, 85,* 772-793.

Lomborg, B. (1996). Nucleus and shield: The evolution of social structure in the iterated prisoner's dilemma. *American Sociological Review, 61,* 278-307.

Luce, R. D., & Raiffa, H. (1957). *Games and decisions.* New York: Wiley.

Marinoff, L. (1992). Maximizing expected utilities in the prisoner's dilemma. *Journal of Conflict Resolution, 36,* 183-216.

Mark, M. M., & Folger, R. (1984). Responses to relative deprivation: A conceptual framework. *Review of Personality and Social Psychology, 5,* 192-218.

Messick, D. M., & Liebrand, W. B. G. (1995). Individual heuristics and the dynamics of cooperation in large groups. *Psychological Review, 102,* 131-145.

Mio, J. S., Thompson, S. C., & Givens, G. H. (1993). The commons dilemma as metaphor: Memory, influence, and implications for environmental conservation. *Metaphor and Symbolic Activity, 8,* 23-42.

Molander, P. (1985). The optimal level of generosity in a selfish, uncertain environment. *Journal of Conflict Resolution, 29,* 611-618.

Mueller, U. (1987). Optimal retaliation for optimal cooperation. *Journal of Conflict Resolution, 31,* 692-724.

Nowak, M., & Sigmund, K. (1993). A strategy of win-stay, lose-shift that outperforms tit-for-tat in the prisoner's dilemma game. *Nature, 364*, 56-58.

Oskamp, S. (1971). Effects of programmed strategies on cooperation in the prisoner's dilemma and other mixed-motive games. *Journal of Conflict Resolution, 15*, 225-259.

Parks, C. D., Henager, R. F., & Scamahorn, S. D. (1996). Trust and reactions to messages of intent in social dilemmas. *Journal of Conflict Resolution, 40*, 134-151.

Parks, C. D., & Komorita, S. S. (1997). Reciprocal strategies for large groups. *Personality and Social Psychology Review*, 314-322.

Parks, C. D., & Scamahorn, S. D. (1997). *Reciprocation as an effective strategy for inducing cooperation in asymmetric social dilemmas.* Manuscript submitted for publication.

Parks, C. D., & Vu, A. D. (1994). Social dilemma behavior of individuals from highly individualist and collectivist cultures. *Journal of Conflict Resolution, 38*, 708-718.

Patchen, M. (1987). Strategies for eliciting cooperation from an adversary: Laboratory and internation findings. *Journal of Conflict Resolution, 31*, 164-185.

Pruitt, D. G. (1981). *Negotiation behavior.* New York: Academic Press.

Rapoport, A., Budescu, D. V., & Suleiman, R. (1993). Sequential requests from randomly distributed shared resources. *Journal of Mathematical Psychology, 37*, 241-265.

Schelling, T. C. (1973). Hockey helmets, concealed weapons, and daylight saving: Binary choices with externalities. *Journal of Conflict Resolution, 17*, 381-428.

Schelling, T. C. (1978). *Micromotives and macrobehavior.* New York: W.W. Norton.

Stern, P. C. (1976). Effect of incentives and education on resource conservation decisions in a simulated commons dilemma. *Journal of Personality and Social Psychology, 34*, 1285-1292.

Suleiman, R., & Rapoport, A. (1992). Provision of step-level public goods with continuous contribution. *Journal of Behavioral Decision Making, 5*, 133-154.

Swistak, P. (1989). How to resist invasion in the repeated prisoner's dilemma game. *Behavioral Science, 34*, 151-153.

To, T. (1988). More realism in the prisoner's dilemma. *Journal of Conflict Resolution, 32*, 402-408.

Wilson, W. (1971). Reciprocation and other techniques for inducing cooperation in the prisoner's dilemma. *Journal of Conflict Resolution, 15*, 167-196.

Wu, J. Z., & Axelrod, R. (1995). How to cope with noise in the iterated prisoner's dilemma. *Journal of Conflict Resolution, 39*, 183-189.

Yamagishi, T. (1986). The structural goal/expectation theory of cooperation in social dilemmas. *Advances in Group Processes, 3*, 51-87.

Young, H. P., & Foster, D. (1991). Cooperation in the short and in the long run. *Games and Economic Behavior, 3*, 145-156.

# 14     Dynamic and Static Theories of Costs and Benefits of Cooperation

**Wim B. G. Liebrand**
*University of Groningen*

**David M. Messick**
*Northwestern University*

The problem of cooperation still triggers the attention of researchers in various disciplines. It is therefore safe to conclude that the problem has not yet been solved. Why do economic agents in a social environment sometimes cooperate at a cost to themselves? To make the question more concrete, why do colleagues or firms in the same neighborhood, in situations where they have a conflict of interest, cooperate rather than compete and maximize their own interest?

This question has had many answers. Within the economic literature the problem has been approached from a macro perspective in which equilibria are selected according to evolutionary criteria like fitness selection. Economic agents may profit from their collaborations and thereby create a relatively strong position compared to agents who share the negative externalities of competition. In this view the problem of cooperation is approached as an adaptation process for groups of economic actors.

Within psychology almost all the relevant research has been focused on the presence or absence of external factors that influence an individual's propensity to cooperate. In this static-level approach, external factors are manipulated in psychological laboratories where individual agents have to make choices in so-called experimental games. Consequently, the theories that are proposed to solve the problem of cooperation rely heavily on the influence of external factors such as what the other person or persons do, what the payoffs are, what the measurable individual differences among subjects are, whether or not players can communicate, and so on.

At a general level, we see that the economist's approach to the problem of cooperation differs from the prevailing approach in social psychology in two major ways. The first difference refers to the contrast between dynamic-level and static-level theories. Dynamic theories of interaction in game contexts have developed rapidly in economics and game theory since the pivotal work of Kreps, Milgrom, Roberts, and Wilson (1982) demonstrated the rationality of cooperation in repeated games. More recent work has focused on the relation between learning processes and cooperative outcomes in dynamic interactions (e.g., Kalai & Lehrer, 1993; Roth & Erev, 1995). Related work is also beginning to appear in the sociological literature (Macy, 1991). Within social psychology, however, experimental work on dynamic social processes is rare although it has witnessed a recent surge (see Vallacher & Nowak, 1994, 1997). Most experimental attention has been paid to static representations of individual psychological phenomena.

The second general difference in approach pertains to the focus on group level phenomena within economics, compared to the individual level approach in experimental social psychology and traditional [static] decision-making theories.

It is our goal to draw attention to the processes that are neglected by both the dynamic-level approach that uses adaptation at a group level and the static-level approach with its emphasis on individual adaptations. We focus on the dynamic interplay between individual-level behavior and the corresponding regularities in the prevalence of cooperation at the macro level. We analyze the dynamic emergence of cooperation in simulated populations in which all participants played prisoners' dilemma games (PDG). Individual economic agents use simple decision heuristics before they apply their pure strategy. In our dynamic explanation, we view the propensity to cooperate as the result of a complex process that involves assumptions about choice rules, outcome evaluations (via social comparison), and social networks. In Simon's (1976) terminology, agents use a procedural rational rule rather than a substantive rational rule as common economics would assume. The present dynamic approach sees cooperation within a society as a dynamic equilibrium, the level of which can change in unexpected and unintuitive ways, depending on the procedurally rational choice heuristics employed by individual economic agents.

The goal of this chapter is to contrast static-level explanations of cooperation that derive from traditional decision-making theories with dynamic explanations assuming procedurally rational agents. Contrasting these levels of analysis raises questions about the external validity and generalizability of the different theories. We analyze cooperation in computer-simulated populations and use the theory developed in Messick and Liebrand (1995) to formulate our predictions. In addition we use formal computational methodology developed by Buskens and Snijders (1996) in an attempt to independently estimate the results of the computer simulations and thereby check the robustness of the results.

It is not our goal to argue that either the dynamic or the static level of explanation is preferable to the other. We demonstrate, however, that simple extensions of static-level explanations to societal levels may be misguided and incorrect. Indeed, as we show, even in circumstances where the two types of

**Table 14.1**
**Illustrative Payoff Structures for a PDG**

### A. Decomposed Structure

|                  | Cooperate | Defect |
|------------------|:---------:|:------:|
| *Payoff to self*  | -5        | 0      |
| *Payoff to other* | 8         | 0      |

### B. Corresponding Matrix Structure

|     |   *C*  |   *D*  |
|-----|--------|--------|
| *C* | 3, 3   | -5, 8  |
| *D* | 8, -5  | 0, 0   |

### C. Cost/Benefit Structure

Cost of cooperation    =   -5
Benefit of cooperation =    8

---

explanations predict the same qualitative pattern of results, they do so for very different reasons and via very different mechanisms.

As we contrast the two different types of theory, it is important to note that the types differ by degrees, not absolutes. Dynamic theories contain two features that many experimental theories lack – an implicit or explicit temporal feature acknowledging that behavior occurs in time and is influenced by prior events, and a reciprocal feature that recognizes that, in social environments, a person is both a source and a target of social causal influence. Thus an event that causes a change in the behavior of a single person in an interacting group may cause secondary changes in the behavior of others who witness the behavior change, or who observe witnesses of the behavior change, and so on. Dynamic theories, in other words, view behavior both as cause and effect in some sort of temporal structure or sequence.

This chapter explores one relationship that is important in explaining cooperation; the interaction between the benefit and cost of cooperation and the level of cooperation. We have selected this particular relationship because it is empirically well established in the context of prisoner dilemma (PD) research. The qualitative finding, which we specify in more detail later, is that as the cost of cooperating decreases, and as the benefit provided to others increases, the level of cooperation increases (Kelley & Grzelak, 1972; Komorita & Ellis, 1995; Komorita & Parks, chap. 13, this volume; Komorita, Sweeney, & Kravitz, 1980; Rapoport, 1967). This qualitative hypothesis has also been explored in contexts in which cooperation is viewed as helping behavior (e.g., Piliavin, Dovidio, Gaertner, & Clark, 1982). Burnstein, Crandall, and Kitayama (1994) went so far as to suggest that the tendency to process social transactions in terms of costs and benefits may be significant from an evolutionary perspective.

To make our comparisons concrete, we outline conditions in which the costs to the cooperator and the benefits to the recipient can be unambiguously specified. In PD we can do this by using "decomposed" games (Messick & McClintock, 1968; Pruitt, 1967). In decomposed games, the payoffs to the two participants can be represented as the additive result of the consequences of their two choices. Each choice for each party specifies a payoff for the chooser and a payoff for the other party. Consider the payoffs presented in Section A of Table 14.1 as an illustration. Assuming symmetry in payoffs, the cooperative choice costs the chooser five points and awards the other eight, whereas the defecting choice provides zero points for both players. (As a scaling convention, we let the payoffs for the defecting choice be zero for both players.) The combined implications of the joint choices for the pair is presented in matrix format in Section B of Table 14.1. Joint cooperation yields three points for each – eight they are given by the other player less the five they cost themselves. Joint defection yields zero points each. (Our scaling convention will always yield zero payoffs for mutual defection.) When one defects and the other cooperates, the defector gets eight and the hapless cooperator loses five.

Each decomposed game like the one in Section A of Table 14.1 yields a unique matrix game like the one in Section B of Table 14.1. However, matrix games (that are decomposable) may have many decompositions, as Messick and McClintock (1968) and Pruitt (1967) demonstrated. One implication of this fact is that a given decomposable matrix game can be represented strictly in terms of a cost/benefit paradigm. By a cost/benefit paradigm we mean that the payoffs can be constructed as if the defecting choice provides equal payoffs to both members of the pair and that the cooperative choice entails a cost to the chooser (the difference between the chooser's cooperative payoff and the defecting one) and provides a benefit to the other person (the difference between the other's payoff for chooser's cooperation and defection). The cost/benefit representation of the matrix in Section B of Table 14.1 is given in Section C of Table 14.1. The cost to the chooser in this example is -5 points and the benefit to the other is 8 points. As long as the benefit exceeds the cost, the game will have the PDG structure. With our scaling simplification we can represent any decomposed game by two parameters: a cost measure, $c < 0$, and a benefit parameter, $b > 0$.

**Table 14.2**
**Symbolic Representation of PDG Payoffs**

---

A.   **Standard Representation of PDG Payoffs.**

|   | _C_ | _D_ |
|---|---|---|
| _C_ | R, R | S, T |
| _D_ | T, S | P, P |

B.   **Cost/Benefit Representation of PDG Payoffs**

|   | _C_ | _D_ |
|---|---|---|
| _C_ | b+c, b+c | c, b |
| _D_ | b, c | 0, 0 |

---

## Static Level Explanations

One advantage to the cost/benefit representation is that it allows us to calculate a measure of the cooperativeness of a PDG matrix in terms of its cost/benefit parameters. Of the 11 cooperation indices that are described by Murnighan and Roth (1983), we selected one frequently used one to explore. The measure is the so-called "$K$ index" that was developed by Rapoport (1967) and extended by Komorita (1976). As illustrated in Table 14.2, the $K$ index is calculated from matrix games by taking the ratio of the difference between the payoff for joint cooperation (**R**eward) and joint defection (**P**unishment) to the difference between the payoff for exploiting the other person (**T**emptation) and being exploited (**S**ucker).

$$K = \frac{R-P}{T-S} \qquad (1)$$

The logic behind this index is explained clearly by Komorita and Parks (1994) as a reinforcement concept. $R$ and $S$, the payoffs associated with a cooperative choice, are positively associated with $K$. The larger $R$ and $S$ are, the larger $K$ will be, and the larger the predicted cooperation. The larger the payoffs associated with the defecting response, $P$ and $T$, the lower the predicted rate of cooperation. In a PDG in which $T$ is the largest payoff and $S$ is the smallest, $K$ ranges between 0, when $R$ and $P$ are equal, to its maximum, 1.

There is a direct connection between the $K$ index and the cost/benefit parameters. If we write the payoffs in terms of the cost/benefit parameters, we see that $S = c$, $T = b$, $R = b + c$, and $P = 0$. Recall that $c$ is a negative number, the cost of cooperation. Therefore,

$$K = \frac{b+c}{b-c} \qquad (2)$$

To illustrate, in the game presented in Section B of Table 14.1, $K = .231$, which can be verified either from the cost/benefit parameters of -5/8, or from the entries in the matrix.

It is clear from Eq. 2 that increasing $b$ while holding $c$ constant leads to increases in $K$; in addition, $K$ increases as $c$ decreases in absolute value. (Recall that $c$ is a negative number so that the numerator is, in fact, the difference between $b$ and the absolute value of $c$, and the denominator is the sum of $b$ and the absolute value of $c$.) Thus cooperation is predicted to increase as $b$ goes up and $|c|$ goes down. Representing the game in cost/benefit terms suggests that players have a positive desire to provide the benefit $b$, but that they may be deterred by the cost, $c$, of doing so. This assumption is made explicitly in models of helping behavior described by Piliavin, Dovidio, Gaertner, and Clark (1982) and it is implicit, as in Hornstein's (1972) theory of promotive tension.

The connotations of these static-level models differ, but they uniformly predict that changing $b$ and $c$ so as to increase $K$ will lead to increases in cooperation.

## Dynamic Level Explanation

If we view individuals as embedded in interdependent networks in which one person's outcomes may influence another person's evaluations, we may reach different predictions about the effects of manipulating $K$, or $c$ and $b$. Messick and Liebrand (1995) described one such theory in which this is the case. In this theory, several assumptions are made about the nature of social networks and about individual psychological processes. The implications of these assumptions are then explored using computer simulations.

Specifically, Messick and Liebrand (1995) assumed that each person is a member of a large group in which each person has eight neighbors. (Think of the neighbors as the sides of a 3 x 3 grid with the person in the center.) People interact only with their neighbors. In each time period, a person from the large group is selected to interact with a randomly selected neighbor. The interaction is via PDG and the person and the neighbor make their choices independently.

The rules that were used for making choices were the major independent variables that Messick and Liebrand (1995) studied. Two of the three rules that they examined are explored here. The first is the "win-stay, lose-change"

(WSLC) rule that Kelley, Thiabut, Radloff, and Mundy (1962) formulated. With this rule, after a person played, the person would repeat the just-made choice if the outcome was a win, but change to the other choice if the outcome was coded as a loss. The neighbor did not update the choice following a play (although for most purposes it makes little difference whether there is simultaneous or single updating).

A crucial psychological process is the coding of outcomes as wins and losses. Accumulating research indicates that the interpretation of events as gains or losses, rewards or punishments, or most generally, as positives or negatives, is the result of complex psychological processes (Brendl & Higgins, 1996). We assumed that the person compared the outcome to a social reference point, $M$, which is the average of the most recent outcomes of the person's eight neighbors. If the person's outcome was equal to or above $M$, the outcome was coded as a win; if it was below the social reference point, the outcome was coded as a loss. Although our coding process is an obvious oversimplification, it is realistic in highlighting the social sources of judgment standards.

This coding or evaluation process, along with the behavior consequences of the coding, represent the psychological assumptions of our simulation. The assumptions can be changed in many ways to explore the consequences of different models that might include levels of aspiration, individual adaptation levels, or memory failures or biases. Messick and Liebrand (1995) explored biases in the classification of outcomes as wins and losses, for instance, and found that relatively small biases could induce relatively large shifts in global levels of cooperation. However, our goal in this chapter is to explore payoff effects, not psychological assumptions, so we restrict our investigations to two heuristics and a single coding process.

A second heuristic that we employed was a "win-cooperate, lose-defect" (WCLD) rule. We argued that this rule, which is a type of affective tit-for-tat (TFT) in which positive acts, namely cooperation, are performed after positive outcomes have been received, and in which negative acts, namely defection, follow negative outcomes, is a realistic abstraction of much research showing that helping behavior is enhanced by the creation of positive moods (Isen, 1987) and that intentionally harmful acts are often reciprocated (Gouldner, 1960). Wins and losses are coded as with WSLC, and the only difference is in the response contingencies.

WSLC is a heuristic that may be thought of as the basic kernel of adaptive behavior. It reflects the principle that rewarded behavior perseveres whereas unrewarded behavior is inhibited. WCLD embodies a slightly different principle, namely the affective TFT mentioned earlier. Positive outcomes (wins) induce positive behavior (cooperation) whereas negative outcomes (losses) induce negative behavior (defection). In both cases, our heuristics represent only one implementation of these adaptation principles.

**Hypothetical distribution of neighbors' mean payoffs**

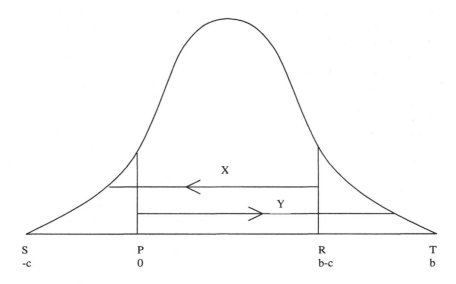

Fig. 14.1. Hypothetical distribution of $M$, mean payoff of eight neighbors.

The dependent variable that we examined is the frequency of cooperation that is induced in the population by these rules. Extremely stable levels of cooperation of .40 and .55 were found for WSLC and WCLD, respectively, when the parameters of the matrix were $R = 2$, $P = 1$, $T = 3$, and $S = 0$. These payoffs correspond to $c = -1$ and $b = 2$ or to a $K$ index of .33.[1]

Predicting cooperation in this context is very different from predicting cooperation in an experiment involving one or two subjects. Variables that are critical in determining the level of cooperation are (a) the probability that joint cooperation will be followed by cooperation ($x = $ P(C|CC)), and (b) the probability that joint defection will be followed by cooperation ($y = $ P(C|DD)). Both probabilities, $x$ and $y$, depend on the distribution of social reference points in the population, which depends on the most recent distribution of outcomes, which depends on the frequency of cooperation, which depends on $x$ and $y$, and so on. The role that $x$ and $y$ play in this dynamic context is crucial. For both WSLC and WCLD, $x$ is the probability that a person's cooperative response, when matched with cooperation by the neighbor, will be followed by cooperation. Because the numerical payoff to the person is $R$, cooperation will occur if $R$ is coded as a win, as it will be if the mean of the neighbors' outcomes,

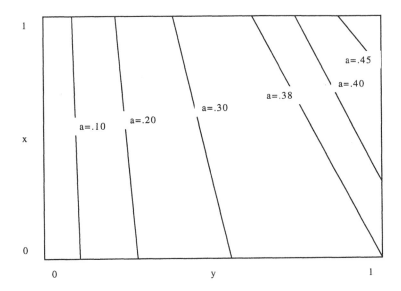

Fig. 14.2. Equicooperation contours for the WSLC heuristic.

$M$, is $R$ or less. This probability can be seen in Fig. 14.1 as the area under the curve to the left of the point $R$. Recall that the random variable here is $M$, not the person's outcome which is fixed at $R$. The uncertainty about the coding of the outcome, whether it is a win or a loss, lies in the social environment.

The form of Fig. 14.1 is not intended to imply that this distribution is normal, symmetric, or even unimodal. We mean only to communicate that $M$ is a random variable whose distribution determines $x$ and $y$.

Figure 14.1 also provides a graphical depiction of $y$, the probability of cooperation following joint defection. Because joint defection provides a payoff of $P$ to a person, with WSLC, the person will cooperate if $P$ is coded as a loss (leading the person to "change"). This will occur if $M$ is greater than $P$, so the probability of cooperation with WSLC is the area to the right of $P$.

With the other rule, WCLD, cooperation will follow if the outcome is coded as a gain. Clearly the probability of that outcome is $(1 - y)$ or the area to the left of $P$ in Fig. 14.1. Understanding how experimental manipulations influence $x$ and $y$ is essential to making predictions about cooperation from the perspective

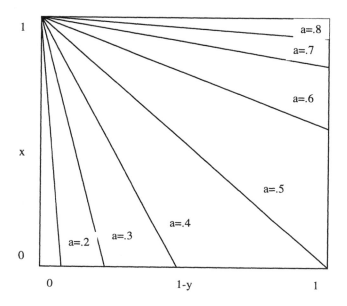

Fig. 14.3. Equicooperation contours for the WCLD heuristic.

of this dynamic theory.

Messick and Liebrand (1995) showed how to find equilibrium conditions that relate the overall level of cooperation to $x$ and $y$. We found that there are many equilibria that can be displayed, as in Figs. 14.2 and 14.3, for WSLC and WCLD, respectively. These figures show the predicted equilibria, the predicted overall level of cooperation, $a$, for any given combination of $x$ and $y$ for the two heuristics. The relationships expressed in these figures become essential to reasoning about how various changes will influence levels of cooperation in the population.

## Formal Computations

It is possible to estimate the complex relations between $x$ and $y$ and the overall level of cooperation $a$, by using the computational methods developed by Buskens and Snijders (1996). This approach uses mathematical problem-solving software to solve higher order polynomials that calculate approximations for each equilibrium. Messick and Liebrand (1995) specified the equilibrium equations in terms of $a$, $x$, and $y$;

$$\text{for WSLC } a = x\left(a^2\right) + y(1 - a)^2;\tag{3}$$

$$\text{for WCLD } a = x\left(a^2\right) + a(-a) + (1 - y)(1 - a)^2\tag{4}$$

In Buskens and Snijders (1996) approach, the propensities $x$ and $y$ are expressed in terms of the overall level of cooperation $a$. This is done by considering each one of all the possible outcome configurations for the 8 neighbors ($4^8 = 65,536$), and selecting those outcome configurations in which the actor would code the CC outcome as a win $(x)$, and similarly select all outcome combinations in which the DD outcome is coded as a loss $(y)$. Because the probability of a CC, CD, DC, DD outcome is $a^2$, $a(1 - a)$, $(1 - a)a$, $(1 - a)^2$, respectively, we are able to calculate the probability of each outcome configuration in which CC is coded as a win, and DD is coded as a loss. Adding all the relevant probabilities yields the values for the propensities $x$ and $y$ and thus leads to equilibrium equations in terms of $a$ only. For the basic PDG in which $S = 0$, $P = 1$, $R = 2$, and $T = 3$, the equation for WSLC is:

$$8a^{16} + 924a^{15} - 859a^{14} + 31507a^{13} - 60354a^{12} + 60578a^{11} - 14098a^{10}$$
$$- 45710a^9 + 71356a^8 - 55985a^7 + 27566a^6 - 8645a^5 + 1540a^4 - 63a^3\tag{5}$$
$$- 34a^2 + 6a = 0$$

and for WCLD:

$$344a^{16} - 372a^{15} + 1646a^{14} - 4074a^{13} + 61236a^{12} - 50288a^{11} + 868a^{10}$$
$$+ 54080a^9 - 74436a^8 + 56643a^7 - 27636a^6 + 8645a^5 - 1540a^4 + 63a^3\tag{6}$$
$$+ 36a^2 - 9a + 1 = 0$$

Solving these 16th degrees polynomials is easy nowadays with the help of mathematical software packages like MAPLE. The equilibrium value is 0.43 for WSLC and 0.53 for WCLD. These values correspond closely to the observed levels of stable cooperation in the simulations which were 0.40 for WSLC and 0.55 for WCLD.

## Computer Simulations

The formal computational method can be used to estimate the equilibria for

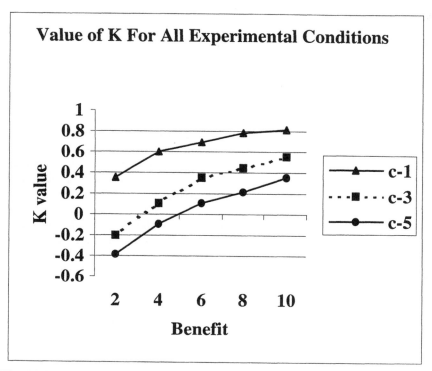

Fig. 14.4. Cooperative index $K$ as a function of the cost/benefit parameters used in the experiment.

different combinations of cost/benefit parameters. However, in order to understand and predict what exactly underlies the different choice heuristics of a simulated population, we consider it necessary to use computer simulations and to base our theorizing on the interrelation between the propensities $x$ and $y$ and the overall level of cooperation $a$. We conducted a computer simulation in which we manipulated the values of cost $(c)$ and benefit $(b)$ orthogonally. $C$ took the values, -1, -3, -5, and we increased $b$ from 2 to 10 in units of 2.

Thus the experimental design was a 3 (cost) by 5 (benefit) completely crossed design. In each of the 15 conditions, we ran 50 simulations with populations of 100, each of which was 100 generations long. A generation consisted of taking a sample with replacement that was the size of the population, that is, a sample of 100. Each simulation was initialized with 50% cooperators and 50% defectors. Details of the simulation methodology are described in Messick and Liebrand (1995) and are summarized later. After 100

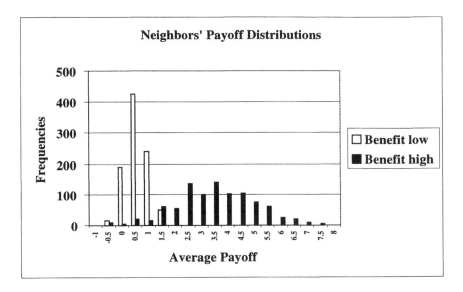

Fig. 14.5. Empirically estimated distribution of $M$, neighbors' mean payoff, for $c = -1$ and either $b = 2$ (low benefit) or $b = 8$ (high benefit).

generations, we recorded the proportion of cooperators in the population.

Before presenting the data from this experiment, we return to the question of making predictions from the two perspectives. From the point of view of the static model, we can calculate the $K$ index for each of our 15 experimental conditions. These values are presented in Fig. 14.4. Inspection of Fig. 14.4 confirms that $K$ increases as benefit increases and as the (absolute value of the) cost decreases. The static-level theory thus predicts that cooperation will increase with increasing $b$ and with decreasing (absolute) cost.

The situation is not so simple from the perspective of the dynamic theory because two important features of the situation change as the payoffs in the matrix change. First, the outcomes change. But these outcome changes also influence the distribution of the social reference outcomes, $M$, because the outcomes change for all the people in the population, not just for the subject on a given trial. One needs to envision what changing the payoffs will do to the distribution of $M$. To this end, consider Fig. 14.5. Here we have plotted two empirically observed distributions of $M$. The distributions were obtained for a fixed cost value of 1, and two different benefit values of 2 and 8 respectively.

Figure 14.5 illustrates the general mechanism that if we hold $c$ constant and increase $b$, the points $T$ and $R$ will both increase (in this case from $T = 2$ and $R =$

1 to $T = 8$ and $R = 7$, respectively) stretching the distribution to the right. The increase in $b$ will *increase* the area under the curve to the left of $R$, thereby increasing $x$. This same movement in $R$ and $T$ should also *increase* the fraction of the distribution to the right of $P$, thereby increasing $y$, and, of course, decreasing $(1 - y)$. To predict changes in cooperation as a function of increasing $b$, we need to refer these changes in $x$ and $y$ to Figs. 14.2 and 14.3 for the two heuristics. In Fig. 14.2, we see that increasing both $x$ and $y$ results in movement toward the upper right-hand corner. Because this movement is crossing contour lines in the direction of greater cooperation, we can predict that increasing $b$ will lead to increasing cooperation. Because the theoretical maximum for WSLC is .50, increasing $b$ should increase cooperation for WSLC, but not beyond .50.[2]

Referring now to Fig. 14.3, we see that for WCLD, $x$ increases and $(1 - y)$ decreases. The direction of movement here is toward the upper left corner of the space. In this case the movement is roughly parallel to the contour lines. This implies that whether cooperation will be increased or decreased will depend on the rate of change in $x$ and $y$ compared to the slopes of the closest contours. It also means that the changes will not be great. Increasing $b$, therefore, should have relatively little impact on cooperation with WCLD.

We can make predictions about the effects of manipulating $c$ by seeing what happens to the distribution in Fig. 14.1 as we move the points labeled $S$ and $R$ to the left, holding $b$ constant. As these points are shifted to the left, more of the distribution can be expected to fall to the right of point $R$, meaning that $x$ will decrease. Furthermore, the proportion of the distribution falling to the right of point $P$ should also decrease as the distribution shifts leftward, implying that $y$ will also decrease as $c$ increases in absolute value. Referring to Fig. 14.2, we can see that when both $x$ and $y$ decrease, movement is to the lower left and cooperation can be expected to decrease for WSLC. Again, for WSLC, the dynamic theory makes predictions that correspond qualitatively to those of the individual model although the reasons for the prediction are very different.

However, in Fig. 14.3, as $x$ decreases and $(1 - y)$ increases, we see that movement is to the lower *right* corner of the space, which is again roughly parallel to the contour lines. Thus for $c$, as for $b$, we can only predict that the level of cooperation will be changed little, if at all, by increasing the cost of cooperation.

To summarize the predictions for this simulation experiment, the static theory predicts that cooperation will increase with increases in $b$ and decrease with increases in (the absolute value of) $c$. More precisely, it predicts that cooperation should be monotonic, increasing with the index $K$. The dynamic theory, on the other hand, makes different predictions as a function of the heuristic that is generating the choices. For WSLC, the predictions are the same as those for the static model. For the WCLD rule, the prediction is that changes in $b$ and $c$ will have little impact on cooperation.

## METHOD

For each combination of benefit and cost, we ran 50 simulations, each of which was 100 generations long. The population size was 100 in all cases. Each simulation began by randomly assigning each person in the population with an initial choice of either cooperate or defect. These were assigned with equal probability. They were also assigned an initial outcome that was the average of the four payoffs in the payoff matrix. On each trial, one person out of the 100 was randomly selected and one of that person's eight neighbors was also randomly selected. They played the appropriate PDG one time and their choices were either those that were randomly assigned (if they had not been selected as the person previously) or the choice that was calculated following their most recent interaction (for those that had been selected previously). Following the interaction, the person's outcome was compared to the mean of that person's neighbors' outcomes (from the last time they had been selected), and the person's next choice was calculated as a function of the appropriate rule, WSLC or WCLD, and the outcome of the comparison. Only the person's choice was updated following a trial, not the neighbor's choice. Next, another of the 100 persons was randomly selected to start a new trial. A generation consisted of 100 trials in which people were selected with replacement. This means that in a given generation, some people may have been selected more than once and others selected not at all. A simulation lasted for 50 generations. Our previous research had shown that the populations converged rapidly from widely differing initial distributions to their asymptotic states, so 50 generations was considered sufficiently long for the populations to stabilize.

Following the 50th generation, we counted the proportion of the 100 persons who were cooperators – who would cooperate the next time they were selected, either as persons or as neighbors. These relative frequencies were the basic dependent variable.

## RESULTS

For each rule, we ran 750 simulations – 50 in each of the 15 experimental conditions. For each combination of heuristic, benefit, and cost, we calculated the mean asymptotic level of cooperation. These means are presented in Table 14.3.

Messick and Liebrand (1995) warned against the overinterpretation of the statistical results of simulation experiments and now we repeat the warning. With 50 cases per cell and small within-cell variability, very small population effects will be statistically significant. The standard error of the mean for these

**Table 14.3**
**Prevalence of Cooperation as a Function of Cost and Benefit for WSLC and WCLD.**

| | Win-Stay, Lose-Change (WSLC) Cost | | |
|---|---|---|---|
| **Benefit** | *1* | *2* | *3* |
| 2 | 41.3 | 15.8 | 11.7 |
| 4 | 48.4 | 30.9 | 16.8 |
| 6 | 48.4 | 40.9 | 29.7 |
| 8 | 50.1 | 44.8 | 37.9 |
| 10 | 48.5 | 48.4 | 40.2 |

| | Win-Cooperate, Lose-Defect (WCLD) Cost | | |
|---|---|---|---|
| **Benefit** | *1* | *2* | *3* |
| 2 | 54.3 | 52.1 | 49.5 |
| 4 | 53.5 | 52.4 | 51.7 |
| 6 | 54.4 | 53.6 | 51.2 |
| 8 | 52.5 | 51.9 | 49.2 |
| 10 | 51.3 | 52.7 | 55.6 |

*Note.* Population size is 100. Each mean is based on 50 simulations.

proportions is typically less than .01. The important thing is to observe the large effects that make major impacts on the system.

To illustrate this sensitivity, when the data from Table 14.3 are subjected to a 2 (heuristic) by 3 (cost) by 5 (benefit) ANOVA with the simulation runs as the replicate, all three main effects and all four interactions are statistically significant. The smallest $F$ ratio is 15.56. This is based on the three-way interaction with df = 8 and 1470. For the remainder of the data, we forego description of statistical significance with the assurance that everything is statistically, but not necessarily psychologically, significant.

The main finding of concern to us is that the two choice rules react very differently to the cost/benefit manipulations. As predicted from the dynamic theory, the data for WCLD show very little dependence on changes in the cost and benefit parameters. The lowest level of cooperation is 49.2 and the largest is 55.6. As expected, this rule is relatively insensitive to changes in these payoff parameters. We need to point out that this rule is not insensitive to *all* changes in payoff parameters. Messick and Liebrand (1995) showed the WCLD was *more* sensitive than WSLC to changes in the $T$ or Temptation parameter.

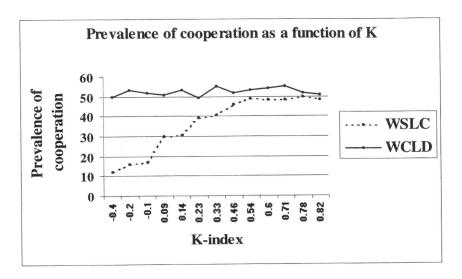

Fig. 14.6. Mean levels of cooperation as a function of *K*.

The second feature of the data we note is that with WSLC, the levels of cooperation show the pattern predicted by both the static level theory and the dynamic theory. Cooperation clearly increases as *b* increases and decreases as *c* increases absolutely. Moreover, cooperation is very low in the three conditions in which cost exceeds benefit, that is, in games that are not PDGs but in which maximum joint outcomes result from joint defection. A strategic analysis of these three games suggests that cooperation should be 0 because the maximum joint outcome results from both parties using their dominating choices. However, none of the theories that we mentioned thus far claims to be a "rational" or prescriptive theory.

With WSLC, the level of cooperation does not exceed 50%, the theoretical maximum for cooperation for WSLC. In the one cell in which the average is greater than 50% (50.1%), the mean is not significantly greater than 50%. A 95% confidence interval around this mean is [48.7, 51.5]. These results further support the Messick and Liebrand (1995) equilibrium predictions that WSLC, under these assumptions, cannot exceed 50% cooperation.

In Fig. 14.6 we have plotted the cooperation level for each condition against the *K* index for that condition for both heuristics. For WSLC, it is clear that there is a positive relationship between these numbers. When $K > .50$, the level of cooperation appears to be close to the maximum of 50%. For $K < .50$, there is a perfect monotonic relationship between *K* and the level of cooperation. With

**Table 14.4**

**Predictions (Using the Buskens-Snijders Method) of Cooperation Levels as a Function of Cost and Benefit for WSLC and WCLD**

| | Win-Stay, Lose-Change (WSLC) | | |
| | Cost | | |
| **Benefit** | *1* | *2* | *3* |
|---|---|---|---|
| 2 | 43.3 | 20.9 | 16.6 |
| 4 | 48.5 | 35.5 | 23.2 |
| 6 | 49.5 | 43.3 | 34.2 |
| 8 | 49.6 | 47.0 | 40.6 |
| 10 | 49.6 | 48.2 | 43.3 |

| | Win-Cooperate, Lose-Defect (WCLD) | | |
| | Cost | | |
| **Benefit** | *1* | *2* | *3* |
|---|---|---|---|
| 2 | 53.6 | 51.2 | 50.4 |
| 4 | 52.4 | 52.1 | 51.0 |
| 6 | 51.0 | 53.6 | 50.3 |
| 8 | 50.0 | 50.0 | 50.0 |
| 10 | 50.0 | 50.0 | 53.6 |

WCLD, there appears to be little if any relationship between cooperation and $K$.

## Comparison With the Formal Computational Method

As shown earlier, the equilibria for different cost/level combinations can also be estimated by the formal computational method. Table 14.4 displays the predictions generated from the Buskens and Snijders (1996) model of the equilibrium. The means are presented to facilitate comparison with the data in Table 14.3. With regard to the WSLC comparison, three points merit notice. First, the patterns of means are remarkably close. Cooperation increases as costs decrease and as benefits increase and the rate of increase is greater when costs are high and benefits are low. Second, the predictions tend to be higher than the observed simulation results. This is certainly due to the simplifying assumption that is made in the calculations that the outcomes are independent. We know that they are not. Finally, the model predicts a maximum of 50% cooperation in agreement with our earlier calculations.

The comparison of the predictions with the WCLD simulation data is highly instructive. The data in Table 14.3 hint at a nonmonotonic relationship between costs and benefits. When the cost is one, cooperation seems to decrease as benefits increase, and when the cost is three, there is the suggestion that cooperation is maximal when benefits equal six, twice the cost. However, the magnitude of these changes is so small that one cannot discern whether they reflect noise or real changes in the equilibrium. Seeing precisely the same pattern reflected in the predictions assures us that these small effects are real. Cooperation is predicted to decrease with benefit when cost is one, and to be maximal when benefit is six when the cost is three. The Buskens-Snijders method allows us thus to place confidence in the theoretical underpinnings of the complex interaction of cost and benefit with the WCLD heuristic.

## DISCUSSION

This study deviates from the approaches commonly used in economics and social psychology to study the problem of cooperation. We focus on the emergence of equilibria in simulated populations as a consequence of individual behavioral adaptations that are procedurally rational. This perspective deviates from the traditional economic approach because it does not assume substantive rationality on the part of the economic agents. It differs from the standard social psychology approach by providing a dynamic theory for the emergence of stable levels of cooperation.

We used this study to compare two classes of theories in terms of their predictions of cooperation in a PDG, or games resembling PDGs, when the costs and benefits of cooperation were systematically varied. The static-level theory represents intuitions about individual human impulses and the factors that would tend to make individuals more or less willing to help another person. Whether the theory is based on an implicit trade-off between cost to self and benefit to another person or based on an intuition about accumulating points, money, or reinforcers, the prediction is that cooperation is more likely when costs are lower and benefits higher than when costs are higher and benefits lower.

The other type of theory is a dynamic one that assumes an adaptive behavioral mechanism or heuristic, either WSLC or WCLD, that is responsive to past outcomes. One component of the mechanism is an evaluation process that behaves differently as a function of whether the current outcome is coded as a win or a loss. The coding process itself compares the current outcome to a social reference point. The dynamic theory relates the rule or heuristic to the aggregate level of cooperation in a population. The theory can be used to make predictions about the impact of independent variables, such as the cost and benefit parameters, on cooperation. Explaining cooperation from this perspective entails postulating individual psychological mechanisms and also the forms of social interdependence and systems of mutual influence that affect global levels of cooperation.

The results of the simulation suggest that although the two classes of theory explain the effects of $b$ and $c$ on cooperation with the WSLC rule, the static level account fails to explain why cooperation does not increase with the WCLD rule. This failure results from the fact that the static level theories do not explicitly consider choice mechanisms and how they might differ in terms of dynamic impact.

The dynamic theory, on the other hand, can explain why the cost/benefit manipulations have little impact with the WCLD rule as well as why they do have an impact with WSLC rule. The explanation is somewhat complex, involving changes in one's own and others' outcomes that influence the distribution of social reference points, $M$, and, hence, the conditional probabilities $x$ and $y$. These changes must then be referred to Figs. 14.2 and 14.3 to grasp their impact on equilibrium levels of cooperation.

The explanation, at this level, has little intuitive appeal. It is the logical consequence of the assumptions, as is any theoretical derivation. We see no intuitive reason, for instance, why WSLC cannot generate more than 50% cooperation, but, mathematically, the theory does not permit more than this level and we have never observed more than 50% with this heuristic. Creating a dynamic theory requires that we suspend our reliance on intuitive understanding of psychological processes.

With WSLC, where both types of theory make the same, accurate qualitative predictions about cooperation, we cannot say which is better. We cannot make a judgment about relative accuracy because they are equally accurate, but we can judge the underlying reasons for the predictions, which are very different. Cooperation is the result of a complex process involving a particular rule, a particular social comparison and coding process, and a particular definition of neighborhoods on which the social comparison process rests. Nothing was programmed into the psychology of the decision process that calls for a cost/benefit trade-off of the sort that we found. Moreover, if one observed these results with WSLC and concluded that the pattern provided support for the psychological process postulated by the static-level theory, one would be deceived. Different processes, having nothing directly to do with cost/benefit considerations, produce the same monotonic relationship predicted by the static-level approach.

The contrast we have offered can be accused of being unfair or biased. It is wrong to conclude that the dynamic theory is better than the static-level theory because the aggregate, dynamic model was developed for precisely the context embodied in the simulation, and the static-level theory was not. To phrase this allegation somewhat differently, the simulation was designed to incorporate all the features of the dynamic model, so it should not be surprising that its qualitative predictions are more accurate than those arising from the static-level model. It would be similarly inappropriate to apply the dynamic theory to a two-person interaction in a PDG and to "evaluate" the dynamic theory against data from such experiments.

But our goal is not to pit the two types of theory against each other in a competition. Rather, we want to emphasize that the theories are more or less appropriate to different contexts. The explanations of cooperation are not mutually exclusive. As we said earlier, they explain different phenomena. The static-level theory explains human impulses in isolated environments with short time perspectives, little or no contextual sensitivity, and no knowledge of the payoffs of others. The dynamic-level theory looks at large networks in an interrelated system in which behaviors reciprocally influence the very environments that evoked them.

The fact that we can have theories on different levels yielding different predictions about cooperation challenges us with the question of which type of theory is more appropriate when we want to think about increasing cooperation in schools, organizations, families, or society in general. Most of the research that is done by social psychologists, especially on the topic of cooperation, is done, we presume, with the more or less remote goal of enhancing cooperation in our normal social ecology. How do we generalize the results of our scientific findings to this ecology? Which types of theory do we generalize? Our warning is that it may be as inappropriate to apply static level theories to real social environments as it is to apply them to the simulations described here. This warning also reminds us that the assumptions of the dynamic theory may be incorrect and may not generalize to real social contexts.

Our argument resembles the one made about cognitive biases and organizational effectiveness by Tyler and Hastie (1991). They investigated the organizational implications of the egocentric biases that lead people to feel that their contributions to their groups are underappreciated. In particular, the computer simulation they used was designed to explore whether it was the more or less talented employees who would be most dissatisfied with their outcomes, relative to the other employees. Although their simulation represented an oversimplified theory of organizational satisfaction, our theory is an oversimplified statement of the determinants of cooperation in groups. Nevertheless, we propose that these oversimplified models do incorporate the essential structures of interdependent social processes and, therefore, that some application of aggregate level, dynamic theory will be better than none for most real social environments.

Imagine, for instance, that a proposal has been made in a high school that teachers explicitly reward students with praise or tokens for acts of generosity and helpfulness to other students. Although such a proposal raises many questions, the one we pose is: What type of theory of cooperation should one rely on to predict the ultimate outcome of the proposal with regard to its ultimate impact on cooperation levels? By increasing the benefit for cooperation, static-level theories would predict that cooperation would increase. Dynamic considerations should give us pause, however. If these new, higher rewards raise expectations and comparison levels (Thibaut & Kelley, 1959) and shift the social reference point upward, previous rewards may appear less attractive or be coded as losses, reducing the total support for cooperation. It is plausible that increasing rewards for cooperation would fail to increase the overall level of cooperation in the school, and the reasons for this failure might be very similar to the dynamics captured by the WCLD heuristic.

We make no claim that the particular dynamic theory we described here and in Messick and Liebrand (1995) is the definitive word on dynamic theories of cooperation. On the contrary, we believe that such ideas are in their infancy in social psychology, and that much of the theory we have proposed will turn out to be inadequate, oversimplified, or flat-out wrong. Nevertheless, it does seem clear that if we want to predict and explain cooperation in real situations, where behavior is embedded in social networks, and where social comparisons influence outcome coding processes, we may be more successful using an oversimplified view of these complexities than by ignoring them totally. Our specific theory of cooperation in groups is relatively unimportant to the general point of this chapter. What is far more important is the possibility that dynamic theories may prove more useful as explanations of cooperation and other sorts of social behavior than static-level theories. Thus, we are suggesting that it may be time to revisit the levels of analysis distinction that was so clearly articulated nearly 50 years ago by Kretch and Crutchfield (1948).

## ACKNOWLEDGMENTS

Preparation of this chapter was supported by the Institute for Social Science Information Technology of the University of Groningen, the Center for the Study of Ethical Issues in Business of the Kellogg Graduate School of Management, Northwestern University, and the International Molluscan Society.

## ENDNOTES

1. These payoffs were scaled so that $S = 0$. Rescaling so that $P = 0$ merely involves subtracting 1 from each cell. Neither the static theory nor the dynamic theory predict any effect for adding a constant to the cells in the matrix.
2. The equilibrium specification for WSLC is $a = x(a^2) + y(1 - a)^2$. This expression does not have a solution for $a > .50$ when $0 \leq x, y \leq 1$. Thus, the maximum value level of cooperation for WSLC is .50.

# REFERENCES

Brendl, C. M., & Higgins, E. T. (1996). Principles of judging valence: What makes events positive or negative. In M.P. Zanna (Ed.), *Advances in experimental social psychology, Vol. 28.* (pp. 95-160). San Diego, CA: Academic Press.

Burnstein, E., Crandall, C., & Kitayama, S. (1994). Some neo-Darwinian rules for altruism: Weighing cues for inclusive fitness as a function of the biological importance of the decision. *Journal of Personality and Social Psychology, 67*, 773-789.

Buskens, V., & Snijders, C. (1996). *Individual heuristics and the dynamics of cooperation in large groups: Comment.* Unpublished manuscript, University of Utrecht.

Gouldner, A. W. (1960). The norm of reciprocity: A preliminary statement. *American Sociological Review, 25*, 161-178.

Hornstein, H. A. (1972). Promotive tension: The basis of prosocial behavior from a Lewinian perspective. *Journal of Social Issues, 28*, 191-218.

Isen, A. M. (1987). Positive affect, cognitive processes, and social behavior. In L. Berkowitz (Ed.), *Advances in experimental social psychology, Vol. 20* (pp. 203-254). New York, NY: Academic Press.

Kalai, E., & Lehrer, E. (1993). Rational learning leads to Nash equilibrium. *Econometrica, 61,* 1019-1045.

Kelley, H. H., & Grzelak, J. (1972). Conflict between individual and common interest in an n-person relationship. *Journal of Personality and Social Psychology, 21*, 190-197.

Kelley, H. H., Thibaut, J. W., Radloff, R., & Mundy, D. (1962). The development of cooperation in the "minimal social situation." *Psychological Monographs, 76*, Whole # 19.

Komorita, S. S. (1976). A model of the N-person dilemma-type game. *Journal of Experimental Social Psychology, 12,* 357-373.

Komorita, S. S., & Ellis, A. L. (1995). Reward structure and cooperation in the n-person prisoner's dilemma. In D. A. Schroeder (Ed.), *Social dilemmas* (pp. 15-30). Westport, CT: Praeger.

Komorita, S. S., & Parks, C. D. (1994). *Social dilemmas.* Madison, WI: Brown & Benchmark

Komorita, S. S., Sweeney, J., & Kravitz, D. A. (1980). Cooperative choice in the n-person dilemma situation. *Journal of Personality and Social Psychology, 38*, 504-516.

Kreps, D., Milgrom, P., Roberts, J., & Wilson, R. (1982). Rational cooperation in the finitely repeated prisoners' dilemma. *Journal of Economic Theory, 27*, 245-252.

Kretch, D., & Crutchfield, R. (1948). *Theory and problems of social psychology.* New York, NY: McGraw-Hill.

Macy, M. W. (1991). Learning to cooperate: Stochastic and tacit collusion in social exchange. *American Journal of Sociology, 97*, 808-843.

Messick, D. M., & Liebrand, W. B. G. (1995). Individual heuristics and the dynamics of cooperation in large groups. *Psychological Review, 102*, 131-145.

Messick, D. M., & McClintock, C. G. (1968). Motivational bases of choice in experimental games. *Journal of Experimental Social Psychology, 4*, 1-25.

Murnighan, J. K., & Roth, A. E. (1983). Expecting continued play in prisoner's dilemma games. *Journal of Conflict Resolution, 27,* 279-300.

Piliavin, J. A., Dovidio, J. F., Gaertner, S. L., & Clark R. D. (1982). Responsive bystanders: The process of intervention. In V. J. Derlega & J. Grzelak (Eds.), *Cooperation and helping behavior* (pp. 281-305). New York, NY: Academic Press.

Pruitt, D. G. (1967). Reward structure and cooperation: The decomposed prisoners' dilemma. *Journal of Personality and Social Psychology, 7,* 21-27.

Rapoport, A. (1967). A note on the "index of cooperation" for prisoners' dilemma. *Journal of Conflict Resolution, 11,* 101-103.

Roth, A. E., & Erev, I. (1995). Learning in extensive-form games: Experimental data and simple dynamic models in the intermediate term. *Games and Economic Behavior, 8,* 164-212.

Simon, H. A. (1976). From substantive to procedural rationality. In S. J. Latsis (Ed.), *Methods and appraisal in economics* (pp. 87-111). New York, NY: Cambridge University Press.

Thibaut, J. W., & Kelley, H. H. (1959). *The social psychology of groups.* New York, NY: Wiley.

Tyler, T., & Hastie, R. (1991). The social consequences of cognitive illusions. In M. H. Bazerman, R. J. Lewicki, & B. H. Sheppard (Eds.), *Research on negotiation in organizations, Vol. 3.* Greenwich, CT: JAI Press.

Vallacher, R. R., & Nowak, A. (1994). *Dynamical systems in social psychology.* San Diego, CA: Academic Press.

Vallacher, R. R., & Nowak, A. (1997). The emergence of dynamical social psychology. *Psychological Inquiry, 8,* 73-99.

# 15    Determinants of Trust

## Chris Snijders
*Utrecht University*

## Gideon Keren
*Technical University of Eindhoven*

## TRUST IN SOCIAL DILEMMAS

Trust is to some extent inherent in any social dilemma. In the process of achieving a mutually beneficial outcome, actors face egoistic incentives that can be subdued only by ignoring these incentives and trusting in the willingness of other actors to do the same. Surprisingly, this subject has received little attention. Only recently has a game theoretic paradigm of trust been introduced in the form of the Trust Game (see Fig 15.1; Dasgupta, 1988; Kreps, 1990).

The Trust Game is an example of such a social dilemma (for reviews, see Colman, 1982; Dawes, 1980): Strict economic rationality (i.e., rationality combined with pure self-interest) implies Actor 2 will not honor trust and Actor 1 will therefore decide not to trust Actor 2, which yields both Actors a payoff $P$, whereas both would have been better off had they been able to reach the $(R,R)$ outcome. Theoretically, there is no need to assume that the game is symmetrical. A more general definition of the Trust Game could introduce potentially different monetary payoffs to Actor 1 and Actor 2 $(P_1,P_2)$ if Actor 1 decides not to trust Actor 2, and monetary payoffs $(R_1,R_2)$ if Actor 2 abuses Actor 1's trust. Such a generalization would classify as a Trust Game if (and only if) $T > R_2$, $S < P_1 < R_1$, and $P_2 < R_2$. Throughout, we only consider symmetrical Trust Games (i.e., $P_1 = P_2$ and $R_1 = R_2$). A Trust Game is therefore completely characterized by $(S, P, R, T)$.

The Trust Game can be viewed as a sequential and one-sided version of the well known Prisoner's Dilemma (PD). PD has been widely used as a paradigmatic example of problematic social interaction (for extensive references, see Campbell & Sowden, 1985). Trust is implicitly encapsulated in PD because actors have to decide whether or not to choose cooperatively without knowing

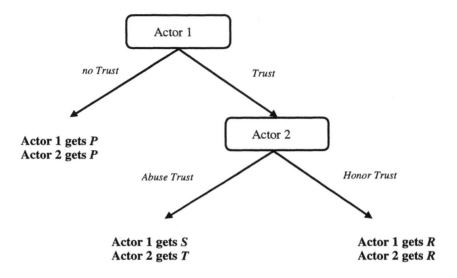

Fig. 15.1. The Trust Game $S < P < R < T$.

whether the other actor has chosen cooperatively. This implies that both a certain notion of trust *and* of honoring trust is implicit in PD. In the Trust Game, actors are explicitly and unequivocally confronted with the question of trust: Actor 1 has to decide whether or not to trust Actor 2, and Actor 2 has to decide whether to honor this trust. In PD these two decisions, namely trusting and honoring trust, are confounded whereas the Trust Game explicitly disentangles these two decisions.

Trust can be conceived to be based on three main factors (Snijders, 1996). First, trust depends on *disposition*: some individuals may be more prone to trust than others (Parks, Henager, & Scamahorn, 1996; Yamagishi, 1986). For instance, research on social dilemmas suggests that economists tend to be less cooperative (Frank, Gilovich, & Regan, 1993). Similarly, one could hypothesize that economists are also less likely to trust and more likely to abuse trust. Daily experience further supports the allegation of individual differences with regard to trust.

A second important factor seems to be based on social perceptions namely one's ability to "read" the other's intentions and inclinations (Korniol, 1990). For instance, trust depends on the anticipated reciprocation of the other actor, and that anticipation may be determined by previous knowledge and experience with that individual, or by appearance such as facial outlook and other behavioral signals (Van Lange & Kuhlman, 1994).

Third, trust would seem to depend on the stakes involved, and their relative importance for each of the parties. For instance, the likelihood of trust would decrease under circumstances in which abused trust would have devastating results for the trustor or when there is anyway not much to gain by trusting the other. To some extent, research on the effect of the stakes in PD is also about trust (for a review, see Murnighan & Roth, 1983). The focus of this chapter is on this third aspect.

This chapter analyzes the strict economic interpretation of game theory and points out its inadequacies from a descriptive viewpoint. Psychological components are explicitly added to the game theoretical model with respect to the decision to trust (and honor trust). Two main variables that drive the decision to trust and honor trust are identified: we label them *risk* and *temptation*. We also describe an experiment to test the effect of risk and temptation, discuss the sequential nature of the Trust Game, and report an experiment that was designed to capture the effect of this inherent sequentiality.

# THE NORMATIVE VIEW

Strict economic rationality in the Trust Game can be characterized by three factors: (a) all actors try to maximize their own utility, (b) utility is derived from own monetary payoffs only, and (c) all actors know that all other actors behave as rationally as they do themselves. Under such strict assumptions trust will not be established: Actor 2 will not honor trust since $T > R$ and because all Actors know that no Actor 1 will be willing to trust Actor 2 because $S < P$.

This prediction was tested in a pilot experiment. Subjects were students from the university of Utrecht who were asked to participate in the experiment at the beginning or the end of a lecture (the size of the class varied between 25 and 61 students). Subjects were first given instructions explaining the Trust Game, then they had to make a decision in the role of Actor 1 and subsequently in the role of Actor 2 in one Trust Game. They were further told that two of the subjects in the classroom would be randomly chosen and accordingly paid in real monetary terms, and that the payments would be in accordance with their choices.[1]

As can be seen in Table 15.1, the strict predictions of game theory are not corroborated: both the percentage of subjects who chose to trust Actor 2 and the percentage of subjects who chose to honor given trust by Actor 1 is significantly different from zero.[2] Further, these percentages seem to differ across different Trust Games.

The observation that people tend to cooperate in situations that are structured to induce noncooperative behavior is obviously not novel (e.g., Colman, 1982; Dawes, 1988). Under question is the extent to which deviations from the standard prediction of noncooperative behavior are systematic. More

**Table 15.1**
**Percentage of Cooperators in Trust Games**

| _S_ | _P_ | _R_ | _T_ | _n_ | % Trust | % Honor |
|---|---|---|---|---|---|---|
| 1 | 2 | 4 | 5 | 26 | 69 | 63 |
| 10 | 20 | 40 | 50 | 61 | 70 | 75 |
| 10 | 20 | 40 | 70 | 25 | 76 | 48 |
| 0 | 20 | 40 | 70 | 25 | 36 | 44 |
| -5 | 20 | 40 | 70 | 47 | 30 | 43 |

Note. $S$, $P$, $R$, and $T$ denote payoffs in the Trust Game, $n$ the number of subjects for that game.

specifically, what are the circumstances and variables that determine the magnitude of cooperative behavior, or in our context the proportion of people who choose to trust (or honor trust).

## MODELING PSYCHOLOGICAL COMPONENTS

Casual observations as well as controlled experimental results suggest that a narrow economic interpretation of game theory (utility only depends on money to ego) may lead to inaccurate predictions regarding human behavior. Consequently, the underlying assumption adopted here is that monetary outcomes to self are not the sole cause determining people's behavior: People are assumed to behave in accordance with a social utility function that incorporates elements other than monetary payoffs to self (see, e.g., Loewenstein, Thompson, & Bazerman, 1989).

Consider Actor 1's decision whether or not to trust in a Trust Game ($S$, $P$, $R$, $T$). Actor 1 is willing to trust Actor 2 if Actor 1's subjective probability $p_{2,1}$ that Actor 2 will honor trust is large enough. If we define Actor $i$'s utility function $U_i$ as $U_i(M_i, M_j)$ if actor $i$ gets $M_i$ and actor $j$ gets $M_j$, then we see that Actor 1 trusts Actor 2 if and only if $p_{2,1}U_1(R, R) + (1 - p_{2,1}) U_1(S, T) > U_1(P, P)$, so that "large enough" can be made explicit:

Actor 1 trusts Actor 2 in a Trust Game ($S$, $P$, $R$, $T$) if and only if

$$p_{2,1} > \frac{U_1(P,P)-U_1(S,T)}{U_1(R,R)-U_1(S,T)}. \tag{1}$$

Depending on the utility function $U_1$ and on the subjective probability $p_{2,1}$, different predictions can be made (see Braun, 1992). In other words, different underlying conjectures about what constitutes the psychological component in the utility function lead to different implications about how the monetary Trust Game payoffs are related to behavior in Trust Games.

In the following subsections, we consider three different ways to model the psychological component: one based on social orientations, one based on guilt, and one on regret. Instead of focusing on the differences between these models, we focus on their similarities. Specifically, we identify two constructs, expressed as ratios of the monetary Trust Game payoffs, which are of particular interest because they affect the likelihood of trusting (and honoring trust) in all three models. We label these two constructs risk (which is based on the payoffs $S$, $P$, and $R$) and temptation (which is based on the payoffs $S$, $R$, and $T$).[3]

## Social Orientations

A parsimonious procedure that can handle the transformation from a given to an effective matrix (or Trust Game) is what may be termed the social orientation model according to which utility is defined as a linear combination of monetary outcomes to self and monetary outcomes to others (McClintock, 1972; McClintock & Liebrand, 1988).

In the social orientation model, a person's behavior is assumed to be led by a utility function, $U_i(M_i, M_j) = M_i + \vartheta_i M_j$, where $\vartheta_i$ stands for a person's social orientation, and the weight person $i$ attaches to $M_i$ has been set equal to 1. This representation is without loss of generality under the assumption that more money renders more utility. In the Trust Game, Actor 1 and Actor 2's utilities can then be summarized as in Fig. 15.2.

Following the social orientation model, Actor 2 honors trust if and only if $R + \vartheta_2 R > T + \vartheta_2 S$. Hence, Actor 2 honors trust if and only if that Actor's social orientation is large enough, $\vartheta_2 > (T - R) / (R - S)$. Suppose that all Actors 2 indeed posses a personal social orientation (assumed to be stable over time) and behave accordingly. Then, as $(T - R) / (R - S)$ increases, the percentage of Actors 2 with a sufficiently strong social orientation to be willing to honor trust will decrease. Hence, the probability that Actor 2 honors trust in a Trust Game $(S, P, R, T)$ decreases with increasing $(T - R) / (R - S)$. Note that this implication (like all subsequent implications of other models) can be deduced *without* actual measurement of a person's social orientation, and holds for arbitrary distributions of social orientations over the population.[4]

For Actor 1, the situation is slightly more complicated. Actor 1 will decide to trust Actor 2 if and only if

$$p_{2,1}(R + \vartheta_1 R) + (1 - p_{2,1})(S + \vartheta_1 T) > P + \vartheta_1 P. \qquad (2)$$

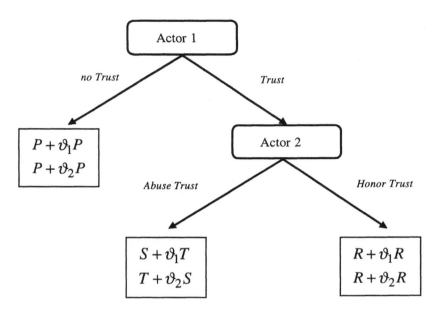

Fig. 15.2. The Trust Game based on the social orientations model.

_____

The added complexity arises because exploitation of Actor 1 may in fact be associated with an additional positive component. Specifically, a large value of $T$ is of high value not just to Actor 2 but, according to the social orientations model, also of some value (namely $\vartheta_1 T$) to Actor 1. In fact, Actors 1 with a large social orientation (larger than $(P - S) / (T - P)$) are not really playing a Trust Game in terms of utility. They will trust Actor 2 because they prefer both their trust being honored _and_ their trust being abused over not trusting Actor 2 (because they derive utility from $\vartheta_1 T$). Actors 1 with a small social orientation (smaller than $(P - S) / (T - P)$) will trust Actor 2 if and only if

$$p_{2,1} > \frac{P - S - \vartheta_1(T - P)}{R - S - \vartheta_1(T - R)} \approx \frac{P - S}{R - S} - \vartheta_1 \frac{(T - S)(R - P)}{(R - S)^2} = \left(1 + \vartheta_1 \frac{T - S}{R - S}\right)\frac{P - S}{R - S} - \vartheta_1 \frac{T - S}{R - S}.$$

(3)

where the approximation is brought about by applying the first order Taylor approximation (in $\vartheta_1 = 0$).

Note that the ratio $(P - S) / (R - S)$ is related to whether Actor 1 is willing to trust Actor 2. If we assume that all subjects have their own probability

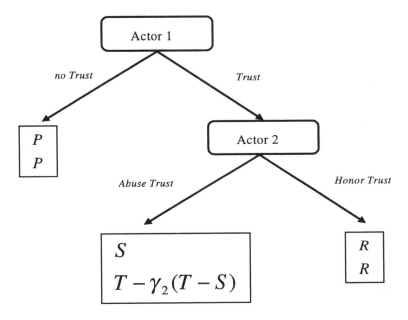

Fig. 15.3. The Trust Game based on the guilt model.

---

assessment $p_{2,1}$ independent of the value of this ratio (which is a plausible assumption), then as $(P - S) / (R - S)$ increases, the percentage of subjects with a large enough $p_{2,1}$-value decreases if $1 + \vartheta_1(T - S) / (R - S) > 0$. We can conclude that trust decreases with increasing $(P - S) / (R - S)$ for those individuals with social orientations between $- (R - S) / (T - S)$ and $(P - S) / (T - P)$.

## Guilt

A second way to model the psychological components of utility is by assuming that abusing the trust of others is associated with a negative component of utility. This can be accomplished by adding an egalitarian component to the utility function (Knight & Dubro, 1984). The intuition underlying this egalitarian component is straightforward. Given a similar amount of invested effort, people want to get neither more nor less than others. The extent to which people are agonized by departures of an equal split is a personal trait $\gamma_i$ and could be labeled a person's *egalitarian orientation* or *guilt parameter*. The corresponding utility function can then be expressed by $U_i(M_i, M_j) = M_i - \gamma_i \max (0, M_i - M_j)$, with $\gamma_i > 0$, which implies an effective Trust Game as in Fig. 15.3.[5]

In the guilt model, depicted in Fig. 15.3., Actor 2 honors trust if and only if that Actor's "guilt parameter" $\gamma_2 > (T - R) / (T - S)$. As stated earlier, the model assumes that the reason why Actor 2 may not abuse Actor 1's trust is due to Actor's 2 guilt feeling about pocketing more cash than Actor 1 ($T$ for Actor 2, as opposed to $S$ for Actor 1), in a situation where Actor 1's decision is precisely what allowed Actor 2 to receive more money in the first place. Now suppose that indeed all Actors 2 are characterized by their personal guilt parameter and behave accordingly. Then as $(T - R) / (T - S)$ increases, the percentage of Actors 2 with a guilt parameter that is sufficiently large to be willing to honor trust decreases. Note that Actor 1 has nothing to feel guilty about and thus is not assumed to feel guilty about his or her trust being abused (consequently, the guilt model is *not* equivalent to the social orientation model).

In the guilt model, Actors 1 will decide to trust Actors 2 if and only if

$$p_{2,1} > \frac{P - S}{R - S}.$$ (4)

Again, we can conclude that the ratio $(P - S) / (R - S)$ is apparently linked with Actor 1's decision to trust Actor 2. Assuming that $p_{2,1}$ is independent of the value of this ratio, implies that, according to the guilt model, trusts decreases with increasing $(P - S) / (R - S)$.

## Regret

Another psychological component that could be explicitly incorporated in the utility function is *regret* (e.g., Loomes & Sugden, 1982; Luce & Raiffa, 1957; Savage, 1954). Actor 1 can be assumed to anticipate regret associated with trust being abused. We assume that this implies a utility loss proportional to the loss Actor 1 incurs $(P - S)$, and that the extent to which this loss is amplified is a personal trait. That is, $U_1 (S, T) = S - v_1(P - S)$. The utility of Actor 2 is left unspecified. Actor 2 may also experience regret at a later stage for choosing to abuse the trust that was given by Actor 1, but the motives for such possible regret are not related directly to Actor 1. The Trust Game based on the regret model can be seen in Fig. 15.4.

Actor 1 trusts Actor 2 if and only if

$$p_{2,1} > \frac{P - S + v_1(P - S)}{R - S + v_1(P - S)} \approx \frac{P - S}{R - S} + v_1 \frac{(R - P)(P - S)}{(R - S)^2} = \frac{P - S}{R - S}\left(1 + v_1\left(1 - \frac{P - S}{R - S}\right)\right).$$ (5)

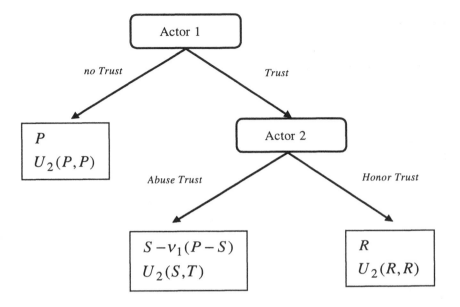

Fig. 15.4. The Trust Game based on the regret model $0 < v_1 < 1$.

---

again using the first order Taylor approximation (in $v_1 = 0$).

Once more, it is observed that $(P - S) / (R - S)$ has an impact on trust. Because $0 < v_1 < 1$, it can be easily seen that $(P - S) / (R - S) [1 + v_1(1 - (P - S) / (R - S))]$ increases in $(P - S) / (R - S)$. In other words, it becomes less likely that $p_{2,1}$ is large enough to trust as $(P - S) / (R - S)$ increases. This implies that, assuming that $p_{2,1}$ is independent of the value of $(P - S) / (R - S)$, the regret model predicts that trust decreases with increasing $(P - S) / (R - S)$.

## Trust Depends on Risk and Temptation

Theoretically, the three models (social orientations, guilt, and regret) are discernable. They can be distinguished, for instance, by the different ways in which the probability that Actor 1 trusts Actor 2 is affected by changes in the payoffs. The guilt model predicts that trust is dependent on $(P - S) / (R - S)$ only, the social orientations model predicts that it depends on $(P - S) / (R - S)$ and $(T - S)(R - P) / (R - S)^2$ (and $\vartheta_1$), and the regret model predicts that trust depends on $(P - S) / (R - S)$ and $(P - S) (R - P)/ (R - S)^2$ (and $v_1$).

Empirically, however, there are difficulties in constructing appropriate tests that would distinguish between these models. For example, both the social orientations and the regret models imply an effect of the risk-variable $(P - S) / (R - S)$ on trust that varies with the monetary payoffs *and* among individuals, which complicates statistical testing. Moreover, the other relevant variables are likely to be correlated. Finally, it is possible that models that have a different behavioral interpretation lead to identical predictions with respect to the effect of the monetary payoffs on trust (and honoring trust). It is therefore not likely that an analysis of the effect of payoffs on trustfulness and trustworthiness will easily result in one of the models being the definite winner (this is discussed later). Consequently, we adopt an approach that focuses on elements that are common to all the models and base our hypotheses on these common factors. Given that the models are a reasonable representation of the arguments underlying trusting and honoring trust, these common factors should capture the dependency of actors' behavior on payoffs in the Trust Game.

**Temptation.** *In both models that operationalize Actor 2's decision, his or her decision appears to be led by a construct of S, R, and T (namely $(T - R) / (R - S)$ and $(T - R) / (T - S)$ respectively).*

Intuitively, this makes perfect sense: Actor 2's decision will be led by the monetary amounts that Actor 2 can end up with ($T$ and $R$), and if one allows for a component in the utility function in which Actor 2 will experience displeasure if Actor 1 would only get a small amount of money, then dependency on $S$ is a natural result. For all the models, we find that honoring trust increases with decreasing values of $(T - R) / (T - S)$ (and hence also with $(T - R) / (R - S)$). The variable $(T - R) / (T - S)$ (and also $(T - R) / (R - S)$) captures Actor 2's *temptation* to abuse trust. This suggests the following hypothesis regarding stakes.

**Hypothesis 1.** *Consider a Trust Game (S, P, R, T). The larger the temptation ($(T - R) / (T - S)$ or $(T - R) / (R - S)$), the less likely that Actor 2 will honor trust.*

Given the qualitative (and monotonic) nature of this hypothesis, it makes no sense to favor either of the two ratios. Because $(T - R) / (T - S) = f((T - R) / (R - S))$ with $f$ an increasing function, it is impossible to distinguish between whether the probability of honoring trust increases linearly in $(T - R) / (T - S) = f((T - R) / (R - S))$, or nonlinearly (but according to $f$) in $(T - R) / (R - S)$. Later, we use $(T - R) / (T - S)$ as the operationalization of Actor 2's temptation.

**Risk.** In all the models, Actor 1's decision appears to be led by a construct of $S$, $P$, and $R$. The variable $(P - S) / (R - S)$ is embedded in all the models describing Actor 1's behavior. This ratio and its interpretation as risk also make intuitive sense. The worst (in terms of monetary outcomes) Actor 1 can get is $S$. At best, Actor 1 gets $R$. That is, Actor 1 is certain to get $S$, but playing the game and being lucky will yield an extra $R$-$S$. By not taking a chance (i.e., choosing not to trust Actor 2), Actor 1 is certain to get an extra $P$-$S$. In other words, Actor 1 can gain $R$-$S$ in addition to $S$ in a Trust Game and $(P - S) / (R - S)$ represents the proportion of that potential gain covered by simply refusing to trust Actor 2. The larger $(P - S) / (R - S)$, the more of this gain there is to lose by taking a chance and trusting Actor 2. We therefore use the label risk for the ratio $(P - S) / (R - S)$ (cf. Koller, 1988).

**Hypothesis 2.** *Consider a Trust Game (S, P, R, T). The larger the risk ((P − S) / (R − S)), the less likely that Actor 1 will trust Actor 2.*

Because Actor 2's temptation is a predictor for the probability that Actor 2 honors trust and Actor 1 is assumed to take this probability into account, we can conjecture that:

**Hypothesis 3.** *Consider a Trust Game (S, P, R, T). The larger the temptation for Actor 2, the less likely that Actor 1 will trust Actor 2.*

Note that one may wonder about the game theoretical validity of the approach just outlined. Specifically, given the use of "personal trait" parameters like $\vartheta$, $\gamma$, and $v$, one can expect an adequate extensive form for a game theoretical analysis of the Trust Game to include "nature" moving first and selecting both Actor 1's and Actor 2's personal parameters (i.e., either $\vartheta$, $\gamma$, and $v$ for Actors 1 and 2) from a given distribution of parameters that is assumed to be common knowledge. This seems at odds with the reasoning above, because nothing has been assumed about the Actors' knowledge about the distribution of the personal trait parameters. The sequentiality of the Trust Game ensures that such an assumption is not necessary. Actor 2 does not need to have information about the basis on which Actor 1 decided to trust Actor 2.[6] Actor 2 does not even need to know the initial distribution of parameters. Actor 2 needs only to know the value of his or her own parameter. This implies that essential for an adequate game theoretical analysis of behavior in the Trust Games, is *only* Actor 1's (subjective) assessment about Actor 2's decision. This estimate may be derived with the help of knowledge about the initial distribution of parameters (which is the standard game theoretical assumption), but this is not necessary here.

In our first experiment, we analyze whether the ratios associated with risk and temptation indeed affect the probability to trust (and honor trust) in a Trust Game. In addition, we focus on the extent to which the variation in behavior caused by differences in the monetary payoffs can be captured by these two ratios.

# EXPERIMENT 1

## Subjects

Five different studies were conducted with subjects from four different Dutch universities (Amsterdam, Utrecht, Nijmegen, and Groningen). They were recruited by campus advertisements and were promised at least 10 Dutch guilders (and the possibility for a larger reward) for participation. Nearly all participants were undergraduates from a variety of disciplines with the exception of the study in Amsterdam in which 71 out of the 120 (59%) subjects were students of economics (or econometrics). The purpose of this later sample was to test whether these students may respond differently because previous research (cf. Frank et al., 1993) suggests that economic students were more likely to behave in accordance with the strict economic interpretation of game theory. Two subjects were removed from the data set because it was clear from the questions they asked during the session that they did not understand the essentials of the task. A few other subjects failed to make a choice (e.g., one subject wrote "my choice depends on who Actor 2 will be") or responded in an unclear manner. Hence, 24 out of the 490 subjects (who participated in the five studies) were eliminated from further analysis.

## Procedure

Subjects were seated in a room with either seven (the experiments in Utrecht and Nijmegen) or fourteen participants such that they were always able to see each other. The experimenter informed subjects that the experiment would consist of a number of different tasks, some of which would concern choices regarding monetary outcomes. They were further instructed to think carefully about their choices because it was possible that (at the end of the session) some of them would be paid in accordance with one of their choices. The procedure to determine which subjects would be paid and the specific game were explicitly outlined. First, one of the games was to be randomly selected followed by a random selection of two subjects who would then be paid according to their choices in that particular game. The procedure was explained by means of a hypothetical example.

The purpose of applying such a procedure was to exclude "wealth effects" (e.g., Davis & Holt, 1993; Kahneman & Tversky, 1979). Because each decision situation is selected with equal probability, choices in each situation enter a subject's overall expected utility as additively separable components. Consequently, each component can be maximized separately and potential earnings in one game should not affect decisions in other games. The method is supposed to increase subjects' motivation as there were considerable sums of

**Table 15.2**
**Percentage of Trust and Honoring Trust in Trust Games in Extensive Form**

| Trust Game (*S-P-R-T*) | Risk | Temptation | % Trust | % Honor Trust |
|---|---|---|---|---|
| 1.  15-20-80-100 | .08 | .24 | 46 | 48 |
| 2.   5-15-70- 90 | .15 | .24 | 78 | 83 |
| 3.  10-20-70- 95 | .17 | .29 | 92 | 58 |
| 4.   0-10-45- 95 | .22 | .53 | 56 | 54 |
| 5.  15-30-80-100 | .23 | .24 | 61 | 69 |
| 6.   5-20-70- 90 | .23 | .24 | 70 | 57 |
| 7.  15-30-65- 70 | .30 | .09 | 74 | 87 |
| 8.   0-20-65- 85 | .31 | .24 | 50 | 54 |
| 9.  20-40-80-100 | .33 | .25 | 57 | 60 |
| 10.   0-15-45- 85 | .33 | .47 | 60 | 52 |
| 11.  10-25-55- 95 | .33 | .47 | 44 | 40 |
| 12.  20-40-80-140 | .33 | .50 | 44 | 24 |
| 13.   0-15-45- 95 | .33. | .53 | 60 | 27 |
| 14.  10-20-40-140 | .33 | .77 | 43 | 9 |
| 15.   0-25-65-105 | .38 | .38 | 38 | 37 |
| 16.  10-30-60- 75 | .40 | .23 | 76 | 68 |
| 17.  10-30-60- 80 | .40 | .29 | 42 | 44 |
| 18.   5-35-75- 95 | .43 | .22 | 52 | 74 |
| 19.  10-40-80-115 | .43 | .33 | 43 | 43 |
| 20.   5-35-75-120 | .43 | .39 | 50 | 46 |
| 21.   5-35-75-140 | .43 | .48 | 17 | 14 |
| 22.   5-25-50-135 | .44 | .65 | 31 | 15 |
| 23.   0-20-40- 50 | .50 | .20 | 52 | 64 |
| 24.   0-40-80-100 | .50 | .20 | 35 | 54 |
| 25.   0-40-80-140 | .50 | .43 | 30 | 43 |
| 26.  10-30-50- 90 | .50 | .50 | 41 | 41 |
| 27.   5-20-35-100 | .50 | .68 | 36 | 29 |
| 28.  15-30-45-110 | .50 | .68 | 47 | 20 |
| 29.   0-20-40-200 | .50 | .80 | 31 | 8 |
| 30.  10-35-55- 65 | .56 | .18 | 42 | 52 |
| 31.  10-30-45- 70 | .57 | .42 | 27 | 46 |
| 32.  10-30-45-100 | .57 | .61 | 21 | 17 |
| 33.   0-15-25-150 | .60 | .83 | 20 | 4 |
| 34.  10-30-40-120 | .67 | .73 | 30 | 9 |
| 35.  15-40-50- 75 | .71 | .42 | 5 | 24 |
| 36.  15-40-50- 85 | .71 | .50 | 12 | 33 |

money at stake. The maximum amount a subject could earn was 120 Dutch guilders (about U. S. $75) which, according to student standards, is certainly a substantial amount.

Subjects were explicitly told that there were no right or wrong answers. They were instructed to complete their tasks in the order in which they were presented in the instruction text, and were given the possibility to ask the experimenter for assistance. In each study, subjects performed three or four decision making tasks in which the Trust Game task was the first one.

## Tasks

Subjects were told that they would participate in a two-player game in which they would have to make choices in the role of Player 1 and in the role of Player 2. The game was described (without mentioning concepts like trust or fairness) by referring to a card with a display of a Trust Game in its extensive form. Subjects were asked to make their choice as Actor 1 and their choice as Actor 2 in several different games, each game represented by a separate card. For each card they were told to make their choice as Actor 1 and as Actor 2, leaving the order in which the cards had to be dealt with up to the subjects. Across the different studies, subjects responded on average to five different Trust Games (the 36 different games employed in the different studies are presented in Table 15.2). The subjects' choices in the role of Actor 1 and Actor 2 constitute the dummy variables *Trust* and *Honor Trust*. The variable *Risk* equals $(P - S) / (R - S)$ and *Temptation* equals $(T - R) / (T - S)$.

Following their choices on the Trust Game subjects were asked to fill out a questionnaire that included questions about their sex, age, field of study, knowledge of game theory, whether they were a blood donor, whether they carried a donor codicil, and composition of their high school final examinations (whether it included math, physics, economics, French, and/or history). The answers to these questions constitute the variables *Male*, *Age*, *Economist*, *Game Theory*, *Blood Donor*, and *Donor Codicil*. A factor analysis of the composition of subjects' examination package constitutes a single variable labeled *School*. As mentioned before, the literature on social dilemmas suggests economists trust and honor trust less often. Basically, the other variables served as crude proxies of subjects' disposition to trust.

## RESULTS

Across the 36 different Trust Games, the percentage of subjects in the role of Actor 1 who opted for choosing trust varied between 5% and 92%, with a mean of 45%. The percentage of subjects in the role of Actor 2 who chose to honor trust varied between 4% and 87%, with a mean of 42% (see Table 15.2).

In the following analyses an attempt is made to account for this large variation (in both trusting and honoring trust) by means of variation in risk $((P - S) / (R - S))$ and temptation $((T - R) / (T - S))$.

## Violation of Independence

The main dependent variable in our analysis is the choice made by Actor 1 in a Trust Game. Our theoretical models can be translated in statistically testable probit models that regress the behavior of Actor 1 on individual attributes and characteristics of the game as reflected in the payoffs (see the Appendix). The data, however, consist of multiple observations within subjects. It is therefore likely that the necessary requirement of standard probit models, that all observations should be independent, is violated. This kind of "clustering" in the data can lead to underestimation of the standard errors of the coefficients of the statistical model, consequently yielding artificial significant effects. Huber (1967) proposed a method of estimating standard errors that takes such possible effects into account. The following results are based on Huber's method with each subject representing a single cluster.[7]

It is a nontrivial question whether Honor Trust should be incorporated as an independent variable in the analyses. On the one hand, it would allow to control for the degree to which Actors 1 are guided by what they would do themselves if they were in the role of Actor 2.[8] On the other hand, our theoretical models suggest that Honor Trust and temptation $((T - R) / (T - S))$ measure, at least partly, the same thing. We therefore ran our analyses with Trust as the dependent variable twice: once using only Temptation as an estimate of Actor 2's behavior, and once with Honor Trust *and* Temptation as an estimate of Actor 2's behavior.

## Data and Controls

Four variables in the data were eventually disregarded in the analyses: Age, Blood Donor, Game Theory, and School. None of these variables approached significance in the analyses. Other dummies that were included in the analyses were *Experimenter* (a dummy variable that captured whether the first author or someone else was the experimenter), *Session* (session dummies), and *First Trust Game* (a dummy that captured whether the first few Trust Games were involved or the last few) to control for carry-over effects. None of these variables approached significance. Analyses are displayed without incorporating these control variables. To control for effects that are somehow related to the five different experiments, a categorical variable *City* was incorporated in the analyses (with five categories, one for each city, Groningen-1 and Groningen-2 being taken as two cities). The analyses revealed that significant differences occurred between the two experiments in Groningen, the experiment in Nijmegen, and the experiments in Utrecht and Amsterdam. Consequently, the

**Table 15.3**

**Probit Analysis of the Probability That Actor 1 Trusts Actor 2 in Experiment 1**

| Indep. Variable | Honor Trust Excluded | | | Honor Trust Included | | |
|---|---|---|---|---|---|---|
| | *Unstand. Coeff.* | *p-value* | *Effect* | *Unstand. Coeff.* | *p-value* | *Effect* |
| *Stakes* | | | | | | |
| Risk | -2.32** | 0.00 | -0.85 | -2.68** | 0.00 | -0.73 |
| Temptation | -.50** | 0.00 | -0.18 | 0.68** | 0.00 | 0.24 |
| Honor trust | -- | -- | -- | 1.27** | 0.00 | 0.46 |
| *Disposition* | | | | | | |
| Male | 0.07 | 0.47 | | -0.20* | 0.04 | 0.07 |
| Codicil | 0.23* | 0.02 | 0.08 | 0.30** | 0.00 | 0.11 |
| Economist | -0.20 | 0.23 | | -0.16 | 0.29 | |
| *Controls* | | | | | | |
| Groningen | 0.54** | 0.00 | 0.20 | 0.44** | 0.00 | 0.16 |
| Nijmegen | 0.36* | 0.02 | 0.14 | 0.03 | 0.85 | |
| Constant | 0.76 | 0.00 | | -0.04 | 0.90 | |

Pseudo-$R^2$ = 0.12                     Pseudo-$R^2$ = 0.25
Number of obs. = 2254               Number of obs. = 2247
Log likelihood = -1303.5           Log Likelihood = -1112.6
Effects at $p$ = 0.34                    Effects at $p$ = 0.33

variable City was replaced by two dummy variables: *Groningen* and *Nijmegen*, which were included in the models as separate additive components.

In all the following tables containing probit analyses, we add a column in which the effect of a variable that turns out to have a statistically significant effect on the estimated probability to trust (or honor trust) is stated.[9] We first consider the decision to trust in Table 15.3.

The effect of Risk is in the right direction, and has a coefficient that is relatively robust against adding the Honor Trust variable, which supports Hypothesis 2. When Honor Trust is excluded from the analysis, the coefficient for Temptation is significant and negative, supporting Hypothesis 3. Note that this coefficient is significant and positive when Honor Trust is excluded, which seems to be incompatible with the theoretical arguments and common sense: a positive coefficient suggests that subjects are more likely to trust when the

**Table 15.4**
**Probit Analysis of the Probability That Actor 2 Honors Trust in Experiment 1**

| Independent Variable | Unstandardized Coefficent | $p$-value | Effect |
|---|---|---|---|
| *Stakes* | | | |
| Temptation | -2.56** | 0.00 | -0.94 |
| | | | |
| *Disposition* | | | |
| Male | -0.24* | 0.02 | -0.09 |
| Codicil | -0.08 | 0.43 | |
| Economist | -0.14 | 0.42 | |
| | | | |
| *Controls* | | | |
| Groningen | 0.42** | 0.00 | 0.15 |
| Nijmegen | 0.87** | 0.00 | 0.34 |
| | | | |
| Constant | 0.35 | 0.21 | |

Pseudo-$R^2$ = 0.13
Number of obs. = 2247
Log Likelihood = -1276.6
Effects at $p$ = 0.34

temptation for Actor 2 is larger. A plausible explanation relies on the fact that Honor Trust is a decreasing function of Temptation itself. The effect of Groningen and Codicil is consistent across both analyses. The subjects in the Groningen sessions and subjects carrying a donor codicil are more likely to trust others (an approximate effect of 0.18 and 0.10 on the estimated probability to trust). The effect of Nijmegen disappears after controlling for Honor Trust. This suggests that subjects in Nijmegen were more likely to honor trust (additional analyses confirm these findings, see Snijders, 1996). We have no explanation for the differences among different cities (separate analyses reveal that the effects of the other variables are robust). The variable Economist had no significant effect. The Male subjects were more likely to trust, after controlling for Honor Trust. Without controlling for Honor Trust there was no effect. Taken together, this suggests that given that men and women do not differ in the extent to which they base their behavior on whether they would honor trust themselves, men are more

**Table 15.5**
**Goodness of Fit With Respect to Trust in Experiment 1**

|  | Independent Variables | Log Likelihood | Likelihood Ratio Test |
|---|---|---|---|
| Model 1: | Constant | -1495.7 | 0.00 |
| Model 2: | Model 1 + male + . . . + Nijmegen | -1392.0 | 0.00 |
| Model 3: | model 2 + risk + temptation | -1303.5 | 0.02 |
| Model 4: | Model 2 + risk$^2$ + temptation | -1299.4 | 0.09 |
| Model 5: | Model 2 + 36 Game dummies | -1277.4 |  |

*Note.* Likelihood Ratio Test compared to model 5, the saturated model.

likely to trust intrinsically (as opposed to "because they are more likely to believe that Actor 2 honors trust"). The difference is rather small: an effect of 0.07 on the estimated average probability to trust.

Table 15.4 shows that temptation has a strong negative effect on the probability to honor trust, which supports Hypothesis 1. Relatively large differences exist between the sessions in Groningen and Nijmegen and the others.[10] Males are somewhat less likely to honor trust (an effect of -0.09 on the estimated probability). Somewhat surprisingly, subjects who study economics do not abuse trust more often.

## Goodness of Fit

Although the previous analyses tend to support our first three hypotheses, it remains to be seen to what extent the variation in trust and honoring trust can be explained by the variation in risk and temptation. To assess the goodness of fit of the models with respect to stakes, we compare the likelihood of the saturated probit model

$$\text{Trust} = \beta_0 + \beta_1 \text{game}_1 + \beta_2 \text{game}_2 + \ldots + \beta_{36} \text{game}_{36} + \beta_{37} \text{Male} + \ldots + \tau \text{Nijmegen} \tag{6}$$

where game$_i$ represents a dummy variable for game $i = 1 \ldots 36$, with the likelihood of the theoretical model

$$\text{Trust} = \beta_0 + \beta_1 (P - S)/(R - S) + \beta_2 \text{Male} + \ldots + \tau \text{Nijmegen}. \tag{7}$$

In the saturated model each game gets its own dummy. Therefore, the

**Table 15.6**
**Goodness of Fit With Respect to Honoring Trust in Experiment 1**

|  | Independent Variables | Log Likelihood | Likelihood Ratio Test |
|---|---|---|---|
| Model 1: | Constant | -1485.8 | 0.00 |
| Model 2: | Model 1 + male + . . . + Nijmegen | -1394.6 | 0.00 |
| Model 3: | model 2 + risk + temptation | -1276.6 | 0.81 |
| Model 4: | Model 2 + 36 Game dummies | -1263.2 |  |

*Note.* Likelihood Ratio Test compared to model 4, the saturated model.

likelihood of this model provides an upper limit for the likelihood that can be attained with any model based on the monetary payoffs alone, while controlling for the other variables like the sex of the subject. Table 15.5 summarizes the results.

The last column in Table 15.5 reports the likelihood ratio test compared to the saturated model.[11] As can be seen, the saturated model still performs significantly better in describing the effect of the payoffs than our theoretical model (model 3). Replacing Risk $(P - S)/(R - S)$ by its square (or just adding its square) renders a model that captures the effects of the monetary payoffs (almost) as well as the saturated model, which suggests that the variation in the payoffs can be explained reasonably well with the help of the variables risk and temptation.

Table 15.6 shows the results of identical analyses on honoring trust. Temptation seems to perform well with respect to honoring trust. As the last column of Table 15.6 shows, the saturated model does not perform significantly better in describing the effects of the Trust Game payoffs in the data than the theoretical model. The variable temptation adequately captures the variance that can be ascribed to the payoffs with respect to honoring trust.

## Other Indices

As mentioned before, there is evidence in the literature of the effect of stakes in social dilemmas. For instance, Murnighan and Roth (1983) discussed the relation of 10 different indices to the probability of cooperation in PD. Whereas we feel our ratios have a "theoretical edge" in the sense that they can be derived rigorously from assumptions on utility functions, we briefly elaborate on Murnighan and Roth's (1983) indices. First, it should be noted that as long as only monotonicity hypotheses are considered (the larger the index, the more/less cooperation), it does not make sense to distinguish between indices that can be transformed into each other by a monotonic transformation. This was the reason why distinguishing between $(T - R)/(T - S)$ and $(T - R)/(R - S)$ does not make much sense in our empirical analyses and the reason why the 10 indices in Murnighan and Roth (1983) reduce to seven for our purpose.[12] From these seven, none performs better in explaining honoring trust than temptation, and none performs better in explaining trust than risk, which renders some additional support for our indices.

To summarize, we started out by claiming that utility, defined in terms of money to ego only, cannot explain behavior in Trust Games. We then suggested that explaining trust would require the incorporation of some psychological components in the utility function. Different ways to include such psychological components – social orientations, guilt and regret – were proposed. Ultimately, we identified two variables that seem to emerge from our different models: risk $((P - S)/(R - S))$ and temptation $((T - R)/(T - S))$. These two variables properly account for the variation in behavior due to variation in the monetary payoffs. Moreover, the effects of potential "disposition variables" appeared small (for gender and carrying a donor codicil) or absent (for age and studying economics).

## THE SEQUENTIALITY OF TRUST

Incorporating psychological components in the utility function seems a substantial improvement. However, one could argue that the essence of trust is not contained in the different monetary payoffs at the endnodes of the Trust Game, but in the way in which these endnodes are reached. The emphatic sequentiality of trust, the voluntarily handing over of control over one's own resources, that is what trust is all about. Likewise, honoring trust has to do with not having the heart to betray someone who has just put his or her fate in your hands. One could expect such an effect to go beyond the direct effect of the monetary payoffs. From a game theoretical perspective this is an obvious extension. We first assumed behavior to be explained by money to ego (a single column of payoffs in the game tree), then by money to ego and alter (both columns of payoffs in the game tree) and now by the way in which money to ego and alter comes about (both columns of payoffs in the game tree and the path leading to these columns).

We would expect that the more salient the sequentiality of subjects' choices is, the more trust will be honored.[13] In anticipation of this, trust will then also be more likely. To test these predictions, we compared subjects' choices in Trust Games in extensive form with their choices in Trust Games in normal form.

In the extensive form Trust Game, Actor 2 knows Actor 1 has trusted him or her and in the normal form Trust Game, Actor 2 could argue that the choice is

**Table 15.7**
**Percentage of Trust and Honoring Trust in Trust Games in Normal Form**

| Trust Game (*S-P-R-T*) | | Risk | Temptation | % Trust | % Honor Trust |
|---|---|---|---|---|---|
| 1. | 10-20-70- 95 | .17 | .29 | 68 | 50 |
| 2. | 15-30-65- 70 | .30 | .09 | 44 | 56 |
| 3. | 0-20-65- 85 | .31 | .24 | 50 | 57 |
| 4. | 20-40-80-140 | .33 | .50 | 42 | 46 |
| 5. | 10-20-40-140 | .33 | .77 | 46 | 31 |
| 6. | 10-40-80-115 | .43 | .33 | 36 | 42 |
| 7. | 5-25-50-135 | .44 | .65 | 32 | 14 |
| 8. | 0-20-40- 50 | .50 | .20 | 35 | 58 |
| 9. | 0-40-80-140 | .50 | .43 | 36 | 52 |
| 10. | 10-30-50- 90 | .50 | .50 | 29 | 29 |
| 11. | 0-15-25-150 | .60 | .83 | 35 | 27 |
| 12. | 10-30-40-120 | .67 | .73 | 30 | 8 |

important only in case Actor 1 has decided to trust him or her. Therefore, these two representations of the Trust Game are formally equivalent. However, the notion of trust is much more salient in the extensive form case, which suggests our fourth and fifth hypothesis.

**Hypothesis 4.** *In Trust Games, trusting is more likely in the extensive than in the normal form.*

**Hypothesis 5.** *In Trust Games, honoring trust is more likely in the extensive than in the normal form.*

## EXPERIMENT 2

The experimental setup described earlier (for the second experiment in Groningen) included a Trust Game in normal form task. Subjects in these sessions were asked to choose a move for five Trust Games in extensive form, and subsequently for four Trust Games in normal form. As in the previous experiment, subjects could actually win the amounts of money at stake in the Trust Games in its normal form. Table 15.7 summarizes the Trust Games in normal form that were used and the proportion of subjects trusting and honoring

**Table 15.8**
**Probit Analysis of the Probability That Actor 1 Trusts Actor 2**

| Independent Variable | Unstandardized Coefficient | p-value | Effect |
|---|---|---|---|
| *Sequentiality* | | | |
| Normal form | -0.23* | 0.04 | -0.09 |
| | | | |
| *Stakes* | | | |
| Risk | -3.27** | 0.00 | -1.23 |
| Honor trust | 1.19** | 0.00 | 0.44 |
| | | | |
| *Disposition* | | | |
| Male | 0.18 | 0.29 | |
| Codicil | 0.25 | 0.16 | |
| | | | |
| Constant | -0.33 | 0.67 | |

Pseudo-$R^2$ = 0.19
Number of obs. = 935
Log Likelihood = -506.0
Effects at $p$ = 0.37

*Note.* Normal form included.

trust.

The analyses mentioned earlier were repeated including all Trust Games (i.e., those in extensive and in normal form). The model to be estimated was derived as in the previous sections, but a dummy variable *Normal Form* was included as a separate additive component in the model. Table 15.8 displays the analysis including the variable Honor Trust and excluding the variable *Temptation*.[14] The major interest of this analysis was the variable Normal Form.

The data revealed a tendency to trust less in normal form games than in extensive form games (an estimated probability to trust of 0.28 vs. 0.37), supporting Hypothesis 4. The explicit sequentiality of the extensive form Trust Game increases the salience of the risk Actor 1 takes to trust Actor 2; to trust when it is obvious that this may result in a considerable loss to the trustor is more likely to be rewarded. Therefore, Actors 1 can rely more on reciprocation of their cooperative decision to trust in the extensive than in the normal form of Trust Games. However, it is still unclear whether this increased probability to trust caused by the salience of reciprocation is justified (in the sense that Actors

**Table 15.9**
**Probit Analysis of the Probability That Actor 2 Honors Trust**

| Independent Variable | Unstandardized Coefficient | p-value | Effect |
|---|---|---|---|
| *Sequentiality* | | | |
| Normal form | -0.14* | -.13 | |
| *Stakes* | | | |
| Temptation | -1.93** | 0.00 | -0.75 |
| *Disposition* | | | |
| Male | -0.43* | 0.04 | -0.16 |
| Codicil | -0.03 | 0.86 | |
| Constant | -0.43 | 0.63 | |

Pseudo-$R^2$ = 0.08
Number of obs. = 935
Log Likelihood = -588.8
Effects at $p$ = 0.42

*Note.* Normal form included.

2 are indeed more likely to reciprocate trust in the normal form Trust Games).

Surprisingly, although Actors 1 behave as if they anticipate a bonus for deciding to trust in a Trust Game in extensive form, Actors 2 do *not* live up to that expectation, which refutes Hypothesis 5 (see Table 15.9). It seems that at the moment Actor 2 has to decide what to do, the past becomes of minor importance.[15] The contrast between these results and the results from bargaining experiments is striking. In bargaining experiments, subjects are typically reported to reciprocate a first move that leads to a distribution of money that is considered "unfair" by a second move that diminishes the monetary payoff of the first mover even at the expense of the second mover. In other words, negative first moves trigger negative second moves in bargaining. In Trust Games, positive first moves do not seem to trigger positive second moves.

# CAN WE TRUST OUR KNOWLEDGE ABOUT TRUST? SOME REFLECTIONS

In this study we investigated how the pattern of payoffs influences the extent to which trust can be established, specifically the degree to which Actor 1 is willing to put trust in Actor 2 and the extent to which the latter will honor it. Contrary to the rigorous dictates of standard game theory, our empirical results show that a substantial proportion of people are willing to trust others under a wide range of conditions. Correspondingly, many people will tend not to abuse the trust given to them, thus choosing for the cooperative move. Similar results have been reported by Dufwenberg and Gneezy (1996). These authors employed an experimental setup (which they labeled the "lost wallet game") where Actor 1 can take $x$ guilders (in which case Actor 2 gets nothing) and end the game, or let Actor 2 divide a fixed sum between the two players such that $y$ percent will go to Actor 1. Similar to our results, these authors report a high proportion of subjects who, as Actor 1, chose for the cooperative move and trusted the other Actor (the extent of such cooperative behavior varied between 12% and 100%, depending on the game).

Our results suggest that the extent to which mutual trust will be established depends on the notions of temptation and risk. It is important to realize that we basically adopted a game-theoretic framework in which the ratios that we labeled temptation and risk are directly derived from this framework. In that sense, the psychological arguments underlying the different models constitute themselves the intuitive justification of the ratios. Basically, our analyses imply that Actor 2's decision whether or not to honor trust depends on temptation, but not on risk. That is, honoring trust depends on $S$, $R$, and $T$, but not on $P$.[16] Actor 1's decision to trust is based on both temptation and risk, of which the latter has the strongest effect. The ratio $(P - S)/(R - S)$, which we used as our operational definition of risk, is a way of balancing or weighing the potential losses against the potential gains. Indeed, the importance of the weighing of possible losses against possible gains has also been observed by Dufwenberg and Gneezy (1996): They report that the tendency of Actor 1 to trust decreases as the amount $(x)$ associated with the move of "not trusting" increases.

An unexpected finding across all our studies is the fact that Actor 2's decisions were apparently not based on the payoffs that could have been reached if Actor 1 had not trusted Actor 2. This finding is incompatible with the intuition that part of the reason why trust is honored is an acknowledgment of the degree to which the trustor has put himself or herself in a vulnerable position. Again, Dufwenberg and Gneezy (1996) reported similar results: The amount of money Actors 2 keep for themselves $(y)$ does not depend on the amount of money that Actor 1 would have received $(x)$ if he or she had not trusted.

Although the empirical results reported here have been replicated in several experiments and are thus robust, we may still pose the question of how much do we know about the intricate and complex concept of trust? Our feeling is best captured by Lykken (1991), who, paraphrasing Mark Twain, proposed that "it is not so much what we don't know that hurts us, as those things we do know that aren't so" (p. 8). In the remainder of this chapter, we briefly outline some critical comments. We first mention some possible reservations directly applicable to our approach and end with some general remarks.

The game-theoretic model we adopted is based on four parameters ($S$, $P$, $R$, and $T$). Consequently, as we hinted earlier, one may quickly get to the point at which different psychological accounts would converge to essentially identical models. Further refinements and possibilities to distinguish between different models could be attained by applying the different models to asymmetrical payoff matrices.

In the present framework, hypotheses are derived by estimating the probabilities that Actor 1 will trust and Actor 2 will honor trust. These probabilities are assessed solely on payoffs and largely disregard other variables. For instance, it was shown that physical appearance affects the likelihood of trusting and honoring trust. Indeed, in an experiment not reported here (Snijders & Keren, 1996), we have shown that physical appearance affected trust. The effect was statistically significant yet rather small, but one cannot rule out that in a different experimental setting the size of the effect will be much larger.

Perhaps the most basic question, and one for which game theory can at best offer indirect answers, is whether the process of establishing trust is dominated by rational considerations. Game theory is in essence a rational theory and deviations from the theory may suggest considerations other than rational ones. We believe that trust is, at least partly, strongly associated with noncognitive components, only some of which can be captured by a game-theoretic framework. For instance, as we mentioned earlier, the possibility of dispositions to trust. Although we were unable to detect such dispositions in our studies, these cannot be ruled out because our experiments were not designed explicitly to detect such dispositions. Other studies (e.g., Parks et al., 1996; Yamagishi, 1986) suggest that such dispositions do exist though their relative importance remains to be unknown.

One of the more important clues we obtained from our data was the reaction of one of the subjects (while in the role of Actor 1) who refused to make a choice. He said that he could not respond because his choice depended on who Actor 2 was. It is certainly conceivable that many other subjects had similar feelings, yet because they were paid for their services they gave a response to satisfy the experimenter. Indeed, there is evidence that different cues such as physical outlook, first impressions (e.g., Quigley-Fernandez, Malkis, & Tedeschi 1985), and others all seem to influence the judgement of trust. It is certainly not our claim that judgements based on such cues are necessarily accurate, only that these cues play an important role regardless of their predictive validity.

The decision whether to put trust in another person and to what extent may be conceived as a prediction based on a large number of predictors. Real-life observations suggest that such predictions regarding trust may often be characterized as what has been termed "clinical predictions." Dawes, Faust, and Meehl (1989, 1993) showed (across a broad number of applications) the shortcomings and dangers associated with clinical judgments. Regardless of their inaccuracy and potential misleading outcomes, clinical judgments remain indispensable if we are to accurately describe human behavior, the judgment of trust being no exception. Our study provides partial insight into the processes underlying the establishment of trust. A further understanding may be obtained by the analysis of clinical judgements associated with the determination of trust.

## ACKNOWLEDGMENTS

Useful comments on earlier versions of this chapter by Werner Raub, Jeroen Weesie, Robyn Dawes (who suggested the second experiment), J. Keith Murnighan, an anonymous reviewer, and David Budescu are gratefully acknowledged. Financial support was provided by the Netherlands Organization for Scientific Research (NWO) under grant PGS 50-370.

## ENDNOTES

1. All monetary amounts are in Dutch guilders, where 100 Dutch guilders were approximately equal to U. S. $60.
2. In the previous experiments, subjects responded in both the role of Actor 1 and Actor 2 (i.e., a within-subjects design). In one condition, using $S = 1$, $P = 2$, $R = 4$, and $T = 5$, we employed a between-subjects design in which each participant played either the role of Actor 1 or the role of Actor 2 (but not both). The percentage of subjects trusting as Actor 1 was 69% and the percentage of subjects honoring trust was 63%.
3. In this chapter, our arguments in favor of these constructs are based on utility functions of three theoretical models. They can, however, be shown to affect the probability of trust and honoring trust for a larger class of utility functions.
4. Arbitrary may be too strong a term. However, assuming that the distribution of social orientations is continuous on $[a, b]$ and that $\Pr\{\vartheta \in [a,b]\}=1$ (for some $a$ and $b$), is enough to claim that the probability that Actors 2 honor trust decreases with increasing $(T - R)/(R - S)$ on $[a, b]$.
5. Different assumptions about the exact operationalization of the model can be made that may represent guilt more adequately. For instance, it is possible that guilt increases as Actor 2 gains more $(T_2 - R_2)$, and as Actor 1 gets less $(R_1 - S_1)$. Instead of a model of guilt with $U_2(S_1, T_2) = T_2 - \gamma_2(T_2 - S_1)$, a guilt model could then be characterized by $U_2(S_1, T_2) = T_2 - \gamma_2(T_2 - R_2) / (R_1 - S_1)$. The latter model would be more capable of capturing effects brought about by asymmetry in the payoffs. For simplicity, we stick to the model specification in the text.
6. At least as long as models such as the ones presented here are considered. Actor 2

could also be assumed to (be known to) base the decision to honor trust on the value of the personal parameter of Actor 1. For instance, Actor 2 may be willing to honor trust based on genuine altruistic grounds. In that case, Actor 2 would need to consider on what grounds Actor 1 decided to trust Actor 2, in order to infer the value of Actor 1's parameter.

7. Other ways to cope with possible dependencies in the observations are available. For instance, we compared the Huber (1967) parameter estimates with the mean of the parameter estimates of 5,000 "standard" probit analyses on a single randomly chosen observation per subject. Such a bootstrap analysis leads to results that are only marginally different from the Huber estimates. In addition, we estimated a model that introduces two error terms: an error term on the individual level and an error term on the observation level. Taken together, comparison of the different statistical techniques suggest that the Huber standard errors as reported in our analyses are fairly conservative.
8. The so-called "consensus effect" (Dawes, 1989; Ross, Greene, & House, 1977).
9. For dummy variables, the magnitude of the effects were calculated by comparing the estimated probability at the means of the other independent variables with the dummy equaling 0 and 1. For (quasi) continuous variables, the slope of the probability function at the mean of the other independent variables was approximated.
10. Separate analyses per city revealed that the strong effect of temptation is robust.
11. This employs the fact that the difference in the log likelihood times $-2$ is $\chi^2$ distributed with $d_0 - d_1$ degrees of freedom, where $d_0$ and $d_1$ are the degrees of freedom associated with the saturated and "constrained" model.
12. Murnighan and Roth (1983) consider indices labeled $r_1$ through $r_4$, $e_1$ and $e_2$, and $k_1$ through $k_4$. Because $r_2 = (R - S) / (T - S) = 1 - (T - R) / (T - S) = 1 - r_4$, and $e_2 = 1/r_2 - 1$, the indices $r_2$, $r_4$, and $e_2$ cannot be distinguished.
13. Erev and Rapoport (1990) for related arguments in the context of public goods.
14. The effect of Normal Form does not change substantially by including Temptation and excluding Honor Trust.
15. Additional support for this claim can be based on the fact that including P or P-S in the analysis of Table 15.4 has no significant effect on the probability that trust will be honored.
16. We chose to operationalize temptation by $(T - R) / (T - S)$, but choosing $(T - R) / (R - S)$ makes just as much sense.
17. The derivation of a statistical model that incorporates visible characteristics of Actor 2 and of a statistical model of Actor 2's decision whether or not to honor Actor 1's trust, run analogous to the derivation of the model for Actor 1. See Snijders (1996).

# REFERENCES

Braun, N. (1992). Altruismus, moralitaet und vertrauen [Altruism, morality, and trust]. *Analyse und Kritik, 14*(2), 177-186.
Campbell, R., & Sowden, L. (Eds.). (1985). *Paradoxes of rationality and cooperation. Prisoner's dilemma and Newcomb's problem.* Vancouver: University of British Columbia Press.
Colman, A. (1982). *Game theory and experimental games.* Hillsdale, NJ: Lawrence

Erlbaum Associates.

Dasgupta, P. (1988). Trust as a commodity. In D. Gambetta (Ed.), *Trust, making and breaking cooperative relations* (pp. 49-72). Oxford, England: Basil Blackwell.

Davis, D. D., & Holt, C. A. (1993). *Experimental economics*. Princeton, NJ: Princeton University Press.

Dawes, R. M. (1980). Social dilemmas. *Annual Review of Psychology, 25*, 1-17.

Dawes, R. M. (1988). Anomalies: Cooperation. *Journal of Economic Perspectives, 2*, 187-197.

Dawes, R. M. (1989). Statistical criteria for establishing a truly false consensus effect. *Journal of Experimental Social Psychology, 25*, 1-17.

Dawes, R. M., Faust, D., & Meehl, P. E. (1989). Clinical versus actuarial judgement. *Science, 243*(4899), 1668-1674.

Dawes, R. M., Faust, D., & Meehl, P. E. (1993). Statistical prediction versus clinical prediction: Improving what works. In G. Keren & C. Lewis (Eds.), *A handbook for data analysis in the behavioral sciences: Methodological issues* (pp. 351-367). Hillsdale, NJ: Lawrence Erlbaum Associates.

Dufwenberg, M., & Gneezy, U. (1996). *Efficiency and expectations in an experimental Game*. Working paper, Center for Economic Research, Tilburg University, The Netherlands.

Erev, I., & Rapoport, A. (1990). Provision of step-level public goods: The sequential contribution mechanism. *Journal of Conflict Resolution, 34*, 401-425.

Frank, R. H, Gilovich, T., & Regan, D. T. (1993). Does studying economics inhibit cooperation? *Journal of Economic Perspectives, 7*, 159-171.

Huber, P. J. (1967). The behavior of maximum likelihood estimates under non-standard conditions. *Proceedings of the Fifth Berkeley Symposium on Mathematical Statistics and Probability, 1*, 221-233.

Kahneman, D., & Tversky, A. (1979). Prospect theory: An analysis of decision under risk. *Econometrica, 47*, 263-291.

Knight, G. P., & Dubro, A. F. (1984). Cooperative, competitive, and individualistic social values: An individualized regression and clustering approach. *Journal of Personality and Social Psychology, 46*, 98-105.

Koller, M. (1988). Risk as a determinant of trust. *Basic and Applied Social Psychology, 9*, 265-276.

Korniol, R. (1990). Reading people's minds: A transformation rule model for predicting others' thoughts and feelings. *Advancements in Experimental Social Psychology, 23*, 211-247.

Kreps, D. M. (1990). Corporate culture and economic theory. In J. E. Alt & K. A. Shepsle (Eds.), *Perspectives on positive political economy* (pp. 90-143). Cambridge, England: Cambridge University Press.

Loewenstein, G. F., Thompson, L., & Bazerman, M. H. (1989). Social utility and decision making in interpersonal contexts. *Journal of Personality and Social Psychology, 57*, 426-441.

Loomes, G., & Sugden, R. (1982). Regret theory: An alternative theory of rational choice under uncertainty. *The Economic Journal, 92*, 805-824.

Luce, R. D., & Raiffa, H. (1957). *Games and decisions: Introduction and critical survey*. New York, NY: Wiley.

Lykken, D. T. (1991). What's wrong with psychology anyway? In D. Cicchetti & W. M. Grove (Eds.), *Thinking clearly about psychology, Vol.1: Matters of public interest* (pp. 3-39). Minneapolis, MN: University of Minnesota Press.

McClintock, C. G. (1972). Social motivation – A set of propositions. *Behavioral Science*, *17*, 438-454.

McClintock, C. G., & Liebrand, W. B. G. (1988). Role of interdependence structure, individual value orientation, and another's strategy in social decision making: A transformational analysis. *Journal of Personality and Social Psychology*, *55*, 396-409.

Murnighan, J. K., & Roth, A. E. (1983). Expecting continued play in prisoner's dilemma games. *Journal of Conflict Resolution*, *27*, 279-300.

Parks, C. D., Henager, R. F., & Scamahorn, S. D. (1996). Trust and reactions to messages of intent in social dilemmas. *Journal of Conflict Resolution*, *40*, 134-151.

Quigley-Fernandez, B., Malkis, F. S., & Tedeschi, J. T. (1985). Effects of first impressions and reliability of promises on trust and cooperation. *British Journal of Social Psychology*, *24*, 29-36.

Ross, L., Greene, D., & House, P. (1977). An egocentric bias in social perception and attribution processes. *Journal of Experimental Social Psychology*, *13*, 279-301.

Savage, L. J. (1954). *The Foundations of statistics*. New York, NY: Wiley.

Snijders, C. (1996). *Trust and commitments*. Amsterdam, Netherlands: Thesis Publishers.

Snijders, C., & Keren, G. (1996). *Trust is in the eye of the beholder: The effect of physical appearance on trust*. ISCORE Paper No. 35., Utrecht University.

Van Lange, P. A. M., & Kuhlman, D. M. (1994). Social value orientations and impressions of partner's honesty and intelligence: A test of the might versus morality effect. *Journal of Personality and Social Psychology*, *67*, 126-141.

Yamagishi, T. (1986). The provision of a sanctioning system as a public good. *Journal of Personality and Social Psychology*, *51*, 110-116.

# APPENDIX

## From Game Theoretical to Statistical Models

Earlier we showed that Actor 1 trusts Actor 2 in a Trust Game $(S, P, R, T)$ if and only if $p_{2,1} > \dfrac{U_1(P,P) - U_1(S,T)}{U_1(R,R) - U_1(S,T)}$, and subsequently considered different "effective" utility functions $U$. We now add an assumption about the effective probability $p_{2,1}$, which enables statistical testing of our hypotheses.

For ease of exposition, consider the guilt model as an example. In the guilt model, Actor 2 honors trust if and only if $\gamma_2 > (T - R) / (T - S)$. We assume that the way in which subject $i$ in the role of Actor 1 assesses the probability that $\gamma_2 > (T - R) / (T - S)$, depends linearly on personality characteristics of Actor $i$ and on the relevant characteristic of the game $g$, $(T - R) / (T - S)$:

$$p_{2,1}^{ijg} = \Pr\left\{ \left[ \gamma_2^i > \frac{T-R}{T-S} \right]_g \right\} = \Phi\left( \alpha_0 + \alpha_i'\zeta_i + \alpha_2 \left[ \frac{T-R}{T-S} \right]_g + \varepsilon_1^{ijg} \right), \quad (8)$$

with $\alpha_2 < 0$, $\zeta_i$ the (vector of) characteristics of individual $i$, $(T - R) / (T - S)$ the relevant characteristic with respect to honoring trust in the Trust Game $g$ for the guilt model, and the $\varepsilon$'s independently distributed error terms with $\varepsilon_1^{ijg} \sim N(0, \sigma^2)$. The standard normal cumulative distribution function $\Phi$ was added to make sure that $0 \le p_{2,1}^{ijg} \le 1$. It then follows by substitution and rearranging that

$$\Pr\{\text{Actor 1 trusts}\} = \Pr\left\{ p_{2,1}^{ijg} > \left[ \frac{P-S}{R-S} \right]_g \right\} =$$

$$= \Pr\left\{ \varepsilon_1^{ijg} > \left[ \Phi^{-1}\left( \frac{P-S}{R-S} \right) \right]_g - \alpha_0 - \alpha_1'\zeta_i - \alpha_2 \left[ \frac{T-R}{T-S} \right]_g \right\} \quad (9)$$

$$= \Phi\left( \frac{\alpha_0}{\sigma} + \frac{\alpha_1'\zeta_i}{\sigma} + \frac{\alpha_2}{\sigma}\left[ \frac{T-R}{T-S} \right]_g - \frac{1}{\sigma}\left[ \Phi^{-1}\left( \frac{P-S}{R-S} \right) \right]_g \right).$$

Hence, this renders a statistically testable probit model

$$\text{Trust} = \frac{\alpha_0}{\sigma} + \frac{\alpha_1'}{\sigma}\zeta_i + \frac{\alpha_2}{\sigma}\left[ \frac{T-R}{T-S} \right]_g - \frac{1}{\sigma}\left[ \Phi^{-1}\left( \frac{P-S}{R-S} \right) \right]_g, \quad (10)$$

which incorporates (vectors of) Actor $i$'s characteristics, and characteristics of the Trust Game $g$. For convenience and ease of interpretation because $\Phi^{-1}(P - S) / (R - S) \approx 2.86(P$

$- S) / (R - S) - 1.44$ for $0.07 < (P - S) / (R - S) < 0.80$ (as will be the case in our data), we transform the model to the probit model

$$\text{Trust} = \frac{\alpha_0}{\sigma} + \frac{\alpha_1'}{\sigma} \zeta_i + \frac{\alpha_2}{\sigma} \left[ \frac{T - R}{T - S} \right]_g - \frac{2.86}{\sigma} \left[ \frac{P - S}{R - S} \right]_g + \frac{1.44}{\sigma} . \tag{11}$$

In this model, the estimated coefficient of $(P - S) / (R - S)$ renders an explicit estimate for $\sigma$ (the estimated coefficient should accordingly be negative). Therefore, contrary to standard applications of probit models, the model is identifiable. Because $\alpha_2$ should be negative (the larger $(T - R) / (T - S)$, the less likely that Actor 1 trusts Actor 2), the estimated coefficient of $(T - R) / (T - S)$ should also be negative. Hence, the analyses with the decision to trust as the dependent variable and $(P - S) / (R - S)$ and $(T - R) / (T - S)$ as the game indices test a probit model

$$\text{Trust} = \beta_0 + \beta_1' \zeta_i + \beta_2 \left[ \frac{T - R}{T - S} \right]_g + \beta_3 \left[ \frac{P - S}{R - S} \right]_g \tag{12}$$

with $\zeta_i$ an operationalization of variables that characterize Actor 1's personal trait and $(P - S) / (R - S)$ and $(T - R) / (T - S)$ as the operationalization of variables that characterize the game at stake.[17]

# 16 Common Pool Resource (CPR) Dilemmas With Incomplete Information

**Ramzi Suleiman**
*University of Haifa*

**David V. Budescu**
*University of Illinois at Urbana-Champaign*

Numerous societies are facing rapid exhaustion of their natural resources because of overconsumption. The disappearance of rain forests, depletion of fresh water resources in arid areas, pollution of breathable air in our congested cities, and the rapid decline of whale and lobster populations are only some of the many pernicious problems plaguing industrial and agricultural societies alike. The control and distribution of these rapidly shrinking resources constitute serious policy and management problems. They also raise new theoretical issues, which in turn have stimulated much experimental investigation by social scientists.

Following the seminal work of Olson (1965) and Hardin (1968), recent theories of collective choice appear to have concluded that individuals competing for limited resources are locked into a struggle that in extreme cases, may lead to the destruction of the resource. This theoretical conclusion has received only limited empirical support. There is empirical evidence from many societies that people using Common Pool Resources (CPR) have devised their own rules to limit or regulate individual requests in many ingenious ways that avoid, or at least delay, the "tragedy of the commons" (Ostrom, Walker, & Gardner, 1992). There is additional evidence that individuals engage in cooperative and pro-social behavior even in the absence of such societal mechanisms (Dawes & Thaler, 1988). This apparent contradiction between theoretical predictions and empirical evidence has given rise to a systematic program of experimental research on requests from limited shared resources (e.g., Allison & Messick, 1990; Gardner, Ostrom & Walker, 1990; Hackett,

388 SULEIMAN AND BUDESCU

Schlager, & Walker, 1994; Kramer & Brewer, 1984; Rutte, Wilke & Messick, 1987; Samuelson & Messick, 1986a, 1986b; Samuelson, Messick, Rutte, & Wilke, 1984).

The dilemma faced by each group member in these experiments is between the individual interest in harvesting as large a share of the CPR as possible and the collective interest in reaching Pareto optimal solutions. This dilemma has been often characterized as a clash between collective rationality, which induces and fosters cooperation, and individual rationality, which induces selfish and competitive behavior.

A major dimension on which these experiments differ from one another concerns the possibility of replenishment of the CPR. Resources are *renewable* when a natural replacement rate (typically greater than one) can be defined; they are *exhaustible*, otherwise. The former kind of resources has led to the construction of multistage decision tasks, and the latter to the construction of a sequence of independent single-stage tasks.

A second dimension concerns the presence or absence of face-to-face communication among the users of CPR. Experimental research on face-to-face communication in CPR tasks and more general public goods experiments has shown that communication is a powerful tool for enhancing efficiency by increasing cooperation (Dawes, 1980; Ledyard, 1995).

A third dimension concerns the type and amount of information that users have about CPR. A common assumption underlying the just-mentioned studies is that the size of CPR or its productivity are known with precision by all the group members. The plausibility and generality of this assumption have been questioned by Suleiman and Rapoport (1988), who argued that typical CPR dilemmas are characterized by some degree of uncertainty. Such uncertainty reflects incomplete, unreliable, or possibly biased information regarding the size of the resource in question. For example, a few nations (Norway, Japan) have decided recently not to respect the internationally imposed quotas on whaling. Their reasoning has been that the estimates used to determine those quotas are outdated and systematically undercount the whale population. Similar disagreements among experts have been expressed with regard to the size of water reserves in many arid areas or size of underground oil reserves.

Uncertainty about the size of CPR reflects private information, optimistic (wishful) or pessimistic thinking, or other self-serving biases. It is, of course, impossible to capture all these factors (which are to a large degree context dependent) in laboratory experiments. To incorporate this (environmental) uncertainty in the experimental investigation of CPR dilemmas, we have assumed – as is common in experimental studies of noncooperative games with incomplete information – that the size of CPR is a random variable with a commonly known distribution function, and constructed an experimental research paradigm to study it. A major purpose of our research on CPR problems was to investigate – both theoretically and experimentally – the effects of systematic changes in the amount of uncertainty about the size of CPR on the appropriators' consumption, and on the groups' efficiency in managing the uncertain resource.

A fourth dimension, which was not systematically studied in earlier CPR experiments, concerns the protocol of play (Harrison & Hirshleifer, 1989), which determines the information that each player has about the behavior of the other group members when it is his or her turn to state a request from CPR. In the studies reported here, we investigated, both theoretically and experimentally, several protocols of play, corresponding to different information structures. Under the simultaneous protocol of play, players make their requests from the common pool simultaneously and anonymously. Under the sequential protocol of play, individual requests are made in an exogenously determined order, which is common knowledge, such that each player knows his or her position in the sequence and the requests of the players who have preceded him or her in the sequence. A third protocol examined in our experiments is the positional order protocol of play. Under this protocol, each player is informed about his or her position in the sequence, but not about the requests of those who have preceded him or her.

To motivate the positional order protocol of play, notice that the sequential protocol is characterized by two distinctive features: each member $j$ of the group is informed accurately about his or her position in the sequence ($j = 1, 2, \ldots, n$), and the total requests of players $1, 2, \ldots, j$-1, who preceded him or her in the sequence, denoted by $k_{j-1}$. Under the positional order protocol of play, the first assumption is satisfied but the second is not. The positional order protocol raises an important issue concerning a major distinction between *priority in time* and *priority in information*. We talk about priority in information if knowledge of the outcomes of event A is given when event B takes place, and about priority in time if the occurrence of event A is known to precede in time the occurrence of event B. von Neumann and Morgenstern (1947) explicitly recognized this distinction and considered it in some length when comparing preliminarity (priority in information) and anteriority (priority in time). Priority in information implies priority in time, but the reverse is not necessarily true, as event A may be known to occur before event B but its outcome remains unknown.

Modern game theory does not recognize priority in time; only priority in information is captured by the conceptual structure of games in extensive form. Therefore, the positional order protocol allows the examination of a fundamental question, namely, whether priority in time, which is not accompanied by priority in information, affects interactive behavior in a systematic manner.

A fourth protocol of play, which we mention briefly, is the cumulative protocol of play (Budescu, Au, & Chen, 1997). Under this protocol, each player is informed about the total amount requested, $k$, but not about his or her position in the sequence. This implies that under this protocol, players have priority in information, rather than time.

The major goals of the research program described here were to investigate the effects of resource uncertainty, and of different information structures – embedded in different protocols of play – on individual and group behavior in CPR situations. This chapter outlines the research paradigm implemented in our studies, describes theoretical models for predicting behavior in CPR situations under uncertainty and under different protocols of play, derives qualitative predictions based on these models, describes several experiments, and summarizes their major findings.

## THE CPR DILEMMA GAME

The CPR dilemma game is a single-stage noncooperative $n$-person game in which a group of $n$ players have access to a CPR whose size, denoted by $X$, is unknown. Rather, $X$ is a random variable with a commonly known distribution function. Each group member $j$ ($j = 1, 2, \ldots, n$) can request any amount, $r_j$, from the CPR. The individual payoff, $p_j$, is determined by comparing the total group request $r = \sum r_j$ with the random resource. If the resource contains $x$ units, then the payoff, $p_j$, is given by:

$$p_j = \begin{cases} r_j, & \text{if } r \leq x \\ 0, & \text{otherwise.} \end{cases} \qquad (1)$$

This payoff function is used to model cases where the units of the common resource are not provided in smoothly increasing amounts as the level of requests increases. Rather, it assumes the existence of a critical value or a threshold that, if exceeded, prevents provision of the requests. Although this type of payoff function seems restrictive, Taylor (1987) noted that some ecological systems such as lakes, rivers, the atmosphere, and fisheries can normally be exploited up to some critical level while largely maintaining much of their use value. If exploitation rates go beyond this critical level, use value falls catastrophically. With many fisheries, for example, once the population has fallen below some critical value that is necessary to maintain a viable breeding stock, the species will rapidly cease to be commercially exploitable or disappear altogether. Similarly, river water will become undrinkable once the pollution level exceeds some critical value. Examples of man-made CPRs for which this rule applies are electric power stations and large mainframe computers that fail under excessive demand.

In all of our experiments we have assumed that the CPR is distributed uniformly over the interval $[\alpha, \beta]$. Thus,

$$f(x) = \begin{cases} 1/(\beta - \alpha), & \text{if } \alpha \le x \le \beta \\ 0, & \text{otherwise.} \end{cases} \tag{2}$$

This assumption is introduced to simplify the task, as the uniform distribution can be easily explained and illustrated to subjects. To prevent unreasonable requests, which are irrelevant to the game but can distort certain statistics computed from the data, we restrict the individual requests by imposing $0 \le r_j \le \beta, j = 1, 2, \ldots, n$.

## THEORY

Our experimental research has been driven by noncooperative $n$-person game theory for which the Nash equilibrium is the major solution concept. To derive the equilibrium solution, the utility functions of the $n$ players must be specified. We have assumed that the $n$ players have a power utility function $u(p_j) = (p_j)^c$ with a common exponent $c$ ($c > 0$). Power utility functions allow for risk aversion ($c < 1$), risk seeking ($c > 1$), and risk neutrality ($c = 1$). There is ample evidence supporting the use of this function in studies of both individual decision making (e.g., Galanter, 1962; Galanter & Hollman, 1967; Tversky & Kahneman, 1992) and interactive behavior (Rapoport & Suleiman, 1993; Suleiman & Rapoport, 1992).

Assuming a power utility function with a common parameter c, the symmetric Nash equilibrium solution for the simultaneous protocol of play has been derived by Rapoport and Suleiman (1992):

$$r_s^* = \begin{cases} \alpha/n, & \text{if } \alpha \ge cn(\beta - \alpha) \\ c\beta/(1 + nc) & \text{if } \alpha < cn(\beta - \alpha) \end{cases} \tag{3}$$

for $= 1, 2, \ldots, n$. In the special case of linear utility functions ($c = 1$), Eq. 3 reduces to

$$r_s^* = \begin{cases} \alpha/n, & \text{if } \alpha \ge n(\beta - \alpha) \\ \beta/(n+1) & \text{if } \alpha < n(\beta - \alpha). \end{cases} \tag{4}$$

Under the same assumption about the players' utility functions, the subgame perfect equilibrium (SPE) solution (a refinement of the Nash equilibrium for games played in extensive form) for the sequential protocol of play has been derived by Rapoport, Budescu, and Suleiman (1993):

$$r_j^* = \begin{cases} (1+c)^{n-j}\alpha - [(1+c)^{n-j}-1]\beta - k_{j-1}, & \text{if } 0 \le k_{j-1} \le \omega \\ [c(\beta - k_{j-1})]/(1+c), & \text{if } \omega \le k_{j-1} \le \beta \\ 0, & \text{if } k_{j-1} > \beta \end{cases} \quad (5)$$

where $j = 1, 2, \ldots, n$, and $\omega = (1 + c)^{n-j+1}\alpha - [(1 + c)^{n-j+1} - 1]\beta$. In the special case of linear utility functions, Equation 5 reduces to

$$r_j^* = \begin{cases} 2^{n-j}\alpha - (2^{n-k}-1)\beta - k_{j-1}, & \text{if } 0 \le k_{j-1} \le \eta \\ (\beta - k_{j-1})/2, & \text{if } \eta \le k_{j-1} \le \beta \\ 0, & \text{if } k_{j-1} > \beta \end{cases} \quad (6)$$

where $\eta = 2^{n-j+1}\alpha - (2^{n-j+1} - 1)\beta$.

Game theory considers information about priority in time irrelevant. Hence, it predicts that the simultaneous and positional order protocols will elicit the same behavior. In light of Schelling's (1960) analysis of coordination games and questions raised by Kreps (1990) about priority in time, we (Budescu, Suleiman, & Rapoport, 1995a; Rapoport, 1997; Suleiman, Budescu, & Rapoport, 1994) formulated an alternative hypothesis asserting that information about the order of play – or priority in time – affects interactive behavior in a systematic manner. The strong version of this hypothesis asserts that each player assumes that *all* the group members will take advantage of their position in the sequence and expect others to do so. As a result, players will behave as if the requests of all the players preceding them in the sequence are known. Consequently, a player will expect each of the other players to make requests that are consistent with SPE for the sequential protocol (Equations 5 and 6). The weak version of the alternative hypothesis states that only *some* of the players will interpret the positional order protocol as just described, whereas the others will treat information about priority in time as irrelevant. As a result, the positional order protocol under this weak version will yield mean requests that fall between the requests obtained under the simultaneous and sequential protocols.

Figure 16.1 portrays the equilibrium requests for the simultaneous (Equation 4) and sequential (Equation 6) protocols of play. The figure depicts the equilibrium request functions for members of groups of size $n = 5$. It assumes risk neutrality (linear utility functions) and a family of uniform resource distributions with a common expected value of $\mu = 500$ and ranges from 0 ($\alpha = 500$, $\beta = 500$) – the case of no uncertainty – to 1000 ($\alpha = 0$, $\beta = 1000$) – the case of maximal uncertainty. The broken line ($r_s^*$) shows the Nash equilibrium request function for the simultaneous protocol (Equation 4), and the five solid lines ($r_j^*$, $j = 1, 2, 3, 4, 5$) show the SPE request functions for the five players under the sequential protocol (Equation 6). Figure 16.2 portrays similar request

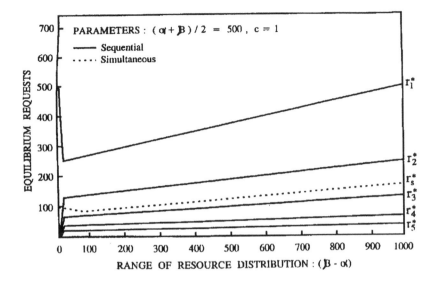

Fig. 16.1. The equilibrium requests for the simultaneous and sequential protocols under the assumption of risk neutrality ($c = 1$).

functions for the same parameters for risk-averse players (with $c = \frac{1}{2}$).

## QUALITATIVE PREDICTIONS

The equilibrium solutions allow for quantitative predictions (see Figures 16.1 and 16.2); testing them requires the assessment of individual utility functions. It is well known that utility functions in interactive decision tasks are task-dependent and notoriously difficult to assess (Bazerman, Lowenstein, & White, 1992; Lowenstein, Thompson, & Bazerman, 1989), even if one accepts the assumption that they are of the same form. Because of these difficulties, the emphasis in most of our research has been on *qualitative* predictions derived from the equilibrium solution. The major predictions are listed here; most of them can be visually verified directly from Figs. 16.1 and 16.2.

1. *Provision of the requests.* The equilibrium solution for the simultaneous protocol is a piece-wise linear function with a "kink" point at $\alpha^* = cn(\beta - \alpha)$. If $c = 1$, as in Fig. 16.1, then $\alpha^* = 90.91$. The equilibrium solution implies

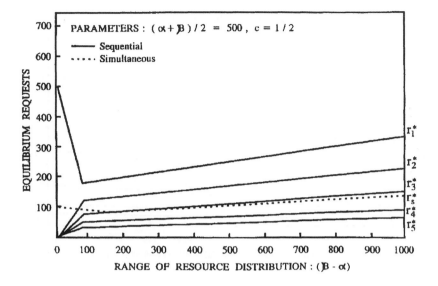

Fig. 16.2. The equilibrium requests for the simultaneous and sequential protocols for risk averse players with $c = 0.5$.

---

that requests will be granted with certainty below $\alpha^*$, and will only be granted probabilistically, otherwise. We can label the two segments of the function to the left and right of the "kink" point the "certainty range" and "uncertainty range," respectively. A similar prediction applies to the sequential protocol, but with a different "kink point".

2. *The CPR uncertainty effect.* For the simultaneous and sequential protocols and all players, the segments of the equilibrium lines that are in the uncertainty range increase linearly in the CPR range, $\beta - \alpha$. Therefore, individual requests in this range are predicted to increase linearly as the uncertainty about the exact value of the CPR increases. It follows that this prediction also holds for the positional order protocol (regardless of whether the players approach it as a sequential or simultaneous protocol).

3. *The position effect.* Under the sequential protocol the equilibrium requests of the n players in the uncertainty range form a geometric series, such that:

$$r_{j+1}^* = \frac{r_j^*}{1+c},$$

(7)

$j = 1, 2, \ldots, n$. As a result, players appearing earlier in the sequence should request more and regard their positions as more advantageous. A similar, although weaker, effect can be predicted to exist under the positional order protocol.

4. *The protocol effect.* Let h denote the minimum of the two "kink" points (see Equations 3 and 5). Assuming the same group size, $n$, and utility parameter, $c$, under the simultaneous and the sequential protocols, it follows that for $(\beta-\alpha) \leq h$, the group equilibrium request under the two protocols is equal to $\alpha$. Alternatively, for $(\beta-\alpha) > h$ it is possible to show that equal size groups will never demand less under the sequential than the simultaneous protocol, and that they will request more as the uncertainty about the resource size increases. For the positional order protocol, the weak hypothesis predicts that requests will be intermediary between the demands of the sequential and simultaneous protocols.

5. *The nonmonotonicity effect.* Under the simultaneous protocol, individual requests will first decrease linearly and then increase linearly as the range of the CPR increases. Under the sequential protocol, this piece-wise pattern is only predicted for the first player in the sequence. The request functions for the other $n - 1$ players will be monotonically increasing (see Figs. 16.1 and 16.2).

# THE EXPERIMENTAL PARADIGM

Several experiments have been designed to test the various implications of the equilibrium solutions just described and compare them to other, psychologically motivated, models, which are not described in the current chapter (Budescu, Rapoport, & Suleiman, 1992; Rapoport, Budescu, & Suleiman, 1993). Although these experiments were designed to test distinct predictions and, as such, used different variations of the CPR game and manipulated a variety of independent variables, they all used the same basic paradigm and methodology. The experimental paradigm assured that all the assumptions underlying the equilibrium solutions for the single-stage CPR game were satisfied, and the subjects were properly motivated.

In all the studies, subjects (primarily undergraduate students at the University of Haifa in Israel) were recruited to participate in group decision making experiments by advertisements posted on bulletin boards on campus. The advertisements informed (potential) participants that they would receive monetary rewards contingent on performance. Subjects were run in groups of size $n$. Every possible effort was made not to include acquaintances in the same group.

On arrival to the laboratory, subjects were randomly assigned to private and soundproof cubicles, each containing a terminal connected to a computer. No communication or coordination was permitted during the study. Subjects were given on-screen and written descriptions of the experiment explaining the nature of the task, its various parameters, the payoffs, and the experimental setup.

In a typical experiment, several CPR games with various levels of uncertainty were presented to the subjects in some random order and replicated several times. A subset of the games (typically half) were followed by few simple questions asking subjects to estimate some key quantities such as the amount requested by others in the group and the size of the random resource. These quantities were used in some of the secondary analyses. We never found any evidence indicating that posing these questions biased the subjects' decisions, so in the sequel we do not distinguish between trials with and without questions.

To eliminate reciprocal learning, reputation, and other sequential effects, the subjects' identities were not revealed (players were identified as number 1, 2, etc.), and no trial-by-trial feedback was provided about individual or total group requests, the actual value of the resource, and the outcome for the trial. Hence, we treat the requests on the various replications as if they were gathered in independent single-stage games. During the experiment the resource and the requests were described in terms of points. However, in all the experiments the subjects earned real money contingent on their (and the other group members) requests on a subset of trials, and according to a predetermined points-to-money conversion rate.

In a typical experiment conducted under the simultaneous protocol all subjects were instructed to key in their requests at the same time. A game was completed after all n requests were registered. In experiments conducted under the sequential or positional order protocols, each player was assigned a position at the beginning of the trial, and was instructed to make a request only after the previous players registered their demands. In the sequential protocol the subject assigned to the j'th position (j=1, 2, . . ., n) was also informed of the total amount requested by the (j-1) previous players (but not their individual requests). Under the cumulative protocol subjects knew only the total amount already requested, but not their position in the sequence. No time limits were enforced, and subjects were allowed to key in the requests at their own pace.

The instructions emphasized that:

1. Each group consists of $n$ players.
2. No communication is allowed before or during the experiment.
3. The experiment consists of several independent trials with no feedback between trials about requests or outcomes.
4. At the beginning of each trial specific information (e.g., trial number, limits of the resource distribution, player's position, etc.) will be provided.
5. Each subject may request any amount from the resource. If the total group request exceeds the actual resource for that trial, subjects get nothing. Otherwise, each subject is granted his or her request.

**TABLE 16.1**
**List of Experiments on CPR Games**

| Study Number | Reference | Protocol(s) | Ranges of Resource | Group Size (n) | Sample Size |
|---|---|---|---|---|---|
| 1 | Rapoport et al., 1992 (Study 1) | Sim. | 0,250,500, 750, 1000. | 5 | 55 |
| 2 | Rapoport et al., 1992 (Study 2) | Sim. | 0,500,1000. | 5 | 25 |
| 3 | Rapoport et al., 1993 | Seq. | 0,500,1000. | 5 | 45 |
| 4 | Budescu, Suleiman, et al., 1995 (Study 1) | Pos. | 0,500,1000. | 5 | 45 |
| 5 | Budescu, Suleiman, et al., 1995 (Study 2) | Sim., Seq., Pos. | 0,60,100, 160,520,760, 880,1000. | 2 | 72 |
| 6 | Budescu, Suleiman, et al., 1995 (Study 2) | Sim., Seq., Pos. | 0,40,160, 760,1000. | 3 | 108 |
| 7 | Budescu, Suleiman, et al., 1995 (Study 1) | Sim. | 5,70,200, 380,560. | 5 | 60 |
| 8 | Budescu, Suleiman, et al., 1995 (Study 2) | Sim., Seq. | 5,200,560. | 5 | 60 |
| 9 | Suleiman et al., 1996 (Study 1) | Seq. | 0,500,1000. | 5 | 90 |
| 10 | Suleiman et al., 1996 (Study 2) | Seq. | 0,500,1000. | 5 | 90 |
| 11 | Budescu et al., 1996 | Sim.,Seq., Pos.,Cum. | 0. | 5 | 87 |

6. At the conclusion of the experiment a subset of games will be selected and the amounts won by each subject on these trials will be calculated and paid in full.

## Independent Variables

A large number of independent variables were manipulated in the various studies using both between- and within-subjects designs. These included:

1. The group size ($n = 2$, 3 or 5).
2. The protocol of play (simultaneous, sequential, positional, or cumulative).
3. The level of environmental uncertainty: In all cases the subjects were informed of the lower ($\alpha$) and upper ($\beta$) bound of the uniform resource. The mean value of the resource was kept constant at $\mu = (\alpha + \beta)/2 = 500$ points. This allowed for distributions with a range of $R = (\beta - \alpha)$ from 0 to 1,000.
4. The position in the sequence: In the sequential and positional protocols subjects were assigned to the first, second, . . ., n'th position in the sequence. In most cases subjects were rotated among the $n$ positions, but in one study (Suleiman, Rapoport, & Budescu, 1966) subjects were assigned fixed position in all trials.
5. Assignment of positions: In most experiments subjects were arbitrarily assigned to positions. In a recent study of the sequential protocol (Suleiman et al., 1996), position rights were "acquired" by the subjects.
6. Monetary payoffs: The money to points conversion rates were equal for all players, except in one study (Budescu, Rapoport, & Suleiman, 1990), in which asymmetry was induced by using different (logarithmic) points-to-money conversion rates.

Table 16.1 provides a summary of the 11 experiments that are reviewed in this chapter.

# RESULTS

Rather than describing each study separately, the experimental findings are briefly summarized in terms of the major predictions of the equilibrium solution outlined above. First, we discuss the results obtained under the simultaneous protocol, then the results of the sequential protocol, and finally the closely related positional order.

## The Simultaneous Protocol

The expected requests for any individual in a group of n players with a common power utility function with exponent, $c$, are characterized by the following three properties:

**TABLE 16.2**
**Mean and Standard Deviation of Individual Requests As a Function of the Range of the CPR Under the Simultaneous Protocol in Groups of Size 5**

| Range of Resource | Source of Data | Sample Size | Mean Request | Pooled SD |
|---|---|---|---|---|
| 0 | Exps. 1,2 11 | 167 | 106 | 55 |
| 5 | Exps. 7,8 | 120 | 113 | 75 |
| 70 | Exp. 7 | 60 | 115 | 78 |
| 200 | Exps. 7,8 | 120 | 122 | 85 |
| 250 | Exp. 1 | 55 | 125 | 96 |
| 380 | Exp. 7 | 60 | 110 | 72 |
| 500 | Exps. 1,2 | 80 | 122 | 103 |
| 560 | Exps. 7,8 | 120 | 137 | 109 |
| 750 | Exp. 1 | 55 | 135 | 112 |
| 1000 | Exps. 1,2 | 80 | 162 | 130 |

*Note.* Rounded to nearest integer.

1. For precisely specified resources, that is, for $\beta-\alpha = 0$, the players should request a "fair share" of the resource: $r^* = \alpha/n$;
2. As the uncertainty increases up to the "kink" point, $(\beta-\alpha) = 2\mu/(2nc+1)$, the requests should *decrease* linearly. The lowest predicted request is $r^* = 2\mu c/(2nc+1)$;
3. From the kink point up to most extreme uncertainty, the requests are expected to *increase* linearly. For the highest uncertainty the predicted request is $r^* = 2\mu c/(nc+1)$.

These three predictions imply that the request is a piece-wise linear, single dipped function of $(\beta-\alpha)$. The location of the "kink" point and the two slopes of the function depend on the expected resource size, $\mu$, the size of the group, $n$, and the exponent of the utility function, $c$. In general, for more risk-averse subjects, the "kink" point will be located closer to the upper end of the resource range. For example, if $n = 5$ and $\mu = 500$, subjects with $c = 2$ (risk seeking), $c = 1$ (risk neutral) and, $c = 0.5$ (risk-averse) should request least when $(\beta-\alpha) = 48$, 91, and 167, respectively. Given that the range of the resource can be as high as 1,000, we expect that for most subjects the mean requests should increase as a function of resource uncertainty. However, the exact location of the "kink" point

TABLE 16.3
Proportion of Cases in Which the Total Group Request Was Less Than, or Equal, to the CPR's Expected Value ($\mu=500$) Under the Simultaneous Protocol, as a Function of the CPR's Range

| Range of Resource | Group Size | Source of Data | Number of Groups | Percentage of Provision |
|---|---|---|---|---|
| 0 | 5 | Exps. 1,2 | 16 | 47 |
| 1000 | 5 | Exps. 1,2 | 16 | 11 |
| 0 | 3 | Exp. 6 | 36 | 64 |
| 1000 | 3 | Exp. 6 | 36 | 29 |
| 0 | 2 | Exp. 5 | 36 | 96 |
| 1000 | 2 | Exp. 5 | 36 | 29 |

cannot be precisely predicted because all samples consisted, as expected, of subjects with heterogeneous attitudes towards risk (i.e., various $c$'s).

Table 16.2 summarizes the individual requests across all the games (from five different studies) in which n = 5 players made simultaneous requests from a resource with a mean of $\mu$ = 500. For each range examined, we list the relevant studies, the total number of subjects, the mean group request, and the pooled standard deviation of these requests. [1]

In all the experiments that we have conducted, the effect of the CPR range was significant. For certain resources (range = 0) the mean request is close to the "fair" request $\alpha/n$. In fact when $\beta = \alpha$, the modal request (e.g., in 81% of the cases in Experiments 1 & 2) was 100 points. When the range of the CPR was small (e.g., 10 or 70), most of the subjects requested approximately an equal share of the lower bound of the resource. But when the range of the CPR increased, the percentage of the subjects requesting $\alpha/n$ declined rapidly and, despite substantial individual differences, the mean individual requests increased. The Spearman rank correlation between the CPR range and the mean request was 0.82. The single deviation from this monotonic pattern is observed in the case of $(\beta-\alpha) = 380$, which displays an unexpected and unexplainable drop.

Similar results were obtained for smaller groups (n = 2, 3 in Budescu, Suleiman, et al., 1995) but, as predicted by the model, the effects of the CPR range were more modest for smaller groups. For example, for n = 2 the mean request was in the vicinity of (or substantially under) $\alpha/n$ for almost all ranges of the CPR. In one of our experiments (Study 1 of Budescu, Rapoport, et al., 1995), we made a special effort to locate the subjects' kink points and validate the counterintuitive nonmonotonicity effect. We found that the group results were best fitted by a single-dipped piece-wise linear pattern. The dip was located at 146, implying that most subjects were risk-averse ($c = 0.58$). More impressive results were obtained in an individual analysis: the requests of 31 (52%) of the 60 subjects were ordinally consistent with the non-monotonic prediction (compared to 13%, the expected value under chance).

Table 16.2 also shows that the variance between requests increases monotonically with the range of the resource. This result can not be accounted for by the equilibrium solution in Equation 3, which assumes uniformity in risk attitudes among all players. Rapoport and Suleiman (1992) derived an asymmetric equilibrium solution for the more general case of players with unequal risk indices. In essence, the asymmetric solution predicts that players' $j$ request, $r_j$, can be expressed as $F_j(c_1, c_2, \ldots, c_j, \ldots, c_n)\beta$, where $F_j(..)$ is a function of all the subjects' risk indices $c_1, c_2, \ldots, c_j, \ldots, c_n$, and $\beta$ is the upper limit of the resource distribution (see Rapoport & Suleiman, 1992). It can be easily shown that the standard deviation of the asymmetric equilibrium requests, $\sigma(r_j)$ is a linear function of $\beta$. To test this prediction, we calculated the ratio $\beta/\sigma(r_j)$ for the results of Study 1 from Rapoport, Budescu, Suleiman, and Weg (1992), and Study 1 from Budescu, Rapoport, et al. (1995). The $\beta$ values in the Rapoport et al. (1992) study were 500, 625, 750, 875, and 1,000. The $\beta/\sigma(r_j)$ ratios are 7.25, 6.51, 7.0, 7.81, and 7.41 respectively. For the Budescu, Rapoport, et al. (1995) study, the $\beta$ values were 505, 535, 600, 690, and 780, and the $\beta/\sigma(r_j)$ ratios are 6.01, 6.86, 7.41, 9.58, and 7.57, respectively. Thus, most ratios are, approximately, equal and are quite consistent with this model prediction.

A corollary of the systematic increase in the individual requests as a function of the CPR's range is that the likelihood of provision of the resource, at the group level, should decrease, accordingly. The test of this hypothesis depends, in part, on the (randomly sampled) size of the CPR. In order to eliminate the spurious effects of this random component, we compared the total group request with $\mu$, the expected size of the CPR, which was identical (500) in all cases. Table 16.3 presents the provision rates for groups of size 2, 3, and 5 for the two extreme cases ($\beta - \alpha = 0$ and 1,000). Table 16.3 shows a sharp drop in the rate of provision as uncertainty increases in groups of all sizes. Note, however, that coordination resulting in provision of the CPR is invariably more difficult in larger groups.

## The Sequential Protocol

Table 16.4 summarizes the mean requests made by subjects in several experiments using the sequential protocol. In all reported experiments, players participated in groups of size n = 5, and were rotated across all $n$ positions (by random assignment). The table reveals several consistent and robust trends.

**TABLE 16.4**

**Mean Individual Requests As a Function of the Range of the CPR and the Player's (Randomly Rotating) Position Under the Sequential Protocol in Groups of Size 5**

| Range of Resource | Sample Size | Player's Position | | | | | Group Total |
|---|---|---|---|---|---|---|---|
| | | 1st | 2nd | 3rd | 4th | 5th | |
| 0 (Exps. 3,9,10) | 180 | 171 | 120 | 109 | 85 | 64 | 543 |
| 5 (Exp. 8) | 60 | 162 | 112 | 110 | 81 | 61 | 525 |
| 200 (Exp. 8) | 60 | 161 | 115 | 101 | 90 | 70 | 540 |
| 500 (Exps. 3,9,10) | 180 | 160 | 117 | 106 | 124 | 110 | 617 |
| 560 (Exp. 8) | 60 | 169 | 135 | 118 | 107 | 119 | 650 |
| 1000 (Exps. 3,9,10) | 180 | 209 | 166 | 141 | 138 | 121 | 775 |
| Mean | 720 | 176 | 131 | 116 | 110 | 95 | 627 |

*Note.* All values rounded to nearest integer.

Consistent with the CPR uncertainty effect, and replicating the results from the simultaneous protocol, subjects tend to request more as the range of the CPR increases. And, confirming the position effect, there is an inverse relationship between a player's position and his or her requests. Of the 60 relevant pair-wise comparisons (10 pairs of positions for each of the six levels of the CPR range) only 6 (10%) violated the predicted ordering. The two effects were additive (none of the studies found an interaction between the position and the CPR's range) and were quite substantial.

Similar effects were found for smaller groups (Budescu, Suleiman, et al., 1995). When the CPR was shared by only n = 2 players, the first player requested, on the average, 50% more than the second (296/195), and for n = 3 the mean requests in the three positions were 254, 168, and 135, respectively. In passing, we note that a CPR with n = 2 players and a fixed resource is identical in all respects to the ultimatum game (e.g. Güth, Schmittberger, & Schwarze, 1982; Thaler, 1988). The predicted CPR "position effect" is consistent with the expectation that the sender should offer only $\varepsilon$ (barely greater than 0) to the receiver. Our results are fully consistent with the common observation that a vast

**TABLE 16.5**
**Mean Individual Requests As a Function of the Range of the CPR and the Player's (Fixed) Position Under the Sequential Protocol in Groups of Size 5**

| Range of Resource | Sample Size | Player's Position | | | | | Group Total |
|---|---|---|---|---|---|---|---|
| | | 1st | 2nd | 3rd | 4th | 5th | |
| 0 | 180 | 178 | 120 | 119 | 100 | 76 | 577 |
| 500 | 180 | 182 | 130 | 121 | 146 | 121 | 635 |
| 1000 | 180 | 241 | 168 | 181 | 166 | 150 | 907 |
| | *Mean* | 200 | 139 | 134 | 137 | 116 | 726 |

*Note.* All values rounded to nearest integer. Source: Experiments 9 and 10

majority of the offers are biased in favor of the sender (i.e., the first player), but are much more egalitarian than predicted by the equilibrium prediction.

Budescu, Rapoport, et al. (1995) analyzed the sequential requests at *the individual level*. They compared requests made by each subject in various positions, contingent on the total amount requested by the previous players, and found that in 72% of the valid cases (i.e., excluding out of range requests and the ambiguous case of equal requests), the pattern of results was consistent with the position effect predicted by the equilibrium model.

The equilibrium solution is, of course, not sensitive to the process by which players acquire their position, nor the degree of permanence of their positioning. However, the empirical results are slightly different when players are assigned (or acquire) a fixed position in the sequence. Table 16.5 summarizes results from two studies (Suleiman et al., 1996) in which subjects played multiple games in the same position, averaged across several assignment methods (for more details, see Suleiman et al., 1996). The uncertainty effect is replicated (actually it is a bit stronger) but the position effect is only partially supported. Although we observe a first mover advantage and a last mover handicap, the requests in the three central positions are practically identical. This pattern may be attributed to the stronger perceived threat of retaliation by players in the less advantageous positions.

As in the simultaneous case, systematic increases in the individual requests should affect the provision rate at the group level. Table 16.6 presents the provision rates for groups of size 2, 3, and 5 for the two extreme cases (ranges of 0 and 1,000). In all cases there is a sharp drop in the rate of provision as the uncertainty level increases. Also, similar to the simultaneous protocol, the

**TABLE 16.6**
**Proportion of Cases in Which the Total Group Request Was Less Than, or Equal, to the CPR's Expected Value ($\mu$=500) Under the Sequential Protocol, as a Function of the CPR's Range**

| Range of Resource | Group Size | Source of Data | Number of Groups | Percent of Provision |
|---|---|---|---|---|
| 0 | 5 | Exp. 3 | 15 | 64 |
| 1000 | 5 | Exp. 3 | 15 | 23 |
| 0 | 3 | Exp. 6 | 36 | 86 |
| 1000 | 3 | Exp. 6 | 36 | 19 |
| 0 | 2 | Exp. 5 | 36 | 96 |
| 1000 | 2 | Exp. 5 | 36 | 42 |

coordination required for the provision of the CPR is, invariably, more difficult in larger groups.

## The Positional Order Protocol

As explained earlier, this is a variation of the sequential protocol in which information about previous requests is withheld. This protocol was implemented in two studies with n = 5 players (Budescu, Suleiman, et al., 1995, Study 1 and Budescu et al., 1997), as well as in smaller (n = 2, 3) groups (Budescu, Suleiman, et al., 1995, Study 2). In all these experiments, the uncertainty effect was replicated. More interesting, however, is the fact that we also obtained a significant position effect. The effect was weaker than in the full information sequential protocol. This is revealed in two statistics: The requests of the players in the various positions are more equal (i.e., the slope of the mean requests on players' positions is flatter), and the percentage of individual subjects displaying this pattern is smaller. For example, Budescu, Suleiman, et al. (1995) report that for n = 2, 3, and 5 the proportion of subjects who request more when assigned to the first position than when assigned to the last one are 0.62, 0.55, and 0.64, respectively. By contrast, the corresponding proportions for the sequential protocol are 0.87, 0.78, and 0.82.

These findings indicate that the mere positioning of players in positions that are typically perceived as advantageous or disadvantageous, is sufficient to induce differential requests, but cannot account for the full effect, that is, they support the weak hypothesis outlined earlier (see Rapoport, 1997, for similar examples in other games). This effect was clearly supported by the subjects' reports about the behavior of other players. When subjects in various positions were asked to estimate the total requests of all previous and subsequent movers, they consistently expected the first $X$ players to request more than the last $X$ players in the group ($X = 1,2, \ldots$, n-1). For example, Budescu, Suleiman, et al. (1995) reported that when subjects in the triad experiment were assigned to the middle position, they estimated that the first mover requested 196 points and anticipated that the last will settle for 162 (interestingly, and consistent with the position effect, the mean request in the second position was 170, i.e., between these two values[2]).

## The Protocol Effect

In a variety of studies we have compared the total requests made by groups of a given size using different protocols of play. For example, Budescu et al. (1992) compared the requests of independent groups of n = 5 using the simultaneous and sequential protocols; Budescu, Rapoport, et al. (1995, Study 2) compared the same two protocols in a within group design (i.e., the same subjects played under the two protocols); and Budescu, Suleiman, et al. (1995, Study 2) compared performance of the simultaneous, sequential and positional order protocols for $n = 2, 3$. In all of these cases we found no significant differences between the total group requests, nor any interaction with the level of resource uncertainty.[3] This invariance of the total group requests across various protocols contradicts the equilibrium predictions. We speculate that these results are partly due to the relatively small differences between the predicted equilibrium requests under the various protocols (see Figs. 16.1 and 16.2) and the (relatively) small size of the groups.

# SUMMARY AND DISCUSSION

The results of the experiments reviewed in this chapter support several nontrivial, and occasionally counterintuitive, predictions of the game theoretical model. The uncertainty effect was confirmed under all three protocols of play (simultaneous, sequential, and positional order), and for groups of various size ($n = 2, 3, 5$). Our results also support the position effect predicted for the sequential and the positional protocols, and the nonmonotonicity effect predicted for the simultaneous protocol. We believe that the uncertainty effect, replicated in all our studies, can be of particular practical importance for helping policy makers in predicting the effect of environmental uncertainty on demands from real common resources.

Notwithstanding the relative success of the equilibrium model, note that some of its major predictions can be derived from simple, yet plausible heuristic models based on focal points considerations. Specifically, Budescu et al. (1992)

proposed two such models capable of predicting the uncertainty and nonmonotonicity effects under the simultaneous protocol, and the uncertainty and position effects under the sequential protocol (for a detailed description of these models, see Budescu et al., 1992).

From a theoretical point of view, perhaps the most interesting finding of the reviewed studies is that information about positional order was sufficient to induce a position effect similar, although weaker, to the one obtained under the sequential protocol. The significance of this finding stems from the challenge it poses to game theory, which recognizes priority in information but not priority in time. In the absence of information regarding the requests of preceding players, game theory views the CPR game played under the positional protocol as a game with symmetric information, just like the simultaneous game. The finding that a position effect emerges under these circumstances should not be viewed as a failure or weakness of game theory as a descriptive model. Instead, we opt to attribute the discrepancy between our data and the game-theoretic prediction to the theory's normative insufficiency. Specifically, we contend that temporal information is informative, independently of any additional information about actions and outcomes. For example, the sheer information that a player is preceded by others who have already played their strategies, implies that the consequences of the player's actions will be contingent on actions that had already been taken by others.

The results of the positional order experiments call for a theoretical modification of game theory that may render it capable of independently modeling the two types of information. Of course, incorporating information about time priority is fully consistent with the essence of strategic thinking. Consider the simple example of CPR with no uncertainty. Assume that there are two symmetric and rational players, that rationality is common knowledge, and that the resource consists of 10 distinct and indivisible units. The equilibrium solution under the simultaneous protocol prescribes that each player request an equal share of five units. Assume that temporal asymmetry is introduced, and Player A is the first to request from the pool. If this information is common knowledge, Player A will take advantage of the priority in time and request as much as possible from the resource. For practical reasons, Player A will request nine units, leaving only one unit to Player B. Player B, who recognizes the possible strategies available to Player A will anticipate Player A's choice, and request only one unit. This reasoning shows that common knowledge about priority in time leads to the same equilibrium solution as in the sequential protocol, even in the absence of any information about the first player choice.

The distinction between the two types of information applies to the sequential CPR as well. When Player B is informed that the first mover has requested a given amount, say seven units, the player learns not only the quantity of resources available in the impoverished pool. He or she also learns that Player A has already committed to an irreversible action and has created a new reality that one must accommodate to when choosing his or her actions.

## CPR and the Ultimatum Game

For the certainty condition ($\beta$-$\alpha$ = 0), the two players sequential CPR dilemma is structurally identical to the well-known ultimatum game. Larrick and Blount (1995) pointed out that despite their structural similarity, the ultimatum and CPR games are quite different in terms of their social contexts. In contrast to ultimatum bargaining games, which are perceived in the context of power relations, CPR games are perceived in the context of affinity relations. They found that under the ultimatum condition, subjects behaved in a more self interested manner than they did under the resource dilemma condition. Our results from the dyadic case (n = 2) and a fixed resource ($\beta$-$\alpha$ = 0) of 500 points (Budescu, Suleiman, et al., 1995, Experiment 2) show that the average requests made by the first and second players were 253, and 211 points respectively. Thus, the mean request of the first player (the "offer" in ultimatum terms) constitutes 50.6% of the resource, that is, only slightly more than an equal split, and considerably less than the almost 60% mean demand obtained in several ultimatum experiments (Güth et al., 1982; Kahneman et al., 1986; Suleiman, 1996). However, when we look only at those cases where the payoffs of the two players add to the total resource (500) the typical ultimatum game results reappear, with the first mover requesting 292 points (58.3% of the CPR).

In the same spirit, the $n$-person sequential CPR game under certainty can be viewed as a generalization of the ultimatum game for $n > 2$ players. In this generalized game, a player occupying the $j$'th position in the sequence ($1 < j \leq n$) is informed about the total requests of the preceding j-1 players. The player can "reject" the offer by requesting an amount that exceeds the remaining portion of the resource, that is, $r_j > (x - k_{j-1})$. The SPE for the generalized ultimatum game prescribes that the first player should demand almost all the "pie." Our results for n = 3 (Budescu, Suleiman, et al., 1995), and n = 5 (Rapoport et al., 1993; and summary in Table 16.5), illustrate that the subgame equilibrium for the generalized ultimatum games is not a good descriptive model of behavior. On the average, neither the first player, nor any of the following players, took advantage of their ultimatum position vis a vis their successors. In those cases where late movers thought the previous players requested too much, they did not hesitate to reject their insultingly low offers. It seems that the shift towards less egalitarian requests is more pronounced in games with larger groups ($n$ = 3, 5), than in the dyadic game. We hope that future experiments with structurally equivalent games framed as $n$-person CPRs and $n$-person ultimatum games will shed further light on the relationship between the two games.

# ACKNOWLEDGMENTS

Professor Amnon Rapoport was a full partner in most papers reviewed in this chapter. We thank him for shaping our thinking and guiding our work on this topic.

Doctors Gideon Keren and Craig Parks provided useful comments on an earlier version of this chapter.

The work summarized in this chapter was supported by grants SES 9107439 and 9122686 from NSF, and by a grant from the Israeli National Academy of Science and Humanities.

# ENDNOTES

1. The pooled variance is the average of the within-study variances, weighted by the respective degrees of freedom.
2. These results are based on 90 subjects and 5 levels of resource uncertainty.
3. In fact, the subjects' estimates of the size of the random resource are identical in the various protocols.

# REFERENCES

Allison, S. T., & Messick D. M. (1990). Social decision heuristics and the use of shared resources. *Journal of Behavioral Decision Making, 3*, 195-204.

Bazerman, M. H., Lowenstein, G. F., & White, S. B. (1992). Reversals of preferences in allocating decisions: Judging an alternative vs. choosing among alternatives. *Administrative Science Quarterly, 37*, 220-240.

Budescu, D. V., Au, W., & Chen, X. (1997). Effects of protocol of play and social orientation in resource dilemmas. *Organizational Behavior and Human Decision Processes, 69*, 179-193.

Budescu, D. V., Rapoport, A., & Suleiman, R. (1990). Resource dilemmas with environmental uncertainty and asymmetric players. *European Journal of Social Psychology, 20*, 475-487.

Budescu, D. V., Rapoport, A., & Suleiman, R. (1992). Simultaneous vs. sequential requests in resource dilemmas with incomplete information. *Acta Psychologica, 80*, 297-310.

Budescu, D. V., Suleiman, R., & Rapoport, A. (1995). Positional order and group size effects in resource dilemmas with uncertain resources. *Organizational Behavior and Human Decision Processes, 61*, 225-238.

Budescu, D. V., Rapoport, A., & Suleiman, R. (1995). Common pools dilemmas under uncertainty: Qualitative tests of equilibrium solutions. *Games and Economic Behavior, 10*, 171-201.

Dawes, R. M. (1980). Social dilemmas. *Annual Review of Psychology, 31*, 169-193.

Dawes, R. M., & Thaler, R. (1988). Anomalies: Cooperation. *Journal of Economic Perspectives, 2*, 187-197.

Galanter, E. (1962). The direct measurement of utility and subjective probability. *American Journal of Psychology, 75*, 208-220.

Galanter, E., & Hollman, G. L. (1967). Some invariances of the isosensitivity function and their implications for the utility function of money. *Journal of Experimental Psychology, 73*, 333-339.

Gardner, R., Ostrom, E., & Walker, J. (1990). The nature of common-pool resource problems. *Rationality and Society, 2*, 335-358.

Güth, W., Schmittberger, R., & Schwarze, B. (1982). An experimental analysis of ultimatum bargaining. *Journal of Economic Behavior and Organization, 3*, 367-388.

Hackett, S., Schlager, E., & Walker, J. (1994). The role of communication in resolving common dilemmas: Experimental evidence with heterogeneous appropriators. *Journal of Environmental Economics and Management, 27*, 99-126.

Hardin, G. R. (1968). The tragedy of the commons. *Science, 162*, 1243-1248.

Harrison, G., & Hirshleifer, J. (1989). An experimental evaluation of weakest-link/best-shot models of public goods. *Journal of Public Economics, 97*, 201-225.

Kahneman, D., Kaetsch, J. L. & Thaler, R. H. (1986). Fairness and the assumptions of economics. *Journal of Business, 59*, 285-300.

Kramer, R. M., & Brewer, M. B. (1984). Effects of group identity on resource use in a simulated commons dilemma. *Journal of Personality and Social Psychology, 46*, 1044-1056.

Kreps, D. M. (1990). *Game theory and economic modelling.* Oxford, England: Clarendon Press.

Larrick, R. P., & Blount, S. (1995). Social context in tacit bargaining games. In R. M. Kramer & D. M. Messick (Eds.), *Negotiations as a social process* (pp. 268-284). Newbury Park, CA: Sage.

Ledyard, J. O. (1995). Public goods: A survey of experimental research. In J. Kagel & A. E. Roth (Eds.), *Handbook of experimental economics* (pp. 111-194). Princeton, NJ: Princeton University Press.

Lowenstein, G. F., Thompson, L., & Bazerman, M. H. (1989). Social utility and decision making in interpersonal contexts. Journal of Personality and Social Psychology, 57, 426-441.

Olson, M. (1965). *The logic of collective action.* Cambridge, MA: Harvard University Press.

Ostrom, E., Walker, J., & Gardner, R. (1992). Covenants with and without a sword: Self governance is possible. *American Political Science Review, 86*, 1-14.

Rapoport, A. (1997). Order of play in strategically equivalent games in extensive form. *International Journal of Game Theory, 26*, 113-136.

Rapoport, A., & Suleiman, R. (1992). Equilibrium solutions for resource dilemmas. *Group Decision and Negotiations, 1*, 269-294.

Rapoport, A., & Suleiman, R. (1993). Incremental contribution in step-level public good games with asymmetric players. *Organizational Behavior and Human Decision Processes, 55*, 171-194.

Rapoport, A., Budescu, D. V., & Suleiman, R. (1993). Sequential requests from randomly distributed shared resources. *Journal of Mathematical Psychology, 37*, 241-265.

Rapoport, A., Budescu, D. V., Suleiman, R. & Weg, E. (1992). Social dilemmas with uniformly distributed resources. In W. G. Liebrand, D. M. Messick, & H. A. M. Wilke (Eds.), *Social dilemmas: Theoretical issues and research findings* (pp. 41-55). New York: Pergamon Press.

Rutte, C. G., Wilke, H. A. M., and Messick, D. M. (1987). Scarcity or abundance caused by people or the environment as determinants of behavior in the resource dilemma. *Journal of Experimental Social Psychology, 23*, 208-216.

Samuelson, C. D., & Messick, D. M. (1986a). Alternative structural solutions to resource dilemmas. *Organizational Behavior and Human Decision Processes, 37*, 139-155.

Samuelson, C. D., & Messick, D. M. (1986b). Inequities in access to and use of shared resources in social dilemmas. *Journal of Personality and Social Psychology, 51*, 960-967.

Samuelson, C. D., Messick, D. M., Rutte, C. G., & Wilke, H. A. M. (1984). Individual and structural solutions to resource dilemmas in two cultures. *Journal of Personality and Social Psychology, 47*, 94-104.

Schelling, T. C. (1960). *The strategy of conflict*. Cambridge, MA: Harvard University Press.

Suleiman, R. (1996). Expectations and fairness in a modified ultimatum game. *Journal of Economic Psychology, 17*, 531-554.

Suleiman, R., & Rapoport, A. (1988). Environmental and social uncertainty in single-trial resource dilemmas. *Acta Psychologica, 68*, 99-112.

Suleiman, R., & Rapoport, A. (1992). Provision of step-level public goods with continuous contribution. *Journal of Behavioral Decision Making, 5*, 133-153.

Suleiman, R., Budescu, D. V., & Rapoport, A. (1994). Positional order effects in resource dilemma games. In U. Schulz, W. Albers, & U. Mueller (Eds.), *Social dilemmas and cooperation* (pp. 55-73).Heidelberg: Springer-Verlag.

Suleiman, R., Rapoport, A., & Budescu, D. V. (1996). Fixed position and property rights in sequential resource dilemmas under uncertainty. *Acta Psychologica, 93*, 229-245.

Taylor, M. (1987). *The possibility of cooperation*. Cambridge, England: Cambridge University Press.

Thaler, R. H. (1988). Anomalies: The ultimatum game. *Journal of Economic Perspectives, 2*, 195-206.

Tversky, A., & Kahneman, D. (1992). Advances in prospect theory: Cumulative representation of uncertainty. *Journal of Risk and Uncertainty, 5*, 297-323.

von Neumann, J., & Morgenstern, D. (1947). *Theory of games and economic behavior* (2nd ed.). Princeton, NJ: Princeton University Press.

# AUTHOR INDEX

Fudenberg, D., 32, 40, 42, 50, 54,
76, 322, 328

## G

Gaebelein, J. W., 319, 328
Gaertner, S. L., 334, 336, 353
Galanter, E., 391, 408
Gale, J., 233, 235
Gardner, R., 387, 408, 409
Gary-Bobo, R., 176, 200
Gigerenzer, G., 74, 76
Gilat, S., 74, 76
Gilovich, T., 356, 382
Givens, G. H., 324, 329
Gneezy, U., 378, 382
Goldstein, D., 107, 139
Gonzalez-Vallejo, C., 70, 77
Gopher, D., 6, 19, 74-76
Goren, H., 53, 75, 299, 302, 313,
322, 328
Gouldner, A. W., 327, 328, 337,
353
Graetz, K. A., 323, 329
Green, D. M., 69, 76
Green, L., 68, 76
Greene, D., 381, 383
Greenshpan, Y., 74, 75
Grossman, S., 173, 200
Grzelak, J., 334, 353
Güth, W., 176, 200, 206, 207, 224,
232, 234, 235, 237-239, 241,
253, 266, 272, 295, 402, 407,
408
Guttman, J. M., 302, 314
Guzzo, R. A., 327, 328

## H

Hackett, S., 387, 409
Halsey, J., 327, 328
Hamburger, M., 68, 76
Hamilton, W. D., 317, 328
Hardin, G. R., 387, 409

Harley, C. B., 54, 76, 302, 314
Harrison, G. W., 97, 102, 216, 217,
235, 389, 409
Harsanyi, J. C., 139, 140, 199, 200,
229, 235, 293, 295
Harstad, R. M., 79, 102
Hastie, R., 351, 354
Healy, A. F., 66, 70, 76
Henager, R. F., 324, 330, 356, 383
Herman, P. G., 70, 77
Herrnstein, R. J., 54, 76
Hessel, S. J., 70, 77
Higgins, E. T., 337, 352
Higgs, A. C., 327, 328
Hilty, J. A., 318, 329
Hirshleifer, J., 217, 235, 389, 409
Ho, T. H., 31, 32, 34, 37, 39, 48-51,
53, 66, 70, 73, 74, 106, 110,
111, 114, 116-118, 120-125,
127-129, 132-140
Hoffman, E., 216, 217, 223, 225,
227, 235, 294, 295
Hogarth, R. M., 4, 18
Hollman, G. L., 391, 408
Holt, C. A, 366, 381
Hornstein, H. A., 336, 353
Horowitz, J., 222, 235
House, P., 381, 383
Howard, J. C., 274, 276, 277, 279,
287, 289, 292, 296
Hoyle, R. H., 323, 329
Huber, P. J., 369, 381, 382
Huck, S., 224, 232, 235
Hulbert, L. G., 320, 324, 325, 329

## I – J

Insko, C. A., 323, 329
Isen, A. M., 337, 353
Itkin, R., 74, 75
Ivanova, R., 253
Jacobson, E., 138, 140
Johnson, E. J., 8, 19, 36, 50, 74, 76,
216, 235

# SUBJECT INDEX

## A

Abstraction, 13, 17, 67, 72, 292, 337
Accuracy, 8, 9, 36, 60, 71, 180, 197, 320, 350
Adaptation, 14, 31, 67, 155, 168, 302, 311, 331, 332, 337
Adjustable reference point, 63
Alternations, 190
Altruism, 23, 27, 203, 205, 214, 224, 226, 228, 233, 352
Anonymity hypothesis, 217, 220, 227
Arithmetic depreciation, 261
Asymmetric, 90, 139, 147, 160, 178, 200, 229, 235, 321, 330, 401, 408, 409
Auction, 24, 80, 81, 85, 97, 102, 237, 238, 240-242, 244, 248-250, 252

## B

Backwards induction, 206, 212, 214, 216
Bargaining, 18, 50, 63, 88, 102, 138, 146, 170, 203, 205, 212, 214, 229-236, 326, 329, 377, 407, 409
    axiomatic, 259
    comparative model of, 234
    cube, 283
    non-cooperative, 267

Benefit, 15, 65, 196, 333-336, 342, 343, 345-347, 349-351
Best reply, 70, 72, 128, 129
Bid
    change hypothesis, 88, 89, 90, 92, 93, 94, 97, 101
    function, 79-85, 88, 90-94, 97-101, 253
    successful, 88, 89, 90, 93, 101
Bidding behavior, 237, 239, 241, 242
Bounded rationality, 7, 16, 80, 87, 105

## C

Cheap talk, 173, 174, 175, 176, 177, 178, 196, 197, 198, 199
Cognition, 77
Cognitive game theory, 54, 74, 75, 171, 200
Common pool resources (CPR), 387-390, 394-396, 400-402, 404, 406, 407
Communication, 5, 143, 144, 170, 173-176, 197, 198, 314, 317, 324, 328, 329, 388, 395, 396, 409
Computer simulation, 58, 310, 311, 315, 321, 332, 336, 342, 351
Conformity, 25, 90, 93, 97, 166
Conservative behavior, 282, 287
Cooperation, 11, 19, 28, 51, 65, 73, 87, 127, 141, 170, 299, 302,

# The Authors

**The Editors:**

Dr. David Budescu
Department of Psychology
University of Illinois at Urbana-Champaign
603 E. Daniel Street
Champaign, IL 61820
USA
dbudescu@uiuc.edu

Dr. Ido Erev
Faculty of Management and Industrial Engineering
Technion – Israel Institute of Technology
Haifa 32000
ISRAEL
erev@techunix.technion.ac.il

Dr. Rami Zwick
Department of Marketing
The Hong Kong University of Science and Technology
Clear Water Bay, Kowloon
HONG KONG
mkzwick@ust.hk

## Chapter Contributors

Dr. Gary Bolton
Smeal College of Business
Pennsylvania State University
University Park, PA 16802
USA
geb3@psu.edu

Dr. Gary Bornstein
Department of Psychology
The Hebrew University
Jerusalem, 91905
ISRAEL
msgary@pluto.mscc.huji.ac.il

Joachim Buchta
Laboratorium fuer experimentelle
Wirtschaftsforschung
Universitaet Bonn
Adenauerallee 24-42
D-53113 Bonn
GERMANY

Dr. Colin Camerer
Division of Social Sciences
California Institute of Technology
Pasadena CA 91125
USA
camerer@hss.caltech.edu

Dr. Robyn Dawes
Social and Decision Sciences
Carnegie Mellon University
Pittsburgh, PA 15213
USA
rd1b@andrew.cmu.edu

Dr. Harel Goren
Department of Psychology
The Hebrew University
Jerusalem, 91905
ISRAEL
msharel@mscc.huji.ac.il

Dr. Werner Güth
Humboldt University
Insititut fur Wirtschaftstheorie
Spandauer Str. 1
D-10178 Berlin
GERMANY
gueth@wiwi.hu-berlin.de

Dr. Teck-Hua Ho
Marketing Department
The Wharton School
University of Pennsylvania
3620 Locust Walk
Philadelphia, PA 19104
USA
teck.ho@ upenn.edu

Dr. Gideon Keren
Philosophy & Social Sciences
University of Technology,
Eindhoven
P.O. Box 513
5600 MB Eindhoven
The NETHERLANDS
G.B.Keren@tm.tue.nl

Dr. Samuel Komorita
Department of Psychology
University of Illinois at Urbana-
Champaign
603 E. Daniel street
Champaign, IL 61820
USA
skomorit@uiuc.edu

Dr. Wim Liebrand
Computing Center
University of Groningen
Groningen
The NETHERLANDS
liebrand@rc.rug.nl

Dr. David Messick
Kellog Graduate School of
Management
Northwestern University
Evanston, Il 60208
USA
dmessick@nwu.edu

Dr. Rosemarie Nagel
Department of Economics
Universitat Pompeu Fabra
Balmes 132
08008 Barcelona
SPAIN
nagel@upf.es

Dr. Jack Ochs
Department of Economics
University of Pittsburgh
Pittsburgh, PA 15260
USA
jochs@vms.cis.pitt.edu

Dr. Craig Parks
Department of Psychology
Washington State University
Pullman, WA 99164
USA
parkscd@mail.wsu.edu

Dr. Alvin Roth
Department of Economics
Harvard University
Cambridge, MA 02138
and
Harvard Business School
Boston, MA 02163
USA
al_roth@harvard.edu

Dr. Darryl A. Seale
Department of Administrative
Sciences
Kent State University
Kent, OH 44242
USA
dseale@bsa3.kent.edu

Dr. Reinhard Selten
Laboratorium fuer experimentelle
Wirtschaftsforschung
Universitaet Bonn
Adenauerallee 24-42
D-53113 Bonn
GERMANY

Dr. Chris Snijders
Department of Sociology
University of Utrecht
Heidelberglaan 1
3584 CS Utrecht
The NETHERLANDS
C.Snijders@fss.uu.nl

Dr. Ramzi Suleiman
Department of Psychology
University of Haifa
Haifa, 31905
ISRAEL
suleiman@psy.haifa.ac.il

Dr. James Sundali
Managerial Sciences / 028
University of Nevada, Reno
Reno, NV 89557
USA
jsundali@scs.unr.edu

Dr. Eythan Weg
Department of Psychology
Indiana University
Bloomington, IN 47405
USA
weg@indiana.edu

For Product Safety Concerns and Information please contact our EU
representative  GPSR@taylorandfrancis.com
Taylor & Francis Verlag GmbH, Kaufingerstraße 24, 80331 München, Germany

www.ingramcontent.com/pod-product-compliance
Ingram Content Group UK Ltd.
Pitfield, Milton Keynes, MK11 3LW, UK
UKHW021605240425
457818UK00018B/395